The Psychology
of Television

The Psychology of Television

John Condry
Cornell University

LEA LAWRENCE ERLBAUM ASSOCIATES, PUBLISHERS
1989 Hillsdale, New Jersey   Hove and London

Lawrence Erlbaum Associates, Inc., Publishers
365 Broadway
Hillsdale, New Jersey 07642

Library of Congress Cataloging-in-Publication Data

Condry, John C.
The psychology of television.

Includes index.
1. Television broadcasting—United States—Psychological
aspects. I. Title
PN1992.6.C65 1989   302.2'345'0973   88-30929
ISBN 0-89859-818-4

Printed in the United States of America
10 9 8 7 6 5 4 3 2

This book is dedicated to:

Ian,
Kirsten, and
Jennifer

Who, after long and patient instruction, taught me
to look at television through the eyes of children.

Contents

CHAPTER 6
Cognitive Mechanisms II: Attention, Comprehension,
and Perceived Reality   144

CHAPTER 7
NonProgram Content of Television:
Mechanisms of Persuasion
John Condry and Cynthia Schiebe   173

PART III
REGULATIONS AND SPECULATIONS

CHAPTER 8
Social Policy and the Regulation of Television
for Children   233

CHAPTER 9
The Future of Television   263

Preface

This book had its conception about 10 years ago while I was teaching courses in Social Development at Cornell University. Social development is the study of all of the influences that impinge on a person in order to make him or her a functioning member of society. Listing the usual influences on social development such as parents, peers, and social institutions like the church and schools, always left an important question unanswered: What about television? It became a litany in my classes, sung by the students, and it resulted in the nagging worry that I was leaving something important out. It bothered me that I had no clear answer to that question, nor could I find the answer in a single place. There were a few books and many articles, often in obscure journals, that had to be described in order to answer this question.

Eventually, I decided to organize all of the research I could find on the psychological influence of television, and not just to list it but to organize and make sense of it to the best of my ability. This book is the result. It turned out to be no simple task. There is a great deal written about television, and much of it is worthless, idle speculation. But there is also a large and serious literature out there about the psychological influence of television, covering a wide range of issues and topics. I have done my best to summarize that literature here, working historically from the early studies that form the bedrock of the research, to the most recent that I know. In describing research, I have often begun with early studies so I could help the reader understand the paradigm of the researchers and the basic questions they were trying to answer. It is important to understand research in the context in which it was done. I am sure I have omitted some important studies, but I hope they are few. I have tried to organize what is there into a coherent whole while retaining the perspective of the various researchers involved.

I have called the book *The Psychology of Television* because it is an attempt to organize and make sense of the psychological literature about the influence of television. I have tried to describe neither the sociological literature, which in any case is relatively small, nor, except occasionally, the literature of the field of communications. Much of the television research in communications is done by psychologists, however, and where it fits it is discussed, as for example with the research on "needs and gratifications" described in chapter 2.

Whenever possible I have tried to describe the psychological mechanisms that are responsible for the influence of television, and I hope that description proves useful. A mechanism is simply a causal route linking some event in the world (on television in this case) to some behavioral event or cognitive structure within the individual. If violence on television has the consequence of making those who are exposed to it more violent, then there must be some mechanism (actually there are several) that allow this cause to have this effect. Knowing these mechanisms allows us to be more precise about the effects of television, and in some cases it allows us to deny the existence of an effect. Consider, for example, the case of "subliminals."

It is widely contended that some kind of subliminal message may be inserted in visual or auditory material that will directly influence the subconscious mind, bypassing the conscious mind entirely, and having direct effects on some behavior. Such messages are credited with helping people lose weight, cope with stress, and improve their sex lives, among other things. But because there is no known mechanism for such effects we have reason to doubt their existence. For any cause to have an effect there must be some causal route that makes it possible. There are many such mechanisms for the influence of television, but there are none for the influence of subliminal messages, so we know that there is no such effect, regardless of how many people believe that there is. Any scientific inquiry should be able to help us sort the real from the fantastic, and that is just what I have tried to do by describing the findings of research in terms of the known mechanisms of influence.

The book is organized into three broad sections each with its own brief introduction: Part I: Essential Facts and Initial Effects, Part II: The Psychology of Television, and Part III: Regulations and Speculations. The heart and soul of the book is the second part, The Psychology of Television, but the other parts have their place. The material in the first three chapters on essential facts and initial effects is useful and important to an understanding of the topic. It contains a description of the history of the television industry and the federal regulatory agencies whose responsibility it is to oversee the industry. It discusses the initial effects of the introduction of television into society, effects largely due to the displacement of time. The first part also contains descriptions of the audience of television, which includes just about everybody and which has remained quite stable for about the last 20 years, and the program content of television which changes with such regularity that one can never be quite up-to-date. I left the description of the advertising content of television to a later chapter on mechanisms of persuasion, chapter 7.

The second part of the book focuses on the psychological mechanisms of influence. It starts with the question of violence, the dominant image of television, and the dominant research question for the first two decades of psychological research. But it goes on to describe much more recent research on attention to television, especially in the young, the comprehension of television, and the perceived reality of television, issues that have little or nothing to do with the question of violence. Analyzing this research in terms of the psychological mechanisms that are responsible for the influence television has on us will help us better understand both the impact of television and what can be done to counteract it when that is deemed necessary.

The final two chapters are slightly different from the rest in that they describe less research and more practice, and they contain considerably more speculation than the earlier chapters. Chapter 8 describes several attempts on the part of federal regulatory agencies to regulate the content of television and to reduce its influence on children, and ends with some brief descriptions of private (nongovernmental) efforts to do the same. Chapter 9 is entirely speculative and concerns what the future of television, and particularly research on television, is likely to bring. Even though each chapter has a summary, the final chapter is something like a summary of everything, an attempt to put the whole thing in context without being too repetitive.

This book has been, for me, a labor of love. Larry Erlbaum encouraged me to write it, and promised to publish it if I did. But the motivation and the sleepless nights were mine. I wrote this book for my students, because they wanted to know, and for my colleagues because they should know more about the influence of television. But I didn't do it alone. I had a lot of help. First and foremost I am indebted, more than I can repay, to my wife and constant companion Sandy Beth. Without her love and support I would not have been able to accomplish half of what I have accomplished, and this book, in particular, would not have been written. She was there when I bottomed out, when I was ready to give up and discard the entire project. She listened to my diatribes, encouraged me to go on, and helped me over the rough spots. She believed in me, which is more than I can say for myself sometimes, and it was enough. What can I say? Thanks, Babe, I love you.

The most important professional influence on the book has been my colleague Dr. Cyndy Scheibe, formerly a graduate student who studied with me, and currently a professor of psychology at Ithaca College. Cyndy encouraged my interest in television, and we have collaborated on most of the television research that I have done over the last several years. Cyndy was the driving spirit behind the archive of television content that I developed and have maintained in the Department of Human Development and Family Studies at Cornell, and she is co-director of the Archive and Research Lab. Cyndy did practically all of the figures in the book, working with a small computer in our research lab and using our data and that of our students. Cyndy is also the co-author of chapter 7, on the Non-Program Content of Television. That chapter reports research which was done entirely in collaboration with Dr. Scheibe. I wrote the rest of the book, for better or worse, but that one chapter is a collaborative effort and Cyndy deserves at least half of the credit. In a close collaborative effort such as ours has been, it is difficult to divide the credit into that which is due to A and that which is due to B. More to the point, there is not any need to. The co-authorship of chapter 7 signals the fact that it is a unified effort, a single product, of two different people working toward the same end. This is the best that can be hoped of scientific collaboration, and ours has been a special one.

I have been blessed, since coming to Cornell, with many excellent and inspiring students. I hope they will forgive me if I do not list them all, but I do recognize and appreciate their help. They provided much of the motivation required to write this book by their persistent curiosity and their hunger for the truth. They provided enthusiasm whenever mine waned. I am particularly appreciative of the efforts of Sue Freund, an outstanding undergraduate student, who has been a pleasure to work with and an immense help in running the Research Lab in my absence. Sue and others like her provide inspiration because they make teaching a pure unmitigated joy, and if they are the future of television, it is in good hands.

I thank my long-suffering secretary, Shawn Lovelace, who has put up with more unreasonable demands than any reasonable person should have to, and who has always done so with good humor. I thank Robin Weisberg, editor at Erlbaum, for copyediting the manuscript, and for her support in the final stages of the project. Finally, a very special thanks to Dr. John Wright and Dr. Aletha Huston, co-directors of the Center for Research on the Influences of Television on Children (CRITC) at the University of Kansas. Drs. Wright and Huston gave me a home away from home, a secure and meaningful place, while I was on sabbatic leave from Cornell. It is there that I put the final touches on the book in the relaxed but intellectually challenging atmosphere of their television research laboratory. For their personal and intellectual companionship I am deeply grateful.

John Condry

ESSENTIAL FACTS
AND
INITIAL EFFECTS

In order to begin the study of the psychological influence of television, it is first necessary to become acquainted with certain basic facts about television itself. We need to know what television is, who watches it, and why. We also need to know what people see when they watch television. These fundamental questions are essential to an understanding of the topic.

When was television invented, and what happened when it was first introduced into society? What kind of industry grew up around television? What do people in this industry do, how do they make their money? To what extent is the television industry regulated by the government, by what federal agencies, and with what history of success or failure? In short, if we are to try to understand the influence of television on human beings, we must first begin by describing what we mean by "television."

When responding to the question "what is television?" three different answers seem appropriate and true. First, television is a *device* for receiving pictures and sound broadcast over the air. If I say "was that shown on television?" you would know I meant the device, the machine. This machine, like all machines, has a history and a structure; it has certain limitations and certain strengths. The device was invented at a certain time in human history, and later it was distributed across society. Once television became widely available, it was immediately embraced by the population. The device gained an audience and thereby a degree of importance.

But television is secondly an *industry*, as in the phrase "Television is responsible for the huge salaries paid to sports stars. . . ." The television industry has emerged in order to program, or use, the device. This industry, the "broadcast industry," includes radio from which television derived its history and form.

Finally, television is *what is shown* on the device, designed by the industry. That is, television is all of the programs, the commercials, and the rest of the visual and verbal clutter that together fill up all the time during the "broadcast day."

This last definition of television in terms of its content is, in fact, the most difficult to get a handle on, the hardest to pin down. Television (the device) and television (the industry) are both understandable, given that they remain much the same over time. But television (the content), the programs and ads, changes with some regularity.

It is impossible, therefore, to describe television and television effects without being clear about which of these three aspects of television (the device, the industry, the content) we mean. Except for the first two chapters (which discuss the history and audience of television) and chapter 8 on regulation of the industry, I refer to the *content* of television and its effects on viewers.

In the first chapter in this section, we see how television as a device for the broadcast transmission of voice and pictures was invented in the mid-1920s and introduced into American society shortly after the end of World War II (in the late 1940s and the early 1950s). Like radio, it became immediately popular; within a decade television reached almost 90% of the homes in the country. Television appealed to an even wider range of the population than radio had because, unlike radio, it was powerfully attractive to children. This fact, in the long run, led the American government to the only serious attempt it has ever made to regulate the content of television, that part of it which is directed to children.

Television (the device) is a powerful tool of mass communication in part because of this wide appeal. It also provides much more information than radio (with its rich visual images), and requires less education in order to be understood than the print media (newspapers and magazines) do. Since its beginning, broadcasting has been used primarily as a marketing device in the United States, and due to the size of its audience, television is the most powerful of such devices ever invented. Since the early days of radio, broadcast media have served the primary function of providing an audience to advertisers. By the time that television was introduced to American society, the economics, structure, and regulation of the broadcast industry were already well established. The primary job of the industry was to program the device with the kind of material that would draw and hold large audiences for a limited period of time. All other considerations are secondary to this one in the broadcasting industry as it has developed in the United States.

There is nothing inherently right or wrong with this, but it is a fact that is important to keep in mind. Among other things, it helps to explain much of what people in the television industry do, by underlining what gods they serve and what outcomes they value. In this respect it is worth noting that the broadcasting industry is not the same everywhere. In some countries the broadcasting media, both radio and television, are run by the government, publicly rather than privately funded, and in these countries they are not primarily used as marketing devices. In these countries television carries no advertising. In other countries, the advertising messages are clumped together and shown at one time of the broadcast day, without periodic interruptions of the programming. In some places television is broadcast only in the evening, whereas in others it goes on around the clock. In other words, across the planet there are many different forms of the broadcast industry, and many different ways of using the device of television.

In this book I concern myself primarily with broadcasting as it has developed in the United States. With rare exceptions, most of the research I describe was conducted in the United States, and was meant to apply to American television. Therefore, when I talk about the television industry, I mean the American television industry; when I talk about government regulation, I mean the American government's regulation of the American television industry. However, the psychological principles that are outlined in this book should apply to the influence of television anywhere, not just in the United States.

When television was first introduced into this country it had certain initial consequences in terms of the redistribution of time that I call "indirect effects." So the first social consequences of television have to do with the fact that it represents a new demand on a limited supply—the time available in the day. This, in turn, leads to other social consequences. Television has a powerful effect on the amount of time spent reading, which can turn out to be a serious problem with children. We consider these indirect effects as part of the history of television in chapter 1.

After we have considered the history of the device and the industry in the first chapter, the next broad and most basic set of questions concern the audience for television. When television was introduced it became immediately popular. But popular with whom? Who watches it?

When? For what reasons?

In terms of psychological influence, television might have little or no impact if only a few people pay relatively little attention to it. But the opposite is the case: Just about everybody watches some television, it has almost universal appeal. A more detailed analysis of the television audience reveals several interesting facts about who watches what, and why. We consider these questions in chapter 2. The first basic principle of influence has to do with exposure. Although the relationship is not perfectly linear, in general the more exposure the more influence. Certainly the more exposure the more *potential* for influence. Although almost everyone is exposed, one of the most important things to learn from the study of the audience of television is that different slices of the total audience, different categories of people (men, women, children, etc.), watch different categories of programming at different times, and thus are exposed to different information both in terms of programs and ads.

In summary, it is an essential fact about television that the audience is quite substantial in terms of numbers, and is, for the most part, selective in its viewing and thus in the features of the television environment to which it is exposed. On the other hand, a wide range of the audience is exposed during the "prime-time" viewing hours and much of the research on the content of television has focused on this part of the broadcast day.

This brings us to the last definition of television. Most statements made about the *effects* of "television" refer to television content—the programs and the ads. Television is what television does: entertain, inform, and persuade. The content of television is drama, soap opera, religion, game show, news, situation comedy, sports, advertisements, promotions for upcoming material, public service announcements, and so forth. We devote all of chapter 3 and most of chapter 7 to the study of the content of television.

Television content is difficult to define in part because the content is constantly changing. There are many reasons for this, the most important of which is that the audience is easily bored and the industry must keep gathering and holding the audience. The audience is attached, via the ratings services, to a feedback loop reaching into the corporate offices of the industry whose job it is to program the device. In a real sense, the content of television is responsive to the changing tastes and prejudices of the audience.

In 1961, to the consternation of network executives, the Chairman of the Federal Communications Commission, Newton Minow, complained that "television is a vast wasteland." Whether or not that was true (or still is), trying to get a fix on the content of television is a little like trying to map the desert. The winds of change are constantly blowing, and much of what was true at one time will not be true a short time later. Most of what I have to say in this book was true of television in the middle 1980s. By the time this book is published some part of it will no longer be exact in terms of the content.

In chapter 3 on television program content, we look first at the kinds of programs that have been popular (and those that have lost popularity) over the years since television was first introduced. We take a particularly sharp look at the kinds of programs that have been designed for and directed toward children, because their youthful vulnerability makes them particularly susceptible to the information on television.

Viewing the content of television, however, as a set of programs falling within certain categories of programming (and how those appeal to different segments of the viewing audience) is more important to broadcasters and communication specialists than it is to psychologists. From a psychological point of view, the content of television presents an environment that contains certain kinds of information that may be understood by human beings with certain cognitive capacities and certain interests.

In other words, both psychologists and communication specialists are interested in detailed information about the content of television, but for different reasons. Media analysts are often concerned with why television presents the information and portrayals that it does, and how such presentations change according to their popularity with viewers. Although psychologists certainly acknowledge that the information presented on television generally reflects the tastes and attention of the viewers (rather than an accurate reflection of the "real world"), we consider this to be irrelevant in terms of the effects that such portrayals may have on the beliefs and actions of viewers. Regardless of whether the information is presented as fiction or nonfiction, true or not, it is still information to which television viewers are exposed that they may incorporate into their knowledge structures.

For psychologists, then, the most important questions about the content of television concerns the nature of the information presented, and how that information compares to similar kinds of information presented in the other environments to which human beings are exposed. For example, how does the information on television compare to that of everyday life? In portraying a community, a workplace, or a family (even when such portrayals are only fictional), what distortions or biases occur in the television information when compared with the same phenomena in the real human world?

To answer these questions, chapter 3 presents studies of the content of television that use the technique of content analysis. In doing a content analysis, a quantitative study is made of the relevant aspects of the programs or ads (e.g., occupational roles for males and females), and when possible the results are compared to quantitative statistical information about the real world (e.g., from the U.S. Census).

Although such studies frequently document distortions found in the information presented on television compared with similar information about the real world, the point of such studies is not to criticize the television industry for presenting unrealistic portrayals or to make a value judgment about whether television should or should not present accurate information. Instead, the point is that where there are distortions of reality presented on television, it may be possible to trace these distortions in the beliefs and attitudes of the viewers exposed to them and therefore establish, to some extent, the degree of influence that watching television has on the viewers' understanding of the real world. In other words, distortions in the information available on television have a value to psychologists that quite transcends whatever reason they have, however fascinating, for being there in the first place.

In this first section of the book, then, we acquaint ourselves with the basic facts about the history of the television device, the television industry, the television audience, and the content of television programs. It is important for us to know what television is, how its industry functions, who it attracts, and what it presents, before we can begin to try to understand the psychology of the impact of television on viewers. So we begin with the story of television and how it came to be what it is today. What *is* television?

What Is Television?

Television is just another appliance. It's a toaster with pictures.
—Mark Fowler, Chairman, Federal Communications Commission*

Television is a machine. It is an electronic device for encoding and transmitting signals that, with the proper equipment, can be received and decoded as a "picture with sound" ready to be perceived and understood by a human being. This fact alone, together with its amazingly broad appeal, makes television a wonderful machine, a truly marvelous toy. But it is much more than simply that.

Mr. Fowler, a man in a position to know better, is too modest. Television is not just "a toaster with pictures." It is also an industry that manufactures and distributes these pictures to millions of homes, an industry that profits from the sale of the audience gathered in front of the machine. Advertisers pay for the temporary use of these masses of viewers so that they may deliver a short and lively message for their clients, large companies with nationwide distribution systems. This "toaster" has the shape of an octopus with tentacles into almost every home in the United States. It has the power to generate millions of dol-

---

*quoted in Stengel (1983).

lars in revenue for the few who have a license to use it. Some appliance!

Although television is both a *device* and an *industry*, neither of these definitions captures the nature of television for a psychologist. From a psychological point of view, television is a window into a world that contains information of use to human beings. As such, television is what is shown on the television set. Television offers information on 20 to 30 channels (with some satellite receivers getting over 100) every second of every minute of every day. With the coming of television the world has changed, particularly the world of the young.

Given the facts that large numbers of people watch television and that its content contains information in a suitable form for learning, we can be reasonably sure that people who are exposed to television are influenced by it. But which ones of them are most influenced, and how?

We begin with a brief look at the history of television (the device), and the history of the industry that grew up around it. When was the device first imagined, and when was the first working model produced? When was television finally mass produced and distributed throughout the society? What were the initial consequences of having this device?

A BRIEF HISTORY OF TELEVISION— THE DEVICE

In the Beginning

The invention of radio by Marconi in 1896 made the invention of television inevitable. But the *idea* of having a picture and sound device in the home, in the living room being watched by the entire family, was first conceived much earlier; shortly after the invention of the telephone in 1876. Cartoons showing people watching screens in their living rooms and being entertained, taught, shown current news events, even shopping from the home, all appeared in popular magazines between 1879 and 1895, 10 years before young Marconi left the seclusion of his bedroom laboratory with his new invention (Barnouw, 1982).

But although these pictures illustrated a futuristic fantasy, Marconi's radio changed those dreams into possibilities. Once it became possible to send signals over long distances without a wire, farsighted individuals realized that it would soon be possible to send a picture and the search for a way to do this was begun in earnest. Meanwhile, radio broadcasting became immediately popular just after the turn of the century when Marconi introduced it to the United States.

At first, the radio industry existed merely to sell radios. These radios were used by businesses in far flung locations and also by the military, especially the Navy with its need to communicate with ships at sea. Radio was very popular with amateurs who built studios in their homes and broadcast their favorite music to whoever would listen. These amateur broadcasting facilities eventually became stations with call letters.

In 1922, something happened that would revolutionize the broadcasting industry. One of these radio stations, WEAF in the New York City area, produced a 10-minute advertisement to sell real estate on Long Island (Tuchman, 1974). At last broadcasting had a purpose beyond mere entertainment, and a means of subsidizing itself beyond the selling of broadcast receivers. People who gathered together around a radio set could be periodically given commercial messages, and advertisers would willingly pay for access to this audience. Most importantly, advertisers would pay "by the head": the larger the audience, the more money was to be made by the broadcasters. And from these humble beginnings a huge and powerful industry was born.

Government Regulation

At about the same time as television (the device) was being invented in the mid-1920s, the radio industry was already experiencing problems. The industry suffered from excessive clutter—a form of electronic gridlock. Too many broadcasters were arrayed across too small a space on the electromagnetic band. Interference between stations was widespread, disputes were hard to settle, and eventually the fledgling industry begged for government regulation. The government was asked to decide who should get a license to broadcast and to see that the broadcasting frequencies of stations within a given area did not overlap with one another. The government was specifically asked to stay out of the regulation of the content of programs, however, in accord with the First Amendment to the Constitution (Emery, 1971).

In 1926 the Radio Act was passed by Congress establishing the Federal Radio Commission, later changed to the Federal Communications Commission (FCC), which was given charge of all of broadcasting including television. It is important to note that the power of the FCC, historically, has been in the ability to grant licenses, not to interfere in any way with programming (Tuchman, 1974).

According to one source, the first broadcast of television was made in 1927, when Herbert Hoover (then secretary of the treasury) gave a speech in Washington, DC and it was picked up "live" in New York.

Few people saw this historic feat, of course, because almost nobody had a television set. Nonetheless, it marked the beginning of the television industry as we know it today (Barnouw, 1982).

Introduction of TV to Society

Research on television as a working device progressed during the next two decades from 1930 to 1950, but the Great Depression and World War II slowed down both the development and distribution of television sets. Throughout this period there were few TV stations broadcasting, and very few families had a means of receiving the broadcasts. Home ownership of a television set was both a novelty and a luxury.

By the late 1940s, however, this picture began to change dramatically and permanently. The war was over and the economy was humming. More people were more affluent than at any time in history. Families separated by the war were back together, settling into a life-style that had been no more than a dream just a decade before. Television sets became available at ever decreasing prices and television stations sprouted up all over.

By 1950, the cost of a TV set had dropped to the point where most moderately affluent families could afford one. There were more stations broadcasting, more hours of the day during which there were programs, and more channels to choose from. Figure 1.1 shows the prime-time schedules taken from early *TV Guides* (Brooks & Marsh, 1981) for the years 1946–1949, illustrating how rapidly the TV broadcast hours were filled with programs.

During these years, most television stations began broadcasting during the early evening (my friends and I would watch the "test pattern" for an hour before the first program), and stations would go off the air by 10:30 p.m. In many places today (e.g., Israel), this is still a typical broadcast day. But in this country, as advertising revenue poured in, more and more of the broadcast day became filled and television began to take the form and shape that it has today.

During the decade of the 1950s, ownership of television sets increased at what is termed an *exponential rate*. Figure 1.2 gives the actual rate of change over time for the introduction of television (the device) into the United States. In 1949, only 2% of American homes had a television set; a year later that figure had risen to 10%, and by 1960 nearly 90% of all American homes had television (Nielsen, 1956, 1960).

Television, the device, had nearly saturated the population by 1960, and its popularity continued to increase over the next two decades until virtually everyone had a set. Statistics from the Nielsen Reports (1986) indicate that in 1985 there were 85.9 million households in the con-

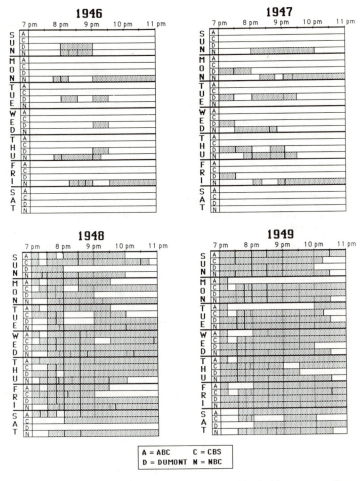

FIG. 1.1. Proportion of the prime time schedule filled with programs, for 1946–1949. (Information from Brooks & Marsh, 1981.)

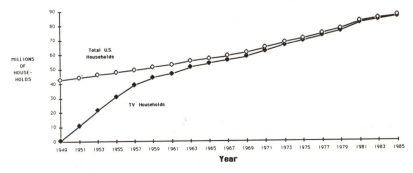

FIG. 1.2. Number of TV households and total U.S. households, for 1949–1985. (Information from Nielsens, 1953 through 1986.)

tinental United States, and 99% of them had at least one television set. Nearly all of these households had sets that were color (93%), and well over half (57%) had two or more sets. The American population is completely saturated with television, both in terms of total numbers and in terms of the age of its viewers.

The story of that first decade from 1950 to 1960 is the story of the first phase of the introduction of a new technological device into a society. It was also a period during which the television industry underwent dramatic growth. What happened in the United States during those early years of television has been repeated again and again in other countries to which television spread after its adoption here, and the changing nature of television in all its forms (device, industry, and content) can be observed in those societies and communities that have only begun to receive television in recent years (Corteen, 1977; Murray & Kippax, 1978; Williams, 1986).

INITIAL CONSEQUENCES OF TELEVISION: INDIRECT EFFECTS

Compared to such inventions as the car, the washing machine, and the radio, television spread very rapidly across American society as soon as it first became available. More people got one, and in a shorter period of time, than had been the case with any previous invention.

There were two important consequences to this rapid diffusion and adoption of television. First, because using the device (i.e., watching it) takes time, other activities formerly done during this time were lost, or at least diminished. For most individuals, 3 to 4 hours of activities a day were displaced by watching television. And because television was adopted into society so very quickly, the effects of this initial disruption of time were quite strong. Yet, because nearly everyone experienced these changes during the same short span of years, few people were aware of the dramatic impact that television viewing was having on the distribution of their free time.

The second consequence of this rapid introduction of television into our society was that American social scientists missed an important opportunity to do certain kinds of comparative research. After the early 1960s it was no longer possible to compare people who had television with people who did not (but who wanted one), because by 1960 nearly everyone who wanted a television set had one.

This may be a characteristic of any attractive new invention. Presumably for any new technology, there will be a period of time (there is a temptation to call this a "window of vulnerability"), when it is possible to study the initial impact of the device by comparing those who

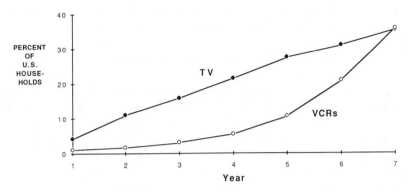

FIG. 1.3. Comparative adoption rates for TV sets (1950–1956) and VCRs (1980–1986). (Information from Nielsen, 1956, and Television & Cable Factbook, 1983, 1986.)

have it with those who do not. Once such a new invention is accessible to the majority of the population, however, this type of comparative research is very difficult, if not impossible.

Some analysts predicted a similar adoption rate to occur for the microcomputer (Condry & Keith, 1983; Lepper, 1982), but the sales of computers has leveled off at about 12 million, approximately 14% of American homes (*Television & Cable Factbook*, 1983, 1986). The video cassette recorder (VCR), another popular invention introduced in the early 1980s, has proven as popular as television once was. Figure 1.3 gives the comparative adoption rates for VCRs (starting in 1980) and television (starting in 1950) for the first 7 years the device was available. As can be seen, the percentage of homes having a VCR is the same as the percentage of homes having a television set 7 years after it was introduced into American society.

Indirect Effects of Television

When a new device such as television (or the VCR) comes into society it has an indirect and a direct effect. *Indirect effects* come about because the distribution of time in daily life changes after the device is introduced. Because watching television takes time that otherwise would be used for other things, the first effect of television is to cause a reallocation of how time is used in everyday life. These kinds of effects are called *indirect* because they result from simply using the device (i.e., time spent watching the television set), regardless of what content is being watched (Maccoby, 1964). *Direct effects*, on the other hand, do relate specifically to the nature of the content watched. For example, the presence of violence in children's programs or the characters portrayed in commercials would both be issues related to the direct effects of television. Direct effects are discussed in much more detail in chapters 3 through 8.

What are the indirect effects of television? In every society into which television has been introduced, there has been a subsequent *decrease* in the time devoted to socializing with friends, sleep, housework, and using other media (i.e., going to the movies, listening to the radio, reading books, magazines, and newspapers) (Furu, 1962; Himmelweit, Oppenheim, & Vince, 1958; Himmelweit & Swift, 1976; Murray & Kippax, 1978; Robinson, 1972, 1981; Schramm, Lyle, & Parker, 1961; Werner, 1971). At the same time, the introduction of television in a country *increases* the total amount of time devoted to "mass media" by a considerable amount, almost all of it due to the fact that people now watch television instead of those other activities.

Although there are some variations among these studies in procedures for measuring time use (see, e.g., Bryant & Gerner, 1981; Robinson, 1972, 1981), there is nevertheless an amazing cross-cultural consistency in documenting the initial consequences of the introduction of television. Robinson (1972) summed up the impact of the introduction of television in 15 countries by saying:

> it is of considerable interest to compare television with other innovations of the twentieth century. Comparing the amount of travel by owners of automobiles with that of non-owners, we were especially surprised that cross-nationally, automobile owners on the average spent only six percent more time in transit than non-owners. While automobile owners were undoubtedly able to cover far more territory in the time they spent traveling, the overall shift is pale indeed to compared to the 58 percent increase in media usage apparently occasioned by the influence of television.... Thus, at least in a temporal sense, television appears to have had a greater influence on the structure of daily life than any other innovation in this century. (p. 428)

These indirect effects of television are extremely widespread; they affect all ages, races, and social classes in the population. For example, not only do adults spend less time with their friends once television is available, but children spend less time with their playmates as well (Furu, 1962; Murray & Kippax, 1978; Werner, 1971). However, what may be relatively harmless for one could be a problem for the other, due to the differential importance of friends in adulthood and childhood.

In summary, once television comes into a society people do not go out as much and they do not have friends over as often as they did before they had television. They spend less time cleaning house, read-

ing, taking the children out, and doing their favorite hobbies. In countries with television, children spend less time with friends, less time
reading and being read to, and less time engaging in imaginative play
(Singer & Singer, 1976; 1981). Television has all these consequences
when it is first introduced, and then those consequences have consequences.

Spend less time with friends, and you become less social; spend less
time reading, and you become to some degree less literate. To the extent that what was done before the introduction of television involved
the practice of skills (such as reading and social interaction), then an
important consequence of the introduction of television is that less time
is spent developing those skills. In the long run, this may mean that
people become less competent in particular endeavors.

In other words, if practice makes perfect, then less practice makes
less than perfect. In the following sections, we look at the research
documenting the effects of the introduction of television on reading,
imagination, social relationships, sports, and frequent hobbies.

Television and Reading. Although television may affect the extent to
which most people in a society take time to read, it will be most disruptive for the skill of reading for those who are still in the process
of learning to read. As a general rule, a skill is most vulnerable to being undermined by extrinsic forces while it is being acquired, whereas
once a skill is relatively stable it is less susceptible to influence by external events (Condry, 1977).

Because we have standardized tests to measure reading skill in children, we can look at what has happened to the reading scores of children as television is introduced into a society. Figure 1.4 shows that
SAT reading scores declined steadily in the United States from the early
1960s until 1982. This decline appears to follow almost directly the rate
of adoption of television in the United States, although there are other
possible contributing factors such as the increase in later-born children
in the population during the post-war baby boom (see Zajonc, 1986).

As previously noted, research conducted in 15 countries where television was being introduced shows unequivocally that the amount of
time devoted to reading of every sort (books, magazines, newspapers,
etc.) declines rapidly as people spend more and more time watching
television (Robinson, 1972). Although most of the decline in reading
for children is in terms of reading comic books (Brown, Cramond, &
Wilde, 1974; Himmelweit et al., 1958; Murray & Kippax, 1978; Schramm
et al., 1961), the consequences are still severe because even reading
comic books may sharpen reading skills. In countries where children
read books rather than comics, such as Norway (Werner, 1971) and

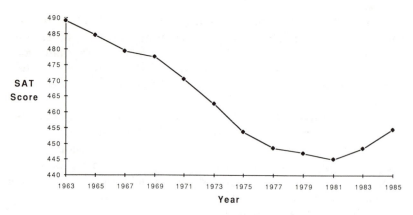

FIG. 1.4.   Average SAT scores, for 1963–1985. (Information from Zajonc, 1986.)

Japan (Furu, 1962, 1971), there was a corresponding decline in book reading following the introduction of television.

All of the studies mentioned so far focused on the amount of time spent reading, but the same results are found when actual reading skill is measured. A study designed specifically to look at the impact of the introduction of television on reading skills was conducted in three Canadian towns (called, for this study, *Notel, Unitel,* and *Multitel* to reflect the condition of television access in each town) (Corteen, 1977). The Notel town had no television, the Unitel town had only one channel, and Multitel had several. In other respects, however, these towns and the people in them were very much alike, differing only in the amount of television available. The results of this study showed that children's reading scores correlated inversely with the amount of television available in the three towns: Reading scores were highest in Notel, next highest in Unitel, and lowest in Multitel (Corteen, 1977).

Eventually cable came to Notel, so a second analysis was done 2 years after television was introduced there to see if reading scores had changed (Corteen, 1977). Corteen found that the reading scores of these children had "deteriorated significantly." It should be noted that these results held true only for children in Grades 2 and 3; the reading skills of children measured in Grade 8 were unaffected by the introduction of television. These last findings suggest that the introduction of television does not as severely undermine the existence of already well-established skills (such as reading for an eighth grader), but having television available does influence the development of undeveloped skills (such as reading for a second and third grader).

A study by Murray and Kippax (1978) offers additional detail about this issue. Doing research in Australia as television was being introduced into parts of that country, these researchers also found that reading in general declined, primarily due to a decrease in time spent reading comics. In their study, however, reading of books actually increased with the introduction of television!

There is much more evidence related to this debate (see, e.g., Morgan & Gross, 1982; Williams, 1986). For the moment it is enough to notice that one important initial effect of television's introduction to society is to reduce the time spent reading, principally reading for leisure. To the extent that one is learning to read, a consequence of having television and watching it is to slow the learning process down (compared to a person without this distraction), because reading, like many other things, is a skill that improves with practice.

Television and Imagination.   Another indirect effect of television, and one more recently discovered, involves a decrease in skills that are important to imagination and creativity. Two of the leading authorities in research on children and the development of imagination are Jerome and Dorothy Singer of Yale University. Since 1977, they have been conducting a large scale investigation of the influence of television on imaginative skills and on aggression in nursery school children (Singer & Singer, 1981; Singer, Singer, & Rapaczynski, 1984).

In this study, very careful records were kept by the parents about the amount of time their children spent watching television and what they watched. At the same time that the children's television viewing was being monitored at home, researchers at the Yale University nursery school were observing the same children in play situations, and recording both imaginative play and aggressive play.

Although the Singers found that television influenced both types of play, we discuss their findings regarding aggression later in the book because they involve a direct effect of television. The influence of television viewing on imagination, however, appears to be an indirect effect. Singer and Singer (1981) reported:

> Our data and observations indicated that heavy TV viewing did not seem to be conducive to the development of imaginative capacities of our middle-class preschoolers. The heavy viewers seemed less likely to be our most imaginative children. (p. 152)

The reason for this finding may be that imagination, like reading, is a skill in the sense that practice typically leads to improvement and that lack of practice leads to a poorer development of the capacity. One reason for suspecting this is that the effect the Singers found was related to amount of viewing, but was not related to the specific content viewed. The mechanism suggested, then, is that heavy television viewing reduces the amount of time available for the child to engage in imaginative play; thus, children who are heavy TV viewers eventually come to be less imaginative due to less frequent practice of this skill.

Television and Sociability.   In addition to the indirect effects of television on reading and imagination, the introduction of television into society also influences the amount of time spent socializing with friends for adults (Robinson, 1972, 1981), and for children (Furu, 1962, 1971; Himmelweit et al., 1958; Murray & Kippax, 1978; Werner, 1971). In a study on the effect of television on children in Australia, for example, Murray and Kippax (1978) compared three towns that differed in the amount of television available. They found "linear decreases across the three towns . . . in general unstructured outdoor activities" (Murray, 1980, p.53). In short, the more time spent with television the less time available for play with friends, especially outdoor play.

Television and Sports.   It is often reported that as television enters a society, attendance at a variety of public functions, including sports and movies, declines. For example, although the population of the United States was increasing dramatically in the period from 1949 to 1969, the time when television was being rapidly adopted into American society, minor league baseball attendance fell from 42 million to 10 million. In the decade from 1946 to 1956, motion picture attendance declined from 82 to 34 million, and although it rose to 41 million in 1960, it declined steadily thereafter, falling to only 19 million in 1970 (Bogart, 1972; Comstock, Chaffee, Katzman, McCombs, & Roberts, 1978).

On the other hand, television has had an obviously beneficial effect on many sports, both professional and non-professional, by directly increasing the public interest in and revenue available to the sport. For example, Belson (1960) found that in England the introduction of television led to a 47% increase in attendance at horse racing and jumping contests. In the United States, *Sports Illustrated* reported that "in 1969 the NCAA championship basketball game attracted 8.2 million viewers . . . [while by 1981], 16.5 million watch the game. The TV audience was 60 million for the 1970 Super Bowl . . . [while in 1981] it drew 100 million viewers" (Johnson, 1981, p. 51.).

So television may have the paradoxical effect of increasing interest and attendance in some sports while decreasing interest and attendance in others. More importantly, the notions of "attendance" and "audience" both change. Audiences for sporting events used to be found in the

stadiums and gymnasiums at which the events occu
the advent of television they are increasingly concen

Television has a similar paradoxical effect on part.
It takes time away from involvement in physical activi
pax, 1978), but it displays sports and sports stars in an a
Mike Lynn, the general manager and vice president o.
Vikings (a professional football team), was quoted in *S* *...ustrated*,
saying: "Pro football will be like the movie industry, and players, like
movie stars, will become so powerful that they will demand — and get —
whatever they want" (Johnson, 1981, p. 53.) On the whole, although the
story has yet to be told in detail, television probably has had a beneficial influence on most professional sports.

Television and Hobbies.   Finally, the introduction of television into society seems to have an important effect on frequent hobbies and activities, according to research done in Great Britain in the early 1950s
as television was being introduced into that country. Belson (1960) asked
a reasonably large sample of people (450 with television, 350 without
it) about their daily activities. He found an initial decrease in all activities, but most infrequent activities tended to "rebound" after the novelty
of television wore off. In a sense, Murray and Kippax (1978) found the
same thing about reading in their Australian study.

In Belson's (1960) study, however, frequent hobbies and activities
did not rebound. If a person visited a home for retired people once
a week, that activity tended to be unaffected by the introduction of television. But frequent hobbies such as stamp collecting and bird watching, to the extent that these hobbies took up a good deal of time, tended
to suffer permanent loss of attention after the coming of television.

Summary of Initial Consequences of Television

The first round of influences that a device like television has as it is
introduced into society is on the way time is distributed and used by
the population. Because television is an attractive and time-consuming
device, as soon as it is introduced it causes powerful and permanent
reallocations of time. These facts are true not only in this country where
relatively little research was done (see, however, Coffin, 1955), but also
in virtually every other country into which television has been introduced (Robinson, 1972, 1981).

Some of these effects might be considered temporary in the sense
that societies may compensate for some of the initial consequences of
the introduction of television. For example, something very much like
this may be happening with reading in the United States. Even though

scores on the Scholastic Aptitude Test in reading declined for several decades following the introduction of television, as we saw in Fig. 1.4, they have now begun to rise again (Zajonc, 1986).

This recent increase in scores may be the result of schools and parents putting more effort into teaching reading and language skills, in order to offset the previous decline. Television producers have also begun to incorporate public service messages about the fun and importance of reading books into children's programs (Condry, Bence, & Scheibe, 1988). To the extent that efforts such as these are successful, some indirect effects of television may not have permanent or long-lasting negative consequences.

We also tend to adapt to some consequences of the amount of time spent watching television without noticing them much. We get used to houses that are less clean and spending less time with friends. Because of this accommodation and adaptation, it is probably the case that indirect effects are most disruptive just as television is being introduced into a society.

This is not to say that they go away completely. Individuals who watch 4 hours of television a day will suffer more indirect effects than those who watch only 2 hours, regardless of what content they watch. The simple act of watching television may lead to serious, long-term consequences both for individuals and for societies, especially to the extent that this behavior is primarily sedentary and precludes strenuous physical activity or time spent outdoors. As a result, heavy television viewing has been tentatively linked to such consequences as obesity, lack of physical fitness, and dental problems (Gerbner, Morgan, & Signorielli, 1982).

THE PSYCHOLOGY OF TELEVISION: EFFECTS AND MECHANISMS

So far, we have seen that the introduction of television has at least one important initial effect, that of displacing and reallocating time. What are the psychological consequences of this? We have already documented the probable link between television viewing and the decline in reading skills among young children. In tracing this link, it was important to demonstrate that there was a strong association between an increase in time spent watching television and a decrease in both time spent reading and in actual reading scores. But in order to explain why these consequences occurred, we also needed to know the relationship between the amount of practice time spent reading and reading skill.

For those individuals just learning to read, this relationship is positive: The more you practice, the better you read.

In explaining the findings concerning television and reading, then, we hypothesized that reading is a skill that needs to be practiced in order for it to be performed well, and that the time spent watching television displaced the time necessary for the reading skills to be practiced. These two steps—documenting the association between television viewing and the second factor, and then providing an explanation for the mechanism by which one factor could cause the other to occur—are essential in any discussion of the psychological effects of television.

In other words, we need to be able to say more than just that television viewing has displaced time spent doing other things. If one of the results of the introduction of television is that less time is spent socializing with friends, then what are the consequences of socializing less with friends? If another effect is to reduce the time spent on frequent hobbies, then what is the psychological consequence of this fact? In each of these cases, there are two things to be established: (a) Is the effect actually related to watching television? Usually this means is there really an association (i.e., a correlation) between some particular behavior (or lack of it) and watching television? And, if so; (b) What is the causal mechanism permitting this effect to occur? Once we are convinced that there is an association between watching television and another factor, then we will want to know exactly how and why it occurs. What is it about human beings that allows television to have such an influence? In this way, we can learn something about the psychology of the individual by studying the influence of watching television on their subsequent beliefs and behaviors.

In summary, trying to understand the psychology of television leads us to study the causal structure of any predicted influence. If television is said to lead to aggression, or passivity, or whatever, we need to evaluate that hypothesis in terms of possible means of being influenced. The effect of television on the development of reading is, for one, to reduce time spent practicing and this, in turn, results in less skill, less ability. We consider this an indirect effect of television because it seems to be independent of the precise content that is being watched. Consequences that are related to television content, what we call direct effects, may be more complicated to document and to explain because there are more factors involved. But like the indirect effects, finding the existence of a direct effect will require that we show not only that there is an association between television viewing and some particular outcome (in terms of the beliefs, attitudes, or behaviors of TV viewers), but also that there exists some plausible causal route that allows this particular influence to occur.

A BRIEF HISTORY OF TELEVISION—
THE INDUSTRY

As of September 30, 1985, there were 1,493 television stations on the air in the United States (1,167 commercial and 326 public; Nielsen, 1986). The people who own, operate, and manage these stations are a large part of another answer to the question: What is television? They make up the television industry, where the decisions are made about what the content of television will be. The television industry has a hand in the production of programs, in negotiating with sports enterprises, in supporting the film industry that provides much of the material seen on television, in the advertising industry, and so on.

The television industry is complex and multifaceted, and a detailed description of it is beyond the scope of this book. Such information can be found in a number of excellent sources, especially those from the field of communications, including: a three-volume study of the history of broadcasting in the United States by Erik Barnouw (1966, 1968, 1970), along with his recent summary volume, *Tube of Plenty* (1982); a thought-provoking analysis by Gaye Tuchman (1974) of the structure of the television industry; and several recent compendiums of television research that include descriptions of the industry by Comstock et al. (1978), Murray (1980), Palmer and Dorr (1980), Liebert and Sprafkin (1988), and Dorr (1986).

Because the focus of this book is on the psychology of television, we do need to understand some of the basic facts about the television industry as it stands today, and a little about how it developed. The structure of the industry dictates a great deal about the nature of the content of television, and all direct effects trace back to this. It is important, therefore, to be able to distinguish between television stations and television networks, to understand what regulations govern the functioning of these stations, and what economic forces underlie the television industry.

The most visible part of the television industry involves the three current major networks: ABC, NBC, and CBS. A *network* is a corporation that attempts to get locally owned stations to affiliate with it. Networks offer programs to affiliated stations, and may also own and operate their own stations. Each major network is allowed to own a certain number of stations (which used to be a maximum of five, but was recently increased to seven), as specified by regulations of the Federal Communications Commission.

What Does the Television Industry Sell?

The steel industry sells steel; the automotive industry sells automobiles; the oil industry sells oil. So what does the television industry sell? It does not sell the content of television, the programs and ads; these are shown "free" to the viewers when they turn on their TV sets. The sets themselves are sold by somebody else. So how do people who own and manage television stations make money? What do they sell?

A television station does not sell time, nor advertisements, nor entertainment, and the television industry does not sell TV sets (although that is how the radio industry started). The business of the television industry is to sell audiences—people in very large numbers who have little else in common except that they are all "tuned in" at the same time. This group of people, who are all exposed to the offerings of a given station, can be counted and sold by that station to interested parties, the advertisers.

Networks, even though they are larger and wealthier than individually owned stations, make their money in the same way stations do: by collecting and selling the largest audience possible to those people who are interested in reaching such an audience, and who can afford the price. The cost of 1 minute of exposure to the millions of people gathered by television networks is difficult to determine, but several private sources suggest that it currently ranges from $200,000 to nearly $1,000,000 a minute! The funny thing is that to the advertiser, it may be worth every penny.

Station owners and network executives alike promise advertisers that they will deliver a certain number of people, having certain demographic characteristics, at a certain time. It is the advertiser's job to come up with a message to show to this audience.

So the business of the television industry is to gather an audience. It is important to keep this in mind because it helps explain a lot of why television broadcasters do what they do, and in particular it explains why they show what they show. Broadcasters are exclusively interested in the attention of the audience, and in the demographic composition of that audience. Within the limits imposed by law and expedience, anything that helps the television industry collect the largest and most demographically attractive audience is allowable. And there are, as we see shortly, few limits imposed by law.

The content of television, designed to attract and hold attention, is made up of two separate components: programs and commercials. These separate components are under the direction of separate authorities within the broadcasting industry. People who supervise the production of entertainment and informational programs, *programmers*, arrange these programs so as to gather and hold as large an audience as possible. *Advertisers* have the task of holding the attention of the same audience, but for a much shorter period of time. Programmers hold the audience's attention by attempting to entertain and/or inform them. Advertisers also frequently entertain and inform, but they have a third, more important goal: to persuade. They hope to change the behaviors of the audience, or at least to change their attitudes.

Programmers and advertisers are somewhat beholden to one another in American network television; each has a very large investment in what the other does. This fact has led to the development of another critical part of the television industry, the Audience Measurement, or Ratings Services. These services are independent of the networks and affiliates, in the sense that they are private organizations hired to count the "house" of television broadcasts for the networks and stations, and those who use them rely on the scientific accuracy of their results.

Audience Measurement: The Ratings Services

If the prime directive of the television industry is to gather and to hold an audience, and both programmers and advertisers are interested in this same question, then how do they measure success? How do they know when they have done a good job? The answer involves using a variety of methods, each with certain strengths and weaknesses, to measure the audience for an individual station or network. Advertisers and programmers know the size and the general composition of the television audience based on the information they receive from these audience counting services, of which there are several. These services draw a sample from the population of television viewers in order to estimate the audience at any given time. Several different sampling techniques are used to determine the information of interest, which includes: (a) when the television set is on and for how long, (b) what channel the set is tuned to, and (c) the demographic characteristics of who is watching.

The best known and most widely used of these ratings services is that of the A.C. Nielsen Company, with corporate offices in Illinois. Although the exact method of sample selection is kept secret by the company, some general facts about it are known. The Nielsen Metered Market Service consists of approximately 2,000 homes in New York, Los Angeles, Chicago, San Francisco, and Detroit, with television sets wired through phone lines to a computer at the Nielsen headquarters in Chicago. The Nielsen company calls this device an "audimeter" and every few seconds each home equipped with one is sampled by the computer to see if the television set is on, and if so, what channel it is tuned to. About 20% of these homes are replaced in the sample each year, giving both continuity and a degree of freshness to the sample.

Because the demographic characteristics of each participating home are known to the Nielsen people, and because data are recorded automatically, there is little room for error. The demographic information concerning who is watching at any given time is much more likely to be subject to bias, of course, because this part is filled out on a "diary" by someone in the home. But the raw data regarding when the sets are on and what they are tuned to has been widely accepted in the television industry as a valid index of exposure (Comstock et al., 1978).

The outcome of this data collection process is the audience rating each program gets. Actually, there are two measures: a *rating*, which is the percentage of the total number of "television homes" that are tuned to a particular program; and a *share,* which is the proportion of all TV sets turned on at that particular time that are tuned to that program. The distinction between these two measures is, for our purposes, not important. What is important is that high quality ratings services such as Nielsens provide us with some of the best information available about the composition of the television audience. Thanks to these services we know some essential facts about the psychology of television: about how much time people spend watching, when they watch, and what they watch. We consider these data in some detail in the next chapter.

In addition to the Nielsen Service using Audimeter instruments, the Nielsen Company also offers for sale the Nielsen Television Index (NTI), which provides an estimate of TV viewing broken down by household characteristics (i.e., demographic information such as the age, sex, income, and education of the people in a given household), from a national sample of homes where diaries are kept on who views what. Although ratings and shares are determined by the audimeter data, the diaries provide evidence of who is watching, at what time, and what stations and programs they are tuned to.

As this book was being written, the A.C. Nielsen Co. introduced a new audience measurement device called "The Peoplemeter." In many ways this device is similar to the audimeter, it is wired directly into the Nielsen computer, for example, but it measures more than just whether the television set is on and what channel it is receiving. In addition, Peoplemeters record who is in the room watching the set. They do this with a hand-held device that is to be used by each person as they watch the show. When the television set is on, every so often a question appears on the television screen: "who is watching?" At this point, everyone in the room is supposed to punch into the hand held device a coded number unique to that person, and this information

In order to get some estimate of how much television you usually watch, we'd like you to shade in
the times that you <u>usually</u> watch TV (in the average week), as illustrated in the example below.
Fill in the first weekly chart for the times you usually watch TV <u>while at college</u>, and the second
one for the times you usually watch TV <u>while at home.</u>

EXAMPLE:

	SUN	MON	TUES	WED	THURS	
7am						for example, if you
8am						usually watch the
9am						Today Show from
10a						8-9 in the morning
11a						and General Hospital
12p						from 3-4 every
1pm						afternoon, and
2pm						usually watch a
3pm						movie or football

game on Sunday
afternoons...

WHILE AT COLLEGE:

	SUN	MON	TUES	WED	THURS	FRI	SAT
7am							
8am							
9am							
10a							
11a							
12p							
1pm							
2pm							
3pm							
4pm							
5pm							
6pm							
7pm							
8pm							
9pm							
10p							
11p							
12p							

WHILE AT HOME:

	SUN	MON	TUES	WED	THURS	FRI	SAT
7am							
8am							
9am							
10a							
11a							
12p							
1pm							
2pm							
3pm							
4pm							
5pm							
6pm							
7pm							
8pm							
9pm							
10p							
11p							
12p							

FIG. 1.5.   Sample of a TV viewing diary. (© Arbitron Ratings Inc.)

is recorded in the computer. Because this device is more a part of the
future of television than the past, a brief description of it is included
in chapter 9 where we discuss the future of television.

Other ratings services use techniques similar to those of the NTI,
with written diaries kept by family members to record the programs
and times that each person watches. Figure 1.5 gives a page from a typical audience survey recording instrument used by The Arbitron Ratings Service. All of these types of self-report diary techniques are subject
to the same limitations, but for the most part they are reliable and valid,
and many experts use the information obtained from them to describe

the characteristics of the television audience and their preferences (Comstock et al., 1978)

Limitations of the Ratings Services. The limitations of the Nielsen data are the same as for any other ratings service, and they arise from the fact that the purpose of the survey is to help television programmers and advertisers determine the size and composition of the audience, and do not constitute a scientific random sample. The users of these services are not particularly interested in how all human beings might react to television; they are mostly interested in those members of the audience who are thought to be the active consumers. This group is known euphemistically as "young adult," and it consists (for the most part) of all the people, ages 18–49, within the reach of television. However, the ratings services make no special effort to reach people who are very poor, those who have no permanent address, and so on. They simply are not interested. And, of course, anyone contacted can refuse to participate.

So the sample is assumed to be slightly biased compared to a completely random sample of the population (although it is hard to tell for certain, because the actual figures are a company secret). It is likely that the Nielsen sample overrepresents the age group from 18 to 49 and it underrepresents the poor, the old, and the transient, relative to what you would get in a more random sample of the entire population of the United States. These slight differences may not be of any real importance to us. We use the Nielsen figures as the best possible estimates of the television audience available at the current time.

In general then, the people in the television industry know they are doing their job of collecting an audience of a given size and composition because they subscribe to the ratings services, whose job it is to carefully and accurately sample the audience and determine who is watching, what, and when. In the next chapter we look in more detail at the picture of the television audience drawn by the Nielsen data.

Agencies of Government Regulation

As we saw in our brief history of broadcasting, the industry has been regulated by the government from practically the earliest days on, and this regulation was initially sought by the industry in order to remove "clutter" from the airwaves. The relationship between the industry and the federal regulatory agencies has always been a cozy one. As one observer explained it (Tuchman, 1974):

that the broadcasting industry requested government regulation certainly suggests that the initial relationship between the industry and the regulatory agency was not exactly an adversary one, but more like a "sweetheart" contract between a business and its house-union. (p. 8)

The one law that regulates all of broadcasting, for both radio and television, was originally written in 1927. This law, the Federal Radio Act, established the Federal Radio Commission. It is noteworthy that this was the year that the first working model of television was demonstrated, although television was not mentioned in the original law. In 1934, however, this same law was amended to include television, and was re-named the Broadcasting Act of 1934. This law established the Federal Communications Commission as the government agency responsible for granting licenses and overseeing the radio and television industry. Because this law continues today to be the only law governing broadcasting in the United States, it is an extremely important law and worthy of study (see, e.g., Emery, 1971).

The FCC has the power to grant licenses, allocate space on the electromagnetic spectrum (the broadcast band), and determine the amount of power a station may use for broadcasting. Licenses are given for 5 years at a time (recently changed from every 3 years), after which the license must be renewed. In granting such a license (worth millions of dollars), the FCC requires that broadcasters "serve the public interest."

There is considerable debate about exactly what this phrase means (Tuchman, 1974), because the definition of "serving the public interest," tends to change over time as different political and economic forces control the FCC. In practice, when a license "renewal" is sought, the FCC requests information from the station about the proportion of programs originated by the station, the proportion of programs devoted to news and public affairs, and the proportion of diverse broadcasting hours, systematically categorized, devoted to such things as commercial advertisements and public service announcements (Emery, 1971; Tuchman, 1974).

Commercials and the FTC.   Although the FCC regulates the licensing of individually owned stations, it has little to do with the actual content that is broadcast by each station other than to specify that it generally serve the public interest. The content of TV programs are not regulated by any other federal agency, although they are subject to internal scrutiny by network and industry officials. Television commercials, however, fall under the supervision of the Federal Trade Commission (FTC) which was formed in 1914 (FTC act, 1914; see also Clayton Anti-trust Act of 1914) whose original mission was protecting businessmen from dishonest competitors. In 1938 the Wheeler–Lea Act amended the original statute to include the protection to *consumers* (not just other businessmen), saying specifically that unfair or deceptive acts and practices were illegal. The Wheeler–Lea Act of 1938 gave the FTC enforcement powers to deal with violators, and it specifically gave the FTC control over food advertising (which had been under the Food and Drug Administration).

It is important to note that although it is true that the FCC and the FTC have the job of regulating the television we watch, it is also true that they regulate very little, especially when it comes to specifying the programming and advertising practices of the stations or networks. The FCC grants licenses and renews them every 5 years. When they do, they require that the stations explain what they are doing to serve the public. But the FCC has never taken away the license of a television station because it failed to serve the public interest (Tuchman, 1974). And although the FTC regulates deception and truth in advertisements, the agency itself does not monitor or preview commercials before they are shown. They wait until some interested party complains, and then they investigate the claims made in an ad. Frequently when the FTC does investigate, it is usually at the behest of one businessman complaining about the practices of another.

SUMMARY

So, what is television? Television is a device, invented in the mid-1920s, capable of sending a picture with sound over the broadcast band. Television is an industry grown up around the use of the device and regulated (more or less) by the federal government. Television is the content of what it shows every minute of every day: the programs and the commercials. Television is all of these things, and it has the potential to be even more.

As it has evolved in the United States, television is a device used to sell goods and services, sometimes to enhance the image of corporations, and occasionally, during elections, used to improve the image of politicians. Television informs us about the world, in part by showing us pictures of the human drama being enacted throughout the world, often as it is actually happening. Television's appeal knows few age, sex, or education barriers. Television is the universal informant. And most of all, television is the most successful marketing device ever invented.

The fact that it is primarily a marketing device has determined, to a very great extent, the nature of what is shown on it. There are very few educational and informational programs on television in the United States because these do not draw the size of audience that other (entertainment) programs do. The themes shown on the dramas are seldom in conflict with the values of the society as a whole, nor with the marketing industry (Barnouw, 1968, 1970; Tuchman, 1974). Because advertisers pay the piper, they get to call the tune.

Television was first introduced into this country at the end of World War II, in the late 1940s and early 1950s. It was quickly adopted by the American people, so that it saturated the country within a decade. During this period of time, television had the first set of effects and influences it was to have: indirect effects. The introduction of television caused the displacement of time (and thus activities) from the lives of many who now watched television rather than follow other pursuits. When television is introduced into any society there is a significant decline in book and magazine reading, in socializing with friends, in attendance at movies and sporting events, and in house cleaning. At the same time, there is an increase in the total amount of daily life devoted to media use — from watching television.

Indirect effects are interesting, but they may be largely temporary. There is reason to believe that such effects on society are only short term because the changes brought about are either adapted to or accommodated in some way. For example, although the introduction of television may have initially reduced literacy, especially among young children just learning to read, gradually the relevant members of society take note of these changes and take actions in order to offset them. Schools and teachers put more pressure on children to improve their reading skills, and concerned parents do the same, so that the constant (indirect) effect of television is met with an equally powerful compensation. Other indirect effects, the ones that are less noticeable such as dirtier houses and fewer friends, we simply accept. We quickly forget what life was like before television.

What about the direct effects of television, those that arise from the content of the programs and commercials themselves? The first step in understanding the direct effects of television is to ask who watches it? If the content has an influence, it will be strongest on those most frequently exposed. It is to this question that we turn our attention in chapter 2.

The Audience:
Who Watches, When,
What, and Why?

Who watches television? Everybody . . .
—George Comstock*

Chapter 1 showed that as soon as television was introduced into this country it became immediately popular, covering nearly the entire U.S. population in about a decade. Part of the reason for this is that unlike radio, its immediate predecessor, the appeal of television is almost universal. People of every age, social class, religion, and cultural background watch it. Children begin watching television before they can talk, and some of the earliest words they speak are learned from it. Immigrants to America (both children and adults) also pick up much of what they know of the English language from television, a device whose colorful visual images allow for comprehension of a simple story even when the words are not fully understood. The average American spends about 4 hours a day watching television, with older adults watching the most of any age group; even teenagers, who watch the least amount

*In Comstock, Chaffee, Katzman, McCombs, and Roberts (1978).

of television, still spend an average of nearly 24 hours a week in front of the TV set.

If we are to understand the nature of the influence of television, we must begin by trying to understand the degree of its attraction across age, sex, race, and other demographic segments of the population. We need to ask not only about the amount of television people watch, but what they watch, when they watch, and why. To begin to answer these questions, we look at some recent facts about the television viewing habits of various categories of Americans, gathered by the A.C. Nielsen Co. as part of their periodic surveys.

TELEVISION VIEWING IN THE AVERAGE HOUSEHOLD

As we saw in chapter 1, television was introduced in the early 1950s and it was quickly adopted into the homes of most Americans. In terms of actual numbers, in 1950 Nielsen estimated that there were 4.6 million homes with a television set. By 1955 this figure had risen to 32 million, and by 1960 it was 45.2 million homes. As of 1985, Nielsen estimated that there were 85.9 million television households in the continental United States, about 99% of the total household population (Nielsen, 1986).

By 1960, almost 90% of American homes had a television set that was, at that time, on for an average of more than 5 hours a day. How has the amount of time devoted to television viewing held up over the decades since? Figure 2.1 shows the number of hours of television usage in the average American household, measured from 1963 through 1985. As the graph illustrates, the number of hours of television viewing has increased almost steadily since the early 1960s, with the current figures showing the average household television usage at a little over 7 hours a day.

It is important to note that these figures represent the number of hours that the television set is on in the average household, and not the number of hours watched by the average person. Because different individuals in a given household tend to watch TV at different times, the average number of hours that a person watches TV is much lower: generally about 4 hours a day, depending on their age and sex. These individual estimates are based on the viewing diaries kept by families in the audience rating service samples, which were described in the last chapter.

These overall figures (4 hours a day per person, 7 hours a day per household) agree fairly well with other estimates of television viewing (see, for example, Bryant & Gerner, 1981; Robinson, 1981), although

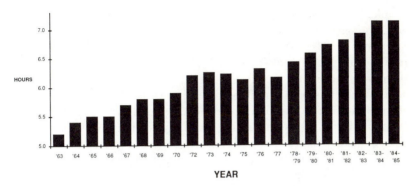

FIG. 2.1.   Average hours of household TV useage per day, for 1963–1985.
(Information from Nielsens, 1982 through 1986.)

when asked directly most people say they watch much less television
than the rating services indicate. Before going further in describing
the demographic differences in viewing behaviors, we need to look
more closely at the validity of each of these types of assessments, and
to examine the psychological reasons why self-report measures of television viewing might be misleading.

Measures of Television Watching:
Self-Report Versus Automatic Devices

As previously mentioned, most social scientists now use and accept the
Nielsen estimates as an accurate assessment of television viewing behavior. These measures have consistently indicated that the average
person watches about 4 hours of television a day; when asked directly
in interviews or surveys, however, the average person reports spending only about 2 hours a day watching TV (see Bryant & Gerner, 1981;
Robinson, 1981). So who is right?

People may not accurately report the actual amount of television
they watch for a variety of reasons, among which is the fact that they
may not really know. Faulty memory, however, should lead to random
error (some overestimation, some underestimation). Most careful
studies done by independent analysts agree, however, that when people err in reporting the amount of television they watch they tend to
do so in only one direction: underestimation (Comstock et al., 1978).
That is, they claim to watch less than they actually do. Why does this
happen?

One important reason has to do with the social desirability, or in
this case the apparent nondesirability, of television viewing. For many

people, it is not considered "proper" or socially desirable to admit to watching television. It is okay to do it, but not to admit to it. Of course, it is permissible to say that one watches educational and cultural programs, but not the average daily fare of commercial television. Moreover, these attitudes do not seem to be held to the same degree in all social classes; the middle and upper classes are more conscious of social desirability, and may therefore be less likely to report the actual amount of television viewing that they do. This bias of underestimation makes us wary of any self-report questionnaires about how much television is watched. In reporting audience and viewing data, therefore, we use the higher estimates reported by the rating services.

Variations in Viewing by Household Demographics

Figure 2.2 breaks down the average weekly viewing of television by three important characteristics of households: size, income, and what kind of selection is available (e.g., broadcast reception, cable, or pay TV). Larger households, not surprisingly, watch significantly more television than smaller households, and households with children watch more than those without. Neither of these findings will raise any eyebrows. But two other facts are of note: First, there is now little variation across the income distribution (unlike the past), and second, this seems to be due to increased viewing by the affluent.

A truism of the first two decades of television research, a fact to have emerged early and one that was repeated often, was that those with less income and education watch more television than those with more income and education. As recently as 1978, for example, a leading text noted that: "Persons in lower-income households watch considerably more television—an additional half-hour a day more in the fall of

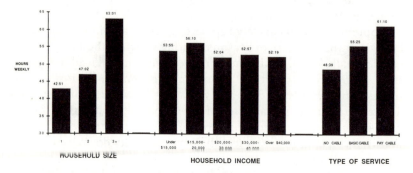

FIG. 2.2. Average hours of viewing per week by various household characteristics. (Information from Nielsen, 1986.)

1976—than the average for all individuals. Higher-income people watch the least television..." (Comstock et al., 1978, p. 94).

But the most recent figures concerning the viewing habits of people in different income brackets in 1985, given in Fig. 2.2, do not agree with this generalization. As can be seen, there are relatively few differences in the amount of weekly television viewing across the five income categories. Why has this happened? Are the less affluent watching less, or are the well-off watching more? The answer, perhaps, lies in the third part of Fig. 2.2, with the viewing statistics for people who have some form of "pay TV" compared to those who do not. As these data show, people who receive television "over the air" in the old-fashioned broadcast way, watch about the same amount of television as do people who get television through a cable, even though the cable offers more channels to choose from. But people who have "pay TV" (one of the several movie channels or a sports channel, costing something over and above the cost of the basic cable) watch an average of 10 hours more a week than either people with cable or people with broadcast only. Because it is the more affluent who are able to afford these extra cost services, this may be the reason for the reduction of the viewing gap between rich and poor. The affluent, it would seem, are watching more.

Channels Received

These considerations raise another series of questions about television: How much has the availability of channels (to some degree a measure of choice) increased? Not only has the amount of time people spend watching steadily increased, but also the number of channels received has increased steadily as well. For many years all of television came over the broadcast band and, in most areas, consisted of no more than the three major networks (the largest cities also had independent stations). In short, throughout most of the country people had only three or four channels available to choose from, and the networks often showed the same kind of program at the same time, so the amount of choice was very limited.

But the coming of cable drastically increased the quantity, if not the quality, of what was available. Now in many areas it is possible to purchase a cable service and get 30–50 channels at one time. Recently, a cable company attempting to get a franchise in an area of New York City (Queens) offered their potential customers over 100 channels! Will people watch all of these channels? Is there a relationship between how much television is offered and how much people will use? Figure 2.3 gives the most recent Nielsen data for channels received versus channels viewed. Two things about this figure seem worth mentioning. First,

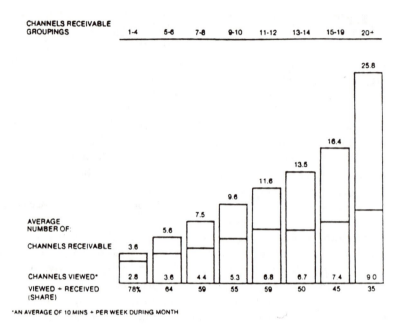

CHANNELS RECEIVABLE
GROUPINGS

| 1-4 | 5-6 | 7-8 | 9-10 | 11-12 | 13-14 | 15-19 | 20+ |

AVERAGE
NUMBER OF:

CHANNELS RECEIVABLE: 3.6 5.6 7.5 9.6 11.6 13.5 16.4 25.8

CHANNELS VIEWED*: 2.8 3.6 4.4 5.3 6.8 6.7 7.4 9.0

VIEWED ÷ RECEIVED (SHARE): 78% 64 59 55 59 50 45 35

*AN AVERAGE OF 10 MINS + PER WEEK DURING MONTH

FIG. 2.3. Number of channels received versus number of channels viewed.
(© A. C. Nielsen, 1982.)

the more channels people have, the more, on the average, they watch. There must be an end to all this (there are only so many hours in a day!) but so far it has not appeared. Second, this increase in viewing is not directly proportional to the increase in channels. So, although people who receive an average of 3.6 channels watch most of them (78%), people who receive an average of 9.6 channels only watch a little more than half (55%), and people who receive 20 or more channels (an average of 25.8) watch 9 of them, or only 35% of the total available. Still, in absolute numbers, the more choice in terms of channels available, the more people tend to watch. Give people a selection and they will use it. (It is not clear, from these figures, how many channels may offer duplicate programming at some times of the day. Thus, the selection among channels may not be completely independent.)

We saw that the television set is on in an average household for a period of 7 hours a day, over 49 hours a week, but this does not tell us anything about who is watching, at what times of the day, or what they watch. For that, we must turn to the demographics of the television audience. Now that we have looked at how much people watch, we turn to who watches, when, and what.

AUDIENCE CHARACTERISTICS: AGE, SEX, RACE, AND SOCIAL CLASS

The A.C. Nielsen Co. divides the over 235 million people in the United States into 85.9 million households, containing a little more than two people (on the average) in each. Of the households in the country, 99% have a television set, which, as we have just seen, is on for nearly 7 hours a day. Of the total population, about half are female. Are their viewing habits different from males? Forty million are children. How much do they watch, and when, and what? How shall we slice the pie of 86 million households? In the following sections, we look at slices by age, sex, race, income, and some of these categories combined.

TV Viewing by Young Children

By all accounts, children begin watching television as a steady habit at around the age of 2½ (Anderson & Levin, 1976), although there is some evidence that children are aware of some things about television, and like it, as early as 6 months of age (Hollenbeck & Slaby, 1979). A recent study demonstrated that infants not only watch television, but they can imitate it as well. In a cleverly designed set of experiments by Meltzoff (1988), infants were shown a simple task on television and given an opportunity to imitate what they had seen either immediately or after a 24-hour delay. Both 14- and 24-month-old infants were able to imitate a television stimulus, both immediately and after a 24-hour delay. These findings suggest that exposure to television in the home may potentially influence the behavior of very young infants moreso than was previously thought. Table 2.1 shows, based on one study, how the habit of watching television develops in children.

TABLE 2.1
Percent of Children Watching Television Regularly for Ages 2–9
(information from Schramm, Lyle, & Parker, 1961)

Age	Percent Watching TV as a Regular Habit
2	14
3	37
4	65
5	82
6	91
7	94
8	95
9	96

As this table shows, the youngest children begin to watch television as a regular habit at 2 years of age, and by 4 over 50% of the children sampled were watching television. By 6 years of age over 90% of American children watch television as a steady habit. The data in Table 2.1 were collected in the early 1960s, but more recent studies confirm these figures (see, e.g., Anderson, Alwitt, Lorch, & Levin, 1979; Anderson & Levin, 1976). Most authorities in the field now agree that at somewhere between 2 to 3 years of age children start watching television as a habit, in the sense of having favorite programs (Anderson et al., 1979).

Not only does the habit of watching television begin very early in life, but it also continues to hold the attention and interests of people well into old age. What a marvelous device to have this range of attraction. It is not clear that a person of 6 and a person of 60 watch television for the same reasons, or that they get the same thing out of it, or even that they pay attention to the same features, but each for their own reasons watches television, and each gets something out of it.

Variations in Viewing by Age and Sex

How does television viewing change over age? If children watch from about 2 years of age on, how much do they watch, and does their sex make a difference? Figure 2.4 gives the hours per week of television viewing broken down by age and sex, based on samples done for the Nielsen Co. in 1985.

These figures show that most children watch an average of between 3 and 4 hours of television daily. Children from 2 to 5 years of age spend more time watching than children from 6 to 11 years, probably

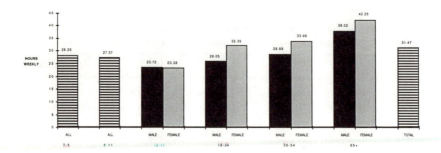

FIG. 2.4. Average hours of TV viewing per week, by age and sex of viewer. (Information from Nielsen, 1986.)

because going to school cuts into the viewing time of older children. During this period there are no obvious sex differences in what children watch, a fact worth noting.

Teenagers (age 12–17) watch significantly less television than any other age group in the population, and teenage boys watch slightly more television than teenage girls. Adolescence is the only age during which the sex difference goes in this direction. At every other age for which sex differences are reported, women watch more television than men. Older individuals (55 and over) watch significantly more television than the national average, and older women watch the most television of any age category, an average of almost 7 hours of television a day, 35 hours over a 5-day week (not counting weekends).

So, although it is true that television captures all ages, it does not capture all ages equally. The very young and the old watch the most, partly because they have more free time, and teenagers watch the least, for reasons that are not clear to anyone. Most adults, as well as most children, watch somewhere between 3 and 4 hours of television a day. Teenage girls watch the least television of any group in the country, whereas women over the age of 55 watch the most television of any group in the country.

We have already noted that one of the basic truths about television is that more women watch than men at every hour of the day and night. The only time women do not make up a majority of the audience is for sporting events, and in the afternoon from 4 p.m. to 5 p.m. when children seem to take over the set (Comstock et al., 1978).

The "gender gap," differences in viewing between men and women, is largest in the early afternoon and reaches a peak at about 3 to 4 p.m. During this time of day television features soap operas, game shows, and reruns of situation comedies. The audience for afternoon television is about one third the size of evening prime-time audiences. For example, at this time a popular afternoon soap opera is "General Hospital," and it draws an audience reported to be about 12 million. A popular evening situation comedy (sitcom) or drama, by contrast, will draw an audience of 35 million.

If we look at the relationship between sex and age, differences do not start to appear in the data until adulthood. Children and teenagers show few sex differences in terms of when they watch television, although adolescent girls watch more than boys from 12 p.m. to 5:30 p.m. After 5:30 p.m., there is a dip in the viewing curve for both sexes, but it is far more pronounced for teenage girls.

These differences reflect two things: (a) girls find the afternoon (soap opera and game show) fare more attractive than do boys, that is, there is a sex difference in the degree of intrinsic interest in watching this type of show; and (b) girls and boys have different roles at suppertime, and the involvement of the girls in preparing and serving dinner probably "cuts into" their television-watching time (Comstock et al., 1978, p. 107).

Aside from these small differences, however, children (ages 2–11) and teenagers (ages 12–17) show few sex differences in terms of either the amount or the type of program they watch. Thus is one of those places where a nondifference is worth mentioning. Children of this age often show large sex differences in play, dress, activity, and peer preferences (Condry, 1984). Children are just learning about sex roles, and they tend to mimic the most blatant and prototypical examples they see in society or on television. Thus, one might expect to find sex differences in television viewing, if not in *time spent* then at least in terms of *program preference*.

It is possible that the sex difference among teenagers in afternoon viewing (from noon to 5:30 p.m.) reflects a sex difference in program preference (for soaps and games) as we noted. But why do there seem to be so few? One possibility is our measures are not sufficiently precise to reflect differences that are actually there. Another is that the fare of television is not sufficiently varied to reflect differences in interest patterns that are really there. So if the programming were more varied, if there were more choices offered, particularly ones that might appeal more to girls than to boys, we might expect to find more sex differences in interest, preference, and program choice.

Variations in Viewing by Race, Income, and Education

These factors should be considered together because they tend to be highly correlated. The last two, education and income, taken together may be used as one definition of "social class." The relationship among these variables is well known: In the country as a whole, Blacks tend to be less affluent and have less education than Whites. The historical reasons for these differences aside, racial differences in television viewing, like sex differences, are of interest if we are going to try to understand the psychology of television.

It is no secret that Blacks and Whites inhabit slightly different worlds. Blacks, on the average, tend to be less affluent and have larger families. In addition to these differences, Blacks and Whites relate differently to television: they watch different amounts (Blacks watch more) and different kinds of programs. Although many of these differences are confounded with income and education, some of them are due to race alone (see, e.g., Bogart, 1972, Bower, 1973; Robinson, 1972, 1981).

Table 2.2 gives the average viewing for Blacks and Whites broken

TABLE 2.2
Average Hours Per Week of Prime-Time Viewing by Race (from Bogart, 1972).

Demographics	Whites	Blacks
Age:		
18–34	8.9	10.4
35–49	9.3	9.1
50 +	10.2	8.0
Income:		
Over $10,000	8.9	10.0
$5,000–9,000	9.7	9.5
Under $5,000	10.1	8.8
Education:		
Some college or more	8.1	8.5
High school	9.8	11.2
Less than high school	10.1	8.7

down by age and income. These data are adapted from an article by Bogart (1972), and the percentages for Whites are based on a larger number of observations ($N = 2,300$–$7,000$) than are the percentages for Blacks ($N = 200$–900).

Blacks watch more television than Whites, as we noted, considerably more. Black viewers watch more during the day than Whites, and they prefer different programs (Comstock et. al., 1978, p.125). Moreover, Blacks hold different attitudes toward the television they watch. Among Whites, the older, poorer, less well educated watch more television than the younger, more affluent, better educated. But among Black Americans these findings are reversed: younger, better educated Blacks with higher incomes watch the most television of all, and hold the most favorable attitudes about it. These class differences, among Blacks, develop early enough to be detected in children (Greenberg & Dervin, 1970).

Unlike the amount viewed, program preference differences between Blacks and Whites are confounded with social class (Greenberg & Dervin, 1970), so it is more difficult to tell whether a particular difference in preference is due to race, or social class, or both acting together. Blacks clearly prefer programs featuring Black performers (Bogart, 1972), and young Blacks prefer shows about families more so than young White adults (Surlin & Dominick, 1970). Blacks watch about the same amount of television as Whites during prime time, but they watch more during the day. Finally, older Blacks watch less television than younger Blacks, and this is the reverse of the trend among White adults.

It is worth noting that these are very limited data and before we are too quick to draw generalizations from this research it should be updated. In general, however, given the evidence we have, Blacks watch more television than Whites from childhood on, and especially during the adult years of 18–49. Social class differences in patterns of viewing are reversed in Blacks and Whites: the poor watch more than the wealthy among Whites, the reverse is true among Blacks. Blacks hold more favorable attitudes toward television than do Whites, they "like it" more, and elderly Blacks watch less than younger Blacks, again the reverse of the trends with Whites.

Before we get too enamoured with the differences, it should be underlined that in most ways the Black viewing audience is similar to the White one: Women watch more than men at every hour of the day and night, for example, and except as we have already noted, the program preferences are the same as those for Whites of every age and social class. Thus, although noting the differences, it is well to keep in mind that the age and class differences found in the population as a whole tend to be reflected as well among the majority of Black viewers (Bogart, 1972).

PROGRAM PREFERENCES

There are so many different kinds of programs available on televi-

TOTAL U.S. TV HOUSEHOLDS	AA%
1. Bill Cosby Show	32.3
2. A Different World	28.5
3. Cheers	26.4
4. Night Court	25.3
5. Growing Pains	24.3
6. 60 Minutes	23.1
7. Who's The Boss?	22.8
8. Murder, She Wrote	22.0
9. Golden Girls	21.5
10. L.A. Law	20.0
11. CBS Sunday Movie	19.6
12. Moonlighting	19.5
13. Family Ties	18.9
14. Alf	18.8
15. NFL Monday Night Football	17.7

MEN 18+	AA%
1. 60 Minutes	17.6
2. Bill Cosby Show	17.3
3. NFL Monday Night Football	16.4
4. Cheers	14.9
5. Night Court	14.6
6. A Different World	14.4
7. Murder, She Wrote	13.9
8. CBS NFL Football Game 1	13.8
9. L.A. Law	13.4
10. CBS Sunday Movie	12.8
11. CBS NFL Football Game 2	12.6
12. NFL Game 2	12.4
13. CBS College Football Game 2	12.2
14. Growing Pains	12.1
15. Family Ties	11.9

CHILDREN 2-11	AA%
1. Bill Cosby Show	22.5
2. A Different World	20.9
3. Alf	20.9
4. Growing Pains	19.2
5. Who's The Boss?	17.6
6. Valerie's Family	17.5
7. Disney Sunday Movie	16.8
8. Family Ties	15.5
9. Pee Wee's Playhouse	14.4
10. My Two Dads	13.9
11. Muppet Babies III	12.3
12. Cheers	12.2
13. Muppet Babies II	11.8
14. Perfect Strangers	11.6
14. Alvin & The Chipmunks	11.6

WOMEN 18+	AA%
1. Bill Cosby Show	26.8
2. A Different World	23.0
3. Cheers	20.8
4. Night Court	19.4
5. Murder, She Wrote	19.1
6. Golden Girls	18.7
7. Growing Pains	18.0
8. Who's The Boss?	17.0
9. CBS Sunday Movie	16.7
10. 60 Minutes	16.3
11. Dallas	15.7
12. L.A. Law	15.6
13. Amen	14.9
14. Matlock	14.8
15. NBC Monday Night Movies	14.5

TEENS 12-17	AA%
1. Growing Pains	25.1
2. Bill Cosby Show	22.9
3. A Different World	22.6
4. Who's The Boss?	21.4
5. Alf	21.2
6. Valerie's Family	19.7
7. Family Ties	19.7
8. My Two Dads	18.2
9. Cheers	17.7
10. Moonlighting	16.9
11. Night Court	16.3
12. Head of The Class	15.9
13. Perfect Strangers	14.0
14. Golden Girls	12.8
15. Facts of Life	12.7

Nielsen Average Audience Estimates
2 or more telecasts (15 minutes or longer)
November 1987

FIG. 2.5. Top 15 regularly scheduled network programs in November 1987. (© Nielsen, 1988.)

sion, and there are so many different kinds of people (age, sex, class, race, etc.), that to attempt any program-by-population category analysis seems an almost impossible task. But just to give a flavor of the pattern of program preferences, Fig. 2.5 shows the breakdown by age and sex for the several categories of program type coded by A. C. Nielsen (based on data collected in 1987.)

Situation comedies, suspense/mystery drama, and feature films have for some time been the most popular program types on television, whereas news and informational programs have always been the least popular. In news, the local news tends to outdraw the national news in audience size. The prime-time shows gather the largest overall audience and also the most diverse audience. Other than this, much of the program preference data is obvious. Specialty programs tend to appeal to the intended group: children's shows mostly to children, soap operas mainly to women, sports mainly to men and boys.

Children watch cartoons and later situation comedies; men prefer adventure, mystery, and sports; women prefer human drama, especially the kind displayed in soap operas and situation comedies. Very few people watch the news, as we noted, yet "60 Minutes," an "informational" program produced by CBS News, was the top-ranking program among all U.S. households in 1982, and has continued to be in the top four programs since. We have more to say about the program content of television in chapter 3.

Public Attitudes About the Media

If a key to the success of television is the audience, what does the audience, the public, think of television? There is no simple answer to this question, in part because public attitudes about television are paradoxical (Comstock, 1988). For example, public evaluation of television has become progressively less favorable over the last 22 years (Bower, 1973, 1985; Steiner, 1963), while at the same time the amount of viewing in the average household has increased steadily (see Fig. 2.1). Public opinion surveys report that about 75% of the public feel there are too many commercials, while an equal proportion (75%) believe that commercials are a fair price to pay for free entertainment (Comstock et al., 1978). As Comstock (1988) put it: "The mass media are accorded a place in social life very much on their own terms; liking them has little to do with whether they are used, how they are used, or even how much they are used" (p. 325). In fact, a study by Neuman (1982) suggests that except for the extreme ends of the range (college professors), even education makes little difference in how one responds to the media.

WHY PEOPLE WATCH TELEVISION:
NEEDS AND GRATIFICATIONS

We have discussed who watches, and when, and what they watch. But none of this tells us why. Why do people watch television? What do they get out of it? How can we tell? We can ask the people who watch, of course, staying conscious of the fact that people may not be fully aware of all the motivations they have, and that people often like to portray themselves in a good light, even if it is not completely true (the problem of "social desirability"). Still, with all of these limitations, researchers have for some time asked people why they watch television, what they get out of it.

One of the earliest studies of this sort was done in 1944. Herzog (1944) interviewed housewives about the gratifications derived from listening to radio soap operas. She found the answers fell into three broad areas: (a) emotional release, (b) as a basis for fantasy, and (3) as a provider of information about the world. Continuing this early line of research with television rather than radio, Katz and Foulkes (1962) posited a single variable model (people watch television in order to "escape"). Finally, in terms of early studies, in their study of children's viewing habits, Schramm et al. (1961) described two reasons children watch television: escape and information.

This category of research is often called a *needs-and-gratifications* approach to understanding television viewing, because it seeks to trace the needs that watching television serves and the gratifications people derive from it (Blumler & Katz, 1975; Galloway & Meek, 1981; Katz, Blumler, & Gurevitch, 1974; Rosengren, Wenner, & Palmgreen, 1985). According to this approach, one job of the social science researcher is to learn what needs can be satisfied by media, and how the various media accomplish this.

McQuail (1972), for example, studied both listeners of radio and viewers of television, and concluded that the reasons people gave for viewing fell into four broad categories: (a) to escape the boredom of everyday life (b) to have something to talk about with others (c) to compare the people and events in the programs with their own experience and (d) to keep in touch with the events in the world.

In a similar study, Katz, Gurevitch, and Haas (1973), working in Israel, asked viewers to explain the role of various media in gratifying needs or in fulfilling expectations. Although agreeing, in general, with the fourfold typology just described, these researchers found that most media were "need specific," that is, different needs were served by different specific media. Books provide escape, for example, and newspapers provide information. Perhaps to no one's surprise, television was the most diverse of the media studied in terms of the needs it served and the gratifications derived from it.

In reviewing two sets of studies conducted in Australia (Kippax & Murray, 1977, 1980), Murray (1980), a well-known researcher commented about the needs-and-gratifications approach:

> television is not only *perceived* as gratifying these needs, it is also *used* as a source of gratification. Individuals who endorse information needs do watch more information programs. Those who endorse social and personal identity needs do watch more of those programs such as popular dramas and movies which can be seen to serve those needs related to vicarious social contact. However there are no specific programs that particularly serve those with escapist needs—for the escapist, any program will do. (p. 28)

Murray suggested that research done in the United States, Australia, Israel, Sweden, Finland, France, and Canada supports the needs-and-gratifications approach.

What Happens When People Give Up Television?

One way to discover how television serves the needs of those who watch it is to ask what happens when people are asked to give it up. Several small-scale investigations of this problem have been conducted, although many of them have been inconclusive. In 1973 in Munich, for example, five families were paid $150 a month for an open-ended period of time not to watch television, and in England, in 1974, the BBC paid five families $200 a month, again for an indefinite period, not to watch television. Both studies were terminated within 2 months because no family was able to continue not watching television beyond this time (Winick, 1988, p. 218). Walters and Stone (1971) studied 76 households in Madison, Wisconson, and Tan (1977) paid 51 households in Lubbock, Texas, $4 a day not to watch. During the time people did not watch, newspapers became the main source of information, including consumer information, and the radio became the main source of entertainment. There were increases in visiting and socializing with others, and family social activities also increased during the time these families did without television.

Winick (1985b, 1988) studied families who were deprived of television sets while they were in repair. Winick (1988) reported:

> The sequence of respondents' reactions to the loss of television was, to some extent, similar for many households. The first 3 or 4 days for most

persons were the worst, even in many homes where viewing was minimal and where there were other ongoing activities. In over half of all the households, during these first few days of loss, the regular routines were disrupted, family members had difficulties in dealing with the newly available time, anxiety and aggressions were expressed, and established expectations for the behavior of other household members were not met. People living alone tended to be bored and irritated. Over four-fifths of the respondents reported moderate to severe dislocations during this period. (pp. 221-222)

Fortunately this situation did not continue. "The fifth to eighth day represented, in many cases, some form of readjustment to the new situation. By the second week, a move toward adaptation to the situation was common" (p. 222). On the basis of his research, Winick concluded that television serves six functions (followed by the proportion of respondents to whom they applied):

1. Surveillance and information—83%
2. Relaxation and entertainment—83%
3. Conversation—72%
4. Social cement—71%
5. Punctuating the day—63%
6. Companionship—60% (Winnick, 1988, p. 223).

Television and Guilt

In addition to meeting certain of our needs, television watching, alone among the other media, seems to engender guilt. At least this is the conclusion of a long-term study of television viewing in England. One of the first investigators to study television use over a long period of time was Hilde Himmelweit, a British psychologist, and a pioneer of television research. In 1951, shortly after the introduction of television in England, as part of a large study of influences on socialization, Himmelweit, Oppenheim, and Vince (1958) interviewed 600 boys, 13–14 years old. Three-quarters of the original subjects were interviewed again when they were 24–25, in 1962; and 246 of the original sample answered additional questions in 1972 when they were 32–33 years old. The study was not originally designed to study television alone, but rather to gather information about the factors that influence lifestyle.

As a result of this research, Himmelweit was one of the first to notice that television watching engendered guilt, especially in middle class viewers. This finding has been replicated by Steiner (1963) in the United States, and Furu (1971) in Japan. Himmelweit found, for example, the more a person engaged in most leisure activities, the more the person said they liked them. There was little "guilt" reported. This was true of everything but television. But heavy TV viewers said they were not satisfied with spending so much time watching it, and they wish they did other things. "Television alone among the major leisure activities evoked guilt" (Himmelweit & Swift, 1976, p. 142).

Himmelweit attributed this to the fact that television is easy to use, being available 24 hours of the day. Going to the theater or to movies, or even getting a book out of the library and reading it, requires a degree of commitment and effort that television does not:

> Guilt may well stem from a feeling of having succumbed to television's attractions too easily merely because it is available, of having taken what is offered rather than having actively sought activities which give greater satisfaction. (Himmelweit & Swift, 1976, p. 142)

Whatever the reason, the guilt-producing effects of television watching has some interesting implications. For one thing, it is probably the reason for such a wide difference between the amount of viewing recorded by survey companies using unobtrusive measures and the amount people admit to watching. As we noted, most surveys show this difference to be on the order of 2 hours a day (Bryant & Gerner, 1981; Robinson, 1972, 1981).

The guilt people feel about watching may also be responsible for the fact that television is not discussed much in the schools, at least not officially. One of the most interesting things about this guilt is that it appears to be confined to the middle class (Himmelweit & Swift, 1976; Steiner, 1963), thus providing a possible confound in research on television. Self-report questionnaires, due to this bias, are likely to underestimate the TV watching of the more affluent.

From another perspective, Himmelweit's findings about the role of television in leisure life offer a sophisticated view of the needs-and-gratifications approach. Leisure choices are viewed as an interplay between a number of different factors: the alternatives available on the one hand, and the socializing experiences of the individual on the other. In short, the accessibility and content of the media are arrayed on one side of the ledger, and the skill, knowledge, and values of the viewer on the other. According to Himmelweit, together these factors predict what media will be used, how the media will be used, and what desires they will satisfy.

Changing Television Tastes Over Time

Some of the most intriguing findings of Himmelweit's long-term study of television use is the evidence she gathered on changing tastes over time. Taste in television fare apparently changes over the course of life. Differences in what one finds "attractive" on television, that is attractive enough to watch, may reflect age differences in both cognitive ability and experience. Himmelweit's research does not include children (we consider the tastes of children in detail in chapters 7 and 8). When Himmelweit first questioned her subjects they were adolescents. According to Himmelweit and Swift (1976) adolescent tastes are centered on the "adventurous and the violent," as they put it: "a taste for strong stimulation."

In adulthood (recall that the oldest of their participants were 33 at the time of their last report, in 1976) tastes were more "differentiated," and preferences had shifted from fantasy to reality. In books, adults preferred technical and nonfiction books to westerns and detective stories, and on television they preferred news, documentaries, and sports programs rather than crime drama and thrillers (Himmelweit & Swift, 1976, p. 154).

In Himmelweit's research, as in other early studies of media usage, education and IQ were significant predictors (the less education and the lower the IQ, the more television watched) of both how much media are used and what programs are watched. Socially active ("gregarious") youngsters were more likely to go to the movies as adolescents and to be heavy viewers of television as adults, for example, suggesting that for a lonely endeavor, television may provide a form of social stimulation to those most in need of it. Himmelweit and Swift (1976) reported that there is a "critical period" in adolescence when children can either learn other leisure pursuits that are more active and more demanding than television, or fail to do so. According to these theorists, habits of leisure pursuit developed during adolescence tend to persist throughout adulthood.

Television and Control

A final perspective on the role of television comes from Ellen Langer, a psychological researcher who has focused much of her research attention on the role of control and predictability in everyday life (Langer, 1983; Langer & Avorn, 1981; Langer & Rodin, 1970). Television offers both predictability and control, "at the least, it provides for the opportunity to engage in conscious instrumental responding" (Langer & Piper, 1988, p. 249). Television provides control, that is, so long as it is not completely predictable, and so long as one uses it in a "mindful" way.

Langer and her colleagues have done a good deal of research on this topic of mindfulness/mindlessness (Langer, Bashner, & Chanowitz, 1985; Langer & Imber, 1979; Langer & Newman, 1987; Langer & Weinman, 1981). *Mindlessness* is seen as a way of doing things predictably, routinely. *Mindfulness*, on the other hand, involves doing the same things but thinking about them, taking another perspective while engaged in the task. Piper and Langer (1986) studied two groups of adults who were asked to watch television in these two different ways. The mindless group was asked to simply relax and enjoy the programs in the way they ordinarily did, but the mindful group was told to take a different perspective each time they viewed. After the viewing was over, participants were given several measures to assess creativity. The results are described by Langer and Piper (1988) as follows: "Several converging measures in this study suggest that watching television in a mindful way apparently results in greater flexibility in one's thinking. Thus it seems that mindful televiewing may indeed be beneficial" (p. 255).

In short, the influence of television and the role it plays in our lives depends as much on how we watch as on what we watch. It is possible to watch the same television stimulus in radically different ways, and to get different things out of it. This is true, of course, of almost everything we do, but as it applies to television this rule takes on a special force. There is sometimes the tendency to think of the "mass" audience of television as one large being, faceless and formless, staring at the tube. Nothing could be further from the truth. What is gotten from the experience of watching television is slightly different for each person, depending on the person's age, background, the program watched, and the manner of watching. All of this must be kept in mind as we study the psychological impact of television.

SUMMARY

Most people watch television, it is hard to avoid. In one study, children who did not have a television set at home still reported to researchers that they watched an average of 2 hours a day (Singer & Singer, personal communication, 1983). They used their friends homes for this purpose, of course. But people who have television certainly watch it, usually more than they notice, or report. The average household has a television set "on" for about 7 hours in the day. The average person, adult or child, watches about 4 hours a day. Teenagers watch somewhat less and older people somewhat more than the average.

If the first big truth about television is that almost everyone watches (for an analysis of nonviewers, see Jackson-Beeck, 1977), the second big truth is that different types of people do so at different times, and they watch different programs. Television seems to offer a little of something for everyone. Women make up a larger proportion of the audience at most times in the day, and a much larger proportion during the afternoon when most of the programs are soap operas. Men watch more than women during the afternoon sports shown on Saturday and Sunday. Children make up a large percentage of the audience on Saturday morning from 7 a.m. to 12 p.m. and during the week in the after-school hours from 4 p.m. to 6 p.m., when many parents are delighted to have such a cheap and effective babysitter.

In addition to differences by age and sex, racial differences are one important area for exploration, especially if race can be separated from income and education as an independent factor in television viewing. In particular, it is interesting that young, affluent, well-educated Blacks are most attracted to television (among Whites it is the opposite). It is also interesting that older Blacks watch less television than younger Blacks (again reversing the trend among Whites). Should these results stand up over time, they could be very informative about why television has whatever influences it has on us.

To determine the influence all of this television watching is having, we need to look in more detail at the content of it, at what people who expose themselves to this world see and hear. There is already enough evidence to suggest that the potential for influence is there. We must now consider the direct effects that are due to the audience being immersed in the content of television, due to "living" in the world shown on the tube.

What is the *world of television* like? What does it consist of? In what ways is it like, in what ways unlike the "real" world? What kind of people are in the world of television and what are they like? In order to understand the influence of television, the direct influence, we must begin an analysis of the "environment," the content, of television.

The Program Content of Television

From 8 to 11 o'clock each night, television is one long lie...
*—David Rintels, Former President, Writers Guild of America**

If the direct effects of television's influence come from the content of television, how can we begin to describe this content? For one thing, we need to adopt a perspective, we need to ask "from what point of view?" The industry's point of view, as we have seen, is that the content of television is a series of programs, divided into types, shown at different times of the day and night, and appealing to certain members of the audience. The content, described in this way, changes with some regularity.

The location of these programming categories varies quite a bit over the day and the week. During the week, the morning is taken up with news and game shows, the afternoon mostly with soap operas and re-runs of situation comedies. The evening begins with more news, more sitcoms, and then the prime-time shows of comedy, drama, entertain-

---

*Waters (1982).

ment, and the like. Finally, late-night talk shows and movies round out the "broadcast day," going well into the night. The content of television on the weekend is different than during the week (and many ratings services keep separate records of weekday vs. weekend viewing).

Much of Saturday morning is given over to shows for children (primarily cartoons) and seasonal professional sports take up most of Saturday afternoon. Sunday morning has both religious and weekly news programs, with Sunday afternoon, like Saturday, being devoted to sports on most of the major networks. (For a more detailed description of the program content and audience for these programs see Comstock et al., 1978.)

HISTORICAL PATTERNS OF PRIME-TIME PROGRAMMING

Although different times of the day have limited and often specific audiences, one time of the day gathers all types and kinds of audience together: prime time, the hours of the week between 8 and 11 p.m. (Nielsen, 1986).

Thanks to an analysis by Patricia Bence (1987), we can get one glimpse of the different programming types to come and go on prime time during the decades of the introduction of television in the United States. Bence analyzed the frequency of different programming types by year, available in a compendium of television programs covering the years 1950–1980 (Castleman & Podrazik, 1984).

Figure 3.1 illustrates the number of programs broadcast each year from 1950 to 1980 for selected program types. Many of the early programs on television drew their format and audience from the days of radio. Westerns, for example, long a staple of radio, became popular on television after 1955 and remained popular throughout most of the decade until 1965, after which time they lost popularity to the point where no additional Westerns appear on prime-time programming after 1980. Likewise, drama anthology, programs like "Playhouse 90" and "The Armstrong Circle Theater," was another program type quite popular in the early days of television, but it too declined in popularity by the 1960s. Essentially, the same pattern of early popularity and decline is seen for prime-time game shows, which decreased after they were mired in scandal (see Barnouw, 1982), and musical variety.

Other programming types have remained consistently popular in prime time over the years: drama, crime drama, movies, and adventure, all have proven to be staples of prime-time programming. The most consistently popular evening prime-time type of program, in Bence's analysis, is the situation comedy (many other content analyses of prime-time programming agree, see, e.g., Comstock et al., 1978).

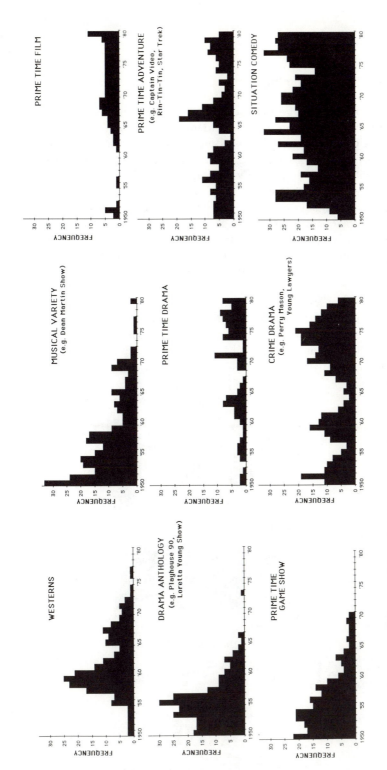

FIG. 3.1. Frequency of different program types as represented by one week, for 1950–1980. (Information from Bence, 1987.)

Children's Programming

The exposure of large numbers of children to the type of content provided by television is new and unique in human history, and deserves to be closely followed. Bence (1987) analyzed network children's programs, again relying primarily on the list of programs aired from 1950–1980, compiled by Castleman and Podrazik (1984).

Children's programs were a popular fare in the early days of television (Fig. 3.2), possibly because they provided a convenient excuse for the family investing a substantial sum of money for a television set ("Buy it for the kids. . ."). A similar argument is made in advertisements today for home computers. But as the number of broadcasting hours increased the number of children's programs decreased, not only as a proportion of the total programming, but also in terms of absolute numbers. As can be seen in Fig. 3.2, there were 84 children's programs per week on network television in 1950, with an average of 14 new programs a season until 1956. Children's programming then declines starting in 1957 and continuing until 1959. From 1960 to 1966 the frequency of children's shows increase to level off at the rate they maintain until

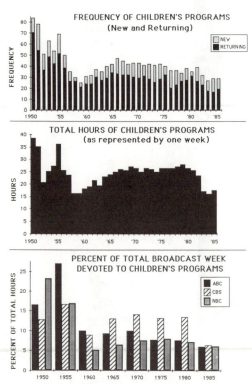

FIG. 3.2.   Changes in children's programming, 1950–1985. (Information from Bence, 1987.)

LIVE VS. ANIMATED CHILDREN'S PROGRAMS

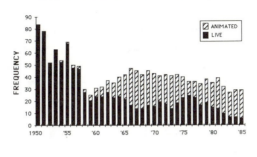

ANIMATED CHILDREN'S PROGRAMS:
NEW VS. RETURNING

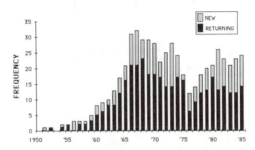

FIG. 3.3.   Changes in animated children's programs, 1950–1985. (Information from Bence, 1987.)

1980. Likewise, the percent of the broadcast week devoted to programs for children (Fig. 3.2), was larger in the 1950s, dips through the early 1960s, and recovers to the rate of about 13% of network programming, where it remains through the early 1980s.

One possible explanation for this pattern is that in the early days many children's shows were on in order to attract family buyers. Many of these programs were sponsored by the stations themselves. As television grew in the mid-1950s, paying customers competed with children's shows, and many of them were driven off the air due to economic forces. Then, in the 1960s, children were "discovered" by the cereal and toy companies as a legitimate audience, and the number of programs for children increases dramatically, sponsored by products designed for them (Adler et al., 1980).

What is the nature of this programming for children, and how has it changed over the years? In the 1950s, the early days of television, most of the programming was live, often featuring performers (Buffalo Bob) who communicated with puppets (Howdy Doody). Beginning in the decade of the 1960s, animated cartoons (Fig. 3.3) made up a larger

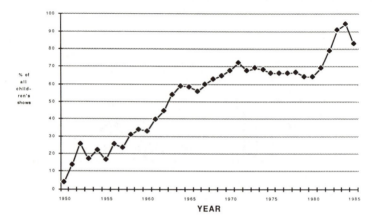

FIG. 3.4.   Percent of all children's programs shown on Saturday and Sunday mornings, 1950–1985. (Information from Bence, 1987.)

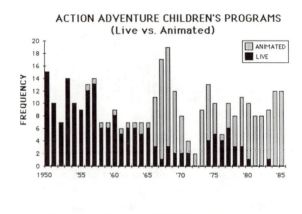

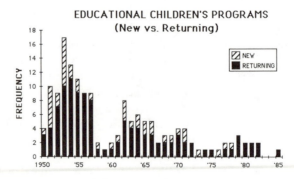

FIG. 3.5.   Changes in action adventure and educational children's programs, 1950–1985. (Information from Bence, 1987.)

and larger share of the programming for children (Bence, 1987).

Between 1960 and 1966, children's programs became a staple of Saturday and Sunday morning time periods (Fig. 3.4). Of the types of programs offered to children, action adventure is one of the most stable program types (Fig. 3.5), whereas educational programs have come and gone, mostly gone. As noted earlier, live puppet shows that were popular in the earliest days of television eventually were completely replaced by animated action adventure stories, often featuring characters that can also be purchased in toy stores. This trend is discussed in more detail in chapter 7. For an excellent analysis of the content of children's programs, see Barcus, 1983.

TELEVISION AS AN "ENVIRONMENT"

From a psychological point of view, however, these programming categories are not as important as understanding the nature of the information contained in each program type. The action adventure category tells us only a little about the content of the material shown. From a psychological perspective it is best to think about television as an *environment,* even though using the term in this way greatly stretches it. For one thing, there is a mutuality about the person and the real environment (Gibson, 1966) that is lacking with television. We change the real environment, and it changes us as well. With the environment of television, the path of influence is more one way: Television changes us more than we change it. We do not "interact" with television, we "encounter" it.

For another thing, no matter how it looks on the surface, the world of television drama is different in a multitude of small ways from the world of everyday life that it is attempting to portray. In fact, as we see here, these little distortions may be critical to tracing the influence of television. Television is not an exact replica of the world of reality in part because it is a "dramatized" world: scripted, directed, and acted; it is designed with the purpose of attracting and holding attention rather than offering an accurate portrayal of "reality." Makers of television drama want to tell a story, and they cannot be constrained by "reality" in doing so.

From each person's perspective, some parts of television drama are "real," whereas other parts are clearly "false." Some part of this depends on what we know, what we understand about the real world. I recall watching doctor shows, popular in the mid-1950s, with my father, a doctor, and listening to him heap scorn on television doctors like Ben Casey and Dr. Kildare (popular doctor programs) because they were "completely false, absurd, and unrealistic." He liked the shows about lawyers, however, he thought they were very true to life. My best friend's father, on the other hand, was a lawyer, and he complained about "Perry Mason" (a lawyer show) because it was so dishonest. But he liked the doctor shows, he thought they were very realistic.

If we agree to view television as an environment, how do we get a handle on the structure of information provided by this environment? What is the world like that is depicted on television? Each person's singular judgment is suspect, as we have seen, and the programmers viewpoint is of very little use. The answer is that we must rely on scientific methods of description: on content analysis.

CONTENT ANALYSIS

A *content analysis* is a careful and replicable way of describing and recording the content of television. After choosing the type of material to be observed, it requires the development of a coding scheme and the training of coders to use the scheme reliably. All of the remaining evidence in this chapter regarding the content of television comes to us through content analyses of the information in the program content of television (in chapter 7, we look at a content analysis of ads). A formal definition of *content analysis* is: "any technique for making inferences by systematically and objectively identifying specified characteristics of messages" (Holsti, 1969, p. 601).

All content analyses of television programming involve decisions about what program material to focus on and what to ignore, what categories of behavior to code and how they will be defined (usually a major bone of contention), and finally how the reliability and validity of the coding scheme will be established.

Reliability and Validity

An item of data about television is *reliable* if the same scene is coded in the same way by different coders, or by the same coder at different times. The first of these is called *interrater reliability,* and the second is *test–retest reliability.* For the most part, we are concerned with interrater reliability. In general, the higher the reliability the better, but the degree of reliability that is attainable, in part depends on the type of event (or character) being coded. Determining the number of characters in a scene can be done very reliably, for example, but coding the "relationship between characters" or the "amount of violence" in a particular scene, is much more difficult. So quantitative events and character portrayals (age, sex, occupation, etc.) are more reliably coded than qualitative characteristics such as power relationships, violence, or values. Interrater reliabilities are determined by correlating the scores of different (independent) viewers coding the same material.

An item of data is *valid* if the coding truly reflects what is there. If a coding scheme measures what it is supposed to measure, then it is valid. The validity of a coding scheme depends, in large part, on the adequacy of the definitions used by the coders. As we see later in this chapter, the *validity* of coding some of the activity on Saturday morning cartoons as violence (or not) is a matter of current debate, although the reliability of these same analyses is not an issue. Most reviewers agree that the analyses are reliable.

In addition to these basic criteria, researchers doing content analyses must design their research so that it may be replicated by others. The decisions made in doing a content analysis therefore must be spelled out in detail and published, so that others, using the same technique (on the same material), should be able to arrive at the same conclusions.

Recurrent Distortions

In our focus on the content of television determined by content analyses, we search for the existence of recurrent distortions, portrayals of the world that depart, in significant ways, from some definition of reality. For example, we look at the number of men on television programs compared to the census statistics for the number of men in everyday life. For the moment, it is not important how those distortions got there, or whether they are accidental or deliberate, only that they exist.

In drama, for example, time is almost always misrepresented relative to "true" time. People in movies and television seldom pay bills, or go to the bathroom, or do the thousand ordinary dull things that the rest of us have to do in order to get through an average day. Stories would be unbearably dull with these included, so they aren't. From the producer's and director's points of view such minor distortions are necessary in order to tell a story in the time allotted.

The importance of such exaggerations and distortions of fact is that they should appear more in the attitudes, beliefs, values, and knowledge systems of heavy viewers compared to light viewers. If the content of television contains small discrepancies, these distorted beliefs should characterize the understanding of those who are more exposed to television than those with less exposure. This is a fundamental fact about research on television and it is important to recognize it.

Cultural Indicators

In the early 1960s a long-standing debate about the effect of violence in media gave rise to a large-scale research project designed to document and analyze the content of television programs to which millions of people were exposed each night.

George Gerbner and his colleagues at the Annenburg School of Communications at The University of Pennsylvania began to collect samples of evening prime-time television and to do content analyses of it. The purpose was to describe the "world" of television. Gerbner called this part of his work "message-system analysis" and it constitutes the first of two stages of research in the Cultural Indicators Research project. The second part of the project involves what Gerbner called "cultivation analysis," where information gleaned from the message system analysis is traced in the attitude and belief systems of heavy viewers. We return to the results of cultivation analysis in a later chapter when we discuss the direct effects of television. For the moment, however, let us consider the findings of Gerbner's message system analysis. What exactly is it, and what does it reveal about the content of television?

Message System Analysis

"Message system analysis is the annual monitoring of samples of prime-time and weekend daytime network dramatic programming. . ." (Gerbner, Gross, Morgan, & Signorielli, 1980, p. 10). Gerbner and his colleagues monitor television, record a sample of the content, and then do a content analysis with a focus on *who, does what, to whom.* A large range of human behavior can be coded using this scheme.

All scenes are coded by pairs of trained coders in order to assure reliability (Gerbner, Gross, Jackson-Beeck, Jeffries-Fox, & Signorielli, 1978), then they are subjected to an extensive reliability analysis. Only those items that meet the project's high standards for reliability are then used in the analysis (Gerbner, 1969, p. 12).

The results of this analysis portray the world of television as a world:

> in which men outnumber women three to one, young people comprise one-third and old people one-fifth of their real numbers, professionals and law-enforcers dominate the occupations, and an average of five acts of violence per prime time hour (and four times that number per weekend daytime hour) involve more than half of all leading characters. (Gerbner et al., 1980, pp. 10–11)

The results of this research have been published in a series of "violence profiles" since 1967 when the project began (Gerbner, 1969,

1972b, 1976; Gerbner, Gross, Eleey, Jackson-Beeck, Jeffries-Fox, & Signorielli, 1977b; Gerbner, Gross, Jackson-Beeck, Jeffries-Fox, & Signorielli, 1978; Gerbner, Gross, Morgan, & Signorielli, 1980, 1986; Gerbner, Gross, Signorielli, Morgan, & Jackson-Beeck, 1979).

The results of other analyses not directly concerned with violence have also been published by members of the Cultural Indicators research team. For example, they report analyses of the portrayal on television of aging (Gerbner, Gross, Signorielli, & Morgan, 1980), sex roles (Gerbner, & Signorelli, 1979; Gross & Jeffries-Fox, 1978), children (Gerbner, 1980a), occupational conceptions (Jeffries-Fox & Signorielli, 1979), educational achievements and aspirations (Morgan, 1980; Morgan & Gross, 1979), family images (Jeffries-Fox & Gerbner, 1977), sexual depictions, and death and dying (Gerbner, 1980b).

We look at the results of some of these other analyses later in this chapter. Now we consider some of the findings of the Cultural Indicators research project about the amount and nature of violence on television, and how it has changed over the years.

VIOLENCE ON TELEVISION

Since the early 1950s there have been several analyses of the program content of television most of which have focused on the programs aired during prime-time (Catton, 1969). Although some of the early studies were of a more general nature (e.g., Head, 1954), most of these descriptions of the world of television have focused primarily on the violent content of television drama.

Two of the earliest studies, for example, were done by Head (1954) and Smythe (1954). Both researchers coded programs "off the air" (there was no videotape available in those days) using trained coders, and both concluded that there was considerable violence in New York City television programming.

Clark and Blankenburg (1972) also coded the amount of violence in television drama but they used a different system. These investigators studied the synopses of programs found in the *TV Guide*. They found that violence on television seems to be cyclical. There were peaks of violent programming in 1955, 1959, 1963, and 1967, about once every 4 years. As we see later in this chapter, this same general conclusion of a high and cyclical rate of violence seems to be true also on the weekend programs designed for children.

Table 3.1 lists several content analyses of violent programming done since the early 1950s with details about what was coded, by whom, and how it was used.

TABLE 3.1
Measuring Violence via Content Analysis

Authors	Phenomenom	Who Codes	Definition	How Used
Cultural Indicators Gerber, Gross, Signorielli, Morgan, & Jackson-Beeck (1979)	Annual weekly samples of prime-time weekend-daytime network dramatic programs	Trained coders (12–16)	Yes	To ascertain content on number of basic issues such as violence, aging, sex-roles, and minority presentation
Harvey, Sprafkin, & Rubinstein (1979)	Week-long sample of prime-time programs (videotaped)	Trained coders	Yes	To determine the impact of family viewing time policy on content; to isolate prosocial and aggressive behavior
Schuetz & Sprafkin (1978)	Week-long sample of Saturday a.m. commercials (videotaped)	Two trained raters	Yes	To isolate prosocial behavior in children's TV commercials
Franzblau, Sprafkin, & Rubinstein (1977)	Week-long sample of prime-time programs (videotaped)	Four trained raters	Yes	To ascertain amount of sexually aggressive (e.g., rape, aggressive touching) behavior in TV programs
CBS, Office of Social Research (1977)	Samples of prime-time programming	Trained coders	Yes	To ascertain the amount of violence in programming

Slaby, Quarfoth, & McConnachie (1976)	Week-long sample of programs (off-air)	Undergraduates (trained & practiced)	Yes (Gerbner Based)	To assess violence on TV and attribute to major sponsors
Dominick (1973)	Week-long sample of prime-time programs (off-air)	7 trained coders	Yes	To ascertain portrayal of criminal victims and law enforcement on TV
Clark & Blankenburg (1972)	TV *Guide* Synopsis (1953–1969)	Coders	Yes	To ascertain trends in amount of violence in prime-time programs
Head (1954)	13-week sample of programs (4 episodes/ programs) (off-air)	4 coders	Yes	To analyze TV content
Smythe (1954)	Samples of programs (off-air)	Trained coders	Yes	To ascertain content of television programs on a number of basic issues

Source: From NIMH report, Morgan et al. (1982) in the public domain.

In addition to scientific researchers interested in the content of television, groups such as the PTA have gotten involved in the debate about the amount of violence on television, and have devised coding schemes of their own. The decision about what kind of content to study depends on one's purposes, as we have seen, thus both the PTA and a group called the National Citizens Committee for Broadcasting (NCCB) have monitored television and done content analyses to determine: (a) who sponsors violent programs (NCCB)? and (b) the amount of "gratuitous" (unnecessary or unrelated to the plot) violence on television (PTA) (Signorielli, Gross, & Morgan, 1982).

Finally, the television networks themselves, especially CBS, and NBC have their own internal research groups that monitor and study violence. There are debates between the academic researchers and the networks about whose definition of television violence should be accepted, and the analyses produced by the networks always end up finding less violence than do the analyses conducted by research scientists located in universities. In a later section of this chapter we consider some of these issues in terms of the debate between CBS and the Cultural Indicators group about the amount of violence on TV.

Messages About Violence

As we noted, Gerbner and his colleagues began, in the mid-1960s, to systematically collect, analyze, and report on the amount of violence on television. They analyzed television broadcasts using week-long samples of prime-time and weekend-daytime network dramatic presentations.

The Cultural Indicators research group used as their definition of violence:

> the overt expression of physical force (with or without a weapon, against self or other) compelling action against one's will on pain of being hurt or killed, or actually hurting or killing. (Signorielli, Gross, & Morgan, 1982, p. 163)

Although it has been a source of much debate, this definition of violence is not very different from that used by other research groups. CBS, for example, in their research project, define violence as: "the use of physical force against persons or animals, or the articulated, explicit threat of physical force to compel particular behavior on the part of a person (CBS Office of Social Research, 1977). The PTA-monitoring project is primarily interested in "gratuitous" violence, which they define as: "violence to maintain interest, violence not necessary for plot development, glorified violence" (cited in Signorielli, Gross, & Morgan, 1982, p. 163).

As the Cultural Indicators group noted:

> for the most part these definitions are remarkably similar—most deal with physical force including hurting and killing. One basic difference is whether or not the definition includes violence to property and emotional or psychological violence. (Signorielli, Gross, & Morgan, 1982, p. 13)

Neither the Cultural Indicators Project nor CBS include violence to property in their definitions. The debate between CBS and the Cultural Indicators Project, instead, focuses on whether certain forms of violence, particularly comic violence and "acts of nature," should be included. Gerbner and his researchers include these two categories in their definition of violence whereas the network researchers do not (Blank, 1977a, 1977b; Coffin & Tuchman, 1972–1973). (For more detail on this debate, see Comstock et al., 1978; Signorielli, Gross, & Morgan, 1982.)

Violence Index

In order to report, on a yearly basis, the amount of violence on television, the Cultural Indicators Project devised a *Violence Index:* a standardized measure of television violence. The index is a combination of three sets of measures, *prevalence, rate,* and *role. Prevalence* is the extent to which violence occurs at all in the program. *Rate* is the frequency and rate of violent episodes, whereas *role* is the number of roles calling for characterizations as violence, victims, or both (Signorielli, Gross, Morgan, 1982, p. 18).

These three sets of data are combined additively into a single score using the formula:

$$VI = (\%P) + (2R/P) + (2R/H) + (\%V) + (\%K).$$

That is, the Violence Index (*VI*) equals the percent of programs containing any violence (*%P*), plus the rate of violent incidents per program times two (*2R/P*), plus the rate of violent incidents per hour times two (*2R/H*), plus the percent of characters involved in any violence (*%V*), plus the percent of characters involved in killing (*%K*). The rates of incidents per program and per hour are weighted by 2 in order to increase their importance. The derivation of this weighting system is discussed in some detail in Gerbner et al. (1977), Gerbner et al. (1978), Gerbner, Gross, Morgan, and Signorielli (1980), and Signorielli, Gross, and Morgan (1982).

Using this standardized measure it is now possible to view the amount of violence, measured in a reliable and valid way, on network prime-time television programming over many years. These basic findings are reported in Fig. 3.6

Several interesting facts appear in this figure. First, the amount of violence, as measured by this index, has remained essentially unchanged in the last 13 years since the project began measuring the amount of violence on television. In fact, using the measure of number of violent acts per hour, instead of the entire index, there has been a steady increase in violence ("a significant linear trend") in the programs shown on prime time since 1967 when these studies were begun (Signorielli, Gross, & Morgan, 1982, p. 23)

The world of television is a violent world, vastly more violent than the none-too-peaceful world of everyday reality. Moreover, television has been this way virtually since its inception in spite of considerable public pressure from organized groups (such as the Parent Teachers Association and the American Medical Association), for reductions in the amount of violence shown on prime-time television programs.

Also noteworthy is that over the years, the Saturday morning children's shows are by far the most violent programs on television, with an average of 93.6%, of the programs containing violence, and an average of 5.77 acts of violence per program (Gerbner, Gross, Morgan, & Signorielli, 1980). Part of the reason for this high rate is that what some would call "comic" violence is included in Gerbner's measure. Even though this is a major point of dispute between the Cultural Indicators Research group and the networks, it is not a question that can be

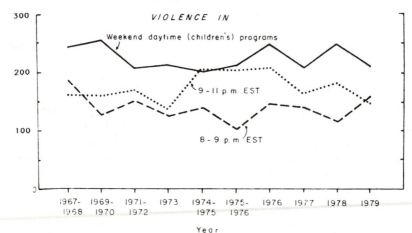

FIG. 3.6. Violence index in children's and prime-time programming, 1967–1979. (© Gerbner, Gross, Morgan, & Signorielli, 1980.)

settled by argument. It may be possible to resolve it with evidence, however.

The point of doing this research in the first place is to, in the long run, understand the effect of watching it. So the question is not whether cartoon violence is or is not violence by one definition, but whether this type of content influences children to be more violent, to act violently. There are several possibilities: For one thing, children could see this material the same way adults do, as fantasy violence, and they might not be influenced by it at all. Presumably this is the point the networks wish to make by insisting that cartoon violence of the "Road Runner" type should not be part of the definition of violence.

On the other hand, the distinction between comic and serious violence may be lost on children, and they may be just as influenced by one kind of violence as another. We come back to this question in chapter 4, which considers evidence for the "effects" of television, and the psychological mechanisms of those effects.

Other Distortions of Violent Behavior

Most of the content analyses we have been discussing have coded the amount of violent behavior without much concern about the nature of it. Yet it is possible for a murder to be depicted either very graphically or very symbolically. Gerbner and his colleagues code "victims" and "violents" (the who and the whom) but not the what, the nature of the actions (killing and injury are, however, separated in Gerbner's analyses).

The violence depicted on television is different in character from violence in real life. The violence on television drama is usually "cleaned up" violence, it is violence shown without the horror and pain and suffering that is characteristic of real violence.

At first glance, it is reasonable to assume that the more horrible aspects of violence are removed to be "tasteful," so as not to disgust the viewer. Although this is probably true, it nonetheless represents a distortion of reality and something we must consider in wondering about the influence of television. Does it matter whether the violence shown is less horrible and gruesome than real violence?

It could matter a great deal. For one thing, part of what keeps people from acting violently may be the horror of it. By denying that part, for whatever reason, we may be making violence seem more acceptable and romantic than it is. Second, there could be powerful and even unexpected consequences of being repeatedly exposed to a false picture of violence. If we are exposed to a false depiction of violence, then we could be greatly *surprised by real violence* when we encounter it. In fact, we might find the real thing more shocking and terrifying. We consider this question in greater detail when we discuss the mechanism of desensitization/arousal in the next chapter. For now, the important point is simply that it is not only the amount of violence that is distorted on television, but the character or nature of violence as well.

OTHER DISTORTIONS AND EXAGGERATIONS ON TELEVISION

Violence is not the only distortion on television, it is just the most obvious and the most extensively studied. But content analyses of the messages on television have revealed other interesting facts about portrayals of sex and gender, of occupations, and of the age distribution of characters. All of these portrayals are "distorted" compared to demographic information about the United States. In addition to violence, *activities* often distorted on television involve sex and sexuality, portrayals of doctors, health, and illness, especially mental illness, and the consumption of alcohol. We consider the evidence regarding the content of television and these various distortions in the next several sections. It is worth keeping in mind that these findings all concern the program and not the advertising content of television.

The Portrayal of Sex and Gender

Even though women make up a majority of the audience, television is a world of men. On prime-time television, men make up a 3:1 majority of characters and the occupations (Gerbner, 1972b; Greenberg, 1982; Signorielli, 1978, 1985; Steinem, 1988; Tedesco, 1974). Other parts of television are more egalitarian: In situation comedies, in family dramas, and on soap operas, for example, the ratio of men to women is more 1:1 — as it is in reality. The ads are more "egalitarian" too, more 50:50 in sex distribution. But the program content of prime time is a world in which the vast majority of characters are men. The stories are, for the most part, written by men about men.

Television's view of sex differences is quite outmoded. Television perpetuates the idea of males and females as opposites, a notion that many current theories of sex roles no longer believe to be true (Condry, 1984). On television, men are portrayed as ambitious, smart, dominant, and violent. In the face of danger or problems, they take care of themselves (Busby, 1974, 1975). Women are portrayed as having exactly the opposite characteristics: On television women are romantic, warm, submissive and timid. Women on television ". . . are portrayed as 'nicer people', being more likely to help, share, and cooperate with others" (Roberts, 1982, p. 214). Women are also depicted on television as being altruistic—caring about others—and socially conforming (Donnager, Poulos, Liebert, & Davidson, 1976). Finally, men and women who are portrayed as alike, for example as both independent, strong willed, achievement oriented, and dominant, are usually characterized as likely to have conflict in their personal lives (Phelps, 1976). "If a woman on television is nurturant and a man independent, their relationship is more likely to be peaceful than if both are independent" (Roberts, 1982, p. 214).

Men and women are shown on television with a different emphasis regarding their bodies as well. Men are concerned with strength and performance—"what can my body do," whereas women emphasize beauty and youth—"how do I look?" (Roberts, 1982). One survey found 85% of women on television to be under 40 years of age (NOW, 1972), whereas another found most women on television to be attractive, well groomed, and well dressed (Long & Simon, 1974). Women are more likely to use their bodies seductively than men in television plots (Silverman, Sprafkin, & Rubenstein, et al., 1979).

Finally, elderly women have few significant roles on television (Aronoff, 1974) and when the elderly are shown, over 90% are male (Peterson, 1973), misrepresenting the actual proportions (the actual population distribution is increasingly female after 55 years of age). We have already mentioned that older women are more likely to be victims of crime on television than in real life (Signorielli & Gerbner, 1977). So women are shown on television, but they are more "of a type" (young, well dressed, submissive) than the range usually found in everyday life.

Some researchers, notably Meehan (1983, 1988) have called attention to the changes in women on television. In her book *Ladies of the Evening: Women Characters of Prime Time Television* (Meehan, 1983) analyzed popular female characters on evening episodic television from 1950 to 1983. Meehan described 10 types of female characters: imp, goodwife, harpy, bitch, victim, decoy, siren, matriarch, witch, and androgyne. In a more recent article, Meehan (1988) added detail to the description of the androgynous character. According to Meehan, androgynes are female characters who are simultaneously strong and autonomous, characters who combine masculine and feminine traits. Meehan argued that these characters, while still very few, add an important dimension to the portrayal of women on television.

On the other hand, a recent annotated bibliography of research on the content of television complied by Nancy Signorielli (1985) comes to this conclusion:

The most striking revelation of this bibliography is the overall similarity and stability of the research findings. In regard to women, study after study reveals that men outnumber women by two or three to one, in addition, women are generally younger than the men and are cast in very traditional and stereotypical roles. Women are less aggressive than men, take more orders than men, and are generally limited in their employment opportunities. Television does not recognize that women can successfully mix marriage, homemaking, and raising children with careers. Programs in which married women work outside the home focus on their home-related roles. (p. xiv; for additional detail on female characterizations see Signorielli, 1987; Steinem, 1988)

The Portrayal of Occupation and Wealth

On television just about everybody is rich. Just about everybody drives a new car and wears new clothes. Just about everybody on television lives in a very expensive house, surrounded by beautiful things. When the producers of television want to show an average middle-class person living in an average middle-class home, they rent the house of a millionaire in Beverly Hills or Brentwood, or one of the many wealthy neighborhoods in Los Angeles.

The income distribution in the United States is approximately like a pyramid (see Fig. 3.7). There is a large base of wage earners who have moderate incomes, the working class; a smaller "middle class" that is more affluent; and an even smaller "wealthy" class. This could be described as a pyramid with a large base and a small top. But the distribution of incomes displayed on television is exactly the opposite: The vast majority of people shown on television are wealthy, and only

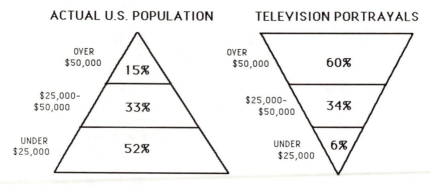

FIG. 3.7. Graphic representation of income disparity between what is shown on television and what is true in the actual U.S. population. (Information from DeFleur, 1964, & U.S. Bureau of the Census, 1970.)

a very small percentage are blue collar. One study estimates the true distribution to be 6% upper class and 60% working class, whereas on television it is the exact reverse: 60% are upper class, and only 6% working class (DeFleur, 1964; see also Gade, 1971; Greenberg, 1982; Long & Simon, 1974; Seggar & Wheeler, 1973). Over and above the distribution of wealth and social class, the occupations displayed on television are also distorted when compared to everyday life (Greenberg, 1980).

Police and law enforcement occupations make up almost half of all the occupations on television (Dominick, 1973; Gerbner, Gross, Morgan, & Signorielli, 1980; Jeffries-Fox & Signorielli, 1979), whereas doctors, lawyers, and managerial professions make up the rest. Many of these professionals are Black and female, unlike the real world. In everyday life, there are few Blacks and women in managerial and professional occupations, but Blacks and women are overrepresented in these occupations on television (Comstock, 1978; Dominick & Greenberg, 1970).

The unemployment rate among women, on television, is between 64% and 70% according to three studies (Dominick & Rauch, 1972; McNeil, 1975; Seggar & Wheeler, 1973). In McNeil's (1975) study, half of the women and one third of the men held jobs in which they were supervised by others. Most of the supervisors (90%) were men. The job opportunities on television are fairly narrow: Seggar and Wheeler (1973) found that 30% of all White males shared only 45 jobs. More than half of all women, from all ethnic groups, shared 5 jobs (Greenberg, 1982).

The Portrayal of Minorities

Amos 'N Andy, a popular radio show of the 1930s and 1940s, ostensibly about Blacks, was performed by two Whites acting as caricatures of Black people. When television came along it was no longer possible to show Whites acting as Blacks, but the portrayal of Blacks was still not much improved. Peoples of color have been both underrepresented and misrepresented since the inception of television. During the early days, nonWhites comprised fewer than 3% of all characters (Smythe, 1954), and they were often cast as either maids or ne'er-do-wells (see MacDonald, 1983 for a review). By the 1970s, however, this figure had increased to approximately 11% (U.S. Commission on Civil Rights, 1977), and there it has remained (Greenberg, 1982; Williams & Condry, 1988).

Stereotypic Black roles of the 1950s and early 1960s gave way to more subtle indicators of racism in the 1970s. For example, Black characters were younger and poorer, and less likely to be cast in professional occupations, dramatic or romantic roles (Berry, 1980, 1982; Graves, 1980; Greenberg, 1982; Stroman, 1984). In addition, Blacks on television were more likely to appear in segregated surroundings, and their appearance was concentrated during a small percentage of the program (Weigel & Howes, 1982; Weigel, Loomis, & Soja, 1980).

A recent analysis of minority portrayals done by Marsha Williams and myself (Williams & Condry, 1988) indicates that the situation has changed very little since the large-scale content analyses of the early 1980s (Greenberg, 1982; Greenberg & Burek-Neuendorf, 1980; Seggar, Hafen, Hannonen-Gladden, 1981; Wilson & Gutierrez, 1985). Analyzing 72 hours of broadcast programming on all three national networks drawn from a representative sample of television for 1987, during times when children comprise a large percentage of the audience, Williams and I found approximately 90.3% White, 7.7% Black, 1.3% Asian, and 0.6% Hispanic characters. For purposes of comparison, it is worth noting that according to the 1980 U.S. Census, the United States population contained 84.5% Whites, 12.2% Blacks, 1.5% Asians, and 6.4% Hispanics. Thus, the figure of 7.7% for Blacks seems like a substantial decline from earlier analyses, but these data are for commercials as well as programs, so the base of comparison is slightly different. In general, however, according to this most recent analysis, Whites are significantly overrepresented and all other minorities are underrepresented. Hispanics are the most underrepresented minority on television, a fact noted some years ago by Greenberg (1982). In addition, Williams noted only one Native American character in the 6,663 characters that she coded.

As we have just seen regarding occupations, the occupational levels for most characters on television is significantly higher than the actual population, but nonWhites continue to be cast in less prestigious occupations than Whites. Williams found that Blacks, Asians, and Hispanics on television were more often cast as blue-collar workers and public safety personnel (law enforcers, firefighters). Moreover, Whites appeared more often as family members and as friends and neighbors than nonWhites. None of the Hispanic characters, for example, appeared cast as a friend or a neighbor, yet their criminal delinquency rate was the highest of all racial groups (Williams & Condry, 1988).

Finally, the types of cross-racial interactions were coded by Williams in terms of tone (either positive or negative) and context (professional or social). A great majority of cross-racial interactions were positive (only 6% were negative), but among adults these tended to be job-related associations rather than social interactions. NonWhite youth were more than three times as likely to engage in positive social interactions with White characters than nonWhite adults were. On television, it would appear, it is safer to show children and youth interacting in a racially integrated manner, especially when they choose to do so (on the playground or at home) rather than when they must (as in school, or for adults in the workplace).

So although minority characters are just as likely to be employed, they hold lower status jobs. They are rarely cast as friends and neighbors, and they appear frequently as both perpetrators and victims of criminal and delinquent acts. Nearly 40% of television's minorities have no contact with Whites, and when cross-racial interactions do occur they are more likely among children than among adults.

The portrayal of minorities on television is no trivial matter, as Berry (1988) explained:

> Whatever else commercial television is or does, one of its primary goals is to entertain. It is a tall order, therefore, to expect television scrupulously to offer the types of portrayals that capture the multifaceted aspects of human behavior and present desirable cultural depictions. Yet, because of television's power to define social reality about viewers' own groups, as well as about people and cultural groups that are different from viewers' own groups, it is important that it's cultural lessons not be distortions of reality. (p. 121)

The Portrayal of Age

Both the young and the old are underrepresented on television in terms of their actual numbers, but they are overrepresented as victims of crime (Gerbner, Gross, Morgan, & Signorielli, 1980; Signorielli, 1978). The typical female on television is younger, clustering around the mid-30s, whereas men are significantly older (Levinson, 1973). It is especially bad to be old on television, and it is terrible to be an old woman. As men get older on television they get more successful and powerful, whereas the opposite is true for women (Beck, 1978).

In the world of television, the worst thing that can happen to a woman is that she get old because she loses her two marketable qualities — beauty and youth — and she gains only aches and pains. That is, if she is lucky. If she is unlucky, she is the victim of a crime. Old women are the most victimized category of individuals on television, being 30 times more likely to be caught up in a violent act than older women actually are in reality (Gerbner, Gross, Morgan, & Signorielli, 1980).

In short, if we look just at characters on television, and we compare them to the U.S. census reports, we find numerous ways in which the world depicted on television is different from the world of reality. There is no particular reason that television should be representative of the real world, and, in fact, it is not. There are lots of reasons for these distortions. The "purpose" of television is to entertain (to gather an audience), not to inform or educate or present an accurate picture of reality. It is not really important why television is so distorted, it is only important that it is consistently so, allowing us to trace the intrusion of these "facts" of the television world, into the beliefs and behaviors of those who view it.

Television's Portrayal of Behaviors
Sexuality and Health

Three areas of the behavior of television characters have been studied, mostly from prime-time shows: violence, sexual behavior, and health portrayals. We have already looked at the research on violence, now let us consider the other two. Both sex and health are important because true information about both is not easy to come by. Parents are concerned that their children do not learn about "sex" too soon, and the field of health has traditionally been full of misinformation with dangerous consequences. The greater danger posed by television is its wide reach and its universal appeal.

Television and Sexuality

Portrayals of overt sex are rare on network commercial television, although cable systems are now showing more sexually oriented material and, in the process, generating considerable controversy. One expert on this topic is Elisabeth Roberts, a researcher with Television Audience Assessment, Inc. of Cambridge, MA. Roberts (1982) pointed out that youngsters have relatively few sources for some kinds of information, and sex is one of those places where the lack of alternative sources of information is most pronounced. Roberts (1982) listed 19 content analyses of sex and sex roles on television.

For example, one study found that during prime time the majority of close relationships shown on television are between those who work together (Gerbner, 1976), and that actual affection or intimacy is rarely shown, especially in the action adventure type of programs. On television, heroes and heroines seldom have a private life, and are rarely tender and loving to one another (Franzblau, Sprafkin, & Rubinstein, 1977). Affectionate relationships are shown most often on situation comedies, rarely in drama.

There are few visual portrayals of explicit erotic activity on commercial television programming, but there are lots of hints of it. There is little actual sex, but lots of sexual innuendo:

> In the past several years, there has been a marked increase in the fre-
> quency of such "cues" and today's television audience is increasingly
> "teased" by flirtatious behavior, subtle and indirect verbal references to
> sex (innuendo) and implied intercourse. (Roberts, 1982, p. 222)

When erotic activity is shown on television, it is frequently linked with violence (Franzblau et al., 1977). When intercourse is mentioned on television, most references to it occur between unmarried partners (five times as often as between married couples); references to intercourse with prostitutes is the second most common. Together, references to either adultery or prostitution account for almost 70% of all allusions to intercourse on prime-time television programs. On television, women can use sex as a weapon (men seldom do), or as a means of achievement. According to Roberts (1982), "For prostitute or police woman, sex is a major vehicle for women in achieving their goals..." (p. 222).

Contraceptive responsibility is not even discussed on television, and television's attitudes toward sex can be summarized as:

> sex is treated as a prelude to, or context for, violence or is viewed as an
> aspect of life to be treated with nervous laughter. On situation comedies
> and variety shows, characters touch, kiss, embrace, and through seduc-
> tive innuendo and flirtation suggest sexual intimacy; these suggestive mes-
> sages are usually accompanied by canned laughter...to make certain
> the humor is not missed. (Roberts, 1982, p. 222)

Television and Health

We have already noted that professionals dominate the occupations shown on television. Next to law officers, doctors dominate the professionals, being five times more frequent on television than in everyday life:

> The typical viewer sees about 12 doctors and 6 nurses each week on prime
> time alone, including 3 doctors and 1 nurse in major roles. By compari-
> son, the same viewer will see only 1 scientist in a weeks prime time view-
> ing, and a scientist will be cast in a major role once every 2 weeks.
> (Gerbner, Morgan, & Signorielli, 1982, p. 293)

Doctors on television symbolize power, authority, and knowledge.

They are seen as ethical, kind, and responsible to their patients, twice as many of whom are female as male (McLaughlin, 1975). Warner (1979) confirmed these findings, and added that 61% of the doctors' duties were performed in house calls and in the field. The television doctor (90% are male) lives for his patients, has great authority over other medical personnel, advises and gives orders to more women than men, and has little or no family life.

Similar portrayals of doctors and of illness dominate the afternoon soap operas (Cassata, Skill, & Boadu, 1979), where nearly half of all characters were involved in health-related occurrences (Katzman, 1972). So television cultivates an excessively high level of interest in health, and it exudes confidence in doctors. Young children who are heavy viewers are more likely to believe of doctors what television says: "that they are all knowing, all seeing, and wise" (Gerbner et al., 1982).

Mental Illness

Katzman's (1972) study of soap operas showed that on television mental illness strikes women more often than men, and usually comes about as a result of guilt, trauma, or inability to cope. Gerbner (1961a, 1961b; Gerbner & Tannenbaum, 1962) found that about 17 percent of prime-time programs involve some significant depiction of mental illness. About 3% of major characters are identified as mentally ill. Earlier studies of the media have noted how the mentally ill are typically portrayed as having some moral flaw which tends to justify their (mis-) treatment. Gerbner and his colleagues found that

> the image of the mentally ill in the mass media was farther removed from the characteristics established by mental health professionals than was the image of the general public. In other words, instead of mediating between the experts and the public, media imagery pulled the public image away from the experts in the direction of traditional prejudices. (Gerbner et al., 1982, p. 293)

The mentally ill are portrayed, on television, as excessively violent. In fact, the mentally ill are more likely to be both violent and victim than other characters. Thus, although 40% of nonmentally ill characters on television were violent (an unusually large percentage anyway), 72% of the mentally ill characters were violent. Although 44% of "normals" on television were victims, 80% of mentally ill persons were. Ten percent of normals were killers, but 23% of the mentally ill were (Gerbner et al., 1982, p. 293).

Alcohol Consumption

Alcohol is the most common and important drug on television (Dillon, 1975a, 1975b, 1975c; Futch, Geller & Lisman, 1980; Greenberg, Fernandez-Collado, Graef, Korzenny & Atkin, 1980) being mentioned in 80% of prime-time programs, and places where alcohol is consumed are frequently the centerpiece of action (as, for example, in a bar). In one study, 40% of 233 scenes with alcohol involved "heavy drinking" and 18% more concerned "chronic" drinkers (Breed & DeFoe, 1981). On television, characters rarely decline a drink or express disapproval of drinking. When disapproval is expressed, it is usually mild, ineffective, and comes from women (Breed & DeFoe, 1981).

TELEVISION AND ADOLESCENTS: THE ROLE OF MTV

As we saw in chapter 2, according to most historical research adolescents watch the least amount of television of any age group in the population, although this is not to say that television has not already had an effect. By the time a child has reached adolescence he or she has already spent more time watching television than going to school, and has been exposed to all of television's diverse messages (Signorielli, 1987). But even these statistics may be changing with the coming of Music Television or MTV (J. Singer & D. Singer, 1987). MTV was first introduced in 1983 and it immediately became a source of debate and controversy (Cocks, 1983; Zorn, 1984). The lyrics of rock music were said to provide a bad influence on children (Cocks, 1985; Dougherty, 1985; Rehman & Reilly, 1985; Zucchino, 1985). Particularly active in this area has been the Parents Music Resource Center (PMRC) founded by Tipper Gore. This group charged in a Congressional hearing that rock music has influences on sexual morality, violence, drug use, and satanism (Gore, 1987).

The importance and role of MTV is too new to have been subjected to extensive research at this time, but there have been some studies of the degree to which adolescents are able to comprehend rock music lyrics (Densioff & Lefine, 1971; Edwards & Singletary, 1984; Gantz, 1977; Robinson & Hirsch, 1969; Rosenbaum & Prinsky, 1987). In a review of the literature, Desmond (1986) concluded: "Taken as a whole, these studies reveal that approximately one-third of any sample of adolescents are able to articulate the meaning of available popular song lyrics" (p. 5). Greenfield et al. (1987) report the findings of three "preliminary" studies of the cognitive effects of rock videos. In line with Desmond's conclusion, Greenfield et al. report that young children often misunderstand the lyrics of rock music, that music videos provide less stimulation to the imagination and are enjoyed less than the songs alone. Apparently the song alone (without the video) allows the listener to conjure up his or her own mental picture, and this makes the music more meaningful and emotionally involving than when it is accompanied by a visual image (see also Greenfield, Farrar, & Beagles-Ross, 1986).

Prinsky and Rosenbaum (1987) found that motivation, experience, and knowledge were all factors in the interpretation of lyrics in rock songs. They discovered that preadolescents and adolescents often missed sexual themes in lyrics, and that the interpretation of song lyrics by various adult organizations (such as the PMRC) was quite different than the interpretation by young people themselves. Prinsky and Rosenbaum found that preadolescents and adolescents interpret their favorite songs in terms of "love, friendship, growing up, life's struggles, having fun, cars, religion, and other topics that relate to teenage life" (Prinsky & Rosenbaum, 1987, p. 393). Greenfield et al. (1987), found that only 10% of fourth graders understood the meaning of Madonna's song "Like a Virgin" and they note that if a child's only knowledge of "virgin" is the Virgin Mary, then the song will have religious not sexual connotations.

SUMMARY

If at first glance television seemed to be a lot like the world of everyday reality, then on second glance it seems a mass of distortion and misrepresentation. As the quote at the beginning of the chapter suggests, "prime-time television is just one long lie..."

Various content analyses have shown that although the biggest lie is about violence, both the amount and the character of it, this is not the only lie told by television. The programs on television also misrepresent men and women, occupation, sexuality, and health issues as well.

It is not particularly important why this is done, although this is an interesting question for people specializing in the study of television as an industry. For a psychologist, the important consideration is whether such "distortions" actually exist on television, and, if they do, how they are represented in the beliefs and values and behaviors of the exposed audience.

The most dramatic distortion, as we have seen, concerns violent action. Thanks to researchers like Gerbner, we now have substantial evidence for the amount and type of violence on television. With the technique of content analysis we learn how much more violence there is on television than in everyday life, and something about when it occurs, who is involved, and against whom the violence is directed. Now we need to ask: What is the consequence of being exposed to all this violent action?

This is, of course, the essential question about the direct effects of television, and in trying to answer it psychologists have discovered several important mechanisms, causal routes, responsible for the influence of television. The first 15 years of psychological research on television was almost exclusively concerned with the question of violence, but in later years the focus of interest has expanded beyond this simple question. From this research, described in detail in the next four chapters, we get our first clear understanding of the various psychological mechanisms that allow television to influence the audience. We turn now to this, the psychology of television.

Part II

THE PSYCHOLOGY OF TELEVISION: PSYCHOLOGICAL MECHANISMS OF INFLUENCE

In the first section we saw how television, the device, was developed and then distributed throughout American society; how it quickly gained a steady audience, and how the program content achieved a degree of stability in its offerings. Most of this happened during the decade from 1950 to 1960.

Once the content of television is sufficiently stable and has an audience, then it is possible to begin to study the influence of this content on this audience. That is, we can begin to study the psychology of television. We saw that to trace an influence of television drama it was useful to know something about how the content was "distorted" relative to the content of the "real world" the drama is attempting to portray. We saw in chapter 3 that there are many such distortions, and that the most common of these was the distortion regarding the amount and nature of violence.

For psychologists, then, the first question regarding influence of television concerned the possible association between the amount and type of violence shown on television and a proclivity to act or think violently on the part of those who viewed it. If so, then the next question becomes: What is the nature of the psychology mechanism that allows this influence to occur? This is the heart of the psychology of television, the unmasking of a variety of psychological mechanisms that permit the information seen on television to effect the viewer's actions, thoughts, and beliefs in and about the world of reality.

In this section, we look at the behavioral mechanisms of imitation/disinhibition, and arousal/desensitization, and the cognitive mechanisms of mainstreaming and resonance. We survey current research bearing on these mechanisms, particularly the cognitive ones. We study the latest research on the nature of attention, comprehension, and the role of the "formal features" of television. And finally, we look at the psychology of advertising, called here *mechanisms of persuasion.*

I divide the mechanisms into "behavioral" and "cognitive" although the distinction is actually hard to defend. It does, however, reflect a division within the science of psychology. Evidence used by those studying "behavioral" mechanisms is typically some activity that can be measured without asking the subject directly. This research comes from a tradition in the science of psychology derived from earlier animal research, and the practitioners tend to favor strict behavioral observations and noncognitive explanations of the relationship between stimuli and responses.

Those doing work on cognitive issues, on the other hand, tend to be more willing to accept the "word" of the subject, and to be more willing to speculate about what is going on in the "mind" of the person they study. These distinctions are overdrawn, but they do reflect an actual and important division of labor and values in the field of psychology. Both types of research are revealing about the manner in which television influences the viewer. In any case, the deeper fact is that all behavioral mechanisms have cognitive components, and vice versa.

The behavioral mechanisms discussed in chapter 4 all tell us something of the structure of the human organism, and about mechanisms that have evolved to serve different purposes (e.g., learning and relaxation). Each of them helps explain how television violence can influence behavior, especially the behavior of acting aggressively and violently. The first two, imitation and disinhibition, both predict that the influence of watching dramatic violence on television will be to increase the probability that a person exposed will act violently. Both predict a "positive" association between viewing violent scences and acting violently, exactly the correlation found by many studies.

Although there are similarities between imitation and disinhibition, there are important differences as well. They represent different causal routes, they are governed by different laws, even though they make the same prediction about the consequences of exposure. Imitation typically refers to learning, acquiring, and performing novel activities, whereas disinhibition refers to already learned or known acts that are "inhibited" through prior experience. One is a theory about the acquisition of novel behavior and the other is a theory about the performance of (inhibited) well-learned behavior. Research on each mechanism has turned up interesting and unexpected evidence. In performing aggressive acts, cartoon figures are imitated as readily as real-life models, and disinhibition is more likely when the violence on television drama is seen to be "justified," in the sense of the victim getting "what he deserved."

Both of these mechanisms are different from arousal/desensitization, particularly in terms of how the effect is measured (by aggressive action on the first case, and physiological measures in the second). All mechanisms have in common the detailing of the circumstances that elicit them, however, and the making explicit of the laws that underlie them.

Arousal/desensitization refers to processes that may be traced to the neural level, to physical habituation. Arousal is typically measured by behaviors such as heart rate, blood pressure, and skin conductance, thought to be largely beyond the control of the subjects. On the other hand, the metaphor is easily understood at a broader level of boredom with often-repeated scenes. The real event does not "arouse" in the sense of interest or draw attention once habituation occurs. The mechanism of arousal/desensitization is central to the most common "use" of television and material on television (films, sports, drama, comedy, etc.) as a way of inducing relaxation, of "unwinding.

Desensitization is what the programmers of television are constantly fighting. The content of television must keep changing, according to this mechanism, because novelty quickly wears thin, and because any new fad is immediately imitated by the other networks.

One of the first attempts to study the cognitive effects of television, the influence of television on attitudes, beliefs, and values, was made by George Gerbner as part of his Cultural Indicators research project. Gerbner, whose analyses of the messages of television was highlighted in chapter 3, has attempted to isolate the effect of television, and television drama alone, on the attitude and belief systems of heavy viewers. Using violent content as the focus of his interests, Gerbner contrasted the attitudes of light and heavy viewers to one another, statistically controlling for such demographic variables as age, sex, social status, education, and other media usage. Doing this, Gerbner and his associates found a small but consistent influence of the content of television on the attitudes of viewers, not about television, but about the world of reality. Gerbner called the basic effect "mainstreaming," and he contended that it is stronger when one identifies with the person victimized in the drama. This latter effect is called *resonance*.

The various studies in chapter 6, go into more detail about the underlying parameters of the mechanisms of mainstreaming and resonance, although the researchers themselves do not view their endeavors in this manner. One line of research focuses on not the content of television in terms of the drama and story line, but the formal features of television. Formal features are all the assorted visual and sound gimmicks that television and film producers use to tell a story. These are detailed by one research group, that of Aletha Huston and John Wright of the University of Kansas.

Another team of researchers, headed by Daniel Anderson at the University of Massachusetts at Amherst, watches children watch television, and studies the role of various visual and auditory features in childrens' attention to television. A third team of researchers out of the University of Minnesota, headed by Andrew Collins, has focused on children's comprehension of television stories compared to the understanding of adults. All of these studies add detail to television's largely unintended cognitive influence on the audience exposed to the informational content of the programs.

The mechanisms underlying advertising, however, the topic of the last chapter in the second part, chapter 7, are the intended persuasive mechanisms utilized in advertising. If the deep intention of the programmers is to capture and hold attention, the deep intention of the advertisers is the same and more. Advertisers want to persuade, they intend to change the attitudes, values, and behaviors of the audience. This fact alone makes the content of advertising especially important. Yet a great deal less public research attention has been focused on advertising, and a great deal less is known about the effects of ads.

Like the programs, the effects of ads will be due to the content, so in the first part of chapter 7 we begin with a description of the world of advertising, using content analyses as we did in chapter 3. We ask who lives in this world, what are they like? What do the ads persuade us to want, to desire? How do the ads on television vary over the television day and week and year? After we have considered the "environment" of television ads, we turn to several theories of their influence: How and why do ads work?

Behavioral Mechanisms: Imitation, Disinhibition, and Arousal/Desensitization

All television is educational. The only question is: what does it teach?
—Nicholas Johnson, Commissioner, FCC*

As we have previously noted, the first step in discovering a direct effect of television is to describe the program content, and particularly that part of the content that may be said to offer a distortion of what we know as "everyday reality." Such distortions, because they misrepresent the world in specific ways, are useful in tracing the effects of television.

In chapter 3, we described a number of these distortions: television has more males, more wealthy persons, and more young upwardly mobile persons (Yuppies) than the mundane world of everyday life. The occupations shown on television are largely professional ones and/or related to law enforcement, and thus are less representative of blue collar and clerical occupations than ordinary reality. We saw that women tended to be presented in stereotypical ways, as are men, but the stereo-

---

*Johnson (1978). Lecture at Cornell University Law School.

typical images are more complimentary to men. The health messages offered on television are not particularly conducive to learning about good health practices. All of these facts represent considerable distortions compared to the world of everyday life. But most of all, we saw that the world of television is an excessively violent world, much more violent than the real communities in which most Americans live.

THE EFFECTS OF VIEWING VIOLENT MATERIAL

What is the influence of watching these repeated displays of violence? Does it affect us in any way at all? Does it make us more violent? Does it make us less so? After we have established the existence of a distortion sufficiently powerful to have some kind of influence, the next question becomes: What is the direction of the effect?

There are three logical possibilities: (a) watching violence on television could make us more violent (Huesmann, 1982; Huesmann & Malamuth, 1986); (b) it could make us less violent (Feshbach, 1972); or (c) it may have no effect whatsoever on our aggressive behavior (the null hypothesis) (Freedman, 1984; Kaplan & Singer, 1976; Milavsky, 1988). All three of these hypotheses have been advanced at one time or another in the research literature on television, but the vast preponderance of evidence supports the first hypothesis of a positive association between viewing television violence and actual aggressive behavior.

In other words, the evidence indicates that the more people are exposed to violent television drama the more they are likely to be violent in their everyday lives. This may be especially true of children. We begin this chapter by reviewing the evidence for this statistical association. Once we have established that a certain outcome is associated with television, then we can begin our search for the psychological mechanisms behind this influence.

Types of Studies

Some of the research on the effect of television has been done in the laboratory, some in the field, some by observation, some by interview. Some studies have included large samples of subjects, but with weak controls on what is watched, or when. Others have had excellent control over what is watched, but the sample sizes were small. No one single method is the best (if so, everyone would use it); each has its strengths and limitations. In the following sections, the research is divided into different types: experimental, correlational, and field studies. Before considering the evidence, we look at the strengths and weaknesses of each of these types of research.

Experimental Studies.   These studies involve the use of small samples of subjects and careful controls on what is watched. Most of the experimental research on television is done with children, although there have been a few studies done with adolescents and adults. The earliest research on television effects was primarily experimental and tended to be criticized for the small number of subjects studied at one time and the fact the materials used were not exactly representative of what was seen on television. Often, for example, films made by the researcher were used (e.g., Bandura, Ross & Ross, 1963), rather than the typical cartoon fare to which most children are exposed. In addition, the viewing conditions were quite far removed from the circumstances under which most children and adults watch television. Thus, although providing great "control" over extraneous variables, the experimental approach to research was criticized for not having enough "ecological validity" (that is, for not replicating the actual conditions under which television is watched, or using the same stimulus materials). Still the experimental study is the best way to test a causal hypothesis (Berkowitz & Donnerstein, 1982).

Correlational Studies.   Larger and done on older populations (who are able to answer interviews or questionnaires), correlational studies tend to be more "ecologically valid" in the sense that they correlate the amount and/or type of television watched by the individuals in their everyday lives with some measure of violent behavior. Compared to experimental studies, however, correlational studies have weaker controls on exactly what the subjects watch, or the conditions under which they watch it. In correlational studies, the person is typically asked two questions: "How much and what kind television do you watch? How violent/aggressive are you?"

Field Studies.   Field studies and field experiments are somewhere in between an experimental/laboratory study and a correlational study. In a field study, a group or "population" (e.g., adolescents in an institution) is exposed to some *specific content* of television (such as violent dramas for one group, nature studies for another) over a particular length of time. All of this is done, however, in the setting in which viewing typically occurs. Afterward, some measure of violent behavior is taken, often by a team of researchers who are unaware of the experimental condition to which the subjects were exposed, and who are unobtrusive in their observations. Field studies have the advantage of being more ecologically meaningful than experimental studies, and they are usually more controlled than correlational studies, although they require a large commitment of time and money.

Several excellent reviews of this literature exist (Andison, 1977; Hap-kiewicz, 1979; Hearold, 1979; Huesmann & Malamuth, 1986), and all provide statistical summaries of the findings of a large number of studies. The account of the evidence given here owes much to recent reviews by Murray (1980), Huesmann, (1982), and Comstock (1980b). The overall conclusion of these and of many other reviewers is un-equivocal: viewing violent drama on television makes people more vio-lent than they would have been if they had not been exposed to such material.

We now consider the evidence in support of this association.

EXPERIMENTAL RESEARCH ON TELEVISION VIOLENCE

Most experimental (laboratory) research has been done with children, although a few studies have been conducted with college students. Some of the earliest research revealing a link between viewing violent material and aggressive behavior was done in the research laboratory of Albert Bandura at Stanford University (Bandura, 1973; Bandura, Ross, & Ross, 1961, 1963; Bandura & Walters, 1963), and by Leonard Berkowitz at the University of Wisconsin (Berkowitz, 1962, 1963, 1973; Berkowitz & Geen, 1966). We consider these studies in far more detail later in discussing the mechanisms of imitation and disinhibition, but in gen-eral all of these studies showed that subjects viewing violent film mate-rial in the laboratory were more likely to exhibit aggressive behavior afterward compared to subjects who either viewed no film or watched arousing but less aggressive material (such as a baseball game).

These early studies were criticized for several reasons, chief among them being the question of "ecological validity" of the film material used. In some cases films were produced specifically for the study (e.g., Bandura et al., 1963), and in other cases only selected parts of films were used (e.g., the fight scene from the movie *The Champion,* used by Berkowitz & Rawlings, 1963). As more experimental evidence was collected, however, these objections were met by additional studies, the findings of which were the same.

For example, in an attempt to use the kind of material actually seen on television, Liebert and Baron (1972) showed children a typical seg-ment from a television show ("The Untouchables") and then gave these same children the opportunity to press control buttons that would either "help" or "hurt" another child. No actual harm was done to any-one, because the actions of hurting and helping were simulated, but they were believable to the children in the study. These investigators found that children who viewed the aggressive program were far more willing to hurt another child than those who had not seen the program. This was especially true of the youngest children. In addition, the same children were later observed in a free play period where they exhibited much more interest in aggressive toys and weapons than the other children.

Experiments with Cartoons

In the last chapter, we saw that there has been a long-standing debate between researchers and the networks concerning whether cartoon or comic violence should be coded as violent content (as Gerbner and his colleagues do), or whether, as the networks insist, cartoons should be viewed as nonviolent "comic action." One way to resolve this debate would be to see if comic violence appears to have any real effects on the aggressive behaviors of viewers exposed to it.

Several researchers have demonstrated that exposure to cartoon violence does lead to increased aggression in children (Bandura et al., 1961; Ellis & Sekura, 1972; Lovaas, 1961; Murray, Hayes, & Smith, 1978; Mussen Rutherford, 1961; Ross, 1972). One study found no effect of violent cartoons on aggression (Hapkiewitz & Roden, 1971), but in this study boys were less likely to cooperate with another child after viewing the violent material.

As this last finding suggests, immediate physical aggression is not the only possible consequence of viewing violent material. Violent drama often involves a story line in which the powerful get what they want and the less powerful must take what is left. One possible consequence of this is to make viewers less kind and altruistic, less cooperative with others. Some studies have looked at this problem by focusing on the way in which children solve conflicts, rather than simply whether or not they display aggression. These studies show that children are more likely to choose violent solutions to conflicts after viewing violent television fare (Collins, 1973; Leifer & Roberts, 1972; Linne, 1971).

The last of these studies, by Linne (1971), was done in Sweden. It involved the comparison of 5- and 6-year-old children who had seen more than 75% of the episodes of a popular violent western ("High Chaparral") with children who had seen half or less of the episodes. A larger proportion of the "high exposure" children selected the aggressive mode of resolving conflicts compared to the "low-exposure" children. Linne also found that the "high-exposure" children tended to watch more televison overall, and that their mothers watched more television than the mothers of the "low-exposure" children (Murray, 1980). Even more striking were the results of a study by Leifer and

Roberts (1972), who found that adolescent males and females were more likely to choose aggressive modes of conflict resolution in direct proportion to the amount of violence contained in the programs they had viewed.

In an article reviewing the experimental research evidence, Comstock (1980b) cited more than 50 laboratory experiments showing a positive relationship between viewing violent content of the type typically shown on television and aggressive behavior immediately following the viewing. Many of these findings are modified, however, by parameters such as how the material is presented in the show or the "psychological state" of the individual who is watching. For example, children are more likely to imitate a model who is reinforced for aggressive behavior than a model who is punished (Bandura & Huston, 1961), and being angered or frustrated before watching a film increases the likelihood of acting aggressively afterwards (Berkowitz, 1973; Berkowitz, Corwin, & Heironimus, 1963; Berkowitz & Geen, 1966; Berkowitz & Rawlings, 1963).

The kind of effect television violence is having on a child is often reflected in the child's facial expression while watching. For example, Ekman et al. (1972) found that by monitoring the emotional reactions of children while they are watching a film, they could tell if the child was likely later to do harm. Those children who showed by their expressions that they were watching and interested (i.e., those who exhibited positive emotions in response to the violence they were viewing) were more likely to hurt another child afterward than were children who displayed disinterest or those who exhibited negative emotions, such as disgust, while viewing. In short, those who seemed to be moved by what they saw, and moved in a positive direction, were the most likely to imitate it (Ekman et al., 1972).

Finally, in research done with adolescents, both Hartman (1969) and Walters and Thomas (1963) found that males who viewed violent films were more likely to give higher voltage shocks to a peer in an experimental setting.

The effects of viewing violent material in the laboratory are all relatively short-term, and explained by increases in arousal, disinhibition, or the evocation of aggressive ideas. In their most recent review of experimental studies, Geen and Thomas (1986) summarize experimental research in the areas of modeling (imitation), cognitive cueing, arousal, media violence as information (the reality–fiction dimension), and symbolic catharsis. Rule and Ferguson (1986) also review experimental (laboratory) research on the impact of media exposure on cognitive processes. We consider television's effects on cognitive processes, on attitudes, beliefs, and values, in more detail in chapters 5 and 6.

The main difficulty with experimental studies is that they typically involve fewer than a hundred subjects, and they are, by their very nature, restricted to the study of only certain variables (Freedman, 1984; Kaplan & Singer, 1976). Correlational studies do not have these problems. They typically involve large samples (by experimental research standards) and include asking the subjects about the television programs they actually watch.

CORRELATIONAL STUDIES: ATTITUDES AND VIEWING PREFERENCES

Dozens of studies have shown that preference for viewing violent television is associated with aggressive attitudes, both in the experimental laboratory (Leifer & Roberts, 1972; Stein & Friedrich, 1972) and in the field (Schramm, Lyle, & Parker, 1961). Furthermore, most of the studies of the introduction of television into various countries have reported an association between the onset of television viewing and aggressive attitudes [Campbell & Keogh, 1962, (Australia); Furu, 1962, 1971, (Japan); Halloran, Brown, & Chaney, 1970, (England); Schramm et al., 1961 (United States)]. In one exception to this rule, Himmelweit, Oppenheim, and Vince (1958), working in England, found no relationship between having a television set and parents' or teachers' ratings of children's aggression); however, their study was done in the very early days of television and measured simply the presence of television (not the kind of content viewed).

In general, the strength of the relationship between amount of television viewing and violent behavior (both assessed through self-report) is weaker in the older studies where total hours of viewing is the usual measure (MacIntyre & Teevan, 1972). But when the type of program is included in the analysis, the relationship between viewing violent programs and acting violently is much stronger (see, for example Dominick & Greenberg, 1972; Greenberg, 1975; Greenberg & Atkin, 1977; Hartnagel, Teevan, & MacIntyre, 1975; Robinson & Bachman, 1972).

Although the positive correlation between viewing violent television content and aggressive behavior continues to be shown in recent studies (Chaffee, 1972; Chaffee & McLeod, 1972; McLeod, Atkin, & Chaffee, 1972a, 1972b), there has always been a debate about the direction of this effect. That is to say, is the association due to the fact that watching violent material makes one more violent, or could it be due to the fact that violent people prefer watching violent material? Strong evidence has not been found to support the second alternative (Murray, 1980), and most researchers now believe that the direction of the relationship does appear to be that of viewing violent television causing one to act more aggressively toward others rather than the reverse. One of the strongest reasons for this belief on the part of researchers has to do with studies using "cross-lagged" correlations to determine the direction of causality.

Cross-Lagged Correlations

In order to answer this question about the direction of the relationship between viewing TV violence and aggressive behavior, several large-scale studies have gone beyond establishing a correlation between the two variables by using statistical techniques that allow for some inferences about the causal direction involved.

One series of studies, for example, obtained peer-rated measures of aggressive behavior and preference for violent television programs when a cohort of children was 8 years old (Eron, 1963). In this study, an association was found between aggressive behavior and preference for violent programs. When this same sample of youngsters was 10 years older, the same investigators returned and measured preference for violent programming and self-reported violent activities (Eron, Huesmann, Lefkowitz, & Walder, 1972; Huesmann, Eron, Lefkowitz, & Walder, 1973, 1984; Lefkowitz, Eron, Walder, & Huesmann, 1972; Lefkowitz & Huesmann, 1980).

Several things of note appear in these findings. First, at age 8 watching violent television and "peer-related aggression" are significantly associated, as other studies have shown. However, preference for violent television at age 18 is unrelated to aggressive behavior at that same age. When looking at the cross-lagged correlations over a 10-year span, the most important finding is the significant positive relationship between preference for watching violent television at age 8 and aggression scores at age 18. The youngsters who preferred violent television programming at 8 years of age reported being more aggressive at age 18 than those who watched less violent programming as 8-year-olds. After examining a number of competing explanations of these findings, Eron et al. (1972) concluded that "The single most plausible causal hypothesis is that a preference for watching violent television in the third grade contributes to the development of aggressive habits . . . (by the 12th grade)" (p. 258).

Several researchers have taken issue with this interpretation on methodological grounds (Becker, 1972; Kaplan, 1972; Kay, 1972), and the authors have responded to many of these criticisms (Huesmann et al., 1973). The evidence does clearly indicate that there is a strong positive correlation between aggressive behavior and watching violent television, and the question of causality is beginning to be more clearly understood.

One correlational study commissioned by a major television network (CBS), was conducted during the 1970s in England with adolescent boys. Belson (1978) interviewed 1,565 boys living in London, ranging in age from 12 to 17. The two major aspects of the interview concerned the youngster's exposure to violent programming in the 10 years preceding the interview, and the youngster's (self-reported) violent behavior in the preceding 6 months. About half of the youngsters in the sample did not engage in any violence during the 6-month period prior to the interview. Of those who did, there was a strong positive correlation between the seriousness of the violent act and the amount of exposure to violent programming. Belson (1978) concluded that "the evidence ... is very strongly supportive of the hypothesis that high exposure to television violence increases the degree to which boys engage in serious violence" (p. 15).

In summary, the correlational studies come to the same conclusion as the experimental studies did: That exposure to television violence increases the likelihood that a person will act violently in his or her everyday life.

Cross-Cultural Studies of Television Violence and Behavior

A series of methodologically sophisticated cross-cultural studies of the influence of television violence on behavior was recently undertaken by Eron, Huesmann, and their colleagues (Eron et al., 1972; Eron & Huesmann, 1980a, 1980b; Huesmann & Eron, 1986; Huesmann, Eron, Klein, Brice, & Fischer, 1981). This large project involved interviews with first and third, and fifth graders in five countries (United States, Australia, Finland, Poland, and Holland). The results that have been obtained so far are summarized in Huesmann and Eron, 1986.

The findings of this large cross-cultural study are summarized by Huesmann (1986) as follows:

> more aggressive children generally watch more television and prefer more violent television. This appears to be true of children in societies with rigidly controlled media and little media violence as of children in free societies with substantial media violence. It also is as true today of girls in the United States as of boys. In fact, the relation disappears only when children are denied individual choice about what is viewed—e.g., among kibbutz children. (p. 126)

In a recent study by this research group, childhood aggression was linked to adult criminality (Huesmann, Eron, Lefkowitz, & Walder,

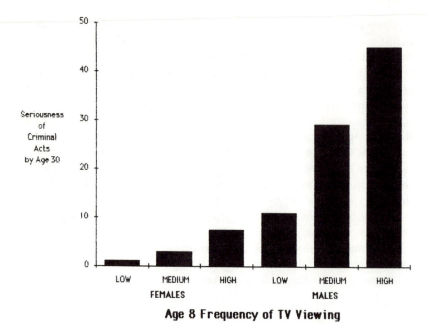

FIG. 4.1.   The relation between age 8 frequency of television viewing and
seriousness of criminal convictions at age 30. High and low subjects at age
8 were in the upper and lower quartiles. (© Huesmann, 1986.)

1984). These researchers argue that aggression, measured by peer nomi-
nation, is a stable trait with correlations between childhood scores of
aggression and adulthood criminality of 0.46. That is, children who
were rated as more aggressive by their peers at age 8 were more likely
to be convicted of crimes by age 30. And if convicted, they committed
more serious crimes. In short, aggressive habits are learned early in
life and once established are not only resistant to change but also predic-
tive of adult criminality (Huesmann, 1986). Figure 4.1 (from Huesmann,
1986) illustrates the relationship between frequency of television viewing at age 8 and seriousness of criminal convictions at age 30 (based
on data from Huesmann et al., 1984).

FIELD EXPERIMENTAL STUDIES

One difficulty with correlational studies is the lack of precision about
exactly how much and what kind of television material is watched
(Chaffee, 1972). This difficulty is overcome, however, in field experiments where either the television watching is controlled, or it is measured much more carefully than is usually the case in correlational
studies.

For example, in a study by Singer and Singer (1981), reliable and valid measures of television viewing were obtained by asking parents to observe in detail their child's viewing during 4 separate weeks of the year. The parents were asked to record each program the child watched, how long they spent watching it and with whom, and the degree of intensity with which the child paid attention to the show.

At the same time, each child's aggressive actions in nursery school were recorded by an independent group of observers who were completely unaware of the television viewing habits of the children who were being studied. As in the study by Eron et al. (1972), the Singers then used a cross-lagged correlation technique to determine the likely direction of the influence.

With respect to TV violence and aggression, the Singers found that viewing violence on television was significantly and positively associated with aggressive behavior in nursery school. Furthermore, because of the design of their study, Singer and Singer (1981) were able to ask the following general question: If a child watches violent TV on a given day, say Monday, is he or she more likely to be aggressive in nursery school the next day, on Tuesday? Conversely, if a child is aggressive in nursery school on a given day, say Wednesday, is he or she more likely to watch violent television later, on Thursday? By looking at the relationship between watching TV and acting aggressively over time, the Singers were able to gather data on the direction of the relationship. They discovered that children who view violent television are more likely to be aggressive in nursery school at a later time, but children who are aggressive in nursery school are not any more likely to view violent television afterwards. So, like Eron and his colleagues, the Singers concluded that the causal direction for this correlation is such that watching TV violence influences aggression, and not the reverse (Singer & Singer, 1980, 1981).

In many field experiments, the amount of TV violence viewing is manipulated by the researchers and the subjects are then observed in terms of their aggressive behaviors (or sometimes both antisocial and prosocial behaviors) (Friedrich & Stein, 1973; Stein & Friedrich, 1972; Steuer, Applefield, & Smith, 1971). For example, Stein and Friedrich (1972), found that children who were initially somewhat more aggressive than other children became significantly more aggressive after viewing "Batman" and "Superman" cartoons, whereas children who viewed "Mister Rogers' Neighborhood" (a program noted for its lack of violence and its deliberate prosocial content) were more cooperative and willing to share toys afterward.

Field Studies in Other Cultures

A field study was described in chapter 1 involving three Canadian towns having different amounts of television available to them, with respect to findings regarding the effects of television on reading (Corteen, 1977). As part of that study, researchers were able to observe aggressive behavior of the children in one town (Notel) both before and after television was introduced (Joy, Kimball, & Zabrack, 1986; Williams, 1978). These investigators reported that after television came to Notel, the children of that town were significantly more aggressive (both verbally and physically) than they had been before television came into their area, and they were more aggressive than the children in Unitel or Multitel, the other two towns that had television for quite a while.

The authors suggest that this difference in aggression was accounted for in terms of a "novelty effect" like that described by Murray and Kippax (1978). Murray and Kippax, in their study of the social behavior of children in three Australian towns, found that when television first comes to town it is watched often and is also likely to be imitated. Once television has been around for a period of time the novelty wears off and there is a subsequent decline in the rate of such imitation.

A similar study, also in Canada, was done by Granzberg and Steinbring (1980). They compared a Cree Indian community into which television was just being introduced with a control Indian community (having no television) and a control nonIndian Canadian town. Although no differences in aggressive behavior were found among the three towns, significant differences in aggressive attitudes were observed on the part of those children who were heavy viewers of television.

It is noteworthy that both in this study and in one by McCarthy, Langner, Gersten, Eisenberg, and Orzeck (1975), the violent attitudes were related to the total amount of TV viewing. Earlier studies (e.g., Eron et al., 1972; Robinson & Bachman, 1972) found no relation between total amount of viewing and aggression. As statistical techniques become more sophisticated, perhaps the relationship between TV viewing and aggression is able to be more precisely established, and begins to appear even for crude measures such as "total viewing." Most modern research takes into account the kind of program viewed as well; when this is done, the correlations between TV viewing and aggression are even stronger (Huesmann, 1982).

Another Canadian field study looked at the impact of violent televised sports on children (McCabe & Moriarity, 1977). Children involved in summer sports camps were shown one of two versions (prosocial vs. antisocial) of a game of hockey, lacrosse, or baseball. The young-sters' behaviors were monitored before, during, and after the showing of the film. The results showed no increase in aggression following ex-posure to the antisocial film and the only trend in the data was a slight increase in prosocial behavior on the part of older children who had seen the prosocial tape. A likely explanation is that the games of hock-ey and lacrosse are already so violent that additional input from the films was of little consequence (Murray, 1980).

A cross-cultural field study by Parke, Berkowitz, Leyens, West, and Sebastian (1977) looked at the effect of filmed violence on adolescents in England and the United States. Youngsters in institutions (where their television viewing could be controlled) were exposed to 5 days of either violent or nonviolent (control) films. In both countries, those who saw the violent films were observed to act more aggressively than those who watched the control films. Similar field studies with adoles-cents done by Leyens, Parke, Camino, and Berkowitz (1975) and Loye, Gorney, and Steele (1977) support these conclusions.

With all of this evidence indicating that watching violence on TV leads to more aggression, it is noteworthy that three other large and well-designed studies failed to find any evidence of a relationship be-tween viewing violent material and aggression. Feshbach and Singer (1971), Milgram and Shotland (1973), and Milavsky, Stipp, Kessler, and Rubens (1982), found no association between viewing violent material and subsequent antisocial behavior in the field experiments they undertook. One other study by Hennigan et al. (1982) also found no relationship between violent criminal activity and television, but they did find an increase in petty larceny with the introduction of television in several cities in the early 1950s.

Even though not all studies show an effect, however, the vast prepon-derance of evidence described so far clearly points in the direction of a substantial positive correlation between viewing TV violence and ag-gressive attitudes and behavior. In fact, the question of whether there is a correlation between viewing violent television and acting violently is not much in dispute anymore (see, however, Freedman, 1984, 1988; Milavsky, 1988; and Friedrich-Cofer & Huston, 1986, for recent discus-sions on the controversy). A bigger issue, still quite unresolved, con-cerns the psychological mechanisms that allow this effect to occur (Huesmann, 1982, Huesmann, 1986; Huesmann & Malamuth, 1986). How does the violence of television "get into" our thoughts and pat-terns of behavior? This is, as we have mentioned, the central psycho-logical question, and we turn to it now.

PSYCHOLOGICAL MECHANISMS OF INFLUENCE

In the remainder of this chapter and in chapters 5 and 6, we look at the psychological mechanisms that allow the violence viewed on television to become part of the behavioral repertoire of those who watch. In this chapter we examine three *behavioral* mechanisms that have been identified, and in the following chapters we analyze several *cognitive* mechanisms.

This distinction between behavior and cognition is only one of convenience. In reality, it is hard to separate acting from thinking. It is obvious, for example, that behavioral mechanisms have cognitive components, and that cognitive mechanisms have behavioral consequences. The distinction is used here because the evidence for the first set of mechanisms (imitation, disinhibition, and arousal/desensitization) tends to be behavioral (physical aggression, lowered restraints and inhibitions, physiological responses such as arousal, etc.), whereas the evidence for the second set of mechanisms (mainstreaming and resonance) is focused on beliefs and attitudes.

Imitation

Different species of animals have different ways of learning, different means of gathering, extracting, and utilizing the information contained in the world. Human beings, for example, have three separate means of learning: direct, observational, and symbolic (Condry, 1987). The first of these involves learning from a direct interchange with the environment, learning by acting and experiencing the consequences. The second capacity to learn is by observation or imitation. This form of learning involves watching other animals like ourselves, and later repeating the same actions (Bandura, 1977). Symbolic learning is learning from the use of language and symbols, either written or spoken.

In other words, we can learn from actually doing something (direct learning), from observing another creature do it (observational learning), or from being told or reading about it (symbolic learning). Each of these forms of learning is more "decontexualized" than the other.

In 1960, Albert Bandura and his colleague Richard Walters were writing a book on socialization, about how children become part of the society into which they are born and how they learn to acquire the skills and behaviors necessary for survival (Bandura & Walters, 1963). Bandura and Walters had come to the conclusion that without the capacity to learn by observation (along with language, which they did not treat as a separate capacity), the human child would simply not have enough time to learn the vast array of behaviors and roles necessary to become part of human culture. As far as these investigators were concerned, observational learning, or *imitation*, was a central feature of the developing child's capacity to acquire knowledge about the world. Imitation was the key learning process of socialization.

It followed from this approach that one should look at the various parts of the world the child might be exposed to as sources of information. Bandura noticed that in addition to the currently recognized sources of information — parents, peers, and school — there was a new source of information available to children in the United States and a few other countries: television. At that point in time, in the early 1960s, it was not yet known whether children would imitate what they saw on television, with its fuzzy screen and fleeting images.

Bandura had published a study in 1961 showing that children would imitate a real-life aggressive model (Bandura & Huston, 1961) and, furthermore, that children would generalize the aggressive responses they had learned to new settings in which the model was absent (Bandura, Ross, & Ross, 1961). But these instances all involved "real-life" models, live human beings present in the same room. Would people (particularly children) imitate a similar model seen on a television set?

In order to answer this question, Bandura designed a now-classic experiment to study what he called "film-mediated aggression." In this study, the researchers compared the extent to which children would imitate real-life, filmed, and "cartoon" models (Bandura et al., 1963). Two questions were of primary interest: (a) would children imitate a television portrayal of aggression *at all*? and (b) if film models *were* imitated, would the imitation extend to clearly fictional models such as a cartoon character?

It is a mark of Bandura's insight that both of these questions highlight central issues regarding children and television that are still of interest today, nearly a quarter of a century later. Bandura realized that if children did not imitate television, then one need go no further in researching its effects. If they did imitate what they saw on television, however, then television must be considered a potentially important source of information available to the child. Furthermore, the issue of cartoon versus real images is still a central one in the field of television research, and Bandura was one of the first to recognize its importance. We are still, as yet, a long way from understanding it.

In designing the original study, Bandura predicted that the film model would be imitated, but not the cartoon model: "It was predicted ... (that) the more remote the model was from reality, the weaker would be the tendency for subjects to imitate the behavior of the model" (Bandura et al., 1963, p. 3). As it turned out Bandura was wrong about this, but he was right about virtually everything else.

To test his ideas, nursery school-aged children of both sexes were exposed to a scene of aggressive actions toward a BoBo doll, in one of three experimental conditions:

1. real person actually in the room acting out the behaviors,
2. real person on film acting out the behaviors,
3. person dressed in a cartoon outfit on film acting out the behaviors.

In the first two conditions, both male and female models were used, in order to determine if the sex of the model was important in how much imitation occurred. The cartoon character, which was actually the female model "costumed as a black cat similar to the many cartoon cats" (Bandura et al., 1963, p. 5), had no obvious sex. In the "cartoon" condition, the background was done in a cartoon-like setting with "artificial grass . . . brightly colored trees, birds, and butterflies, creating a fantasyland setting" (Bandura et al., 1963, p. 5).

In each of these conditions, the model (real or filmed; man, woman, or "cartoon" cat) performed exactly the same sequence of distinctive acts in order to assess the extent to which children actually imitated what they had seen. For example, the model "sat on the BoBo doll and punched it repeatedly in the nose . . . pommeled it on the head with a mallet . . . tossed the doll up in the air aggressively and kicked it about the room" (Bandura et al., 1963, p. 5) In addition to these distinctive physical acts, the model also punctuated the action with specific spoken phrases such as "sock him in the nose," "kick him," and "pow!" (Bandura et al., 1963, p. 5).

All of this was done deliberately in order to be able to trace the influence of the model in the film. Bandura realized that the children might be stimulated to aggress simply by watching the film, without actually imitating what they saw, and he designed the experiment to distinguish between these two possible responses. In order to determine if children were imitating, the experimenters scored only those acts as imitation that involved doing exactly the same thing that the model had done (see Fig. 4.2).

The central findings of Bandura's study are given in Table 4.1. several things are obvious from these results. First, the amount of aggression in both the film-model and the live-model conditions is significantly greater than in the control group (who were not shown an aggressive scene). Thus, children are as likely to imitate a television model as they are a live one. This may not seem like an earthshaking finding today, but it was very important at the time. It proved, beyond doubt, that children could and would imitate the kind of images they see on television.

FIG. 4.2. Examples of imitation of the televised model (top row) by children. (© Bandura, Ross, & Ross, 1963.)

Second, the "cartoon"-film condition was just as effective in promoting imitation of violence as either of the conditions involving real
models. This finding is extremely important, given the fact that most
of the shows that young children watch are cartoon shows, and as we
saw in chapter 3, they are the most violent shows on television. Yet for
years the television networks have responded to objections by saying
that the violence in cartoons was "fantasy," and thus presumably not
imitated by children. Bandura's research demonstrates that cartoon aggression is as likely to be imitated by children as real aggression. From
this standpoint of the outcome, it would appear that Gerbner and his
colleagues were right to code comic violence as violence, because it is
treated this way by children. The distinction between reality and fantasy may not mediate behavioral outcomes for children as it does for
adults.

Bandura also found sex differences in the amount of imitation that
occurred. Boys were, overall, more aggressive than girls (a very common finding in psychological research). There was also some tendency for girls to imitate a female model more than a male model, with
the reverse being true of boys, although this was not true across all conditions. In general, however, it appears that children are more likely
to imitate same-sex models than other-sex ones in circumstances of this
sort (Bandura et al., 1963; see also Bandura et al., 1961).

Since this early research by Bandura, dozens of studies have been
undertaken to expand and refine these basic findings (see reviews by
Bandura, 1973; Friedrich & Stein, 1973; Leyens et al., 1975; Steuer et
al., 1971; Geen & Thomas, 1986) But the central facts have withstood
the test of time.

What these findings mean, quite simply, is that television is an effective tutor, and that it functions as a source of information for children. "All of television is educational," as Nick Johnson, a former commissioner (in 1975) of the FCC, said, ". . . the only question is: what does it teach?" Television provides an infinite variety of behavior models for creatures who can learn by observation and imitation. Both chil-

TABLE 4.1
Aggression Scores for Experimental and Control Groups
(from Bandura, Ross, & Ross, 1963).

Response Category	Real Life Aggressive		Human Film Agressive		Cartoon Aggressive	Control Group
	F Model	M Model	F Model	M Model		
Total Aggression:						
Girls	65.8	57.3	87.0	79.5	80.9	36.4
Boys	76.8	131.8	114.5	85.0	117.2	72.2
Imitative Aggression:						
Girls	19.2	9.2	10.0	8.0	7.8	1.8
Boys	18.4	38.4	34.3	13.3	16.2	3.9
Mallet Aggression:						
Girls	17.2	18.7	49.2	19.5	36.8	13.1
Boys	15.5	28.8	20.5	16.3	12.5	13.5
Sits on Bobo Doll:						
Girls	10.4	5.6	10.3	4.5	15.3	3.3
Boys	1.3	0.7	7.7	0.0	5.6	0.6
Nonimitative Aggression:						
Girls	27.6	24.9	24.0	34.3	27.5	17.8
Boys	35.5	48.6	46.8	31.8	71.8	40.4
Aggressive Gun Play:						
Girls	1.8	4.5	3.8	17.6	8.8	3.7
Boys	7.3	15.9	12.8	23.7	16.6	14.3

Significance Levels: Comparison of Treatment Conditions

Response Category	Live vs. Film	Live vs. Cartoon	Film vs. Cartoon	Live vs. Control	Film vs. Control	Cartoon vs. Control
Total Aggression	ns	ns	ns	<.01	<.01	<.005
Imitative Aggression	ns	<.05	ns	<.001	<.001	<.005
Mallet Aggression	ns	ns	ns	ns	ns	ns
Sits on Bobo Doll	ns	ns	ns	ns	<.05	<.005
Nonimitative Aggression	ns	ns	ns	ns	ns	ns
Aggressive Gun Play	<.01	ns	ns	ns	<.05	ns

dren and adults can learn novel behaviors from television. But the mechanism of imitation is not dependent on portrayals of violence or aggression. If the content of television should change tomorrow to include vastly more examples of loving or prosocial behaviors, then we would expect children to imitate them as well (Leifer, Gordon, & Graves, 1974). Bandura has continued to describe and to elaborate his theory of observational learning since these early days of research on television (Bandura, 1977). He now suggests that learning by observation is governed by four subprocesses: (a) attentional, (b) memory representational, (c) motor productive (which governs the acquisition of knowledge), and (d) motivational (which regulates the performance of observationally learned sequences) (Bandura, 1977, p. 322).

The mechanism of imitation, then, has a great deal of theory and research behind it, making it one of the most widely understood and best researched of the psychological mechanisms. There are many parameters that influence the modeling situation. For example, models are more likely to be imitated if they act vigorously rather than with restraint (Parton & Geshuri, 1971), and what children learn is a specific set of motor responses performed by the model (Dubanoski & Parton, 1971). Adult approval can enhance modeled aggression in children (Eisenberg, 1980), and the presence of other children, especially a peer who also imitates, can also enhance the imitative effect (Leyens, Herman, & Dunand, 1982; O'Carroll, O'Neal, & Macdonald, 1977; O'Neal, Macdonald, Cloninger, & Levine, 1979).

> Collectively, these studies indicate that the presence of others may provide incentives to the child to act out aggressive responses previously learned through observation, or it may threaten disapproval and thereby suppress such acting out. These findings are therefore an extension of Bandura's conclusion that imitative aggression requires both an occasion for learning and a sufficient incentive to carry out the learned behavior. (Geen & Thomas, 1986, p. 11)

It is enough for us to know that learning by observation is accomplished apparently just as easily from a televised stimulus as from direct observation of the event itself. What a host of possibilities this fact opens up for a creature curious about the world and quick to learn! If television had only this influence, and this alone, it would still be an amazingly powerful thing. But there is more to the influence of television on behaviors than imitation alone.

Disinhibition

At about the same time as Bandura was wondering whether children would imitate television, Len Berkowitz, a psychologist at the University of Wisconsin, was becoming interested in a different facet of the problem of television violence. To understand Berkowitz's contribution to the research on television effects, we must begin with a restatement of Bandura's imitation theory.

The theory of imitation goes something like this: An organism introduced to a novel stimulus will, under certain conditions, acquire this novel behavior pattern in the sense of encoding it in memory, simply as a function of paying attention to it. Other variables will then determine when or whether the newly acquired pattern of behavior will ever be *performed*. A key distinction in Bandura's theory of imitation is between *acquisition* and *performance*. Different factors govern each. In terms of aggression, a child who observes a novel pattern of action on the screen (perhaps a model hitting a BoBo doll with a hammer) will, by having seen it, learn how to do it (acquisition). Perhaps later, when and if the conditions are right, the child will repeat that same action (performance).

Berkowitz noted that with adults the knowledge of various forms of aggression is already quite elaborate. Adults know how to hurt one another; they have learned it throughout the course of growing up. With adults, then, acquisition of a novel response pattern is not the problem; performance is. There is not that much new or novel for adults to learn from watching television, so does that mean adults are *not* influenced by television?

Berkowitz reasoned that a second mechanism for the influence of television was *disinhibition*. Television seemed to provide just the kind of information that would release pent-up aggressive behavior, that is, information that released the constraints on one's actions, thereby "disinhibiting" the viewer.

An alternative to this disinhibition theory, exactly the opposite in fact, is the notion of "catharsis." The theory of *catharsis* posits that viewing violence should *reduce* the likelihood of acting violently. As Berkowitz described it: "The symbolic expression of aggressive responses can weaken the instigation to subsequent aggression under appropriate circumstances" (Berkowitz & Rawlings, 1963, p. 406).

In his article, Berkowitz disagreed with the catharsis theory. "Symbolic catharsis is possible. . . but should generally be relatively ineffective as a means of reducing the instigation to aggression" (Berkowitz & Rawlings, 1963, p. 406). Instead, Berkowitz thought that " . . . people seeing fantasy violence under conditions lowering their inhibitions against aggressive responses should display an increased likelihood of subsequent aggression" (Berkowitz & Rawlings, 1963, p. 406).

In short, it was Berkowitz's contention that televised aggression can have a *disinhibiting* effect, making subsequent aggression, after viewing violence, more likely. Not only did Berkowitz think the catharsis theory was wrong, but he thought the opposite of it was true.

Imagine a man coming home from work; he's tired, a little angry from being "pushed around" by the boss, the car has been having trouble, and he is in a rotten mood. He turns on television, gets a beer, and while watching an episode of a violent police drama, his wife comes in and does something to make him madder still. Disinhibition theory says that domestic violence is likely under these circumstances, due to the mechanism of disinhibition. Without television, the man might still feel angry at his wife, but the normal inhibitions that restrain aggression would function to keep him from acting violently. Catharsis theory says just the opposite: After watching the violent television show, the man should be *less* likely to strike out at his wife.

In the early 1960s, at about the same time Bandura was studying imitation, Berkowitz designed a study to choose between these two different predictions, to see which of these two possible mechanisms (disinhibition or catharsis) was more likely to be true. Berkowitz showed college student subjects a film clip of a brutal fight scene from a movie (*The Champion*). Before seeing the film, one group of subjects was made angry as a result of being insulted by one of the experimenter's graduate assistants. After the film, the subjects were given a chance to "aggress" against the same graduate student who insulted them. If disinhibition theory was correct, the angered subjects who saw the violent film should exhibit more aggression afterward than those who were not angered or did not see the violent film.

In addition to comparing disinhibition and catharsis, Berkowitz was also interested in the extent to which the *justifications* for violence given within the story made a difference in a person's response to the material. To see if this factor made any difference, half of the subjects in Berkowitz's study were told before seeing the film that the beating shown was "justified," in the sense that the man beaten in the film "deserved what he got." The other half of the subjects were told that the beating was "unjustified."

Berkowitz's findings confirmed the existence of the disinhibition mechanism of influence. Subjects who saw the aggressive film were more hostile and aggressive toward the graduate student who had made them angry than similarly angered subjects who had not seen the violent film. So, watching televised violence can have disinhibiting effects especially for people who are already angered.

One of the most striking findings of this study concerned the variable of justification. Subjects who had been told that the violence in the film was justified were the most hostile and aggressive of all. This finding raises some important and paradoxical issues for the television industry. Network executives are fond of noting the fact that although there is much violence on television, it is often "justified" in the sense that "good" usually prevails and the villain is caught and punished, so the viewer is reminded that "crime doesn't pay." But, as Berkowitz pointed out:

> the villain is shown being defeated or "punished aggressively"— if he obtains the beating he merited, as is typical in most melodramas—we clearly have a case of *justified aggression*, and this type of fantasy violence may actually increase the likelihood that some recently angered member of a movie or TV audience will attack his own frustrator, or perhaps even some innocent people he happens to associate with the anger instigator. (Berkowitz & Rawlings, 1963, p. 411)

So disinhibition is a second mechanism of influence whereby the content of television may affect how we behave. Like Bandura and his research on imitation, Berkowitz and his students kept up interest in this research area, adding refinement and detail to the picture he drew in 1963 (see Berkowitz, 1965, 1969, 1971, 1974; Berkowitz & Alioto, 1973; Berkowitz & Geen, 1966; Geen 1976; Geen & Berkowitz, 1967; Geen & Stonner, 1974; Geen & Thomas, 1986).

Berkowitz no longer views these results in terms of "disinhibition," a rather narrow concept, but in terms of how the media "activates" ideas, thoughts, emotions, and behavioral tendencies associated with aggression (Berkowitz, 1984). This cognitive–associationist analysis goes far beyond his earlier theory of disinhibition. It can explain many aspects of the data that were not covered by the earlier theory. For example, Berkowitz' new theory explains why the observation of aggression is often followed by aggressive behavior that is substantially different from that shown, and how the sight of weapons or a target person similar to the media portrayal can often elicit aggressive behavior (Geen & Thomas, 1986, p. 21). We have more to say about Berkowitz' 1984 theory when we summarize the psychological theories linking media violence to real-life violence at the end of this chapter.

Both of these mechanisms (imitation and disinhibition) predict effects in the same direction. That is, although each represents a different causal route, the consequence of either mechanism is the same: The more violence viewed on television, the more likely is the viewer to engage in violence. There are, of course, mitigating circumstances: Violence is more likely if the viewer is angry, and if the model observed is "rewarded" for aggression, or is successful in it. Because the overall direction for the association is a positive one, either of these mechanisms could help to explain the positive correlation between viewing violent material and aggression that has been found by dozens of researchers, and described in detail earlier in this chapter.

The Mechanisms Should Be Content-Free. Although the two mechanisms we have just described were discovered in an attempt to understand the effect of watching televised violence, part of their importance from a psychological point of view is that they are not content specific. That is, once we know about a given mechanism and its parameters, this mechanism should allow us to predict similar influences for other kinds of content.

For example, what if the content of television were as sexy as it is now violent. Suppose that in the last chapter, instead of describing the massive exaggeration of violence on television, we had instead noticed that sexual behavior was more frequent and of a different "character" on television than sexual behavior in real life. If this was so, then we would expect the psychological mechanisms of imitation and disinhibition to influence us in the same way they do now. Sexual behaviors shown on television would be imitated, and they would result in disinhibition under certain circumstances.

Rate of Occurrence. Although each of these mechanisms act in the same direction, the psychological mechanisms we have been describing only speak to the possibility of influence. They suggest causal routes that make a positive correlation possible, but they do not tell us the rate of influence. It is one thing to prove that individuals can imitate what they see on television, or that under certain specific circumstances people may become disinhibited, but it is quite another to predict how many people out of a given population will be influenced.

Thus, the issue of rate involves the percent of people in the population watching a particular event who will be likely to imitate it. This is perhaps more properly a sociological question than a psychological one, but several psychologists have tried to determine whether real acts of violence tended to follow televised acts of violence that were spectacular, or in some way thought likely to be imitated.

Berkowitz and Macaulay (1971) studied the deviation from the monthly average crime rate for each month from January 1960 through December 1966, in 40 American cities. They found two dramatic increases in the amount of violent crime during this period, one following the assassination of President Kennedy in November 1963, and the other in the summer of 1966 after the nationally reported mass murders by Richard Speck (in Chicago) and Charles Whitman (in Texas).

In a less-ambitious study, Siegel (1969) found that within 1 week of the showing of a television drama ("The Doomsday Flight"), the plot of which involved money being extorted from an airline company by planting a bomb on a plane, 13 bomb threats were phoned into airline offices! This was twice the number reported in the entire month before the broadcast (Geen, 1976). Berkowitz (1974) also reported evidence of a relationship between airline hijacking and the amount of news coverage given to hijack attempts.

Phillips (1974) conducted a series of studies of popular reaction to several widely publicized suicides. These studies showed that when the media paid lots of attention to a famous person's suicide, there was a subsequent increase in the number of people who took their own lives. Later studies showed this to be also true of car accidents (Phillips, 1979), and well-publicized airplane suicides (in which the effect occurred for other pilots) (Phillips, 1980). According to a recent study, there is also evidence that the portrayal of suicides on soap operas is often followed by a national increase in the suicide rate (Phillips, 1982).

Phillips and Hensley (1984) studied the patterns of 140,000 U.S. homicides after media publicity about prize fights, murder acquittals, life sentences, death sentences, and executions. They found that the number of homicides significantly increased on the third day after a fight. This finding was consistent with earlier research showing that public events have their greatest impact 3–4 days after the event (Phillips, 1983). This research makes a variety of assumptions in order to draw causal inferences (see, e.g., Phillips & Bollen, 1985) and these assumptions have been called into question by several other researchers (Baron & Reiss, 1985; Freedman, 1984; Kessler & Stipp, 1983). An excellent review of these and other naturalistic studies of television violence may be found in Turner, Hesse, and Peterson-Lewis (1986).

Thus, we know that some of the material depicted on television is imitated by at least some of those exposed. We do not yet know how many people will do so in response to any given event, and we cannot predict which particular scenes or events will be likely candidates for imitation or disinhibition. In a celebrated court case several years ago, a television drama ("Born Innocent") portrayed the (simulated) rape of a teenage girl by several other girls in a reformatory. A day or two later, in northern California, a teenage girl was molested in exactly the same way on the beach by a gang of girls. When apprehended, the attackers admitted to getting the idea from the television show (Malamuth & Briere, 1986). In this particular instance, the mother of the assaulted child sued the television network (Olivia v. National Broadcasting Co., Inc., 1978) although the case was eventually dismissed by a judge without going to trial. (For a discussion of the legal issues in this case, see Linz, Penrod, & Donnerstein, 1986, p. 172.)

Because each evening's television fare brings an average of five acts of violence per prime-time hour, and because only some of these are so widely imitated that they make the news, it raises the interesting research question of what it is about a certain scene that makes it a prime candidate for imitation? Are some things simply more "attractive" or attention getting than others? What content characteristics are the most likely to have psychological consequences?

Arousal and Desensitization

The third and final behavioral mechanism is the most poorly understood of all, and yet it is also one of the most fascinating. This mechanism alone could account for the largest single effect that television has, as an "unwinder." Even though they represent apparently opposite reactions, both arousal and desensitization are "positively" related to aggression. That is, the more aroused the greater the potential for violence and the more desensitized, the more violence will likely be tolerated. The activation of either mechanism then, would predict an *increase* in violence after watching violent television.

We consider arousal and desensitization together because both may be part of the *same process* or mechanism. What arouses a person today will be tomorrow's candidate for desensitization. Thus, the two factors seem to be at opposite ends of a continuum.

The Relationship Between Arousal and Desensitization.   Almost any stimulus has less and less capacity to arouse us with each successive presentation. There are physiological mechanisms of habituation that can explain this, but we stick to the psychological data. This lessened capacity for arousal is described psychologically as *desensitization*. If a violent scene arouses and excites the viewer, holding attention for the time being, then the next time it is presented that same scene, or one like it, will have less attention-drawing power, less capacity to arouse. With each repeated presentation, the degree of arousal will decline, until it reaches zero or below.

Arousal and desensitization may play a role in the other behavioral mechanisms, for example, it may be that an arousing television scene such as the rape scene mentioned earlier from "Born Innocent," is also more likely to be imitated (see Linz, Penrod, & Donnerstein, 1986, p. 175). Arousal/desensitization, as a mechanism, may not be independent of the others, but because the research on this mechanism comes from a different research tradition, we describe it as separate. In describing the research, we consider first arousal, then desensitization.

Arousal

Arousal is difficult to define in a precise way, although most of us know what it means. To be aroused is to be excited, and "turned on." Researchers distinguish between two types of arousal: cortical and autonomic

(Routtenberg, 1968, 1971; Zillmann, 1982). *Cortical arousal* involves those processes that govern and serve attention, perception, and response preparation, whereas *autonomic arousal* is related to affective and emotional reactions. The orienting response, the sense of intense awareness that you get when you hear an unusual sound at night, is an example of cortical arousal. Anger is an example of autonomic arousal. The study of cortical arousal involves research on attention, alertness, and vigilance on the one hand and information processing, acquisition, and retrieval on the other. Autonomic arousal pertains to emotional behavior that is activated or altered in response to an event (Zillmann, 1982).

No researchers have studied cortical arousal the way it is usually measured by Alpha Wave blocking on an EEG, but, as we see in chapter 6, Daniel Anderson and his colleagues are beginning to study attention and orienting to television in children. Autonomic arousal has been studied extensively however, measured in a variety of ways: systolic and diastolic blood pressure, heart rate (acceleration and deceleration), vasoconstriction (skin temperature decrease), and skin conductance (Buck, 1976; Zillmann, 1982).

What Program Characteristics Lead to Arousal? Research shows that both suspenseful drama (Zillmann, 1982), and comedy (Tannenbaum, 1971) are especially effective in inducing intense arousal in both children and adults. There is reason to believe, moreover, that these different types of stimuli produce very similar excitatory reactions (Carruthers & Taggart, 1973; Levi, 1965). The indistinguishability of arousal to comedy or drama is congruent with a currently popular psychological theory of emotion: the two factor theory (Schachter, 1964; Schachter & Singer, 1962; Schachter & Wheeler, 1962). In this theory, emotions consist of two factors: an undifferentiated autonomic arousal (excitement), and a cognitive explanation of the feeling state. Thus, the *kind* of emotion is determined cognitively, whereas the intensity of it is determined by the magnitude of the arousal.

In addition to comedy and drama, sports are also capable of causing powerful increases in arousal, and especially so when one identifies with one of the teams (Bryant & Zillmann, 1977). The role of involvement, a factor of some importance in understanding responses to video material, seems to be similar regardless of the arousing stimulus. In drama as in sports, when good things happen to people you like, and bad things befall those you do not like, this heightens the excitation and enjoyment (Tannenbaum, 1972; Zillmann & Bryant, 1974).

What kinds of content leads to the most arousal, what to the least? To consider both ends of the scale: sexually explicit erotic material consistently induces the most autonomic arousal in both sexes (Cantor,

Zillmann, & Einsiedel, 1978; Donnerstein & Hallam, 1978; Levi, 1969; Zillmann, 1971), whereas nature films consistently produce the least arousal (Levi, 1965; Wadeson, Mason, Hamburg, & Handlon, 1963). In fact, nature films often lower arousal below the baseline established before watching a film (Zillmann, 1982).

The kind of material presented by television that has the greatest capacity to arouse is suspenseful drama, hilarious comedy, and sex. Sports could be added, with the caveat that it seems to arouse only certain people (e.g., followers of the team). What do these dramatic events have in common? What makes them arousing? Leaving sex aside for the moment (because of the difference between what is meant by "sex" in this research, and what is meant by sex on television), what do comedy, suspense, and sports have in common that might make them so arousing?

One thing may be "uncertainty." In each of these cases, the greater the uncertainty, the greater the arousal. Each of these program types may induce arousal because of the degree of uncertainty in the plot, coupled with the "involvement" of the viewer. Zillmann (1982) made involvement the centerpiece of his theory of emotional responses to television, because if something is not involving it cannot arouse. A person must "get into" a program, must watch it with some concentration, before it can have an effect on him or her. Once the viewer is "involved," then it would appear that the greater the uncertainty in the plot, the greater the arousal.

The Law of Initial Values.   The degree to which an individual will become aroused in response to televised material depends on the law of initial values (Sternbach, 1966; Wilder, 1957) which states that the magnitude of arousal decreases with increases in the initial arousal state of the subject. Thus, television viewers who are the least aroused initially will have much larger reactions to exciting material than those viewers who are already aroused when they sit down to watch.

The influence of television on a person who is already aroused is an important consideration because one of the most important and commonly reported ways television seems to be used by individuals is as a source of relaxation. Imagine an individual coming home from work, exhausted and somewhat angry about the events of the day. In fact, we imagined such a person earlier and (in our imagination) saw him become "disinhibited" and strike his wife! Could this person have used television as an "unwinder?"

In fact, there is evidence that people do use television just this way. So television can both arouse our mythical person, making it more likely for him to act violently, and/or it can calm him down, making it less likely that he will strike out. Which effect television has will depend on the type of program our mythical person tries to watch.

Arousing and Unwinding.   What are the conditions that lead television to be an "unwinder" or an "arouser?" The answer depends on the relationship of the material to the person's already existing cognitive state. Two factors are involved: (a) whether the television fare is sufficiently absorbing to capture and hold attention, that is, whether it is involving; and (b) the relationship of the communication to the individual's emotional state (Zillmann, 1979).

Exciting material may "unwind" or relax a person who is already excited about something else, but it may make this person even more excited if the story viewed is about the same thing that led to the original arousal. When television does "unwind" a person, when it undermines arousal, it does so because it disrupts the rehearsal processes (thinking about the boss and why he or she made you mad) that tend to keep arousal high. (For more detail see Zillmann, 1982, p. 59.)

Desensitization

Television not only exposes us to arousing, violent material, but it does so repeatedly, night after night, month after month, year after year. Is there any consequence to viewers who are exposed to this type of material over and over again? An obvious consequence is that one could become, in a sense, "callous" and so accustomed to the constant parade of violence, that with each presentation one becomes less and less aroused, less and less interested.

Drabman and Thomas (1974) and Thomas and Drabman (1975) have shown that children of both sexes in elementary school (Grades 1–4) were more insensitive to an apparent real-life violent incident after being exposed to a violent film. In a more carefully controlled study, Cline, Croft, and Courrier (1973) exposed two groups of boys to a violent movie, and measured their physiological response to it. One group of boys had a history of viewing violent television material, and the other group did not. The heavy viewers were less responsive to the violence in the film than the light viewers. This led the investigators to conclude that heavy exposure to violent fare desensitizes the viewer to additional violence. Finally, Thomas, Horton, Lippincott, and Drabman (1977) found a negative relationship between the amount of viewing of television drama and the intensity of arousal reactions to violent portrayals, and Bjorkqvst and Didrikkson (1985) demonstrated significantly decreased arousal to a short violent film after boys were exposed to a long violent film. In all of these cases, the mechanism underlying the response is some sort of "cognitive" desensitization, a lessened arousal and interest in the scene presented. Repeated exposure to "slasher" films can also lower emotional responsiveness (Linz, Donnerstein, & Penrod, 1984).

Habituation/Desensitization to Erotic Material.   Even though graphic sex is seldom seen on television, some of the most extensive research on the process of desensitization to arousing stimuli comes from studies of sexual material on film. Several researchers have exposed subjects to sexual/erotic material over long periods of time and observed decreases in their response to it (Reifler, Howard, Lipton, Liptzin, & Widmann 1971; Zillmann & Bryant, 1980). In all of these studies, individuals habituate very rapidly to the material, regardless of how arousing it was initially. There is also evidence of a strong "rebound" capacity. That is, after a short period of "rest" from exposure, the desensitization effect disappears and response rates to erotic material return to pretreatment levels (Howard, Reifler, & Liptzin, 1971).

These findings suggest a physiological basis for desensitization of one kind, even though the sexual material shown on television is different from the erotic films shown in most of this research (see chapter 2 for a discussion of sex on television).

Studies of media violence of a sexual nature suggest three conclusions according to a recent review by Malamuth and Briere (1986): (a) Males act against female targets in the majority of the depictions (Smith, 1976a, 1976b); (b) Although media sexual aggression has increased in the last 15 years, it is considerably lower than media nonsexual violence (Malamuth, 1986; Malamuth & Spinner, 1980; Palys, 1986; Slade, 1984; Stone, 1985; Winick, 1985a); and (c) Sexual aggression is often depicted quite differently from nonsexual aggression (Malamuth & Briere, 1986, p. 76).

Experimental research on sexual violence has demonstrated that college men's frequency of reading sexually explicit material correlated positively with their beliefs that women enjoy forced sex (Briere, Corne, Runtz, & Malamuth, 1984; Malamuth & Check, 1985). In another experiment, subjects exposed to a "positive rape portrayal" were less negative in their responses to a second rape portrayal (Malamuth & Check, 1980, 1981; Malamuth, Haber, & Feshbach, 1980). In a similar vein, Linz (1985) found that males exposed to sexually violent films were less sympathetic to a rape victim in a simulated trial (see also Linz, Donnerstein, & Penrod, 1984). Ceniti and Malamuth (1984) exposed adults to sexually violent and sexually nonviolent material. Subjects who were classified as "force oriented" (prior to the experiment) showed reduced arousal to sexual scenes—whether violent or nonviolent, while "nonforce"-oriented subjects showed no significant effects of exposure in agreement with desensitization theory (see Malamuth & Briere, 1986, p. 83).

Finally, several studies have shown significant associations between thought patterns justifying sexual agression in college men and self-reported sexual aggression (Briere et al., 1984; Kanin, 1985; Koss, Leonard, Beezley, & Oros, 1985; Mosher & Anderson, 1986; Rapaport & Burkhart, 1984). For an excellent review of the legal and social issues regarding media depictions of sexual aggression, see Linz, Penrod, and Donnerstein (1986).

The fact that people may be desensitized to violent material suggests two consequences of repeated viewing. First, viewers should become more and more accustomed to seeing violence, so that the heavy viewer should not be so aroused by any given act of televised violence, compared to a light viewer. Second, it follows from the first rule that if one is to program television in such a way as to maintain attention, it will be necessary to keep altering the violent material, making it progressively more violent in order to get the same degree of arousal out of the viewer. In this manner, viewing violence on television could be seen to act like an addictive drug. The more one sees, the stronger the next dose must be in order to attain the same level of response. In the view of many researchers and television critics, a trend in the violent programming over the last 20 years of television has been for the violence to become more graphic, more intense (Comstock et al., 1978; Murray, 1980; Winn, 1978; Zillmann, 1982).

The standard fare of television has the capacity to both arouse and desensitize, although the parameters of each of these responses are not well known, both have been shown to happen. There are both immediate and long-term effects. The arousal discussed previously was usually measured in the short term, over a period of hours, whereas "desensitization" is presumed to occur over many presentations, over months and even years of exposure.

Second, it is unclear the extent to which individual's "use" television, like a drug, to change their affective state. People certainly claim this to be the case when asked about why they watch television, as we saw when we discussed the needs-and-gratifications research in chapter 2. Most people say they use television for "escape" and "relaxation." They use television to "unwind," and we have just seen evidence that television has, under certain circumstances, a very powerful capacity to do just this.

This ability to use television for one's own purposes, as an unwinder, for example, raises another important series of questions about the degree of choice available to most viewers. Individuals with cable, or better yet, with a video recorder, should be more able to use television as an "unwinder" because they have a wider selection of material to choose from. Each person knows him or herself better than any other, we know what "turns us on" and what might best "unwind" us. No one has studied it yet, but those with more choice should be better able to accomplish this than those without.

Finally, there is the question we raised earlier of the extent to which television portrays violence honestly or dishonestly. We have suggested that the televised portrayals of violence are "cleaned up" and "not true to life." If this is the case, then heavy viewers should be "desensitized" to the fake violence portrayed on television, but may be even more sensitive to actual violence.

Although it is wildly speculative, something like this could have happened to the first television generation exposed to war. Violence on television drama was quite common by the mid-1960s (see chapter 3), when the images of the war in Vietnam began to be presented on the evening news every night. These real images of war were quite different from the images in the movies. Rather than being romantic and heroic, war was shown to be horrifying, painful, and tragic. It is not possible to gather evidence on this particular question, at this late date, but it would be possible to study the degree to which people who were used to television violence were either more or less sensitive to portrayals of actual (real) violence. Maybe television violence desensitizes us to fantasy or imaginary violence, but not to the real thing. It might even make us more sensitive to the real thing. This is a potentially interesting question for research.

Arousal/desensitization is thus another behavioral mechanism related to the influence of television. Although this mechanism is different from imitation and disinhibition, it may be related to both. It may form the basis of one of the most important uses of television, as an "unwinder."

SUMMARY

In order to discover a direct effect of television, it is necessary to establish two things: First, that some behavioral or attitudinal consequence is, in fact, associated with viewing television; and second, that there exists some psychological mechanism, some causal route, that allows the effect to occur. In the last chapter we saw that the amount of violence on television represented a massive distortion of reality, and, in the chapter before, that this violence is viewed by millions. We began this chapter by asking: Is there any evidence of an association between viewing television shows containing violence and acting or thinking violently? We reviewed evidence from experimental laboratory studies, from correlational studies, and from field studies, all of which point in the same direction: There is a *strong positive relationship* between viewing violence on television and, at some time later, acting violently.

Having established a positive association, our next step in trying to understand a direct effect of television is to look for *psychological mechanisms* that allow this effect, this positive association, to occur. We noted three mechanisms in this chapter: *imitation, disinhibition,* and *arousal/desensitization.* Each mechanism predicts a positive association between viewing violence on television and later acting violently. Although desensitization has more to do with being "tolerant" of violence than with acting violently. We also looked at "catharsis," a mechanism that predicts less aggression after viewing violent material, but we found no solid evidence to support the existence of this mechanism.

We saw that arousal/desensitization is the least well understood of the behavioral mechanisms, yet it may represent the most powerful influence of television: as an unwinder. As much as the arousal that leads to imitation, disinhibition and assault makes the headlines, perhaps the more important fact about television is that it usually functions in just the opposite way. The use of television to relax, to "unwind," as Zillmann called it, may be the most widespread and useful thing to be gained from television.

The psychological theories of imitation/disinhibition and arousal/desensitization were discovered and refined in the 1960s and 1970s. What has happened to these theories in the 1980s? The answer is that they have all become more sophisticated, both about the nature of aggression itself, and about the role of the media in promoting and maintaining it. As noted earlier, for example, Berkowitz (1984) has now expanded his theory to include the stimulation of associative networks of thoughts, ideas, and behavioral inclinations. In Berkowitz' view, violent film and television scripts touch off an associative network in the cognitive structure of the observer. Once primed, this network may be responsible for eliciting, maintaining, elaborating upon, and finally the acting out of aggressive behavioral scripts. This explanation encompasses much of the earlier data on disinhibition, as well as accounts for a number of facts that imitation or disinhibition will not explain. For example, some aggressive behavior is nothing whatsoever like what was seen on the media, yet it may have been "stimulated" by media portrayals nonetheless. Situational cues are important to the emission of aggressive actions, and Berkowitz (1986) has described several of these in a recent article. The presence of others, especially aggressive peers, often serves to enhance aggressive responses, as does the nature of the target person (when he or she is like the target of the media portrayal). The rewarding or punishing nature of the media portrayal is also important, as is the subject's perception of the perceived reality of the scene (a topic we consider in more detail in chapter 6). Finally, the observer's focus of attention, whether on the aggressive acts or other aspects of the portrayal, is another important determinant of the influence of a violent scene.

Current reasoning about aggression is extensively described in a recent whole issue of the *Journal of Social Issues* (Vol. 42. No. 3, 1986), edited by L. Rowell Huesmann and Neil Malamuth, two of the leading researchers in the field. In their introduction to this volume, Huesmann and Malamuth (1986) describe the outlines of a theory of the relation between media violence and subsequent aggression on the part of the viewer. They note, in the beginning, that aggression is a long term and quite stable pattern of behavior that has multiple determinants. In accord with Huesmann and Eron (1986), these authors suggest that a number of "interrelated constitutional and environmental factors" must converge for aggression to emerge. "Aggression is most likely to be the dominant style if the child's environment frustrates and victimizes the child, provides aggressive models, and reinforces aggression" (Huesmann & Malamuth, 1986, p. 3).

Aggressive scripts are learned in three phases, they are "encoded" or acquired from the surrounding environment, including the media; they are maintained over a period of time often becoming more elaborate; and they are emitted under specified circumstances. Violent media play a role in each of these processes. Repeated exposure to violent scripts is important to the initial encoding or acquisition phase, especially if the surrounding real environment is supportive. Encoding is very much dependent on age and attention, and it is well established that more violent aggressive children pay more attention to violent television than less aggressive children (Huesmann & Eron, 1986). It is also worth noting that sometimes people who fear aggression are also, paradoxically, attracted to violent media. Berkowitz explains this attraction as due to the anticipated "reassurance" the viewer gets from seeing the inevitable end of such scripts where the wrongdoer is caught and punished. This thesis, originally stated by Zillmann (1980), is supported by research done by Zillmann and Wakshlag (1985). According to this idea, people who are upset about their personal security in a violent world "greatly enjoy seeing the retaliatory aggression that the forces of law and order direct against the lawbreakers. . .and (they) will find this conclusion comforting" (Berkowitz, 1986, p. 98). Thus, attraction to violent, aggressive material is a complicated matter, but as television executives have known for many years, it excites many different viewers for many different reasons.

Not only does violent media play a role in encoding aggressive scripts, it also plays a central role in the maintenance of aggressive thoughts and ideas (Berkowitz, 1984). People who rehearse violent scripts, who are aroused by them and remember them, are more likely to enact them later. Violent television makes these scripts available on a daily basis, and this can also influence a person's attitudes about violence, as the research cited earlier on sexual violence suggests. So violent television effects long-term attitudes and promotes the elaboration of violent scripts.

Finally, violent media influences the emission of aggressive scripts in a variety of ways, through arousal and providing cues that are similar to the aggressive cues in everyday life. Violent television helps remind violent people that aggression is a socially acceptable way to resolve problems. So, in the emission phase the internal representation, the script, manifests itself in actual behavior partly in response to the current situation and partly in response to acquired and maintained habits of behavior. Again, there is no claim that television alone produces this result, but rather that it encourages and facilitates it (Huesmann & Malamuth, 1986). The striking correlation, described earlier, between viewing aggressive television at age 8 and criminal behavior at age 30 attests to this connection. The violent television at age 8 is not directly related to criminal behavior at age 30, but rather a part of a long cumulative learning process.

As this analysis suggests, both short-term and long-term evidence of an association between violent viewing and violent action is predicted by the most recent theory. The experimental literature has amply demonstrated the short term effects, and longitudinal research on attitudes and aggressive behaviors, such as that done by Huesmann, Eron, et al. (1984) is beginning to document the longer term influences of violent television on aggressive behavior. In explaining these findings, Huesmann (1986) has described a "reciprocal effects model" where aggression is maintained by an interplay between what is seen on television and what is experienced in real-life.

> Aggressive scripts for behavior are acquired from observation of media violence and aggressive behavior itself stimulates the observation of media violence. In both childhood and adulthood, certain cues in the media may trigger the activation of aggressive scripts acquired in any manner and thus stimulate aggressive behavior. A number of intervening variables may mitigate or exacerbate these reciprocal effects. However, if undampened, this cumulative learning process can build enduring schemas for aggressive behavior that persist into adulthood. Thus early childhood television habits are correlated with adult criminality independently of other likely causal factors. Therefore interventions directed at mitigating the effects of media violence on delinquency and criminality should focus on the preadolescent years. (Huesmann, 1986, pp. 138–139)

A study of the psychological mechanisms leads to an understanding of the potential or possible influences of television, but it tells us little of the rate. We know that people imitate what they see, especially children, but we have no way of calculating how many people will imitate any given scene or program. We know that disinhibition can occur under the right circumstances, but we do not have any idea how many people this might involve on any given night, in response to any given program. Finally, we know that television programs can have the function of both arousing and "unwinding," possibly the most powerful influence of all, but we do not have any idea how many people might be aroused or unwound at any given time. The psychology of television cannot answer these questions. It can tell us if a given influence is possible or not, however, and that is quite useful.

All of the mechanisms discussed in this last chapter were "behavioral" in the sense that the measures used, in most cases, involved direct recording of behavior: How much a person aggressed or acted violently or harmfully after viewing violent material, how much or little arousal a person feels after viewing a scene, and so forth.

Television not only influences how we feel and act—what we do—it also influences what we think and understand about the world, and it is to this kind of influence on attitudes and beliefs that we now turn our attention.

Cognitive Mechanisms 1: The Influence of Television on Attitudes, Beliefs, and Judgments

What assumptions does television cultivate about the facts, norms, and values of society?

—George Gerbner

Television influences human behavior because there are "routes" or mechanisms whereby the content of television can have an effect on what we do, and on how we act. Thus, part of television's influence comes about because of how we learn (by observation and imitation), because of how we respond to certain kinds of story material (arousal/desensitization), and because of the structure of our inhibitions and the way television provides the kind of stimulation necessary to release them (disinhibition). I called these *behavioral* mechanisms, because for the most part the influence was shown on some activity.

Television also influences what we believe and think about the world, and it does so, again, because of our make-up, our psychology. Just as the behavioral effects have behavioral mechanisms, the cognitive effects of television have cognitive mechanisms based on the structure of attitudes, beliefs, and judgments, and on the way in which these cognitive structures are acquired.

In traditional social psychology, attitudes are divided into three components: *cognitions* or beliefs; *evaluations* or positive or negative feelings about the object of our cognitions; and *actions* based on judgments derived from these beliefs. We have knowledge about tarantulas, for example, if we know they are large spiders, and if we can discriminate them from other spiders, this is the "cognitive" or belief component of an attitude. In addition, we have feelings and evaluations about tarantulas: some are dangerous, we think, some are poisonous, and this makes tarantulas "bad." These feelings, or values, usually stated in a positive or negative way, are the "evaluative" component of an attitude. Finally, we form judgments and base our "actions" on the knowledge and values we have. If we can discriminate a tarantula from other spiders, for example, and if we value them negatively, then the obvious "action" we would take is to avoid them. A good deal of the research in social psychology has been devoted to how attitudes of this sort develop and function, and particularly to how different components of the attitude structure relate to one another.

It seems obvious from what we already know about television that it provides a great deal of the kind of information that can be used to form attitudes and beliefs. A person who had never seen a real tarantula could still learn what they look like, could learn to discriminate tarantulas from other spiders, and a person watching films on television could learn to fear tarantulas too. But *do* people use this information to form and change their attitudes, beliefs, and values? Like the question of imitation posed in the last chapter, the first question is whether the kind of fantasy information presented on television is used to form real attitudes. If so, how does this work? What are the psychological mechanisms that allow this influence to occur?

In the study of social psychology, the assumption has always been that people learn about the real world from observing it and living in it. The question of whether the world one encountered was real or not was not an issue. But with the coming of television, every person who has one available finds a huge increase in the kind of dramatic and fictional information about the world to which they are exposed. Somehow this should be separated from the real information, but is it? Let's return to the question of tarantulas.

How many people know that although these *are* very large and photogenic spiders (making them useful for film and television), they are also quite harmless and delicate animals? My daughter had one as a pet. They do sting, occasionally, but it is usually no worse than a bee sting. If they are to be feared, it should be no more so than the common everyday honey bee. The fact that they are much more fearful than this we can attribute to movies and television where tarantulas are portrayed as more fearful than they are in reality. Clearly, we learn some attitudes from television, perhaps especially about things like tarantulas where we have little or no real experience.

GERBNER'S CONTRIBUTION II: CULTIVATION ANALYSIS

As we saw in chapter 3, Gerbner, the dean of the Annenberg School of Communications at the University of Pennsylvania, one of the pioneers of television research, began his Cultural Indicators research project in the mid-1960s in an attempt to describe the "world" of television, and particularly the amount of violence in that world. The eventual aim of the project is to discover how watching television drama influences our everyday conceptions of reality.

These two aspects of the Cultural Indicators Project are called: *message system analysis* and *cultivation analysis.* We looked at the findings of message system analysis in chapter 3. As we saw, this part involves a content analysis done by coders who make detailed observations about the characters and the action on television drama. The second aspect, *cultivation analysis*, is to determine what influence these messages have on viewers. How does watching television for 3 to 4 hours a day influence what we think, believe, and value about the world?

In order to determine this, large-scale public opinion organizations are asked by Gerbner and his associates to include in their national probability sample various questions regarding, for example, the amount of true violence in daily life. For each question asked, there is an answer that is more true of television, the "television answer," (derived from *message system analysis*), and a different, "real world" or "true" answer that often goes in the "opposite" direction (Gerbner, Gross, Morgan, & Signorielli, 1980, 1986).

For example, because we know there is more violence on television than just about anywhere in everyday life, an overestimation of the dangers of violence would be considered a "television answer," whereas an accurate estimate, or even an underestimate would constitute the alternative, the "real world" answer.

In Gerbner's cultivation analysis answers to specific questions are then related to amount of television watched, other media habits, and demographic characteristics of the viewers—such as age, sex, income and education (Gerbner & Gross, 1980). Light versus heavy viewers are compared in order to determine the degree of television's influence, and the difference between light and heavy viewers, when all other explanatory variables have been controlled, is what Gerbner and his colleagues call the *cultivation differential* (Gerbner, Gross, Morgan, &

Signorielli, 1980). This is the amount of an attitude that is separately contributed by television. We see some examples later in this chapter.

Cultivating a Violent Outlook

A series of studies provide evidence for a small but significant influence of television's content on attitudes and beliefs about the real world. Heavy viewers exposed to persistent displays of violence and mayhem on television drama come to believe that the real world incidence of such violence is higher than do light viewers of the same age, sex, education, and social class. Apparently the "facts" of the world of television tend to slip into the belief and value systems of individuals who are heavy consumers of it. Gerbner referred to this effect as "mainstreaming" and described it in terms of a "homogeneity" (or sameness) of outlook:

> it is well documented that more educated, higher income groups have the most diversified patterns of cultural opportunities and activities; therefore, they tend to be lighter viewers. We found that, when they are light viewers, they also tend to be the least imbued with the television view of the world. But the heavy viewers in the higher education/high income groups respond differently. Their responses to our question are more like those of the other heavy viewers most of whom have less education and income. It is the college educated, higher income light viewers who diverge from the 'mainstream' cultivated by television; heavy viewers of all groups tend to share a relatively homogeneous outlook. (Gerbner, Gross, Morgan, & Signorielli, 1980, p. 15)

One example of a homogeneous outlook is the misperceiving of the prevalence of true violence in the society. This is sometimes called the "mean world syndrome":

> The results of our ... surveys showed ... that violence laden television not only cultivates aggressive tendencies in a minority but, perhaps more importantly, also generates a pervasive and exaggerated sense of danger and mistrust. Heavy viewers revealed a significantly higher sense of personal risk and suspicion than did light viewers in the same demographic groups who were exposed to the same real risks of life. (Gerbner & Gross, 1980, p. 98)

For example, Gerbner et al. (1977b) asked school children such questions as: "During any week, what are your chances of being involved in some kind of violence? What percent of all males who have jobs work in law enforcement and crime detection? What percent of all crimes are violent crimes? Does most fatal violence occur between strangers or between relatives and acquaintances?"

These questions were combined into an index of perceptions of the prevalence of violence. When correlated with television viewing, the zero-order correlation (with no control variables removed statistically) was positive and significant and with the influence of several variables removed from the equation (sex, grade, newspaper reading, father's education, SES, and IQ) the correlation was reduced but it was still significant.

This evidence suggests that heavy television viewing is associated with increased perceptions of danger, even when comparing individuals who have very similar living circumstances and backgrounds. Wealthy individuals who are heavy viewers, for example, are more fearful than wealthy individuals who are light viewers. These data reveal most clearly Gerbner's view that television has the effect of "homogenizing" the population, resulting in a "flattening of differences" rather than an exaggeration of them.

Figure 5.1 illustrates the cultivation effect of "mainstreaming." In this study, individuals were questioned about their "fear of crime." The responses of three separate income groups are shown in Fig. 5.1, broken down by their television viewing habits: heavy versus light viewers.

Recall that in Gerbner's research scheme, viewers are determined to be "heavy" or "light" in comparison with the social class group to which they belong.

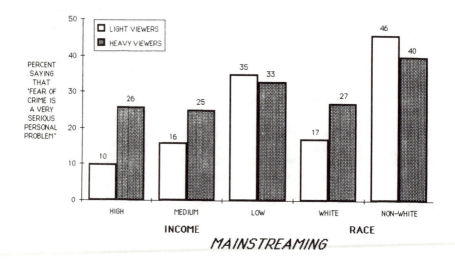

FIG. 5.1. Example of "mainstreaming" in heavy and light TV viewers' fear of crime. (© Gerbner, Gross, Morgan, & Signorielli, 1980.)

The influence of television on beliefs about the prevalence of violence may be seen most clearly if we begin by noting what we might expect if there were no television. Individuals in the high-income group should have the least fear of crime (of the street variety) because of the more secure lifestyle their incomes allow. Middle-income groups should be next, and those in the lowest income group should, realistically, say that "fear of crime" is a serious problem. FBI crime statistics show there is a greater frequency of crime in low-income districts than in middle-or high-income districts.

As can be seen in Fig. 5.1, this pattern of an increasing fear of crime with a decrease of income is exactly what is found for the light viewers. But among the heavy viewers, there were no significant differences across the three income groups. Among heavy viewers, the high-income respondents are just as afraid of crime as the middle-and low-income respondents. In Gerbner's terms, these groups have had their attitudes *cultivated* by heavy television viewing. Even though they live in very different life circumstances in terms of the likelihood of encountering a crime, heavy viewers share a "commonality of outlooks." No such commonality is evident among the light viewers. These findings suggest small but consistent and significant association between viewing television, the content of which is excessively violent, and actual beliefs about violence in the real world.

We cannot yet be sure that television is responsible for this effect, however, because the causal mechanisms are not understood. Even though this is *associative* evidence, and this should not be taken lightly. A correlation does not "prove" that there is a causal relationship, but it suggests the possibility that there may be one. On the other hand, it could be that there is something about heavy viewers in all three of the income groups that both encourages them to watch a lot of television, and makes them more fearful of crime, a common underlying factor influencing both. Until we understand the mechanism, we are never sure.

Mainstreaming and Resonance

Gerbner and his colleagues in the Cultural Indicators Research group call the process described in Fig. 5.1 *mainstreaming* because they believe that it shows how people who are heavy consumers of television come to "live in the mainstream of the television world," and come to adopt its premises and facts as if they were the facts of the world of everyday reality.

In addition to the mechanism of mainstreaming, in their recent ar-

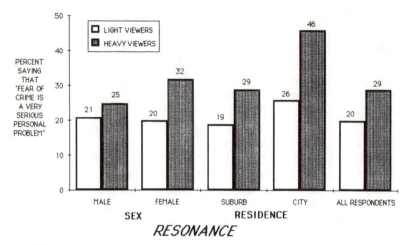

FIG. 5.2. Example of "resonance" in heavy and light TV viewers' fear of crime. (© Gerbner, Gross, Morgan, & Signorielli, 1980.)

ticles Gerbner and his associates have also presented evidence for a second process called *resonance:*

> The relationship of real life experience to television's cultivation of conceptions of reality entails not only this generalized notion of "mainstreaming" but also special cases of particular salience to specific issues. This is what we call "resonance." When what people see on television is most congruent with everyday reality (or even *perceived* reality), the combination may result in a coherent and powerful "double dose" of the television message and significantly boost cultivation. Thus, the congruence of the television world and real life circumstances may "resonate" and lead to markedly amplified cultivation patterns. (Gerbner, Gross, Morgan, & Signorielli, 1980, p. 15)

An example of resonance is given in Fig. 5.2. In the world of television, women are more likely to fall victim to crime.
So women who are heavy viewers of television are exposed to a "double dose" of distortion. First, like everyone else, they see more violence than is really the case, thus they live in the "mainstream" of a violent world. Second, because women are more consistently victimized in this television world, women who are heavy viewers get a second dose of the message that *they* should be especially fearful for themselves. The effect of this is shown in the first part of Fig. 5.2. Females who are also heavy viewers are the most fearful of crime, and, as we have already seen, heavy viewers are more fearful than light viewers. The second part of Fig. 5.2 shows another example of resonance. Because the crime

portrayed on television occurs mainly in cities, the city dwellers who are also heavy viewers get a double dose of the message that they should be fearful. Thus, they "resonate" more with this message than suburban residents. They are, presumably, more influenced by it and this should be reflected in the strength and certainty of their beliefs.

Cross-Cultural Studies of Cultivation

Pingree and Hawkins (1981), working in Australia, set out to test Gerbner's cultivation hypothesis by studying the social attitudes and television viewing of school children in Perth (the largest city in Western Australia). Questionnaires were given to 1,280 elementary school children (2nd through 11th grade) assessing their opinions and knowledge about both life in Australia and life in the United States. At a later time these same children filled out a 4-day television viewing diary. The questions on the questionnaire were designed to get at "television bias" on the part of the children (heavy viewers giving more of the television answer), and to get at beliefs about the prevalence of violence in the world in which they live. The two sets of beliefs were then correlated to determine how much television viewing contributes to attitudes and values.

In general, Pingree and Hawkins found evidence for a cultivation effect of the sort we have been discussing. That is, they found a significant correlation between the total amount of television viewed and a "television-biased" picture of Australia as a "mean and violent" place. Moreover, when these correlations were broken down by what type of content was watched, these authors found that "the most consistent and strongest correlate of television-biased answers to questions about social reality (was). . . one specific type of U.S. program: crime-adventure" (Pingree & Hawkins, 1981, pp. 102–103). So the children who most thought that Australia was a mean and dangerous place were those who most watched U.S. crime adventure programs shown on Australian television.

Interestingly, these same children did not seem to base their conceptions of the United States on these television programs:

> Apparently, Australian children are influenced by U.S. crime-adventure programs in their concepts of social reality for their own country, and to a lesser extent, for the U.S.. . . this argues against the usual notion of greater media effects when direct experience is lacking. (Pingree & Hawkins, 1981, pp. 103–104)

Children from Australia who have no direct experience with America, but who are exposed to television programs made in the United

States do not seem to derive their attitudes about the United States from these same programs. They do, consciously or not, however, seem to form certain of their attitudes and judgments about their *own country* from watching these same programs made in the United States. So in this case, the effect of does not seem to be a conscious one, people are not aware they are being mainstreamed.

Finally, their research has led Hawkins and Pingree to question two of the central assumptions made by Gerbner and his colleagues: First, they suggest that "breakdowns by content type are more useful than the less meaningful measures of total viewing. . ." And second, they suggest that viewing is not "nonselective" as Gerbner and his group have long suggested (Gerbner & Gross, 1980; Gerbner, Gross, Morgan, & Signorielli, 1980). Instead, Hawkins and Pingree find evidence that people do view by content type, that is they view "selectively," and if this is taken into consideration, as they did in their Australian study, stronger correlations would emerge from "cultivation analysis" research (Hawkins & Pingree, 1981, p. 299).

An experimental test of the cultivation hypothesis was conducted by Bryant, Carveth, and Brown (1981). In this study, 90 undergraduates were assigned to watch 30 hours of programming in addition to the television that they normally watched. Half of the subjects were shown program material featuring a "clear restoration of justice," whereas the other half saw programs in which the "outcomes were not just" (p. 108). Subjects who were initially low in manifest anxiety experienced a slight increase in anxiety during exposure to justice-depicting programs, whereas highly anxious students became less anxious as a result of exposure to the same sets of stimuli. "The strongest effect observed, however, was for those students who were heavy viewers of materials in which injustice was habitually depicted: both low anxiety and high anxiety students showed significant increases in anxiety under these viewing conditions, with the greatest increment in anxiety occurring among those students who already highly anxious" (p. 114). The authors view this experiment as support for the cultivation hypothesis: "these findings indicate that heavy exposure to the world of televised action drama does cultivate conceptions of an overly dangerous social reality for some viewers, especially when the adventure drama does not feature the triumph of retributive justice" (Bryant, Carveth, & Brown, 1981, p. 118).

In summary, Gerbner and his colleagues have contended that television drama has a small but significant influence on the attitudes, beliefs, and judgments of viewers about the real world. The direction of this influence is captured in two words: mainstreaming and resonance. People who watch a lot of television live in the mainstream of the television world, and are likely to be more influenced by its information than individuals who watch less. This hypothesis, in turn, requires a continuous analysis of the stream of information, of messages, available on television, and in particular an analysis of the manner in which this information contains distortions and misrepresentations relative to that which is available in the real world. The more a person watches television, the more he or she lives in the mainstream of the television world, and the more of these "distortions" should be found in the cognitive schemata of the heavy viewer.

As one of the researchers in this group put it recently:

> The results of our research on viewer conceptions among both adults and children revealed stable associations betweens of patterns of network dramatic content and conceptions of social reality. Heavy viewers tended to respond to many questions more in terms of the world of television than did light viewers in the same demographic groups (Gerbner, Gross, Morgan, & Signorielli, 1986). This research, using . . . surveys of national probability samples of adults, has shown quite consistently that demographic subgroups of heavy viewers were more likely than comparable groups of light viewers to express the feeling of living in a self-reinforcing cycle of a mean and gloomy world. When asked about the chances of encountering violence, about the percentage of men employed in law enforcement and crime detection, and about the percentage of crimes that were violent, significantly more heavy than light viewers in most demographic subgroups responded in terms more characteristic of the television world than the real world. (Signorielli, 1987, p. 266)

Individuals who are similar to those portrayed as victims on television get a "double dose" of this effect, because they resonate more with what is shown. The primary focus of the early theory has been on violent portrayals but there are many ways in which television presents a distorted, exaggerated, and untrue version of reality, so quite a few avenues of potential influence have yet to be explored. We consider some of these after the discussion of the critics of Gerbner's approach.

Critics of Gerbner

Although few social scientists have questioned the findings of Gerbner's content analysis of television, message system analysis, several researchers have challenged his findings of the effects, of cultivation analysis, just described. Doob and MacDonald (1979), for example, report a study of attitudes toward crime and victimization among Canadians living in Toronto. Individuals were interviewed about their fear of crime using many of the same questions Gerbner used, and they were also asked about their television viewing habits. Doob and MacDonald reported that when neighborhood is used as a control rather than income (which is used by Gerbner) then the correlation between television viewing and fear of crime disappears for all groups but the most poor, living in the most dangerous neighborhoods in the city.

This finding does run contrary to Gerbner's contention that heavy viewing should make all income groups more similar, but it offers some support for the idea of resonance. Doob and MacDonald acknowledge that their results do not unequivocally reject Gerbner's theory, but they take issue with his use of controls for income rather than neighborhood. In addition to finding some support among one social class for Gerbner's theory, Doob and MacDonald also find that when the questions asked are divided into those that are personal in nature ("are *you* afraid of being mugged?") versus those that are about society ("how many muggings were there in your neighborhood last year?"), that there is evidence for a "cultivation effect" with the social questions, but not so much with personal ones:

> Thus, television may well act as a source of information with regard to questions of fact, whereas it does not change people's views of how afraid they should be. (Doob & MacDonald, 1979, p. 179)

As we shall see later in this chapter, because there is other evidence to support it, this insight points to a potentially important modification of the theory of mainstreaming.

Failure to Find Cultivation in England.   Another criticism of Gerbner's theory is offered by Wober (1978) based on research done in Great Britain. Wober analyzed the results of a public-opinion poll asking questions, among other things, about the "prevalence of violence," and "interpersonal distrust," concepts similar to the "mean and dangerous world" idea. The items were summed to form a "security scale" and this was correlated with television viewing. No relationship was found between watching television and feelings of security or a lack thereof, going against the cultivation hypothesis.

But the content of television in Great Britain is much less violent than the content of television in the United States. According to at least some authorities (Hawkins & Pingree, 1982) a heavy viewer of British television sees significantly less violence than many American light viewers, so the comparison drawn by Wober may not be valid. Apparently there must be a certain critical level of a given distortion (like violence) before it is evident in the attitudes of an average viewer. (Recall that Belson, 1978, also working in England, did find a correlation between viewing violent television and acting violently. The difference is that

Belson focused on the specific type of program watched, and he studied only adolescents.)

Reanalyses of the NORC Data.   Another line of criticism of Gerbner's approach comes from two researchers who have reanalyzed the National Opinion Research Center (NORC) data set used by Gerbner and his colleagues (Gerbner et al., 1978) to illustrate the theory of mainstreaming and resonance. Hughes (1980), for example, introduced controls for a number of potential third variables and found that the relationship between television viewing and "fear of walking alone at night" was diminished to nonsignificance when controls were introduced simultaneously (Hawkins & Pingree, 1982). In examining other questions, using simultaneous rather than sequential controls (as Gerbner does), Hughes found curvilinear rather than liner relationships: that is, findings to indicate that moderate viewers seem to be the more influenced by television than either heavy or light viewers (Hughes, 1980).

Thus, it is not that Hughes found Gerbner to be wrong about all of his claims, but he did find differences in places where Gerbner did not. Finally, in reanalyzing two questions, Hughes (1980) found the reverse of what Gerbner found with school children (light viewers were the most likely to approve of violence, unlike what a desensitization or "mean world" analysis would predict).

The Problem of Nonviewers and Extreme Viewers.   A final critic of Gerbner, possibly the most strident, is Paul Hirsch who, like Hughes, also did a reanalysis of the main data set used by Gerbner and his colleagues to establish the validity of the cultivation effect. Hirsch reanalyzed the National Opinion Research Center's *General Social Surveys* of 1975, 1977, and 1978. Although Hirsch does not claim to "disprove" Gerbner's theory or its validity, he suggested that: "the NORC data, properly analyzed, contain precious little which can be found to support cultivation analysis" (Hirsch, 1980, p. 534).

Hirsch's argument with Gerbner involves a *recoding* of demographic variables involving the amount of viewing. When Gerbner and his colleagues do analyses of the data, they do not code the nonviewer of television at the low end of the scale (they start with people who view a little rather than none). At the high end of the scale, Gerbner and his colleagues lump everyone above 4 hours per day as "heavy" viewers. When the group of people who watch no television at all (nonviewers), and the group of very heavy viewers (extreme viewers) are separated out from the analysis and considered separately, as Hirsch (1980) did in his study, results different from those found by Gerbner and his colleagues are found using exactly the same data.

For purposes of analysis, Hirsch separated nonviewers from light viewers (making his category of "light" viewer a person who watches 1–2 hours a day), and at the high end of the scale, Hirsch separated "extreme" viewers (more than 8 hours per day) from "heavy" viewers (4–8 hours a day). So rather than having just light and heavy viewers as Gerbner does, Hirsch looked at nonviewers, light viewers, heavy viewers, and extreme viewers.

Using this scheme, Hirsch (1980, 1981) was able to show that non-viewers are consistently more fearful than light viewers, and that extreme viewers are less perturbed by violence than heavy viewers. These findings "undermine the contention that any relationship between TV-viewing and the provision of 'television answers' to attitude items is linear or even monotonic" (Hirsch, 1980, p. 534).

It is important to understand this claim. Hirsch is not saying that Gerbner is completely wrong and that television has *no effect* on attitudes, beliefs, and values. Rather, Hirsch is arguing that the relationship between amount of television viewing and attitudes and values is much more *complex* than Gerbner has described. From Hirsch's point of view, Gerbner has selected from the data of the NORC survey the evidence that supports his main contention, and he has ignored evidence which does not fit with his mainstreaming theory. Hirsch suggested that Gerbner wanted to show a simple linear relationship, and so he used just the data that support this argument. It is not so much that Gerbner is wrong about this, said Hirsch, but rather that Gerbner is not telling the *whole story,* which is much more complicated than the concept of mainstreaming allows.

Gerbner has begun to respond to these criticisms (Gerbner, Gross, Morgan, & Signorielli, 1980, 1986) by applying different controls when he does analyses (especially simultaneous controls) and asking different questions. One telling point on Gerbner's side of the debate is that the number of people in some of the categories of Hirsch's analysis (for example, nonviewers and extreme viewers) is very small and as a group they may not be representative of the average viewer in this category. So Gerbner may be right about most people, those who range from a little to a lot of television viewing a day, in terms of the association between viewing and fearful attitudes; but he may be wrong about the more extreme viewers. Hirsch is probably right in suggesting that by excluding certain categories and selecting data, Gerbner is not telling the whole story.

Gerbner proposed no clear-cut psychological mechanism, and because he has been shy in describing exactly how the mainstreaming effect works, precise tests of his theory have yet to be made. The NORC survey data, for example, do not go into detail about the kind of programs watched, and Gerbner relies on his assumption that if you've seen some part of television, you've seen it all (viewing is, for all practical purposes, non-selective). As we have noted, this assumption may not be true.

A more precise test of Gerbner's theory would correlate the exact distortions in the television watched for a sample of individuals with their specific attitudes and beliefs. Such an analysis would involve knowing what people watch and the specific information that characterizes those programs. In order to do such an analysis, it is necessary to have good demographic data about who watches what, and good content analytical data about the different types of television content.

PORTRAYAL OF SOCIAL ROLES

Violence is not the only distortion of the content of television, as we saw in chapter 3, and so the "mean world syndrome" is not the only kind of influence we would expect on attitudes and values. Violence is just the most heavily studied. In addition to violence, the content of television drama distorts the distribution of individuals by sex, occupation, and race (Signorielli, 1985, 1987).

Although there have been far fewer studies of the influence of these other distortions, the same mechanisms should function in the manner we have described. It should be possible, just as it was with the study of violence, to trace the effect of these other distortions on the attitudes and beliefs of those who watch. There have been attempts to do this for television's portrayal of gender and family roles, and to a lesser degree for occupation and race and health messages. It is worth reminding ourselves that all of this research concerns the program content of television. The advertising content is considered in chapters 7 and 8.

Sex and Family Role

As we saw in chapter 3, in the content analyses of (evening prime-time) programs, males outnumber females by a ratio of 3:1, and even moreso when only major roles are considered (Gerbner, 1972b, Sternglanz & Serbin, 1974; Tedesco, 1974). Female roles are, for the most part, limited to traditional representations (Leifer, Gordon, & Graves, 1974), and the image of men and women is that of "opposites" (Roberts, 1982). Content analyses of the program content have been done by many people (Aronoff, 1974; Barcus, 1977; Busby, 1975; Butler & Paisley, 1980; Cantor, 1978; Dohrmann, 1975; Franzwa, 1978; Gerbner, 1966; Lemon,

1977; McArthur & Eisen, 1976; Morgan, 1987; Schuetz & Sprafkin, 1978; Stein & Friedrich, 1972; Schwartz & Markham, 1985; Tedesco, 1974; Tuchman, 1978), and there is widespread agreement that the images of women on television are largely traditional and stereotypical.

What is the impact of television exposure on sex-role attitudes? Several researchers have tried to answer this question, and the findings are mixed. Beuf (1974) studied sex-typed occupational choices and found that heavy viewers made more stereotyped choices. Freuh and McGhee (1975) looked at preference for sex-typed activities among heavy and light viewers and found that heavy viewers were more sex typed in their responses to questions on the "it" test (a psychological measure of sex roles). Volgy and Schwartz (1980) found more sexism in adults heavily exposed to entertainment programs, and Rothschild (1979) reported similar findings. Rothschild (1984) discovered that third and fifth graders who watched more television had more stereotypical views of gender roles both in terms of activities (cooking, sports) and values (warmth, independence), findings that are congruent with other recent research by Morgan and Rothschild (1983), and by Williams (1986). Morgan (1982) studied 6th through 10th graders for 2 years, analyzing both sexism and the amount of viewing. Although same-time viewing and sexism was correlated significantly for both boys and girls, longitudinal analyses showed that television viewing predicted sexism scores in girls, whereas for boys sexism scores predicted amount of viewing. The sex-role attitudes of girls in this study were influenced by television, but for boys the amount of viewing was influenced by sexist attitudes. In general then, the weight of evidence supports the view that "television viewing does make an independent contribution to adolescents' sex role orientation" (Morgan, 1987, p. 271).

On the other hand, many studies find no effect of watching television on sex role stereotyping, that is, they find no more sex stereotypical or sexist attitudes in heavy than light viewers (Greer, 1980; Gross & Jeffries-Fox, 1978; Perloff, 1977).

Gerbner and Signorielli (1979) suggested that the cultivation effect of television on sexism is one of "leveling," or "homogenizing" opinion, bringing some people toward more traditional orientations and for some acting in the opposite way. This approach suggests that the degree of television's influence is dependent on the starting place of the individual who watches, not unlike the "law of initial values" in the study of arousal. To some, television presents a more traditional world than the one they live in, and for others it shows a less traditional sex-role environment. This argument says there is no single direction for television's effect other than to predict that heavy viewers should have a "commonality of outlooks," reflecting what is shown on television, compared to light viewers who should be more heterogeneous in their outlooks.

More recent studies (Gerbner & Signorielli, 1979; Greenberg, Simmons, Hogan, & Atkin, 1978; Signorielli, 1987) show greater proportions of females as major characters in dramatic presentations, and as we see in chapter 7, Scheibe (1979, 1983) has shown that the portrayal of women in ads is changing as well.

Family Roles

Portrayals of families are widespread on television (Greenberg, 1982), and several content analyses have focused on these family shows (Buerkel-Rothfuss, Greenberg, & Neuendorf, 1978; Greenberg et al., 1980; Hines, Greenberg, & Buerkel, 1977). Most of these shows depict traditional nuclear families (a father, mother, and children — all living together). The children range in age from middle childhood to adolescence. The storylines revolve around the daily lives of the characters and their various entanglements, mostly humorous (Signorielli, 1987).

One question to crop up again and again concerns the degree to which children are influenced by these images of "ideal" families, and whether they believe that the family portrayed on television is "real" or not (see Dorr, Kovaric, Doubleday, Sims, & Seidner, 1985). Although most researchers find children's notions of television to be less realistic the older they get (Feshbach, 1972; Greenberg, 1972; Noble, 1975), there is no clear agreement about the role of perceived reality in television's influence. We return to this problem in the next chapter, in the section on "Perceived Reality."

Occupation and Race

We noted in chapter 3 that most of the occupations shown on television were those of either law enforcement or professional- managerial types (doctor, lawyer, editor of newspaper, etc.). DeFleur and DeFleur (1967) and Jeffries-Fox and Signorielli (1978) asked children questions regarding selected roles and found conceptions of jobs consistent with those portrayed on television for the heavy viewers.

Both experimental and correlational studies of counterstereotypical occupational roles have been done (Atkin & Miller, 1975; Johnston & Ettema, 1982; Miller & Reeves, 1976; O'Bryant & Corder-Bolz, 1978; Pingree, 1978; Williams, LaRose, & Frost, 1981; Wroblewski & Huston, 1987). For example, Miller and Reeves (1976) studied the impact of female characters in nontraditional occupations among third and fifth graders. Both sexes tended to accept whichever version they were shown. Thus, when the material was stereotyped the children saw this as "typical." When the material was counterstereotyped, subjects were more accepting of girls' aspiring to these occupations and tended to believe that more women participated in these occupations. Williams, LaRose, and Frost (1981) and Johnston and Ettema (1982) studied a program called "Freestyle," intended to increase adolescents' awareness of career options by presenting counterstereotypical occupational roles. These researchers found that "Freestyle" did have a positive influence on the occupational aspirations and stereotypical attitudes of both boys and girls. Moreover, the positive effects of exposure to "Freestyle" were evident 9 months after the posttest, suggesting that specifically designed counterstereotypical portrayals can have a lasting effect on how children view role options.

A recent study of the impact of television on the occupational role understanding of early adolescents was done by Wroblewski and Huston (1987). These researchers questioned 65 children in fifth and sixth grade about their understanding of various common occupational roles in real life and on television, and occupations infrequently encountered in real life and on television. Children knew more about the real life and television jobs than about the uncommon occupations, confirming the prediction that television serves as a source of occupational information. There were also sex differences. Although boys showed evidence that television is associated with polarized occupational aspirations, girls preferred masculine television occupations to feminine real-life occupations. In general, girls were more positive than boys toward counterstereotyped participation in all occupational categories (Wroblewski & Huston, 1987).

Atkin and Miller (1975), O'Bryant and Corder-Bolz (1978), and Pingree (1978) each studied the effects of commercials portraying women in nontraditional occupations on the occupational attitudes of grade-school children. All three groups of researchers found that after exposure to such commercials, the portrayed occupations were seen as more appropriate for women. As in the study by Wroblewski and Huston, this effect was stronger for girls than for boys.

Finally, Greenberg (1982) reported on a study by Abel, Fontes, Greenberg, and Atkin (1980) where over 1,500 children (fourth, fifth, and sixth graders) in two communities with different access to programs portraying occupations, thus permitting an assessment of role evaluation, gender appropriateness of job, rewards, power, and the physical attributes necessary for role, and many other factors (such as job knowledge) related to occupational role choice. The authors concluded that "being exposed to the programs substantially alters selected perceptions of occupational roles and . . . exposure definitely affects the child's aspirations for the occupation and their evaluation of the role" (cited in Greenberg, 1982, p. 186).

Growing Old

As we saw in chapter 3, older individuals are underrepresented on television, and when they are shown, it is often in a negative light. Several studies have shown that heavy viewers of television, especially younger viewers, hold negative beliefs about older individuals. Apparently the older one gets the more perceptions of the elderly (on television) become positive (Bower, 1973; Davis, 1971; Harris, 1975; Korzenny & Neuendorf, 1980). Younger heavy viewers, are more likely to believe that older people are not open minded, not bright, alert, or good at getting things done (Greenberg, 1982). Korzenny and Neuendorf (1980) found that negative reactions of the elderly to perceptions of television's portrayal of them diminished their self-concept. The heaviest viewers were "more likely to perceive the television elderly as hindrances to society" (Greenberg, 1982, p. 188). Gerbner, Gross, Morgan, and Signorielli (1980); Gerbner and Signorielli (1979); and Hawkins and Pingree (1982) report beliefs in heavy viewers that the proportion of older people is declining, (it is actually increasing), that people do not live as long as they used to, (in fact they live longer), and that older people are less healthy than they used to be (whereas, again, the opposite is the case).

Health Portrayals

Does heavy exposure to television's portrayal of health have an influence? We saw earlier that health professionals dominate the occupations, that alcohol consumption was common (it is prohibited in advertisements), and nutritional messages were often one-sided. Leaman (1973) found that children (fourth and sixth graders) who watch more television have lower levels of nutritional knowledge. Young children who are heavy viewers of television hold images of doctors and medical professionals similar to those found on television (Arenstein, 1974; McLaughlin, 1975). Even among adults, Volgy and Schwartz (1980) found that confidence in doctors is higher, and especially among those in the audience who are heavy viewers of doctor shows.

A study by General Mills (1979) asked people to choose their "two or three main sources of health information." Television was the second most-cited source. More importantly, those who did mention television programs (compared to those who did not) were more complacent about health, had older versus modern health views, were poorly informed and less likely to exercise (Gerbner, Morgan, & Signorielli, 1982, p. 299).

Reporting on another study done by the Roper Organization (a survey research organization), Gerbner et al. (1982) offered an example of mainstreaming that contains a mystery. First the data. Figure 5.3 contains responses to the question "how concerned are you about weight?" for three different television viewing groups (light, medium, and heavy), broken down also by income (high, medium, and low).

The figures are given in terms of "lack of concern" but it is evident that the views of the three income groups, while quite well differentiated in the light and medium viewer groups, is nevertheless compacted together for the heavy viewers. This would, indeed, appear to be a good example of mainstreaming, of the "commonality" of outlooks, and the "homogenization" of attitude and opinion brought about by heavy television viewing.

So what is the mystery? Note the direction of increase, in lack of concern. The heaviest viewers are least concerned about their health and weight. Most of the people *shown* on television are underweight, however, relative to the rest of the population, as we noted in chapter 3. The reasons for this are obvious enough: The world portrayed on television is more young and beautiful than the population at large, because the world of television is peopled by actors and actresses. They work harder on their looks than the rest of us. So if heavy viewers are exposed to repeated images of young, thin, beautiful people, why aren't

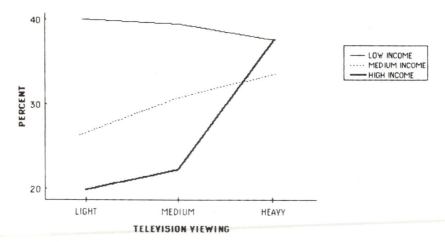

FIG. 5.3. Illustration of "mainstreaming" in association between amount of TV viewing and nutritional complacency, by income level. (From NIMH report, Gerbner, Morgan, & Signorielli, 1982, in the public domain.)

they more, rather than less, concerned with their own weight? Why don't they compare themselves to the people on television, and come out feeling fat and ugly?

Apparently, and this is a very deep truth about television, we do not, for the most part, use the people on television for purposes of "social comparison." That is, we are not bothered by the contrast between how the people on television live and the way we live, we are not disturbed by the way we look relative to the way the people on television look. If we did make such comparisons, then the average level of concern should go in the other direction in Fig. 5.3, the heaviest viewers should be most concerned about weight.

PERSONAL VERSUS SOCIETAL JUDGMENTS

A recently published study may speak to this mystery. Although many studies seem to support Gerbner's contention that heavy television viewing influences judgments about the likelihood of being a victim of a crime (see reviews by Cook, Kendzierski, & Thomas, 1983; Hawkins & Pingree, 1982), as we have just seen many do not (Doob & MacDonald, 1979; Hirsch, 1980, 1981; Hughes, 1980; Skogan & Maxfield, 1981; Tyler, 1980). Tyler and Cook (1984) attempt to resolve the confusion by making a distinction between television's effects on personal versus social attitudes.

According to Tyler and Cook, a *societal level* judgment refers to beliefs about the larger community and about the likelihood of events happening to an "average" person. So a societal level belief about crime would estimate the likelihood of an average citizen being involved in a crime. A *personal level* judgment refers to beliefs about events befalling one's own self, such as *one's own* likelihood of being a victim of a crime. This distinction was apparently first suggested by Furstenberg (1971).

To test this idea Tyler and Cook (1984) present three experiments bearing on the topic. In the first, subjects who were exposed to a television program about nursing home abuse (a 20-minute segment aired on "NBC News Magazine" were compared to a group of subjects asked to watch a similar program ("PM Magazine") having no information about nursing homes, but airing at the same time (shown nationally on May 7, 1981). A sample of subjects was asked, both before and after the program aired, about their beliefs about nursing home abuse, and the degree to which they estimated the likelihood of it happening to them (or someone in their family). These researchers found:

In the case of general judgments, treatment respondents changed their views significantly after viewing the program, perceiving health care as more important, more in need of help, and more fraud-laden. In the case of personal judgment, however, no treatment effect was found; that is, respondents were no more likely to think it would be difficult to find fraud free service for themselves than they were before they saw the program. (Tyler & Cook, 1984, p. 697)

In short, personal and societal level judgments are independent of one another, and that a media intervention, such as watching a television show about nursing home abuse, changed societal level judgments but not personal level judgments. If this finding can be replicated, it could prove an important modification of the mechanism of mainstreaming. It might also explain why people don't make "social comparative" judgments with the people on television, as we noted earlier. But it will raise a lot of questions and problems as well.

Some things on television are designed to persuade and change personal attitudes and behaviors, such as commercials and public service announcements (e.g., for the wearing of seat belts or health-care information). The purpose of these messages is to change personal level judgments and actions not simply to influence the audience's perception about society (Janis, 1980). Are all of these messages doomed to ineffectiveness? What about ads? Don't they try to change "personal" beliefs and actions? Investigation of this problem will allow more parameters about the mechanism of mainstreaming to be known, and more precise predictions made about the influence of television on attitudes, beliefs, and values.

SUMMARY

Television viewing has been shown to have a small but significant influence on attitude and belief systems. The world of television prime-time drama, viewed by large numbers of the population, is a violent and dangerous world, far more so than what most viewers encounter in their daily lives. Heavy viewers of television spend a lot of time paying attention to this world: watching it, studying it, learning from it. When asked about the real world, heavy viewers of television have attitudes about the amount of violence, for example, that reflects more the world of television than the world of reality.

Heavy viewers of television are less trusting and more fearful of crime and violence than light viewers who come from the same social class, and who live in similar neighborhoods. Gerbner and his colleagues call this effect *mainstreaming.* The effect is particularly strong when the world the viewer lives in is, in some manner, similar to that depicted on television. So the most pronounced effects of heavy viewing should be seen in people who come from the high crime areas of the city, as Doob and MacDonald (1979) found. Gerbner called this effect *resonance,* because some facts of the television world resonate more with some of us than others, either because of who we are or where we live. People who resonate with television get a "double dose" of television's influence on their attitudes and cognitions, according to the researchers at the Cultural Indicators Research Project.

The effects of mainstreaming, of the content of television influencing the beliefs of real people about the world, is not confined to the characterization of violence. Older people are shown on television in a negative light, and heavy viewers of television, especially the younger ones, hold negative beliefs about older people compared to light viewers. Heavy viewers of television have less competent views of nutrition and health than light viewers, and they are more trusting of doctors and patent medicine remedies. These same distortions characterized health portrayals (Gerbner et al., 1982). Over a wide range of topics, dozens of studies have shown that the "facts" of the world of television tend to "creep into" the attitude and value systems of those who are heavy consumers of it, and it does this in a quiet, insidious manner. Most heavy viewers are not aware that their attitudes and values have been influenced.

There are many critics of these findings, and the last word is yet to be written about them. To many this evidence is not compelling, and some researchers, using "controls" for several variables simultaneously, find that the "cultivation effect," the difference between light and heavy viewers on any attitude scale, disappears altogether. But the Cultural Indicators Research Project is, relatively speaking, a fairly new approach to the study of the mass media, and the method and theory is just now being spelled out in sufficient detail for the findings to be understood and replicated by others.

Among the many questions raised about mainstreaming, one of the most interesting is the question of television's effect on *personal* versus *societal* levels of judgment. We are not sure yet whether, or under what circumstances this is true, but if it turns out that television's sole influence is on societal judgment alone, then it would still be very important. In democracies citizens must make decisions every year at the local level and at the national level, about how money and political power should be spent. What deserves attention, and what not. Often this decision comes down to a choice: should we put our tax money into police and army, or should we fund education and social welfare programs? Is it to be guns or butter?

In making our political decisions, we must use our beliefs and judgments about what the *real* world is like. If our judgments are systematically altered and influenced by the dramatic content of television, we
must be aware of this influence and try to understand how this influence
might effect a democratic form of government. To do this we need to
understand the mechanism behind an influence.

One psychological concept that may prove to be very useful in understanding the effect of television on attitudes and values is the notion of "script" mentioned first in chapter 4. The idea that people may
code behavior into "scripts" was first described by Abelson (1976). The
fundamental element in a script is an event of short duration that can
be described as a *vignette*, and it consists of both an image and a conceptual representation. A script consists of several of these vignettes
that together provide an adequate description of an event. "Cognitively mediated social behavior depends on the occurrence of two processes:
(a) the selection of a particular script to represent the given situation
and (b) the taking of a participant role within that script" (Abelson,
1976, p. 42). Several researchers have applied the notion of script to
violent scenes on television (Geen & Thomas, 1986; Huesmann, 1986;
Huesmann & Malamuth, 1986; Rule & Ferguson, 1986). According to
Geen and Thomas (1986):

> we may consider the violent episode appearing in the media as a script
> defining a "proper" method of dealing with interpersonal conflict. Such
> a definition is likely to be formulated if the violence is placed in a con-
> text of social approval and justification. Subsequently the observer may
> activate this script as a guide for behavior in some personal situation
> of conflict and, moreover, place himself or herself in the participant role
> of aggressor. Thus violence observed in the media may provide adequate
> explanations for, and guides to behavior within, situations that could
> otherwise remain ambiguous for the person. (p. 9)

The obvious value of this notion of script is that much of what is
seen on television may be coded in this manner, and it provides a well-
recognized psychological mechanism as a focus for research on the
mainstreaming and resonance effects described by Gerbner and his associates. The idea of script can be used to summarize much of the literature described in this chapter on the effect of television on attitudes.
Television provides scripts for how people should behave in occupations, in various gender roles, as older people. Scripts on television relate to healthy and unhealthy behavior. We have reviewed a substantial
amount of evidence that shows how people utilize the scripts shown
on television not only in their conceptions of justice and power, but
in their views of occupational choices, sex roles, and health-related behavior. The script could be both the fundamental level of analysis of

the content of television and the content of a person's behavior. We not only learn scripts, we behave in scripts as well. The notion of script would give Gerbner's analysis the one thing it lacks, a firm grounding in psychological theory.

It is important to know how the viewer comprehends or understands the stream of information that comes to him/her over television. What does the viewer understand television to be? To what extent is the influence of television due to the "form" rather than the content of the medium? These and other questions make up a whole new approach to the study of television which goes beyond violence in order to explore completely different questions. If what we have studied up to now is the psychology of television, then the next chapter begins to take us into an ecological approach to the study of television.

Cognitive Mechanisms II: Attention, Comprehension, and Perceived Reality

In some ways I am the opposite of a magician. A magician gives you illusion disguised as reality, whereas I give you reality disguised as illusion.
—Tennessee Williams

As we have described the effects of television, first indirect and then direct, we have been following along with the research in the historical order in which it was done. Research on indirect effects, for example, described in the first chapter, was mostly done in the 1950s and 1960s, although some of it is still ongoing in countries where television is just being introduced. The research on content and direct effects described in chapters 3, 4, and 5, was begun in the 1960s and continued throughout that decade and into the 1970s. We can broadly classify these studies into (a) those focused on the content and how it may be described, and (b) those focused on the audience, including viewer responses to the content and what implications or consequences these responses might have on a society-wide basis.

This line of research has been called the *dominant-image approach* (Collins, 1983a) because its focus was almost exclusively on the influence of violence, the dominant image of prime-time television. This description fits the research on imitation, disinhibition, and desensitization, as well as the cognitive research we reviewed in the last chapter on mainstreaming and resonance. As we saw, this research left many unanswered questions, especially questions about the nature of the mechanism to account for the cognitive effects.

So in the early 1970s different groups of researchers began to explore a different set of questions and problems about television. In doing so, they introduced issues that go beyond the narrow confines of audience reactions to dramatic violence. Like most research, much of this new work was designed to overcome criticisms of earlier research, especially criticisms about the nature of the stimulus materials used. Much of the early research on television used stimuli such as films that were different from the type of thing actually shown on television. The research described in this chapter utilizes actual samples of television content: and studies people, mostly children, actually watching television. This research has as its focus such fundamental questions as:

1.   What is the nature of attention to television, especially children's attention to television? What are the formal features of television program content, and how is form related to attention and comprehension?

2.   How much of the content of television stories is retained and understood by whom in the audience? That is, to what extent do people, especially children, comprehend television? And how does comprehension change over time, how does it develop? What meaning or consequences do differences in comprehension have for understanding the influence of television?

3.   How do viewers differentially respond to material that they perceive to be "real" compared to material that is dramatic and fictitious? To what extent are people aware of this distinction, and what difference does their awareness make?

ATTENTION TO TELEVISION

Children begin watching television at a very early age, as we saw in chapter 2. Although there is evidence that infants pay some attention to television, steady viewing in the sense of having a "favorite program," begins around 2 years of age. What holds a child's attention at such an early age? It is not likely to be the words. At this age, language has just started to develop and the child grasps only a few simple phrases.

But television has a form that is conducive to grasping and holding attention in a way that makes use of very fundamental perceptual systems. As we noted in the last chapter, television has the capacity to induce what Zillmann (1982) called "cortical arousal," based on biologically mandated "orienting" responses. Our perceptual systems "resonate" (Gibson, 1986) with some kinds of stimulation more than others. Some kinds of stimulation are quick to draw attention. The makers of television are well aware of these. When they want to get our attention they ring bells, break glass, tear cloth, sound gongs, make unusual sights and sounds, flash lights, and blow up cars and buildings. Everybody who watches television is dimly aware of these facts, but until recently, analyses of these formal features were rare.

The Formal Features of Television

The formal features of television include the kinds of visual and auditory "conventions" that television (and film) directors use to tell a story. Sometimes these are necessary, sometimes they are simply "added on." These conventions run from such simple devices as having the music punctuate the visual action (in the early days of silent movies, the music was provided by a local piano player who would improvise in response to the action on the screen), to the use of "fade-in" and "fade-out" to signal the passage of time.

Visual effects can also create distinct *moods* in the viewer. For example, Alfred Hitchcock's well-known technique of flashing scenes at the viewer from unusual visual angles with rapid change of scene and pace, tends to make the viewer anxious, uncomfortable, and confused—to fit with the mood and mental state of the central character in the film. An "emotional tone" is struck in the viewer by the visual action.

Once we know what these "forms" and "conventions" are, we will want to know about their influence on attention to and understanding of television. That is, we will eventually want to know how the form of television makes a contribution to the way we perceive and comprehend the material on it. After a period of growing up with television, of living with it, individuals may evolve different *modes of thinking* about the world, thanks to having the conventions of television woven into the conventions of human thought (Salomon, 1979).

These issues are discussed in the following sections:

• How do programs on television differ in terms of their formal features?
• What are the patterns of childrens' attention to television, and how are these related to perceptually salient features and comprehension?

Marshal McLuhan (1964) was one of the first to suggest that the form of television has an influence that is independent of the content ("the medium is the message"), but it was not until recently that researchers began to attempt a serious taxonomy of the content of television in terms of its formal features.

Form and Stimulus Complexity

One of the earliest attempts to describe the form of television came from "information theory" and involved the concept of "entropy" (Watt & Krull, 1974). *Entropy* or *form complexity* was defined as the number of scenes in a show, the number of characters, and in general the "variability" of the stimulus. The theory suggested that the more complex the stimulus the more attention it would draw.

In one study, form complexity was used to code television shows designed for adults. Programs were found to cluster into two different groups: *dynamism* and *unfamiliarity*, each of which was thought to contribute separately to the popularity of the program (Krull, Watt, & Lichty, 1977). Form complexity was also related to violent programs such that the more violent programs were visually and auditorily complex than the less violent shows. Wartella and Ettema (1974) used this same scheme to code children's attention to commercials. They found that attention was influenced by visual and auditory complexity here as well, such that the more complex commercials drew the greatest attention from the child audience.

Action, Pace, and Perceptual Salience

The most recent and extensive work on a formal description of television, however, has been done by research psychologists Aletha Huston, John Wright, and their colleagues at the University of Kansas at the Center for Research on the Influence of Television on Children (CRITC). For these researchers, television programs can be described using two central dimensions: *action* and *pace*.

Action. *Action* is physical movement, not plot action. Action is further subdivided into "rapid" and "moderate." Rapid action is flying, running, jumping, and the kind of zippity-bang whizzing around that is often found in cartoons and in programs designed for young children (in the age range from 2 to 6). Moderate action, on the other hand, refers to movement at about the speed of walking, action that is less "compelling" from a purely attentional point of view. Interestingly enough, there is an age trend: Older children attend to moderate action more than rapid action, whereas the opposite is the case for the younger ages (Calvert, Huston, Watkins, & Wright, 1981). This finding reveals that moderate action is important for understanding the plot whereas rapid action may just be there to hold the attention of the young audience (Huston et al., 1981).

Pace.   The other important descriptive category of programs is pace. *Pace* refers to the rate of change of scenes and characters. In their analysis, Huston et al. (1981) separate two components of pace: *variability* (the number of different scenes) and *tempo* (rate of change among previously shown scenes and characters). Visual and auditory special effects are also considered. In all, Huston, Wright, and their colleagues coded 13 categories of events, and then compared different programs with respect to these different categories.

In one study by this research group, three kinds of programs were analyzed: (a) Saturday morning cartoon and live shows (b) educational daytime programs (such as "Sesame Street," "The Electric Company," and "Mister Rogers' Neighborhood"), and (c) prime-time programs designed for family viewing.

Programs for children produced commercially were found to be different from other programs, such as educational programs also designed for children: The commercial programs. . .

> are heavily animated and rely extensively on humor, much of which is nonverbal. They are packed with perceptually salient forms—rapid action, frequent changes of scene and character, and considerable variability. They contain both visual and audio gimmicks, and they use non-human characters extensively. . . they contain relatively little child dialogue. . . this pattern of heavy reliance on perceptual salience and relatively sparse use of formal features that might permit reflection, rehearsal, and verbal explanation is true of live programs on Saturday Morning, as well as animated programs. Such programming would appear to be intended for a particular type of child viewer whose attention must presumably be captured and held by constant action, change, noise, and visual onslaught, as well as slapstick violence. (Huston et al., 1981, pp. 45–46)

This is evidence that programs designed for children differ in their formal features, but is there any evidence that the faster paced programs are watched more heavily by the child audience? In order to show that these *perceptually salient* features of action and pace are related to attention, Wright et al. (1984) found that components of a "perceptually salient cluster": pace, movement, auditory and visual special effects, salient music and nonhuman speech occurred more frequently in programs with larger viewing audiences. So programs with more *action* drew larger numbers of children, based on surveys done in the United States.

Surprisingly, violent content was not associated with viewership independently of the formal features of the program (see also Greer, Potts, Wright, & Huston, 1982; Huston & Wright, 1983; Huston et al., 1981). So there is evidence that more rapid paced programs draw large child audiences, and there is reason to believe that the appeal of violence to very young children may be due to the fact that shows containing violence are also very "active," chock full of what Huston and Wright call "perceptually salient features."

The Role of Formal Features In Attention

We have seen that children's programs are replete with perceptually salient features that are designed to attract and hold a child's attention. But are some of these features better at attracting and holding attention than others? Are there developmental changes in what features are most attractive? Investigators have been able to determine (a) how much attention children pay to television, (b) how it changes with age, and (c) what formal features cause children to be most attentive, all by *watching children watch television,* literally placing a television camera behind a television set and videotaping children as they watch the screen.

Attention and Age

Children do not watch television all of the time they are in the room with it on (probably nobody does), but the amount of time spent actually looking at the set is related to both age and to the content of what is shown on the screen. Very young children attend to television only sporadically as we have noted (Hollenbeck & Slaby, 1979), but even infants are aware, as several other studies show, of correlations between action and sound and infants also notice changes in content (Golinkoff & Kerr, 1975).

Starting in infancy, the amount of time children spend looking at a television set while it is on increases steadily with age. The largest increase comes between the ages of 2 and 3. Attention to commercials increases in a linear way with age also (Wartella & Ettema, 1974).

What holds a child's attention at this tender age? What kinds of events on the screen entice the child to watch, and what kinds of events decrease watching? By keeping one eye on children and the other on what was being shown on a television screen, Daniel Anderson and his colleagues at the University of Massachusetts have been able to determine which characteristics of the program are more demanding of at-

TABLE 6.1
Summary of Attribute Analysis

Attribute Type and Name	Occurrence (%)	Main Effect Presence vs. Absence[a]	Differences	Interaction with Age[c]
Adult male:				
Black	21.0	22.95***	−5.1	4.66***
White	20.0	105.94***	−10.1	5.15***
Adult voice	47.8	60.75***	−6.5	N.S.
Adult female:				
Black	5.0	57.08***	11.1	N.S.
Adult voice	6.3	N.S.	...	3.53**
Child:				
Black male...........	12.0	N.S.	...	N.S.
Black female ...	9.8	4.55*	2.5	N.S.
White male	12.0	9.11**	3.0	N.S.
White female.........	6.7	43.43***	9.3	N.S.
Oriental female	8.2	26.04***	7.5	N.S.
Voice	8.8	4.22*	3.5	N.S.
Miscellaneous:				
Eye contact	12.0	17.72***	5.1	N.S.
Body part (not face)....	2.7	57.29***	−11.9	N.S.
Nonhuman characters:				
Puppets	11.0	11.14**	5.4	N.S.
Animals	4.2	14.02***	−6.5	4.97***
Animation	14.0	15.68***	6.7	4.26**
Peculiar voice	19.0	18.46***	5.0	3.69**
No characters:				
Inanimate objects	12.0	N.S.	...	N.S.
Activity:				
Inactive stationary	63.0	55.94***	−5.0	4.44***
Active stationary	21.0	5.77*	1.9	N.S.
Moving through space ..	14.0	17.88***	5.6	2.54*
Dancing	3.9	16.41***	11.2	N.S.
Music:				
Individual singing	8.5	27.51***	7.5	N.S.
Group singing........	6.0	17.72***	6.7	3.80**
Instrumental	46.0	23.95***	3.8	N.S.
Slow	14.7	N.S.	...	N.S.
Lively	31.5	28.03***	5.3	N.S.
Auditory techniques:				
Rhyming, repetition and alliteration	22.0	97.13***	10.3	3.87**
Applause	2.0	N.S.	...	N.S.
Sound effects	12.1	17.16***	3.5	3.76**
Auditory change[d]	41.0	90.29***	7.4	2.95*
Graphics:				
Still drawing	6.7	12.62***	−5.9	2.82*
Script...............	30.0	4.93*	2.1	N.S.
Camera techniques:				
Blank screen	0.7	21.74***	3.8	N.S.
Still camera	76.0	N.S.	...	N.S.

(Continued)

TABLE 6.1
(Continued)

Zoom	12.0	N.S.	. . .	N.S.
Pan	9.4	N.S.	. . .	3.09*
Cut[d]	35.0	N.S.	. . .	2.94*
Change to novel scene[d]	17.7	N.S.	. . .	2.36*
Change to familiar scene[d]	19.2	22.00***	2.8	4.61***
Jerky movement	0.7	N.S.	. . .	N.S.
Slow motion	1.4	N.S.	. . .	N.S.
Fast motion	1.1	N.S.	. . .	N.S.
Reverse motion	20.9	5.01*	7.8	N.S.

[a]F ratio based on 1.56 degrees of freedom.

[b]Percentage of attention in presence of attribute minus percentage of attention in absence of attribute.

[c]F ratio based on 6.56 df.

[d]Indicates sudden transition attribute (see text).

*$p < .05$.

**$p < .01$.

***$p < .001$.

tention in children, and which ones are not. Table 6.1 describes some of the salient features of television programs to which children pay the most and least attention.

Attention and Content

Studies by Anderson and Levin (1976), Levin and Anderson (1976), and Lorch, Anderson, and Levin (1979), where children were observed while watching television, have found that the average preschooler looks at and away from the television screen more than 150 times in an hour. So most young children do not watch television the way adults do—that is, with long periods of full attention. Preschool children show "elevated attention" to: "women, women's voices, eye contact, puppets, animation, peculiar voices, movement, lively music, auditory changes, and rhyming, repetition and alliteration." Children of this age pay relatively less attention to "adult men, men's voices, animals, inactivity, and still drawings" (Anderson, Alwitt, Lorch, & Levin, 1979, p. 344).

It is necessary to be cautious in interpreting the correlational findings described here, because a particular feature (nonhuman characters) may be consistently associated with another even more salient feature (unusual sounds) and the correlation could be due to one, the other, or both in conjunction (for example, see Anderson et al., 1979, pp. 345–347). But keeping this caveat in mind, we can still ask: In addition to the characters, what other features of television hold the attention of young children?

Attention to "Bit Changes."   A *bit change* is defined as the transition point between one segment of a program and another. At this point "all producer-intended message units are terminated and others begin" (Anderson et al., 1979, p. 347). A bit change could signal a change of scene within a story, or a change from one type of content to another— program to commercial for example. Anderson and his colleagues found that if the child was *not looking* at the television screen a *bit change* could elicit a look, whereas if the child was already monitoring the screen, a bit change was often associated with the "termination of looking," especially if the change was from program to commercial.

So bit changes were both negatively and positively associated with attention. If a child was not already watching, a bit change might bring about a look, whereas if the child was watching, a bit change could as well be the occasion for the child to look away. It is not clear how much of this is visual. The bit change on television is usually accompanied by some change in the auditory portion of the program as well, and these auditory changes are often correlated with children looking at the screen (Anderson et al., 1979).

Zooms and Pans.   There are some things a camera can do that the human eye cannot (and vice versa). The eye does not zoom, nor does it cut from one scene to another as can be done with film. What is the role of these camera tricks in getting and holding the attention of children? Anderson et al. (1979) found that zooms, cuts, and pans actually tended to *inhibit* looking.

Attention to Human Characters.   To what degree are children attracted to characters of the human variety? Anderson and his colleagues looked at this factor as well. They found that, in general, when women tended to draw and hold attention but when adult men came on the television screen children would tend to stop watching. An exception, for this sample, occurred for Black men, but the authors noted that because Black men were seen considerably less frequently on television (5.9% as compared to 26% for White men) the effect may be due to novelty. In addition to adult women, children on the screen both elicited and maintained the attention of the children watching (Anderson et al., 1979).

Attention to Nonhuman Characters.   On television programs designed for children, nonhuman characters, such as puppets and animated characters, occur quite frequently, and are generally associated with enhanced attention. But here again we should note that the appearance of nonhuman characters is also typically correlated with unusual sounds. So, although these unusual visual techniques were powerful in eliciting and holding attention, the effect is also due to the auditory structure of the stimulus.

A surprising finding from this research was that the presence of animals did not result in increased attention. Not only did children not pay any more attention when a real animal came on the screen, but instead the presence of animals was *negatively* related to attention. When a real animal came on the screen the children in this study tended to look away! This is surprising because of childrens' well-known affection for real animals. Apparently the television representation of an animal is no substitute for the real thing.

In summary, women's voices, children's voices, auditory changes, unusual voices, movement, sound effects, laughing, and applause were all related to enhanced visual attention to television in preschool children; whereas males, male voices, extended zooms and pans, animals, and still photographs were negatively associated with attention. Some factors, such as bit changes and lively music, were both positively and negatively associated with attention (Anderson et al., 1979; Anderson & Levin, 1976; Levin & Anderson, 1976).

Attentional Inertia

In studying the way in which children watch television, Anderson and his colleagues discovered an interesting fact that deserves mention. Looking at patterns of viewing television among children, a general characteristic of the pattern of children's attention to television was that the longer a child looked, the more you could predict continued looking, and vice versa. That is, it was also the case that the longer a child *avoided looking,* the more you could predict that he or she would continue to avoid.

Anderson et al. (1979) investigated this phenomena using data from children who were observed watching many different television shows. Children spend much time looking at and away from the TV screen, as we have already noted. Most children looked at the screen for only brief times before looking away (54% of all looks were for less than 3 seconds). But once a child started looking: "a child is increasingly likely to continue to look at the TV the longer the look progresses. If a look lasts longer than about 15 seconds, the child has a strong tendency to become progressively "locked in" to the TV screen" (Anderson et al., 1979, p. 339). An illustration of attentional inertia is given in Fig. 6.1.

This tendency toward attentional inertia is the opposite of habituation (where the more you look the *less likely* you will continue looking), and may be related to the "hypnotic" or trance-like quality of televi-

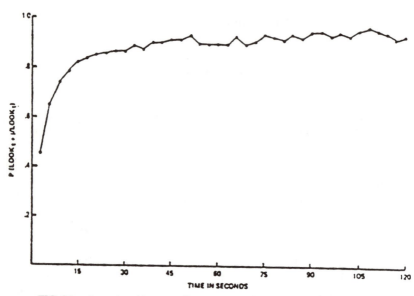

FIG. 6.1. Attentional inertia. (© Anderson, Alwitt, Lorch, & Levin, 1979.)

sion watching. As these researchers note, "if a look continued beyond about 10 seconds, we often observed the child's body relax, head slouch forward, and mouth drop open" (Anderson et al., 1979, p. 340).

Attentional inertia, defined in this manner, is found in children from 1 to 5 years of age and for samples of college-aged adults as well (Anderson et al., 1979). Similar findings for the attention of 4- to 5-year-old children to "Sesame Street" are reported by Krull and Husson (1978).

Attention, Comprehension, and Formal Features

We have seen that perceptually salient formal features are related to attention to television, especially in preschool children. What is the role of these formal features in comprehending television? When they are first exposed to it, children seem to be drawn to television by the sounds and the unusual visual effects, that is, because of basic orienting mechanisms built into the perceptual system. These formal features can be informative, however, and once the "conventions" of television are learned, they may serve as an aid to comprehension.

Salomon (1979) suggested that certain formal features of programs, such as zooming in and out, represent *mental skills* ("now zoom in on that idea"), which are learned from television. These "media-induced skills" may be used in everyday thinking and problem solving. Studies of American and Israeli children support the notion that understanding of media conventions or formal features develops with age and experience (Salomon, 1979).

Aside from the fact that certain conventions of television may find their way into the mental processing of children exposed to it, what is the relationship between formal features and the comprehension of television? The research to date indicates that:

1. Formal features can convey information about central content by signaling what is important (with music, laughter, and other visual and auditory devices) and by highlighting the central aspects of the story (see research by Calvert, Huston, Watkins, & Wright, 1982; Campbell, 1982; Watkins, Huston-Stein, & Wright, 1980).

2. Formal features can convey other important information about time, place, and the context of action. Information that may help the viewer "set the scene" and comprehend the context in which the action takes place (Palmer & McDowell, 1979; Wright & Huston, 1983).

3. Finally, formal features convey information about the degree to which the material may be comprehensible. That is, by the structure of the television program and the formal conventions used, the child is cued into whether it is likely to be a program designed for children or not (Wright & Huston, 1983).

Like the programs, commercials are also replete with formal features designed to signal different sorts of information to the viewer. Some commercials have distinct formats that may make them discriminable. Commercials for toys, for example, designed for either males or females, have distinct formats and visual styles and can be distinguished by children as young as 6 years of age (Huston, Greer, Wright, Welch, & Ross, 1984). We consider this research in more detail when we discuss commercials in chapter 7.

So the form of television is important and useful if the child is experienced enough to have learned the conventions. Not knowing the conventions can undermine comprehension. For example, a typical opening scene in a television show might start with wide angle view, say, of a ribbon of highway disappearing into the distance, and a car on that highway. The next scene is in a car, driving along the road. Most experienced viewers know that the two scenes are related—that the car seen from the outside in the first scene is the same as seen from the inside in the second scene. Salomon (1979) discovered, however, that the youngest viewers did not understand this kind of "cut to close-up" because they did not realize that the two scenes were the same. When a zoom was used instead of a cut, however, the younger children were able to make the connection and understand the scene.

So to some extent the degree to which formal features can be used will depend on what learning has occurred. A related study done in Japan found that school children had little understanding of scene shifts or the technique of montage, and this in turn affected their understanding of a film (Tada, 1969).

The extent to which formal features aid comprehension will depend on the extent to which these features are utilized in the program format for informational purposes. Some television programs designed for children clearly take advantage of this knowledge to make their programs maximally understandable, while others make no such efforts. In one content analysis of "Sesame Street," researchers noted that "producers (of this program) reserved embellishments of the basic messages (with sound and visual effects) for times when critical material was present" (Bryant, Hezel, & Zillmann, 1978, p. 55).

What is the significance of all of this? Clearly, watching television is not a passive experience, it requires activity and is to a degree cognitively demanding (Salomon, 1981, 1983). Over the years, children shift from a low-level monitoring based on perceptually salient features to more focused attention on those parts of the story content and character portrayals that have meaning to them. This "meaning" will change as children get older. For additional research on this topic, see Bryant and Anderson (1983).

COMPREHENSION OF STORY AND PLOT

Another line of new research, not completely independent of the last, involves the study of what children (and to a lesser extent adults) understand of the plot of a typical television drama. In considering this research, we begin with a look at the materials and methods of it, and then summarize the basic findings in terms of retention of material, inferences about motives and interscene relationships, and interventions designed to improve comprehension.

Materials and Methods

The recent research on the comprehension of television drama starts with a movie or story actually shown on television (thus overcoming an objection made to earlier research). For example, a study by Andrew Collins and his colleagues (Collins, Wellman, Keniston, & Westby, 1978) used a 17-minute police drama as the basic stimulus. The plot of the television drama ("Police Story") is described by the researchers as follows:

> an unsuccessful young man steals a check protector from a business-machine repair shop. During the robbery, an elderly panhandler inad-vertently comes on the scene and the young man kills him. The police tie the killer to a series of forged checks written with the stolen check protector and eventually track him down. (Collins et al., 1978, p. 391)

Obtaining a "stimulus" typical of what is shown on television is the first part of the method in this research, and the next step is to de-velop a criterion against which the understanding of this particular plot is to be measured. In his research on children's comprehension, Col-lins showed the stimulus film (described earlier) to adults and asked them to summarize the plot by telling the "gist" of the story, and by selecting events and scenes that were central to understanding the plot.

Events in the story that are named by 70% or more of the adult view-ers are identified as *essential* (Collins et al., 1978, p. 392). The video-tape is now shown to children of different ages, usually in a school setting. After they have seen the drama children are asked to explain what it was about, to tell the "gist" of the story, and to describe the in-formation that is "central" versus "incidental" to the plot, and so on. The responses of the children are then compared to what the adults said about the same show.

Using this research procedure, Collins has been able to draw a fas-cinating picture of what children understand of a television program relative to what adults understand of the same program. The findings of this program of research fall into two categories: (a) retention of content, and especially retention of features of the plot which are con-sidered "essential," and (b) temporal integration of plot elements from scene to scene, especially in terms of what these signal of character moti-vation.

Retention of Essential Detail

As we have noted, to measure what children and adults remember of what they have seen, subjects are shown a movie and then asked to describe the story and to answer questions about it. The most striking finding to have emerged from this research is that even relatively "old" children—in the age range from 8 to 9—retain very little of actions, events, and settings seen in a typical evening drama such as the one studied.

Over age, comprehension improves quite a bit (Collins, 1979, 1983b;

Collins et al., 1978; Leifer & Roberts, 1972; Newcomb & Collins, 1979), eventually reaching adult levels by 13–14 years of age. But it is striking how little children seem to comprehend of television drama, particularly from an adult's perspective. It is not hard to test this finding. Sit down with a 2-year-old sometime and begin watching television. Once there is a break in the action, when the commercial comes on for example, ask the child to explain what has been happening. This research suggests that the younger the child the more the child's description will depart from an adult's understanding.

Why does this happen? The hypothesis advanced by Collins is that, compared to adults, young children are not as able to either *encode* or *remember* the *essential details* of the program. Children often pay attention to peripheral aspects of the plot missing the central information. An example of this finding is given in Table 6.2 from a study in which essential information, implicit information, and predictions were asked of the subjects.

The first two categories (essential information and implicit content) are defined by the responses of the "adult panel" described earlier. These two categories show powerful differences across age, especially between second and fifth grade. Young children grasp a smaller proportion of the essential plot details and they are less good at inferring information that is not explicitly stated in the drama. Memory improves with age so that by eighth grade children remember 90% or better of the explicit, central information in a program. But this means that it is not until about 13 years of age that children are beginning to view some television programs from an "adult perspective."

The third item of data, correct predictions, is not as neat as the other two (the trend is not linear across age) but it reveals a particularly nice bit of methodology. One good mark of understanding a plot should

TABLE 6.2
Children's Comprehension of Television Information

	Grade		
	2	5	8
Implicit information	47%	67%	77%
Essential information	66%	84%	92%
Correct prediction	28%	68%	78%
	n = 292		

Source: Collins et al. (1978).

be the ability to anticipate or *predict* of what is coming next. In general, the better the plot is understood, the more a person should be able to make such predictions accurately. For older subjects, these predictions should be based on knowledge from the program itself—from what has gone before. To measure prediction, Collins used a technique of stopping the film at critical junctures and asking the viewer (child or adult) "what has just happened" and, more important, "what is going to happen next?" The variable of "correct predictions" reveals that younger children are much worse at this than older children.

Why do children have difficulty remembering? One possibility is that young children encode central information differently and/or inadequately. According to this theory, the more children are exposed to the kind of drama television has to offer, the better they will get at recognizing and encoding the central content and the more they learn to filter out extraneous detail (Collins, 1982, 1983a, 1983b).

Another possibility attributes changes in children's processing of central details to developmental changes in attention to salient perceptual features (which decreases with age), and to a greater understanding of the "grammar" of the medium (which increases with age). That is, as children get older they are less and less drawn by the unusual sounds and sights, and more and more taken by the plot itself (Wright & Huston, 1983).

Interscene Relationships and Inferences About Motivation

Comprehension requires more than just being able to pay attention to the right parts of the story and understanding what is "central" to the plot. Comprehension also involves making certain *inferences* about the characters and especially their motivations. Comprehension of television includes the skill of being able to grasp the relationship between characters and scenes that, although related, are separated in time. Each of these capacities, necessary for an "adult" level of comprehension, involves conceptual and knowledge skills that the young child simply may not possess. It may be that children do not focus on this type of information because it is not "salient" or meaningful to them, or that their cognitive skills are so poorly developed that they are unable to keep long sequences of action and plot detail in memory.

Motives and Consequences. The findings of research show that children more clearly recognize consequences than they do the motives behind them. For example, in one study Collins (1973) showed 609 children in kindergarten, second, fifth, and eighth grade an 11-minute version of an action adventure. After it was over, the children were asked about the program and about what happened to whom and why. Young children remember the consequences ("two men got into a fight, and one of them got killed") but not the motivations behind them. So the fight is remembered, but not the fact that one person did it because of some action of the other. Older children remember *both* consequences and motives in their explanations of what happened in a story, making their understanding more like that of adults.

Interscene Relationships. In addition to understanding motives better with age, there are strong age trends in the ability to draw inferences about *implicit* events, and understanding relationships from one scene to another (Collins et al., 1978; Newcomb & Collins, 1979). Young children have a difficult time integrating scenes, and particularly so when commercials are shown in between (Collins, 1982). This inability is not simply due to inadequate memory for explicit events such as we have just described, because even when young children are aware of the essential events they do not make the inferences necessary to understand the story. Older children spontaneously make discrete scenes coherent by *inferring implicit relationships.* This is probably a function of greater awareness of television plots on the part of older children (Wright & Vlietstra, 1975).

Collins is not the only researcher to have found that childrens' comprehension of television is quite low. Studies of "Sesame Street" (Calvert & Watkins, 1979; Friedlander, Wetstone, & Scott, 1974) report that young children retain very little of what they see, even though the material, in this case, is designed to be understood by children. Similar memory deficits for commercials has been found (Wackman, Wartella, & Ward, 1977) and of news stories (Drew & Reeves, 1980).

Interventions to Improve Comprehension

The foregoing suggests that children do not understand television the way adults do. When children and adults watch together, they may be exposed to the same information at the same time, but they often "see" very different stories, and draw very different conclusions about what is happening on the television screen. We now know that the reason for this difference in comprehension between children and adults is that children lack a variety of cognitive skills that are necessary for comprehension.

If children do not encode *essential details* or understand *motivation,* or draw *implicit inferences,* would it help improve their understanding of television if someone, watching at the same time, would draw their attention to these things? To answer this question, Collins, Sobol, and Westby (1981) conducted a clever series of studies using essentially the same materials as in the research described earlier. The researchers began with a prior question: To what extent might the children's performance improve if they were given a stronger incentive to recall, or if they were told in advance that they would be asked questions?

In this study, children from second and eighth grade watched a movie under one of three *incentive* conditions:

1. a "learning set" (you will later be tested on what it is about);
2. an "incentive set" (you will be tested, and you can win a prize); and
3. "no special instructions" (relax and enjoy the film).

Most of the research we have been summarizing was done under the third type of instruction (relax and enjoy). Collins et al. (1981) found that neither of the other cognitive sets: *learning* or *incentive,* were more effective than the *relax and enjoy* instructions in eliciting better comprehension. The authors suggest that the incentive instructions were not effective because the second graders lacked adequate cognitive strategies for improving their comprehension of the program and thus could not perform better even if they were strongly motivated to do so.

In a second study, these same authors studied the effect of an adult who made "facilitating comments about the program." In a second condition of the same study, adults made "neutral comments" about the program. Adults who made *facilitating* comments did indeed influence the childrens' understanding of the plot. Children exposed to the facilitating comments recalled more of the key facts about the story than children who were exposed to the *neutral* comments.

A similar type of intervention involves having adults give cues about what is happening for child viewers (Friedrich & Stein, 1975). For example, in one study adult co-viewers made comments about the nature of program events and how these related to the plot, and this improved the comprehension of kindergarten, third- and fourth-grade children (Watkins, Calvert, Huston-Stein, & Wright, 1980).

Finally, Singer and Singer have done several studies of family mediation and television viewing (Singer & Singer, 1984; Singer, Singer, & Rapaczynski, 1984) showing that generally adults can have important mediating effects on the extent to which television influences children's subsequent aggression and children's understanding of television content. (For a good review of "family mediation" studies, see McLeod, Fitzpatrick, Glynn, & Fallis, 1982.)

What Does It Take to Comprehend?

What does adult comprehension of television content require? Collins speculated that three sets of knowledge are needed:

1. A knowledge of exposition of forms, or the general structure of stories;
2. knowledge of the world; and
3. knowledge of the structure of television and its particular conventions.

The first of these criteria, knowledge of expositional forms, comes from research on children's comprehension of *written* stories rather than television stories (Mandler & Johnson, 1977; Poulsen, Kintsch, Kintsch, & Premack, 1979; Stein & Glenn, 1979). Stein and Glenn, for example, found that third graders elaborated significantly on the plot when they retold a story, and they did so from a knowledge of *basic story structure*. Similar findings are reported by Newcomb and Collins (1979). Collins (1982) commented:

> Apparently, the general knowledge available to the two groups was somewhat different and, for second grade viewers, permitted differential understanding of the programs. At the two older ages, however, viewers from all groups understood both programs equally well, perhaps because their more extensive and varied social knowledge made it possible for them to understand a range of types of portrayals. Thus within the younger age group, in which understanding is generally unreliable, there appeared to be individual differences that are accounted for significantly by variables that summarize viewers' previous social learning experiences. (p. 17)

Knowledge of the world is another aspect that greatly aids comprehension, and this clearly develops and improves with age. An example of the importance of this variable is found in the research on the relationship of life experience to comprehension of television. In one study, children from lower and middle-class homes were shown two different programs: one showing lower class family life and the other showing middle-class family life (Newcomb & Collins, 1979). After seeing the program, children in the second, fifth, and eighth grades were asked questions about their understanding of the plot and events in the story. For the second graders, their understanding was far better if the show was about characters similar to themselves than if it was about characters different from themselves. In the words of the researchers:

> Middle-SES (social class) second graders who viewed the middle class show inferred more about the causes of actions and the feelings and emotions

of the characters that lower SES second graders who watched the lower class character show. (Newcomb & Collins, 1979, p. 422)

Comprehension of television story and plot, obviously, is not a simple matter. Comprehension means many things and there are several different definitions in the research literature. There is some evidence that children do not comprehend because they are not aware of central plot elements and they do not pay attention to them or encode them in memory. Children are not as aware of motivation as adults, and so do not follow a story at that level either. Children are not as good at making inferences especially about information that is not made explicit, or that is carried over from scene to scene. Children understand better television depictions of worlds like their own than worlds that are somehow different than their own.

Finally, it is clear that adults can improve children's comprehension by pointing out central plot elements and important information. Most important of all, perhaps, in helping children understand television is to point out the motivations of characters and how it is based on events in the program.

PERCEIVED REALITY OF TELEVISION

It is an interesting fact about broadcasting that it may contain material that is real or fictitious. Often these two types of content are indistinguishable. The consequences of blurring this distinction are impressive. On Oct. 30, 1938, Orson Welles and the "Mercury Theater of the Air" presented a radio play called "War of the Worlds," based on a novel by the science-fiction writer H. G. Wells. The program was announced as a drama, as a radio play, but it was presented convincingly and in a manner that blurred the distinction between news and drama. Many people who tuned into this program that night were driven into a "panic" not only by what they heard, but also by confirming evidence they gathered from around them, watching what others were doing (Cantril, Gaudet, & Hertzog, 1940). Why did people panic while listening to a radio show about creatures from outer space? Was this a fluke, or could it happen again? What does this event teach us about the *perceived reality* of an event presented on radio or television?

Much of what we know about the radio program "War of the Worlds" comes from a group of psychologists directed by Hadley Cantril, who interviewed people who panicked as a result of the program. A vivid description of what happened to people that night was given to me by one of those who did panic, a man who was interviewed by Cantril. This man lives near the university town where I teach, and he was kind enough to share his recollections of that night with me. At the time of the famous radio broadcast, this man owned a gas station. On the night of Oct. 30, 1938, he was in and out of the house pumping gas, talking with neighbors, and listening to the radio.

When the "Mercury Theater of the Air" came on and the credits were given he must have been otherwise occupied, because he does not remember hearing the part about it being a radio play. After the opening credits, the drama began with dance music "brought to you from the Meridian Room of the Park Plaza Hotel." After a short musical rendition, the program was interrupted by a "news bulletin" reporting unusual explosions on the surface of the planet Mars. The program of music then returned. After another song or two, the program was interrupted again, this time for an interview with an astronomer (Orson Welles). Shortly thereafter, the astronomer and the reporter went to visit the sight of a "small earthquake" not far from the Observatory. Once again, the program lapsed into dance music.

My informant tells me that like many people he believed he was listening to a program of music interrupted by "news bulletins." These were unusual to begin with (explosions on mars, earthquakes in New Jersey) but they soon became extraordinary: Ships from another planet landed in New Jersey (at Grovers Mill) and they seemed to be killing the locals. As the program progressed, my informant became more excited and distressed. His wife did not share in this, because she was inside the house listening to a program of prayer on another channel.

People who were upset started coming into the gas station, filling their tanks in case they had to "make a run for it." Some were already leaving, "heading for the hills." This experience only served to excite and terrify my informant all the more, it gave more validity to the broadcast. My informant decided to join those going off into the woods. He was not "just going to sit there and let the aliens come and get him!" He gave the gas station to his unemployed brother-in-law (a regrettable incident, because when it was over the brother-in-law was unwilling to give it back) and he went off into the woods. After several days he ran out of food and had to return home, only to learn that what had scared him was simply a radio play.

The radio play scared people because they thought it was real, not fictitious. Real events demand action. Fiction may be arousing and exciting, and we can enjoy it partly because we know that the fear we feel is only illusory; there is no real danger. It's a lot like a rollercoaster, it gives the appearance of danger without the substance.

So one lesson of this story is that the distinction between reality and fiction is important because whether an event we hear portrayed is one or the other will determine, to a great extent, how we *should* respond to it. A second and perhaps more important lesson is that the distinction itself is made up of various small discriminations, judgments of the stimuli presented, that result in the belief that the event presented is real.

I recall watching television with my (5-year-old) son when the first men landed on the moon. "It's not real," he said, apparently because he thought the picture too grainy and poor to be "real." The funny thing is that exactly the same thing, the poor quality of the picture, suggested the opposite to me, that the picture was real. So in addition to being able to make the cognitive distinction of real versus fictitious, it is important to know what this distinction is based on, and how the discrimination is learned. As the story of the "War of the Worlds" tells us, we use cues of internal consistency of the story and also cues based on social comparison, on what we see others do in response to it.

In the radio play "War of the Worlds" a bit of internal inconsistency occurs early in the program: Two newsmen drive a distance of 30 miles in less than 5 minutes. But few listeners noticed this oddity. Apparently once one has accepted the premise that a broadcast is real, we do not continue to question its validity, or pay careful attention for inconsistencies. More interesting, perhaps, is how much more real a story about invaders from Mars becomes when other people appear to believe it also.

Psychological Responses to Perceived Reality

What difference does it make whether a bit of television is real or fiction? As the example about the "War of the Worlds" suggests, sometimes it makes a great deal of difference. On the other hand, we have seen evidence in the last chapter that attitudes and beliefs, especially about violence, may be learned from watching fictional material. Clearly, the effect of watching television may be modified by the perceived reality of it, but whether and when people make such discriminations is unclear. Semiotic analysis of children's comprehension of cartoons emphasizes reality distinctions as central to children's cognitive organization of television messages (Hodge & Tripp, 1986), and many programs of media literacy focus on the fictional nature of television in an attempt to lessen the impact of television on children (Corder-Bolz, 1982; Desmond, Singer, Singer, Calam, & Colimore, 1985; Singer, Zuckerman, & Singer, 1980).

A good deal of research has been devoted to the question of the perceived reality of television, and from it is beginning to emerge some important distinctions. Real events are more involving (Halloran, 1969; Osborn & Endsley, 1971) compared to fiction. Real things are also more likely to be acted upon. Violent scenes, for example, when they are real, have a greater likelihood of resulting in aggression (Berkowitz, 1984). In the following sections we review some of the early literature that attempts to get a grasp on this problem, and then we turn our attention to the question of how this distinction is learned in children.

Perception of Television as Real or Fiction. In the early 1970s, several teams of researchers tried to assess the importance of the perceived reality of television by asking: "Are people on TV just like people in real life? Do the same things happen to people on TV as happen to people in real life? Are places on TV just like places in real life? (Greenberg & Reeves, 1976; Reeves & Lometti, 1979).

Using this technique, several studies demonstrated that children and adolescents placed about mid-point on the scales (Dominick & Greenberg, 1970; Greenberg, 1972; Greenberg & Dominick, 1969; Greenberg & Reeves, 1976; McLeod, Atkin, & Chaffee, 1972a, 1972b; Noble, 1975; Reeves, 1978, 1979; Reeves & Greenberg, 1977; Reeves & Miller, 1978), and adults score about the same (Dervin & Greenberg, 1972). That is, in answer to the question "is television real?" most children and adults say that it is mid-way between reality and fantasy. It is difficult, however, to make much sense of this answer because the question is too general.

One interesting suggestion to come from this line of research is that individuals with little experience and information are more likely to accept fictional information as truth on television (Greenberg & Reeves, 1976). This suggestion is supported by Donohue and Donohue (1977) who suggest that a person believing that the portrayal of dating and marriage on television is accurate may experience disillusionment when encountering either situation in real life. This early research established the fact that people do sort television into real and fictional, but the general nature of the question makes the answers hard to interpret.

More recent studies have relied on the technique of showing children bits of television and asking for each bit (or character) whether it is real or pretend. Dorr (1983) suggested three possible ways in which children may attempt to discern whether a particular piece of television programming is real or pretend (a) they may use knowledge of television production, (b) they may use form cues such as animation, and (c) they may use their knowledge of the real world. Other researchers have identified these same features as important (Dorr, Graves, & Phelps, 1980; Kelly, 1981; Leary, Wright, & Huston, 1985; Leifer, Gordon, & Graves, 1974; Streicher & Bonney, 1974).

Morison, McCarthy, and Gardner (1979) studied first, third, and sixth graders' abilities to classify television segments as reality or fantasy, and investigated their explanations for their decision. They found two factors: a willingness to compare television to the "real" world, and an understanding of how and why television programs are put together. Morison, Kelly, and Gardner (1981) found that children's TV–real-life comparisons could be broken down into three different types of decisions: (a) Does this television object or event exist in the real world? (b) Is it possible in the real world? and (c) Is it plausible or possible? Several studies have shown that young children pay attention to and rely upon form cues (such as animation) to establish the reality of the material (Brown, Skeen, & Osborn, 1979; Leary et al., 1985; Quarfoth, 1979; Skeen, Brown, & Osborn, 1982). In a later section, we see how these and other studies of perceived reality may be organized in order to see how the distinction is learned by children.

Perceived Reality and Violence.   If people do make the distinction between real and fictional on television, what difference does this distinction make? One of the first psychologists to study the distinction between reality and fiction in a filmed account was Bandura in a study we discussed extensively in chapter 4 (Bandura, Ross, & Ross, 1963). In that study, recall that Bandura wondered whether children would be more likely to imitate a real person acting in an aggressive manner (either on film or "live") compared to a cartoon character. Bandura hypothesized that the real person would elicit more imitation than the cartoon character (actually a person dressed in a cat outfit) but he found no differences in the rate of imitation across the conditions. Children in his study were as likely to imitate a cartoon character as a real person.

Feshbach (1972) reported two studies of 9- to 11-year-old children watching a news film about a college riot, with scenes of fighting between students and police, labeled *real* or *fictitious*. He studied the youngsters' subsequent aggressive behavior. According to Feshbach, children who viewed the film labeled *real* were subsequently more aggressive than children who viewed the film labeled *fictitious*.

In studies done with adults, males were found to be more aggressive (i.e., more willing to deliver shocks to another student—a confederate of the experimenter who had just provoked them) after seeing a film of combat described as real compared to subjects who had seen the same film described as fictitious (Berkowitz & Alioto, 1973). Similar findings are reported by Thomas and Tell (1974) and Geen (1975). Geen and Rakosky (1973) found that male subjects who were shown a prize fight and reminded throughout that the film was not real manifested less overall arousal than subjects not given these reminders.

In summary, most experimental investigations using children show that factual or real television has more pronounced effects on behavior than fictional television, especially in terms of the imitation of violence (Atkin, 1983; Feshbach, 1972, 1976; Sawin, 1981; Snow, 1974). Correlational studies have focused more on the "realism" of television than the "factuality" of it (Dorr, 1983; Klapper, 1981). They find that the perceived social realism of television violence is correlated with both aggressive behavior and with the amount of television viewed (Huesmann & Eron, 1986).

Perceived Reality and Emotional Response. We may respond with stronger arousal to a television stimulus thought to be real compared to one thought to be make-believe. For example, Geen (1975) found that subjects showed greater arousal, measured by the GSR response, to a film labeled *real* compared to the same film labeled *fiction.* And in a more recent study with adults, males who saw a program about sexual abuse were more emotionally upset by the film when it was described as real than when it was described as fictional (Ross & Condry, 1985).

Whether children show differential emotional responses to real versus fictional television is largely determined by the child's level of cognitive development (Cantor & Wilson, 1984; Hoffner & Cantor, 1985; Sparks & Cantor, 1986; Wilson, Hoffner, & Cantor, 1987). For example, because preschool children are less able to take another person's perspective, they have been shown to react less to fear in facial expression than to when they are able to see the source of the reaction (in this case a mass of threatening bees; Cantor & Wilson, 1984).

The Development of the Perceived Reality Distinction

If television is divided into that which is real and that which is fictitious, and it makes a difference at least in terms of reactions to violence and emotional reactions, then how do children learn the distinction? A precurser, perhaps, to making the real–fiction distinction about television content is the cognitive distinction between how an object appears and what it is "really." Classic studies of this topic involve showing a child a toy car of one color, then putting the car behind a screen that changes the apparent color of the car. The child is then asked: "What color is the car? What color does it appear to be? What color is it really?" In these studies (Flavell, Flavell, & Green, 1987), children of a young age (2–4) seem to possess little or no understanding of the distinction. They fail the simplest tests of the distinction and they are unresponsive to efforts to teach them to make it. The skill seems to be related to the skill of "perspective taking," that is the ability to recognize that another person's perspective on a scene may be different from one's own. Older children, 6–7 years of age, are able to make both distinctions, but they have difficulty reflecting on the task or talking about such concepts as "looks like," "really and truly is," and "looks different from the way it really and truly is." Children of 11–12 years of age have no trouble making these distinctions. They have a body of rich and explicit knowledge in this area.

Wellman and Estes (1986) studied 3, 4, and 5-year-old children's abilities to distinguish between real and mental entities (between a chair and the thought of a chair), and between real and imaginary things (things that do and do not exist). They found that children of all ages make few mistakes in a sorting task. Taylor and Howell (1973) studied 3, 4, and 5-year-olds abilities to distinguish between pictures of clearly real and clearly pretend characters, finding largely the same thing. One difference was this, although most children make few mistakes about what is real, the youngest children (3-year-olds) had some difficulty with fantasy pictures as "things that couldn't happen." This ability to identify fantasy as fantasy increased with age. Although these findings seem to be in conflict with those of Wellman and Estes, the differences are probably due to the different tasks used in the two studies, and the wording of the instructions.

Even though children can distinguish real from fantasy, a second question involves whether children actually do so spontaneously. Two studies have investigated children's spontaneous classification of materials into real and fantasy. Morison and Gardner (1978) gave children three sets of pictures that could be sorted on the basis of two fantasy, or one real and one fantasy paired on some other attribute. Although fantasy pairing was never the predominant mode of classification, there was a steady increase with age (from kindergarten to sixth grade) in the incidence of spontaneous pairing on the basis of fantasy. A second study done by this research team used television programs and asked first, third, and sixth graders to identify which program pairs were more alike (e.g., is "Mike Douglas" more like "Bewitched" or the "News"?). Spontaneous classifications increased with age. Older children both made more spontaneous real–real and fantasy–fantasy classifications and gave this dimension as the basis when they explained their actions.

Thus it would appear that during the preschool years children come to learn to distinguish between the dimensions of fact and fiction. They can sort things into real and fantasy, and they do so spontaneously with increasing frequency as they get older. By the age of 5, whether something is "real" or not greatly depends on factuality, so that a real person (whether an actor or not) is identified as real and a cartoon is identified as fantasy (Hodge & Tripp, 1986; Jaglom & Gardner, 1981).

As children move into middle childhood, the dimension of importance becomes realism rather than factuality (Wright, Kunkel, Pinon, & Huston, 1987). Children are now accurate in distinguishing fictional or nonfactual programs from those showing real world events (Dorr, 1983; Fernie, 1981; Howkins, 1977; Potter, 1982; Morison & Gardner, 1978; Morison, Kelly, & Gardner, 1981). Most 11-year-olds, for example, know that an actor who plays a role does not occupy that role in real life (Dorr, 1985; Hawkins, 1977).

In the age range from 5 to 12 years, children become increasingly sensitive to production formats that signal whether a program is real or not (Leary, Wright, & Huston, 1985). As we have seen, for some program types such as violence, the perceived realism of the material declines with age (Greenberg & Reeves, 1976; Huesmann, Lagerspetz, & Eron, 1984). For other program types there are no changes with age (Dorr, 1983; Klapper, 1981; Wright, Kunkel, Pinon, & Huston, 1987). And for some program types (family comedies) perceived realism increase with age (Dorr, Kovaric, Doubleday, Sims, & Seidner, 1985). The amount of television viewed, in most research, is positively correlated with judging television as realistic (Dorr et al., 1985; Greenberg & Reeves, 1976; Hawkins & Pingree, 1982; Huesmann, Lagerspetz, & Eron, 1984). That is, heavy viewers of all ages see television as more realistic than light viewers.

In summary, children seem to learn first the distinction between fact and fiction, and even very young children can sort television into these two categories. The youngest children studied (3-year-olds) have the most difficulty with fantasy, often calling things that are fantasy (such as a rabbit baking a cake) as real (Taylor & Howell, 1973). At the earlier ages, children make the distinction between fact and fiction on the basis of form cues such as animation (for fantasy) or a news format (for reality) (Wright et al., 1987). As children reach the age of 7 or 8, they begin to rely more on the distinction between realistic and unrealistic rather than on the simpler distinction between fact and fiction made earlier (Dorr, 1983; Hawkins, 1977). The same effects are noted here, television that is more realistic has greater effects than television that is unrealistic, but now the dimensions may cross the boundaries of fact and fiction. That is, there may be television that is realistic but fictional, and there may be television that is factual but uncommon. This shift in thinking on the part of children in the range from 7 to 12 years is characterized by a decrease in the use of *possibility* and an increase in the use of *probability* as the basis of the criterion (Dorr, 1983, 1985; Morison, Kelly, & Gardner, 1981). Thus, rather than defining "real" as something that is possible, individuals at this final stage define real as that which is probable. Things that are probable are called *real* or realistic, whereas things that are improbable are called *unrealistic* or *fictional*. It is notable that one team of researchers studying the way children reason about literature (rather than television) have found the same progression from possible to probable as a definition of the reality of a story (Landry, Kelly, & Gardner, 1982).

Future research on the topic of the perceived reality of television must investigate in more detail the shift from factuality to realism, and must establish what difference the distinction makes to both children and adults. We have seen evidence that the perceived reality of a television stimulus can influence attention and involvement, violent actions, and emotions. What other effects television perceived as real versus not real may have are open to question. But the topic is an important one not only for what it may have to tell us about the nature of these two important cognitive dimensions, but also for research on mitigating the effects of television on children. If young children can be taught that much of television is not real, it may have less influence on them than it currently does.

SUMMARY

In this chapter we have seen some new approaches to the study of television, approaches that go beyond the question of the influence of television violence and focus on issues such as comprehension of television, attention to television, and understanding of the "reality" of a television stimulus and what difference this distinction makes.

These new studies are all characterized by methodological advances compared to the studies of the 1960s. Most of the stimuli used in the research, either as an object of analysis or as a part of an experiment, comes from the kind of television people are exposed to rather than being merely simulations of television programs. New questions have emerged also. What do children understand of the television they see? How much do they really pay attention to it? What aspects of television's form tend to draw attention, and more importantly, how is the form of the program related to a child's comprehension of the material? Is television seen as real or make-believe? And finally, in all of these issues from attention, to comprehension, to perceived reality, what difference does it make?

By studying real television and by expanding the issues and questions, researchers have opened a whole new pandora's box of possibilities. This new approach may be characterized as "ecological" because it attempts to understand television as an environment that certain people expose themselves to at certain times and are treated to certain kinds of information when they do. How an individual or a society will be influenced by this information will be a joint function of the person (age, sex, etc.) and the information contained in the specific environment in question.

This approach is characterized by a content analysis of the kind of material actually watched, and speculations based on how specific real individuals will react to it. We continue with this approach in the next chapter when we take up the question of advertisements. We begin with a content analysis of ads, as we did with programs, and go on to a survey of evidence about how this content influences those who watch it.

Nonprogram Content of Television: Mechanisms of Persuasion

John Condry
Cynthia Scheibe

Ads are the best things on TV . . .
—Jonathan Price*

Ads are the worst thing on TV . . .
—Rose Goldsen**

Whether you love them or hate them, commercials are the whole point of television as it has evolved in the United States, and in many other countries as well. As we saw in chapter 1, the basic economic structure of the broadcast media, since the early 1920s, involves the gathering of audiences in order to sell them to an advertiser. In this respect, television is the most successful marketing device ever invented, and the heart and soul of this device is the television commercial.

There are many questions one can ask about TV commercials. Advertisers, for example, are interested in the *effectiveness* of commercials in promoting a specific product or service. That is, after seeing a commercial, do people remember the product? Do they desire the product? Do they actually buy and consume it? This is what the advertisers have in mind when they talk about the effectiveness of an advertisement.

Psychologists, on the other hand, are more interested in the *effects*

---

*From Price (1978).
**Goldsen (1975).

of ads: how they influence the beliefs, attitudes, values, and behaviors of viewers in ways that go beyond attitudes and behaviors associated with the product itself. Because of these broader interests, we want to know much more about the nature of commercials. What is the "world" that is presented in TV commercials like? What kinds of products are advertised on television? What kinds are not? What information and value judgments are contained in TV commercials? What sort of "messages" are given concerning what people are (or should be) like? What types of people appear in commercials, and what do these people urge the viewer to do? Do commercials have behavioral and cognitive effects in the same ways that programs do? In addition to attitudes and values directly related to the product, what other aspects of beliefs, attitudes, and values might be influenced by commercials?

In several ways commercials are like programs. They are small dramas or comedies, with characters and a plot. They have salient "formal features," such as music and visual effects, that are designed to grasp and hold the attention of the audience. Commercials are also produced in the same manner as programs, with scripts, producers, directors, and actors, although they are much more expensive, per minute of production, than the programs (Arlen, 1979; Price, 1978). They can be studied using the same methods of content analysis that we have applied to the study of programs.

However much they are similar, commercials differ from TV programs in several significant ways. They are much shorter, generally ranging from 10 seconds to 2 minutes in length. They appear with much greater frequency during the broadcast day, and are repeated much more often than individual programs are. These repetitions may occur during the same hour, at many different times of the day and week, and on different channels, so that more people are likely to see a specific commercial than a specific program. Commercials also portray people and situations that are at some level meant to be representative of the real world of the TV viewers because they include products and services that the viewers actually use. Finally, commercials often contain claims and statements that fall under the regulatory jurisdiction of the Federal Trade Commission, as discussed in the next chapter.

In the United States, commercial messages periodically interrupt the program in progress. This simple fact may account for the negative attitude on the part of many viewers toward TV commercials in general: Commercials are seen as annoying and intrusive, something to avoid if at all possible. Part of this negative attitude may also stem from the different types of choices that viewers are able to make for viewing programs versus viewing commercials. Viewers have access to TV guides and listings of the programs that will be shown, but such listings are not available for the commercials. Therefore, although viewers can choose to watch a given program (or not), they cannot tune in to catch a specific commercial; they can only choose *not* to watch the commercials that do appear—by "zapping" to a different station, leaving the room, or turning off the set.

Beyond all of these ways in which programs and commercials differ, the most important difference lies in the *purpose* of commercials compared with programs. Programs are fundamentally designed to hold attention by entertaining and/or informing the audience. The basic purpose of commercials, on the other hand, is one of *persuasion*—changing the beliefs, attitudes and behaviors of viewers. Nearly all of the nonprogram content of television has this persuasive character. Whether the nonprogram content is an advertisement for a product, a public service, or a promotion for a TV program or movie, the purpose of the message is to persuade the viewer. This persuasion could be aimed at getting the viewer to adopt new attitudes or engage in new activities, or it may involve reinforcement of already existing attitudes or behaviors. It could simply encourage viewers to watch the next show, or remind them that there are poor children who need their help. In doing so, these short messages may also entertain and/or inform the viewer, but the primary psychological mechanism is one of persuasion.

Even more so than programs, commercials are designed with a particular audience in mind. Commercials are *targeted* (a favorite term of the advertising industry) toward a specific audience. Commercials targeted toward children (for toys, candy, cereals), for example, usually appear during children's programs (e.g., cartoons) and sitcoms, at times when children are known to be a large percentage of the audience. Commercials for feminine hygiene, beauty, food, cleaners, and other home-related products typically appear during daytime soap operas and game shows, when the vast majority of the audience is known to be female. During sports programs, most commercials are male oriented (e.g., for beer, auto, and financial products), again reflecting the nature of the audience.

In discussing the content of TV commercials and their effects on viewers, then, we must take into account this variation. There are four particular time periods that are useful in exploring these variations because they reflect four different groups of viewers: Saturday morning (7 a.m.–noon), consisting largely of children's programs, with commercials almost entirely directed toward *children;* weekday daytime (9 a.m.–3 p.m.), consisting of soap operas, game shows, and talk shows, with commercials almost entirely directed toward women; weekend afternoon (noon–6 p.m.), consisting of sports and news programs, with commercials primarily directed toward *men;* and prime time (evenings 8–11 p.m.), consisting of a range of different types of programs directed toward the general (largely adult) viewing audience, *everyone*.

In each of the four remaining sections of this chapter, when appropriate, we focus on these different viewing audiences. The topics we consider in this chapter are: (a) the *structure* of the television day, in terms of the frequency and types of nonprogram messages shown; (b) the *content* of the commercials, including character portrayals and values; (c) the nature of commercials directed to children; and (d) the *uses* and *effects* of TV commercials, including issues of advertising effectiveness and effects, mechanisms of persuasion, and the credibility of so-called "subliminal" advertising techniques.

THE STRUCTURE OF COMMERCIALS
WITHIN THE TELEVISION DAY

There is little publicly available research documenting the basic structure of the television broadcast day in terms of how it is broken up into program and nonprogram content. Individual stations keep logs of their own broadcasting schedules and occasionally there are reports of general trends in advertising (e.g., "clutter" resulting from the increasing use of 15-second commercials). But basic descriptive information about the average number of commercials per hour or the amount of time devoted to different types of nonprogram messages has not been readily available.

Yet this type of information is essential if we are to attempt to understand what television is all about and how different types of viewers may be influenced by what they see. Indeed, despite the lack of hard information about the frequency and type of commercials shown, general statements are often made estimating the number of commercials an average viewer is exposed to each year. These figures are usually given for children: "an average child between the ages of 2 and 11 is presented with about 19,000 to 20,000 commercials per year, or about 50 to 55 commercials per average viewing day" (Adler, Lesser et al., 1980, p. 155).

The research conducted by our lab at Cornell University, described later in this chapter, indicates that such estimates may vastly underrepresent the number of commercials an average viewer sees. This lab, the Human Development & Television Lab and Archive (HDTV), was created in order to document the structure of television, both programs and commercials, and to trace changes in this structure over time. The research findings from the HDTV studies are presented in some detail in this chapter, because they constitute the only broad descriptive information of this type that is readily available to psychologists and communications scholars.

But the structure of television involves more than just the number of commercials shown. The HDTV findings that are presented address several questions about the nature of program and nonprogram messages on television. What types of products are advertised in commercials (and what types aren't)? How does this product-type distribution vary across programs and daily and weekly time periods? What seasonal variations exist for different product types? What is the percentage of nonprogram time devoted to messages other than product commercials, such as promotions for upcoming programs (promos) and public service announcements (PSAs)? In short, how does the nonprogram content of television vary by the type of message, program, presumed audience, time of day, and season of the year? Finally, how has the nonprogram structure of television changed since the 1970s?

The HDTV Archive at Cornell University was established in 1983 to begin answering these types of questions. Every 2 years, a large representative sample of network television content is videotaped and stored in the archive. Each year's sample consists of one composite broadcast week selected from each of 4 months (March, June, September, December). On each day selected, broadcast content is taped from 7 a.m. to 1 a.m.; the three major networks (ABC, NBC, CBS) are monitored through their affiliates in Syracuse, New York, with only one station monitored at a time, changing stations hourly using a randomized block design. This produces 18 hours of broadcasting for each day sampled; the 7 different days of the week sampled each month yielded 126 hours each month, or 504 hours each year.

These samples are subsequently analyzed to document the amount of time devoted during each broadcast day to different types of programs and nonprogram messages. The 504 hours were analyzed for program content each year, with a smaller (but representative) subsample of 100 hours analyzed for nonprogram content. The data reported here include analyses of the 1983, 1985, and 1987 samples.

Programs

Before we look at commercials in detail, we discuss the HDTV findings concerning the programs in which the nonprogram content is embedded. Although we have already considered program content in earlier chapters, the HDTV data on the structure of television illustrate several additional points about the types of programs that are shown, and the relationship between programs and commercials.

The relative distribution of the types of programs that appeared during the 1,512 hours of broadcasting in the HDTV samples are shown in Fig. 7.1. More than 20% of the hours between 7 a.m. and 1 a.m. were

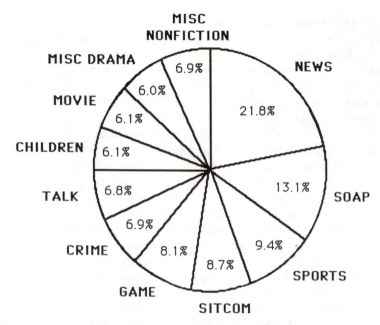

FIG. 7.1. Frequency distribution of program types shown on network tele-vision, 1983–1987 (based on a total of 1512 hours of programs). (Informa-tion from HDTV Archive.)

devoted to news programs of one sort or another (including morning news programs; noon, evening and late night news; prime-time news and newsmagazine shows; and special news reports). Other frequent program types include daytime soap operas (which account for 13.1%), sports (9.4%), situation comedies (8.8%), and game shows (8.1%).

Although this distribution was remarkably consistent across the different seasons and across all years of the sample, there were some trends in relative frequencies of programs from 1983 to 1987. As Fig. 7.2 illustrates, there have been increases in the frequencies of game shows, promotional programs, and courtroom shows (especially dur-ing the "fringe hours" before and after the evening news) and a steady decrease in variety shows and "news/talk" programs (e.g., "Real People", "That's Incredible"). Sports was the only program type that showed a consistent variation by season, with the lowest frequency in June and the highest frequencies in September and December (due largely to prime-time baseball and football broadcasts).

As might be expected, the types of programs shown depends on the time and day sampled. Figure 7.3 compares the program distributions for the four different time periods discussed earlier: Saturday morn-

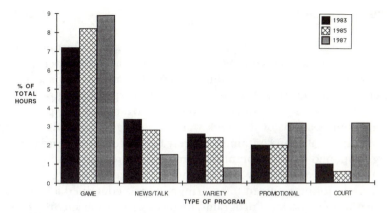

FIG. 7.2. Proportions of selected types of TV programs, by year (based on 504 hours of programs for each year sampled). (Information from HDTV Archive.)

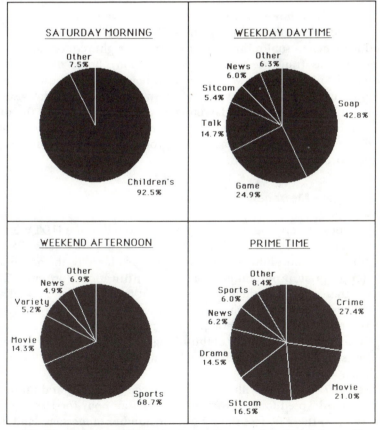

FIG. 7.3. Frequency distribution by program type for selected time periods, 1983–1987. (Information from HDTV Archive.)

ing (children); weekday daytime (women); weekend afternoon (men); and prime time (everyone). Each of the first three time periods contain only a few types of programs designed to appeal to a specific audience, with a much wider range of program types during prime time (crime/action, movies, situation comedies, drama, news, sports, etc.). Other time periods of the week were also program specific: weekday mornings (7–9 a.m.) contained entirely news programs; Sunday morning contained mostly promotional (religious) programs and news. The time periods of weekday late afternoon, after the evening news, and late night (often referred to as "fringe hours") contained a broad mix of syndicated and local programs, including reruns of sitcoms, dramas and crime/action programs, along with game shows, courtroom dramas, children's cartoons, late-night movies, and talk shows.

Much of this information about programs is congruent with what was presented in chapter 3 (derived from older studies). One type of program is new, however. In our sample we have seen an increasing number of "promotional" programs — 60 minute advertisements for products (such as subliminal tapes to help in weight reduction) or services (such as franchise real estate promotion). Some of these are produced to look like news programs, others like talk shows. These promotional programs are typically shown during "fringe" times such as late at night or early Sunday morning. We have also seen the distinction between programs and ads blurred in television designed for children where some programs are for products that can be purchased in the store (such as G.I. Joe).

Nonprogram Messages

Three types of nonprogram messages were coded in the HDTV analyses: (a) product commercials; (b) public service announcements (PSAs) and "drop-ins" (short informational messages produced by the network); and (c) program promotions or station identifications (promos). Together, these nonprogram messages account for more than 20% of all the television content each year. The most recent data from 1987 showed an average of 30.3 nonprogram messages per hour, accounting for more than 13 minutes of the average hour. The majority of these messages are product commercials, which appear an average of 24 times an hour.

Figures 7.4a and 7.4b illustrate the average frequency and number of minutes devoted to nonprogram messages an hour for 1983, 1985, and 1987. As these figures show, both the number of messages and the amount of time devoted to them increased over the 5-year period covered by this analysis. Nearly all of this increase is due to product com-

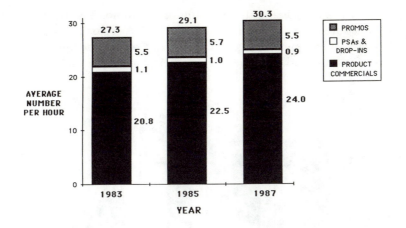

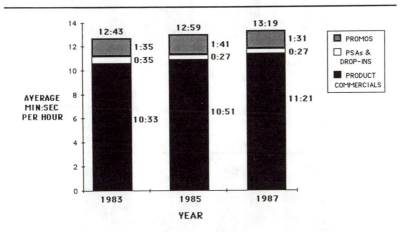

FIG. 7.4.   (a) Average number of nonprogram messages per hour, by message type and year. (b) Average number of minutes of nonprogram messages per hour, by message type and year. (Information from HDTV Archive.)

mercials; promos have stayed about the same, and PSAs have actually declined from 1983–1987.

As these figures illustrate, the number of messages has increased more than the amount of time devoted to them each hour, due to the fact that the messages themselves have gotten shorter. Although the majority of commercials are still 30 seconds long, the number of shorter commercials (usually 10 or 15 seconds long) nearly doubled between 1983 and 1987. In 1987, nearly one third of all nonprogram messages were less than 30 seconds in length, including nearly one fourth of all product commercials and three-fourths of all promos. Figures 7.5a and 7.5b illustrate this decrease in the length that has occurred for all three types of nonprogram messages. The greatest relative decrease has occurred for PSAs and drop-ins — between 1983 and 1987 the number of

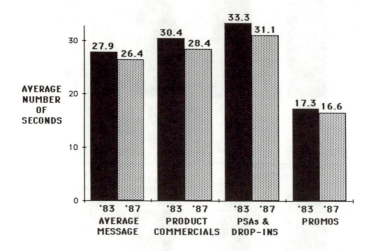

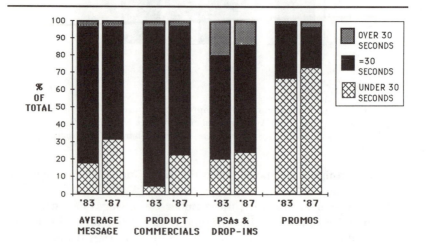

FIG. 7.5. (a) Average length of nonprogram messages by message type and year. (b) Percentage of messages that were over, under, or equal to 30 seconds, by message type and year. (Information from HDTV Archive.)

these longer messages in HDTV Archive sample declined by more than 40%.

The number of minutes per hour devoted to nonprogram content varied widely across the viewing week, as illustrated in Fig. 7.6. Not surprisingly, Sunday morning had the fewest minutes of nonprogram messages per hour (fewer than 5 minutes), whereas weekday daytime (9 a.m.–3 p.m.) had the most (more than 15 minutes per hour). Prime time had the second lowest number of minutes devoted to nonprogram content (10.5 minutes per hour), with the fewest minutes of PSAs but the most minutes of program promos of any time period. Saturday morn-

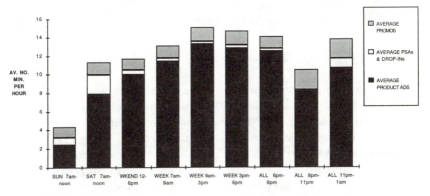

FIG. 7.6.   Minutes of nonprogram messages by time period, 1983–1987. (Information from HDTV Archive.)

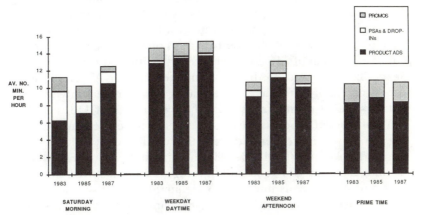

FIG. 7.7.   Minutes of nonprogram messages for selected time periods, by year. (Information from HDTV Archive.)

ing, often criticized for being an advertising "ghetto," actually had the second lowest minutes of product commercials (7.9 per hour) and by far the largest number of minutes devoted to PSAs and drop-ins of any time period (2.1 minutes per hour, nearly 20% of the total non-program time). The other popular children's viewing time period (weekdays 3–6 p.m.) had nearly 13 minutes of product commercials per hour, with almost no PSAs.

The picture of Saturday morning television as being relatively good in terms of the frequency and type of nonprogram messages shown may be changing for the worse, however. As Fig. 7.7 indicates, the proportion of time devoted to PSAs and drop-ins decreased between 1983 and 1987, whereas the proportion of time devoted to product commercials has increased significantly. This trend is discussed in more detail in the section concerning children's programs and commercials.

Product-Type Distribution

As previously mentioned, product commercials were analyzed by drawing a representative sample of 100 hours from each year (about 20% of all content taped). In 1983, the product commercials shown in all 504 hours were analyzed, yielding a sample of more than 11,000 commercials for that year. This sample contained many repetitions of the same commercials, so that there were actually 4,447 different commercials for 2,386 different products and services. Despite public perceptions of the repetitive nature of TV advertising, however, nearly half of the commercials only appeared once in the sample; only 56 commercials were repeated 10 or more times, with the highest number of repetitions of a single commercial being American Family Publisher's Sweepstakes (34). Some products or services had a much larger number of total commercials, but with many different versions shown. For example, there were 50 different versions of commercials for McDonald's, with a total of 146 ads; there were 41 different commercials for Sears (82 total); and 35 different commercials for AT&T (60 total). American Family Publishers Sweepstakes, however, had only 16 different versions of commercials that appeared a total of 113 times.

What types of products are most frequently advertised on television? Fig. 7.8 shows the frequency distribution of different product types in the HDTV Archive (for 1983–1987 combined). Nearly one third of all commercials were for food and beverages or retail stores, supermarkets, and home furnishings. Other frequently advertised products or services include household cleaners, medicines, soda and snacks, financial services, travel and leisure activities, and hygiene products.

The types of products advertised were relatively similar in each of

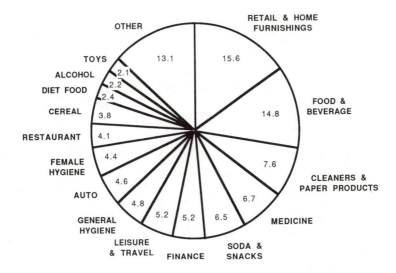

FIG. 7.8. Frequency distribution of product types, 1983–1987. (Information from HDTV Archive.)

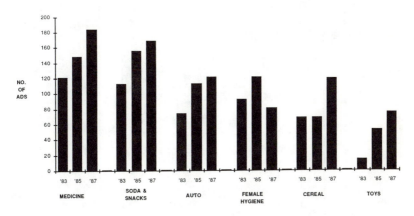

FIG. 7.9. Frequencies of selected product types, by year. (Information from HDTV Archive.)

the 3 years sampled, although some product types do seem to be increasing. Figure 7.9 shows the product types that had the largest increases between 1983 and 1987: medicines, soda and snacks, autos, cereals, and toys. Toys had the largest relative increase (more than 400%), although they still account for only a small percentage of the total commercials shown (3.1%). Female hygiene and beauty ads showed a big increase in 1985, but dropped off again in 1987; they still appear four times

TABLE 7.1

Most Frequently Advertised Product Types for Selected Time Periods, by Year (in Percent of Total Commercials for That Time Period).

Top 10 Product Types (Total Sample)

1983		*1985*		*1987*	
Food & beverage	(16.2)	Retail & home	(15.2)	Retail & home	(15.6)
Retail & home	(14.5)	Food & beverage	(14.6)	Food & beverage	(13.9)
Cleaners & paper	(8.2)	Cleaners & paper	(8.6)	Medicine	(7.7)
Leisure & travel	(6.5)	Soda & snacks	(7.0)	Soda & snacks	(7.1)
Medicine	(5.8)	Medicine	(6.6)	Cleaners & paper	(6.2)
Soda & snacks	(5.4)	Finance	(5.9)	Auto	(5.1)
General hygiene	(5.3)	Female hygiene	(5.4)	General hygiene	(5.1)
Finance	(5.2)	Auto	(5.0)	Cereal	(5.0)
Female hygiene	(4.4)	Leisure & travel	(4.9)	Finance	(4.6)
Restaurant	(4.2)	Restaurant	(4.4)	Leisure & travel	(4.3)

Saturday Morning (7a.m.–noon)

1983		*1985*		*1987*	
Cereal	(32.6)	Toys	(23.6)	Cereal	(34.8)
Soda/snacks	(17.4)	Cereal	(16.4)	Toys	(33.7)
Restaurant	(15.2)	Soda/snacks	(14.6)	Restaurant	(6.7)
Toys	(13.0)	Leisure	(14.6)	Soda/snacks	(4.5)
Leisure	(10.9)	Restaurant	(12.7)	Food/bevg	(3.4)

Weekday Daytime (9a.m.–3p.m.)

1983		1985		1987	
Food/bevg	(25.5)	Food/bevg	(21.6)	Food/bevg	(19.8)
Cleaners	(12.6)	Cleaners	(15.3)	Medicine	(13.2)
Retail/home	(12.3)	Retail/home	(10.6)	Cleaners	(11.7)
Medicine	(7.5)	Medicine	(9.2)	Retail/home	(11.1)
Gen. hygiene	(7.0)	Fem. hygiene	(7.6)	Gen. hygiene	(8.1)

Weekend Afternoon (12–6p.m.)

1983		1985		1987	
Finance	(18.5)	Finance	(24.9)	Retail/home	(18.0)
Auto	(17.8)	Auto	(23.2)	Auto	(11.3)
Retail/home	(13.3)	Leisure	(9.9)	Finance	(8.7)
Leisure	(11.1)	Retail/home	(9.4)	Soda/snacks	(8.0)
Alcohol	(10.4)	Alcohol	(6.1)	Alcohol	(7.3)

Prime Time (8–11p.m.)

1983		1985		1987	
Food/bevg	(10.9)	Fem. hygiene	(11.4)	Auto	(12.2)
Retail/home	(9.4)	Food/bevg	(10.7)	Restaurant	(9.9)
Fem. hygiene	(9.4)	Retail/home	(9.7)	Soda/snacks	(9.2)
Restaurant	(8.2)	Soda/snacks	(9.1)	Food/bevg	(8.8)
Leisure	(7.8)	Restaurant	(8.7)	Medicine	(7.8)

Source: Information from HDTV Archive.

more often than commercials for male hygiene and beauty products.

As with program types, the types of products advertised varied widely depending on the time period sampled. Table 7.1, presents the most frequent product types advertised during each of the four selected time periods (with each years data given separately), along with the top 10 product types for each year as a whole. Although some product types appear frequently during many time periods of the week (e.g., retail stores or food and beverages), most of the time periods are extremely product specific. Weekday daytime television viewers (primarily women), for example, see mostly ads for food, cleaners, medicine, and hygiene; weekend afternoon viewers (primarily men) see mostly ads for finance, autos, retail stores, and alcohol. Children watching on Saturday morning see almost entirely commercials for toys, cereals, soda and snacks, and restaurants.

The product types advertised also undergo seasonal variations, as illustrated in Fig. 7.10 for selected products. Commercials for diet foods/aids appear most frequently during the summer (presumably when people are more conscious of their figures); however an almost identical pattern occurs for candy/snack/soda commercials, which would seem to result in an overall pattern of mixed messages. Medicines, not surprisingly, appear most frequently during the winter months of March and December, whereas travel and leisure commercials are highest during the vacation month of June. Finally, toys and other retail products are advertised most heavily in December when the Christmas season is approaching.

The data reported here represent an extremely large, systematic, and representative sample of network television content broadcast between the hours of 7 a.m. and 1 a.m. Although the sample does have some limitations (e.g., reflecting only the three major networks and only their Syracuse affiliates), it represents the most comprehensive portrayal available of the overall structure of the television environment, especially of the nonprogram content. The findings of this study are numerous, but a few general conclusions can be drawn.

First, this study provides a concrete estimate of the number and minutes of commercials during an average television hour, as well as variations by time and day. As noted earlier, many articles have cited the statistic that the average viewer is exposed to some 20,000 TV commercials a year. This figure, however, seems to be based on frequency data obtained when many commercials were 60 seconds in length. As we have seen, the modal ad is now 30 seconds and getting shorter (5-second ads are even beginning to appear). If the average viewer currently watches about 4 hours of television a day (as the Nielsen figures indicate), then our data would lead us to conclude that with an aver-

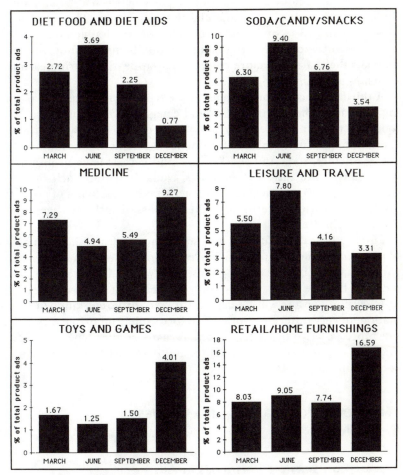

FIG. 7.10. Proportions of all commercials for selected product types, by season (1983–1987). (Information from HDTV Archive.)

age of more than 30 nonprogram messages an hour, an ordinary viewer would be exposed to more than 40,000 such messages a year, including well over 35,000 product commercials. Furthermore, this average alone does not tell the whole story, because the average number of commercials viewed depends on what time of the day and week a viewer generally watches; a person who watches weekday daytime television programs will be exposed to almost twice as many product commercials per hour as a person who watches only prime time or Saturday morning television.

This in turn raises the issue of clutter. Although the number of commercial minutes/hour has risen only slightly between 1983 and 1987, the average length of a commercial has gone down. The number of 10-second and 15-second commercials has nearly doubled during this 4-year period, and this means that in addition to more minutes of commercials there are also more commercials appearing during each advertising minute.

A third point concerns changes in the types of products that are being advertised on television. General categories of products (such as food/beverage and general hygiene) have declined in favor of more specialized products designed for smaller segments of the viewing market. Medicines, soda and snacks, toys, and cereals have proliferated, with many more different products available within each of these categories. The consequences of the increases in these types of products are likely to raise concerns about healthiness of such messages, especially for children.

Finally, these data illustrate the importance of describing the nature of television content. The television "environment" is not homogeneous; wide variations in type of programs, and type and frequency of commercials, by time of day, season, and year mean that different categories of television viewers will be exposed to very different kinds of information, to very different "worlds." To focus solely on prime time as being representative of all television, as many studies have done, may misrepresent the world of television and therefore lead to inaccurate conclusions about its possible effects.

CHARACTER PORTRAYALS AND VALUES IN COMMERCIALS

Research on Sex-Role Portrayals in Ads

Research on the content of commercials on television was initiated by various groups of individuals concerned about the way women were portrayed on television, especially in commercials, and particularly in terms of their occupations and relations with men. Earlier, when we described the program content of television, we saw that television drama was a "man's" world. According to content analyses done by Gerbner and others (reported in chapter 3), on television programs men outnumber women by a ratio of 3:1. Casual observation suggests that the same is not the case with ads.

But even recognizing the more equal sex distribution, many observers felt that the "images" of women in the ads were demeaning and one-sided. It was thought that women were shown almost exclusively as housewives and as "dependent on men." In order to substantiate this claim, researchers did several content analyses of the world of television ads in the 1960s and 1970s.

One long-standing observation, confirmed by early research, was that most of the voices on television ads were male voices, theoretically because the voice of a man carries more "authority" than the voice of a woman. In one early study, 87% of "voice overs" were male, only 6% were female, and almost three times as many women as men were shown in "home settings" (Dominick & Rauch, 1972). In this same study, more than half of the women shown in ads (56%) were housewives. In another early study, Hennessee and Nicholson (1972), concluded that in about one third of the commercials women were shown "dependent on men" and in one quarter of them women were portrayed as "submissive" to men.

Summarizing the findings of these and several other studies of sex-role portrayals in commercials done in the late 1960s and early 1970s, Courtney and Whipple (1974) reported that women were shown in ads primarily doing domestic tasks and demonstrating household products. Women were "overrepresented in home settings, as well as in family/home occupations" (p. 115), presumably relative to their actual numbers in the population (the exact comparison was not specified). Another survey of research on television ads found "the picture presented by television commercials is unchanged—the home is the woman's domain" (O'Donnell & O'Donnell, 1978, p. 158).

Culley and Bennett (1975) concluded that "women are portrayed in most advertisements as being more concerned with personal appearances and household matters, and less concerned with durable good purchases and complex decisions" (p. 168). Another study (Schneider & Schneider, 1979) found that women in television ads were "significantly younger, employed less frequently [and were], inside of residences more often than men" (p. 83). And although Scheibe (1979) found more women portrayed as homemakers (21%) than were shown in occupational roles (18.3%), it was only slightly more. Three groups of researchers (Atkin & Miller, 1975; O'Bryant & Corder-Bolz, 1978; Pingree, 1978) studied the effects of commercials portraying women in nontraditional occupations. All three groups found that after grade school children were exposed to these commercials they believed the nontraditional roles to be appropriate for women. The effect was stronger for girls than for boys.

If there were changes in characters portrayed in TV commercials from the 1960s to the 1970s, these mostly involved changes in the portrayal of women. In the decade of the 1970s, at least on television commercials, the number of occupational roles increased for women, but male characters were shown only rarely in traditionally "female" activity such as child care and housework. On television, at least, things seem to have changed more for women than for men.

Nonetheless, in a summary accompanying an annotated bibliography of research on sex-role stereotyping, Courtney and Whipple (1981) noted that:

> women's place in advertising is seen to be in the home, and their (true) labor force roles are underrepresented. Women are typically portrayed as housewives and mothers, as dependent on men, and sometimes as unintelligent and subservient . . . on the other hand, men are depicted as the voices of authority, the older and wiser advice-givers and demonstrators. They (men) are shown in a wider range of occupations and roles in their working and leisure lives or as beneficiaries of women's work in the home. (p. vii)

For additional research on this topic, see Signorielli (1985, 1988) and Steinem (1988).

Recent Research on Character Portrayals

Although this line of research reveals an honest attempt to study advertising, there are many problems with the methods used. In particular, the analyses were often based on a small number of ads drawn in a haphazard way from television. No careful sampling procedure was used to assure that the ads were representative of those shown. In order to overcome these objections, Scheibe (1983) completed a content analysis of character portrayals and values using a large representative sample of commercials drawn from a composite week in March 1981. Scheibe analyzed 2,135 commercials containing more than 6,000 characters, coding each character's sex, age, occupation, "concerns," and social power. It is possible to use the findings of this study to draw a picture of the "world" of television commercials in 1981, and to compare the demographics of that world to same demographic information about the real world in which we live.

Sex.   As previously noted, research on the sex of characters in television programs, described in chapter 3, found three times as many males as females. By contrast, Scheibe found the commercials in her sample to have a nearly equal sex distribution, with about 52% of the characters being male and 48% female. Even though this is still distorted from the real world (U.S. Census figures indicate that about 52% of the actual population is female), it is a much more realistic presentation than that of TV programs.

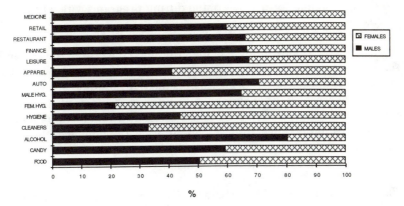

FIG. 7.11. Ratio of male to female characters in TV commercials, by product type. (Information from Scheibe, 1983.)

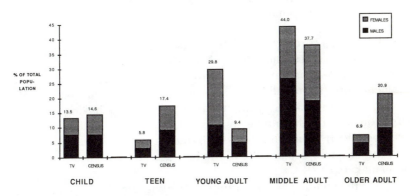

FIG. 7.12. Age and sex distributions for TV commercial characters versus U.S. Census. (Information from Scheibe, 1983.)

Not every product type presents such an egalitarian picture, however. As Fig. 7.11 illustrates, the ratio of female to male characters varied widely by product type. As is apparent from Fig. 7.11, females made up the majority of characters only in commercials for cleaners, hygiene, feminine hygiene/beauty products, apparel, and toys. Males dominated 12 of the 22 product categories, and were most likely to appear in alcohol, autos, leisure/travel, and financial services. As with program–product relationships, the distribution of male and female characters in TV commercials seems to be determined by the target audience. Men advertise products shown during sports programs that are primarily directed toward men, whereas women are more often found selling products designed for use by women during programs with a large audience.

Age. Figure 7.12 illustrates Scheibe's findings concerning the age and sex of TV commercial characters compared with age and sex demographics from the 1980 U.S. Census. As the figure shows, the TV commercials overrepresented young adults by about 3:1 (with the majority being female) and underrepresented teens and older adults. Older adults were underrepresented by about 3:1 with about two thirds of the older adults that were shown being male (whereas in the actual population about two thirds are female).

Race. Just about all of the characters on the TV commercials were white (94%); nearly all of the rest were Black (84% of the remainder). All racial minorities are underrepresented (relative to their true distribution in the population), with Hispanics being the most underrepresented (making up only .2% of the commercials, compared with 6.2% the actual population).

Occupation. According to Scheibe's findings, most characters were shown with no discernable or obvious occupational role. Of the 40% who were shown as having an occupation, only 5% were shown as "homemakers" (almost all female), leaving 35% of the characters (44.5% of the males and 23.6% of the females) portrayed as having some occupation outside the home. In marked contrast to earlier research, Scheibe (1983) found that female characters were shown more often in occupational roles outside of the home (23.6%), than they were as homemakers (9.7%).

When the character demographics found in the world of television commercials are compared to the U.S. Census, the proportion of men to women in most occupational categories was fairly accurate. However, commercials significantly overrepresented white-collar, managerial, and professional occupations (for both males and females) and underrepresented clerical and blue-collar occupations.

Concerns. Scheibe (1983) also described what the characters were "concerned about" in the commercials, what "bothered" the central character (e.g., beauty, or the lack of it; hemorrhoids; rust spots; old age; health and safety of the family). She found that the one overriding concern of characters in TV commercials was having fun. More than anything else, having a good time is what commercials "sell." Drink our beer and you'll have a good time. Drive our car, eat our food, wear our clothes, use our acne medicine, or mouthwash, or toothpaste—and you will have fun.

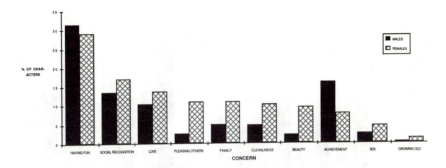

FIG. 7.13. Personal concerns of TV commercial characters, by sex. (Information from Scheibe, 1983.)

Scheibe also found that female characters exhibited more concerns, both product-related and personal, than did male characters. Figure 7.13 shows the frequency distribution of "concerns" for male and female characters. The largest sex differences occur for concerns involving beauty, cleanliness, family, and pleasing others, all of which concerned female characters more than male characters. Males, on the other hand, were significantly more concerned only with achievement and having fun.

Social Power. In order to more clearly investigate earlier claims that women were portrayed as "powerless" or "helpless," Scheibe (1983) coded the social power exhibited by each character (using French & Raven's, 1960, categories of social power). These include four categories of power: power of approval/reward; its antithesis, seeking approval or reward; expert power (based on knowledge or ability); and its antithesis, seeking expertise. Characters frequently exhibited more than one type of power. According to Scheibe (1983), this is illustrated by:

> the typical food commercial in which the wife knows how to prepare a meal . . . but seeks approval from her family when she serves it, while her husband gives his approval for a well-prepared meal, but also asks for help or information ("How do you make your fried chicken so crisp?") (p. 60)

Surprisingly, Scheibe found few differences between male and female characters in the social power they exhibited. Males and females were equally likely to have power of approval, expert power, and to

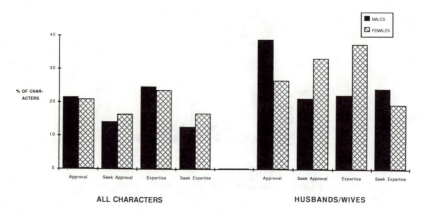

FIG. 7.14. Social power of TV commercial characters, by sex. (Information from Scheibe, 1983.)

seek approval, although female characters were more likely to seek expertise from others than male characters were. These similarities were also true when the characters were shown in occupational roles. In spouse or parent roles, however, significant sex differences did emerge. As shown in Fig. 7.14, female characters shown as either wives or mothers were much more likely to have expert power and to seek approval from others, whereas males shown as husbands and fathers were more likely to have power of approval.

So, although there are differences in what males and females in commercials are "concerned about" and what kinds of power they are shown as having, there are many similarities as well. When the characters were shown as having an occupation, the male and female characters were portrayed as having largely equivalent amounts and kinds of power. However, when characters were shown in a family context, as either spouses or parents, females were more often shown as the expert (they know how to bake a pie or cure a pesky cough), whereas males were more commonly portrayed as having final approval ("What a tasty, flakey pie!" "My cough is better now, you sure know how to fix it.").

Social Values in Commercials

In addition to presenting characters in various roles with concerns and social power, commercials have strong general value orientations. In commercials it is good to have certain qualities (clean teeth, clean floors, pleasant breath), and it is bad to have other qualities (soiled collars, itchy dandruff, body odor). Commercials, by what they portray and how they portray it, express a set of values, and it is possible to analyze these and thus to establish a "value profile" for a given product. Commercials often express what is positively valued by what you may *gain* from the use of their product, and what is negatively valued by what the viewer will *avoid* by using the product. If we are interested in studying the kinds of effects commercials have on individuals who are exposed to them, an analysis of the values presented in commercials may be one of the most fruitful ways to do so (Ball-Rokeach, Rokeach, & Grube, 1985).

Scheibe (1983) analyzed the values expressed in commercials using a scale developed by Rokeach (1979). In this scheme, values are divided into those traits that are a "means" to a goal (called *instrumental* values) and those traits that represent the goals themselves (*terminal* values). A person might value hard work because it leads to financial security, for example; hard work would be the instrumental value, and financial security the terminal value. Figure 7.15 gives the frequency distribution for values found in all commercials coded by Scheibe in her 1983 study.

The most frequently occurring instrumental values were "capable," "helpful," and "smart," whereas the least frequent instrumental values were "courageous," "forgiving," and "physically powerful." Of the values related to personal appearance, the most frequently stressed were "beautiful" and "youthful." Surprisingly, given the amount of criticism concerning sex in advertising (Courtney & Whipple, 1981; Komisar, 1971), Scheibe found the instrumental value "sexy" appeared relatively infrequently—in only about 6% of the commercials she analyzed.

In contrast to the instrumental values, one terminal value clearly dominated the rest: "happiness." The value of "happiness" was present in nearly 60% of all commercials, appearing more than twice as often as any other value. "Social recognition" was the second most frequent terminal value, followed by "family well-being." Self-serving or self-oriented terminal values (e.g., personal happiness, an exciting life, social recognition) appeared much more frequently than those more altruistic or "other-oriented" values (e.g., equality, friendship). Apparently sex as a terminal value is not a central concern either; the terminal value "sexual gratification" occurred infrequently as a desirable goal (only 3.5% of the time).

The values projected in commercials differed depending on the time, and program during which they were shown, and even more so by product type. Some values were almost entirely product specific. Medicine commercials accounted for nearly all commercials stressing "free-

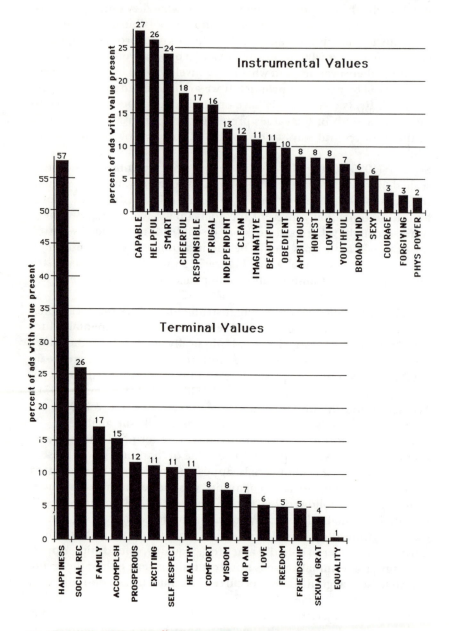

FIG. 7.15. Frequency distribution of instrumental and terminal values in TV commercials. (Information from Scheibe, 1983.)

dom from pain" (but for only 8% of commercials stressing "a healthy life"). Ads for feminine hygiene/beauty and apparel accounted for nearly 50% of all commercials stressing "beautiful," "sexy," and "sexual gratification." More than 70% of ads stressing "a prosperous life" were for retail products, finance, or autos.

As noted, the value "happiness" or "having fun" was the most common value stressed in commercials. Overall, 57.4% of the commercials stressed happiness. Happiness ranged from a low of 16.7% during religious programs to a high of 84.3% for commercials shown during children's programs. The product types *least* frequently showing "happiness" were male hygiene/beauty (33.3%), PSAs (28.4%), and medicines (26.3%); those showing "happiness" most frequently were for soda (88.6%), toys (85.2%), and restaurants (84.4%).

As the aforementioned suggests, it was possible to develop a "value profile" for a particular type of program, product or time period, as well as to determine the values for programs having a high proportion of a specific audience. Value profiles for the four time periods described earlier in this chapter (Saturday morning, weekday daytime, weekend afternoon, and prime time) are shown in Fig. 7.16.

Commercials on children's programs were very different from the overall sample, stressing much *more* frequently the "capable," "imaginative," "physically powerful," "happiness," "an exciting life," and "friendship," and *less* frequently the values of "helpful," "smart," "frugal," "clean," "responsible," "obedient," and "a healthy life." In short, commercials designed for children had lower frequencies than the overall sample for nearly all altruistic values; they tend, instead, to stress playing hard, having fun, and being happy. They rarely stress being helpful, or obedient, or the value of good health.

Figure 7.16 also illustrates the differences between the values in ads aimed at women (shown during weekday daytime) and the ads aimed at men (weekend afternoon). Women's ads were more likely to stress being "helpful," "cheerful," "beautiful," "youthful," "family well-being," and "social recognition." Men's ads were more likely to stress being "ambitious," "capable," "powerful," "physical comfort," "an exciting life," and "sexual gratification."

TV commercials reflect some of America's obsession with youthfulness, dieting, cleanliness, pets, sugared cereals, and the like. They also reflect the values and interests of the product makers, of course. But the reasons *why* such values are shown in commercials is irrelevant to an analysis of their influence on the audience. What is important is to draw some profile of the information contained on television commercials, and then to study the influence of this information on those exposed to it.

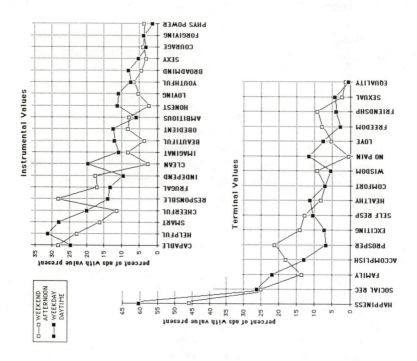

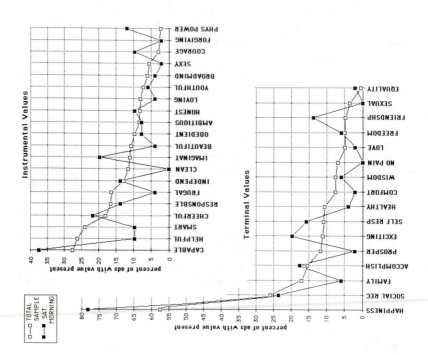

FIG. 7.16. (a) Value profile for Saturday morning commercials versus all TV commercials. (b) Value profile for weekend afternoon (men's) commercials versus weekday daytime (women's) commercials. (Information from Schnibe, 1992.)

Commercials on television do not run the gamut of all products, goods and services, available to the average citizen. Rather, the companies who find it profitable to advertise on network television are those that sell packaged food, and who are large enough to have a nationwide distribution network. In a field where there are several products all containing essentially the same ingredient, advertising helps to set one product apart from the others. Aspirin is a good example. Because the Food and Drug Administration (FDA) limits the name "aspirin" to products containing a given drug—acetoacetic acid—all aspirin products on the market are essentially the same in their basic ingredient.

Regulation of the Content of Commercials

As we saw in chapter 1, although the program content of television is not regulated due to constitutional limitations on government interference in free speech, the same is not true of commercials. Advertisements on television are subject to regulation, they are not considered "protected speech."

The Federal Trade Commission is the governmental body charged with the regulation of advertisements, including those on television, and the networks have their own guidelines about what can and cannot be said on a commercial. Rules that govern the rest of broadcasting apply to commercials as well: It is not permissible, for example, to use obscenity or to display nudity. In addition, as we see in chapter 8, the FTC defines as inappropriate ads that are "false" and/or "deceptive," and these terms have specific definitions that have the effect of limiting the content of commercials (we consider these terms with respect to ads for children in chapter 8).

Rules limiting the content of commercials often do not accomplish what they were intended to accomplish. Consider beer drinking, for example. The FTC has a rule that prohibits showing the drinking of alcohol. This rule only applies to advertisements not programs. The rule is enforced in such a way that only the actual act of drinking is prohibited, the ad *may* show a person in a bar, holding a bottle of beer; the ad may show a person holding a bottle full at one time and empty at another, and so on. As such, there is a serious question of whether this regulation accomplishes it purpose.

Most of the rules seem to come down to a matter of "taste." Nudity is not shown because it is not considered "tasteful" in the family content in which viewing may occur. Intimate personal sanitation has become more tasteful over the years, from being forbidden in the early days of television to one of the most frequently advertised product types on television (Scheibe & Condry, 1988). It is now permissible to show "feminine hygiene" products (douches, vaginal sprays, sanitary napkins, etc.), even though this kind of product was rarely seen in the early days of television. In fact, toilet paper was once considered difficult to market in a "tasteful" way.

So, although television commercials are bound by some rules of good taste, on the whole there is little regulation of commercials on television directed toward adults. In the world of television, the motto *caveat emptor* (buyer beware) is assumed to apply. Adults, by and large, are assumed to be able to "defend themselves" against the claims made by commercial makers. The same is not true of children, as we see in some detail in chapter 8. In the next section, we look at the structure and content of ads directed toward children. What are children who watch television, nearly all children in the United States, persuaded to want and consume? What types of products and how many are advertised on television designed for children? How do these commercials compare to advertisements at other times of the day and week, when other audiences are watching?

COMMERCIALS DESIGNED FOR CHILDREN

Of special interest in the study of ads on television has been the characteristics of commercials designed for children. There are many obvious reasons for this concern, foremost among them the relative helplessness of children and the ease with which they can be manipulated.

In this section, we look at a description of the ads on television that are directed toward children. Are commercials directed to children somehow different in either form or content from other ads? We have already seen that the value profile of children's ads differs in certain ways compared to the values expressed in all ads. How else are commercials for children different?

A Brief History of Programs and Ads for Children

In the 1950s, the early days of television broadcasting, a relatively large proportion of the programs were for children, but few of these had paid sponsors (Adler et al., 1980). The networks and local stations put them on as part of a wider campaign to sell television sets to families just reunited after World War II ("Buy it for the kids"). It is perhaps worth noting that the same claims are now being made for why a family should purchase a computer.

As the number of sponsored programs began to increase, however, programs for children were slowly pushed off the air to make room for paying customers" (Adler et al., 1980; Barnouw, 1982). Thus, in the early days of television, children were seen as a convenient excuse to sell the sets, but they were not viewed as a major consumer group. Then, in the early 1960s, cereal manufacturers "discovered" the child audience, and they began to sponsor Saturday morning programs and ads designed to attract and hold the attention of a child audience (Melody, 1973).

What is an ad "directed toward children?" Although it is true that child viewing is not exclusively confined to any particular time of the day, week, or year (see chapter 2) the audience ranging in age from 2 to 12 is especially large after school (from 4 p.m. to 6 p.m. on weekdays) and on Saturday mornings from 7 a.m. until noon (Adler et al., 1980; Nielsen, 1984). It is not unreasonable to call programs during these times "children's programs," in that they are clearly and obviously designed for children and watched, primarily, by children (Nielsen, 1984).

Commercials during these programs may be called "children's commercials," for much the same reason: They are clearly designed for and attractive to children. They feature products consumed by children (toys, cereals, and candy), they show children consuming the product, and they have design characteristics (such as the use of animation) known to be particularly effective with children.

What Products are Advertised to Children?

During the 1970s, F. Earle Barcus, a professor of communication at Boston University, was commissioned by Action for Children's Television, a consumer group, to survey and describe the *nature* and *content* of commercials designed for children. Throughout the decade of the 1970s, Barcus conducted a number of surveys and issued several reports of his findings. These studies provide important historical evidence about commercials for children. In the following sections we look at Barcus' findings and compare them to a study conducted in our research lab at Cornell of the "nonprogram" content of Saturday morning children's television.

Drawing his first sample in the Boston area in June 1971, Barcus found that, on the average, 20% of each Saturday morning hour was devoted to commercials. Some stations in his sample devoted as much as 25% of the hour to nonprogram material on Saturday morning and weekday (after school) television programs. According to Barcus' initial report, in 1971, an average hour of children's programming contained 26 commercial messages (one every 2.8 minutes). In a second sample taken in November 1971, Barcus found 24% of the average hour of children's television time was devoted to commercials.

Drawing another sample in 1975, Barcus found that the amount of time devoted to commercials had *decreased substantially* (20% to 15.9%) between 1971 and 1975, although the number of messages remained about the same. This was due partly to the introduction of the 30-second commercial.

Barcus' last reported survey of nonprogram content on children's programs (of 33 hours of programming in the Boston area) was released in 1978, and it included a detailed analysis of both types of products advertised to children, and techniques used by advertisers in these commercials. This study found that "on the average the child is exposed to 15 commercial messages, five program promotions and two public service announcements per viewing hours" (Barcus, 1980, p. 275); 80% of all ads fell into one of four product categories: cereals, toys, candy, and fast food restaurants.

What Techniques are Used in Children's Ads?

Different product types vary in basic presentational formats, as we have already noted when looking at values in commercials. Within any category of ads, the formats are usually similar, so that most car ads resemble one another, as do most soap ads, and insurance ads and so on.

Children's ads differ from adult ads in that they use more animation and more references to "magical" events or people (Atkin, 1980). By contrast, most toy ads are *nonanimated* using live action scenes to illustrate the product. Other than toy ads, products advertised to children lean heavily on animation, often in conjunction with nonanimated scenes (Barcus, 1980). There are fewer testimonials on children's ads, and also fewer straight sales messages by announcers or performers. Children's ads seldom urge the child to pressure the parent to buy the product, although there is substantial evidence that such pressure exists (Sheikh & Moleski, 1977). Finally, the use of premium offers (Atkin, 1982) and celebrities (Ross, Wartella, & Lovelace, 1982), are two techniques known to be especially effective in ads for children. Barcus (1980) reported that "premiums were offered in 28% of cereal ads in 1971, 47% in 1975, and 25% in 1977" (p. 277).

Recent Data on Children's Commercials

One of the most recent analysis of ads designed for children was done in our research lab at Cornell, based on data collected from 1983 to 1987 (Condry, Bence, & Scheibe, 1988). The purpose of the study was to replicate and extend the work described earlier by Barcus and his colleagues on the content and structure of "children's" ads.

Bence, Scheibe, and Condry drew a sample of 60 hours of Saturday morning television from our archive of television content at Cornell University: the 5 hours between 7 a.m. and 12 noon on one Saturday in each of 4 months (March, June, September, and December) for 1983, 1985, and 1987. These 60 hours were distributed evenly across the three major networks.

The content of the hour of programming was divided for analysis into program and nonprogram content. Nonprogram content consisted of commercials, Public Service Announcements (PSAs), and program promotions (promos), and drop-ins. The content of each commercial, the product advertised, was coded using categories collapsed for "cereals," "soda, candy, and snacks," "sugared foods, snacks, and beverages," "restaurants," "toys and games," and the general category "other products" (e.g., hygiene, retail, medicine, apparel, etc.).

Average Hour of Saturday Morning Television. Combining the data for all 3 years sampled, an average hour of Saturday morning television contains 11.8 minutes of nonprogram material, with product commercials taking up an average of 8.3 minutes of the hour (69.3% of all nonprogram minutes), PSAs 1.4 minutes (12.3%), promos 1.1 minutes (9.4%), and drop-ins 1.0 minutes (9.0%).

The average number of minutes devoted to each of these four types of nonprogram messages on Saturday morning can be compared to the same data for other time periods of the week, as illustrated in Fig. 7.6. It will be recalled that the number of total minutes devoted to nonprogram messages varied widely across the broadcast week, with the fewest on Sunday morning (about 5 minutes per hour) and the most during weekday daytime (nearly 16 minutes per hour). As Fig. 7.6 illustrated, the Saturday morning time period had the third lowest number of minutes devoted to product commercials and to total nonprogram material, and highest number of minutes devoted to PSAs and drop-ins.

The relative proportion of different types of nonprogram messages depends on whether the measure is time (average number of minutes per hour) or frequency (average number of messages per hour). Because the different message types vary a great deal in length, the measure used makes a difference, especially for PSAs, promos, and drop-ins. Promos are generally short (3–20 seconds) and therefore appear with high frequency but take up little overall time in the average hour. PSAs and drop-ins, on the other hand, are generally longer (sometimes 1–2 minutes in length) and therefore take up a larger proportion of time in the average hour than their relative frequency would suggest. In an average hour of Saturday morning television, there are 16–17 product commercials (66.9% of all non-program messages), 4–5 program promos (18.4%), 2–3 PSAs (11.4%), and 1 drop-in (3.7%).

Variations in Frequency of Nonprogram Messages by Year. There was no significant change in the total number of minutes devoted to nonprogram content in the average hour of Saturday morning programming across the 3 years of the sample (1983, 1985, and 1987). However, there was a significant increase in the overall number of nonprogram messages per hour, from 22.1 in 1983 to 26.9 in 1987, due in part to the shortening of the messages (as previously shown in Fig. 7.5).

There were also significant changes in both the frequency and amount of time devoted to the different types of messages presented during the average hour, as shown in Fig. 7.17. The average number of product commercials per hour has steadily increased, from 13.8 in 1963 to 19.3 in 1987. Also, although the total time devoted to nonprogram messages did not change, the number of minutes devoted to product commercials increased significantly each year. The proportion of nonprogram message time devoted to commercials rose significantly from 62.8% in 1983, to 66.4% in 1985, to 78.6% in 1987.

Promos declined in 1985, and then rose slightly in 1987. Drop-ins rose in 1985 and then almost disappeared in 1987; drop-ins accounted

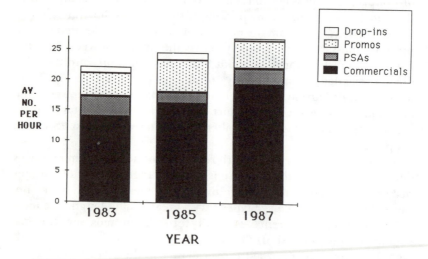

FIG. 7.17. Average number of nonprogram messages per hour on Saturday morning television, by message type and year. (Information from Condry, Bence, & Scheibe, 1988.)

for 13.4% of all nonprogram minutes in 1985, but only 3.3% in 1987 (less than one every 2 hours).

The average number of PSAs per hour dropped in 1985 (from 3.5 to 2.0), and then rose again to 2.8 in 1987. However, the decrease in 1985 came almost entirely for general-audience PSAs, with most of the remaining PSAs ($N = 28$, or 70% of the total) being directed specifically at children or teens. The subsequent rise in total PSAs in 1987 occurred primarily in general-audience PSAs, whereas the number of PSAs for children actually declined ($N = 25$), with over half of those containing anti-drug, anti-alcohol, or anti-smoking messages. Although health and nutrition ads directed toward children or teens were frequent in the earlier years, they had disappeared by 1987.

Variations by Time Slot.   Although the overall number of minutes per hour increased since 1983, the relative distribution of messages and total time across the five hourly time slots of Saturday morning (7 a.m. to noon) did not change significantly over the 5 years covered by the study. In general, the total time devoted to nonprogram messages ranged from 11 to 12.5 minutes per hour across the five time slots of the Saturday morning period, with the highest number of advertising minutes during the middle hour of the morning (9–10 a.m.).

The way in which the time is distributed among the four types of messages did vary across the time slots, however. The percentage time devoted to product commercials in each of the five time slots reflects an inverted U-shaped curve, with the highest percentage (85.8%) during the middle of the morning and the lowest (53.2%) during the 7–8 a.m. time slot. Conversely, other types of messages are more likely to be shown during the early or later hours of the morning. This is especially true for PSAs, which account for a large percentage of the first hour (18.3%) and last hour (11.5%) of the morning, but are rarely shown between 9 and 11 a.m. when the audience is largest.

Frequency Distribution by Product Type.   As we have noted, the average number of product commercials has increased steadily over the 3 years sampled. Commercial messages were also identified by the type of product advertised, and as Fig. 7.18 illustrates, the number of commercials increased in nearly all product categories. This increase was most dramatic for toys and games; cereal, candy and snacks, and restaurant ads all dipped slightly in 1985 and then rose again substantially in 1987.

Variations by Season (Month) of Year.   As noted earlier, the number of

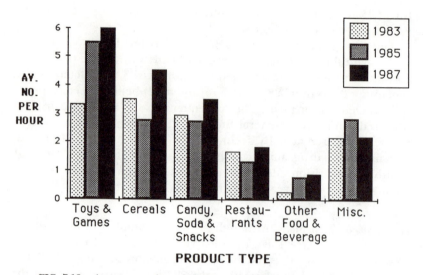

FIG. 7.18. Average number of commercial messages per hour on Saturday morning for selected product types, by year. (Information from Condry, Bence, & Scheibe, 1988.)

minutes and relative distribution of nonprogram messages varies somewhat across the seasons of the year, with December generally being quite different from the other 3 months (March, June, September), the same is true of children's ads. Nearly half of all commercials on Saturday morning in December were advertising toys and games (46.6%), twice the proportion found in the other 3 months (23%–26%). December consequently contained fewer ads for cereals (16.2%, compared with 20%–28% in the other months) and candy/snacks (7.7%, compared with 21%–24% in the other months). In all 3 years, December had the fewest number of minutes devoted to product commercials and the most minutes of PSAs.

Variations by Network. The distribution of nonprogram messages and product types varied a great deal across the three networks in 1983, although these differences decreased substantially over the 3 years of the study. As Fig. 7.19 shows, the NBC affiliate devoted the largest percentage of nonprogram message minutes to product commercials in all 3 years of the study, and the smallest to promos and PSAs (showing only about one third of the number of PSAs presented on the other two networks). The ABC affiliate had the highest number of total minutes of nonprogram messages in all 3 years, due largely to PSAs

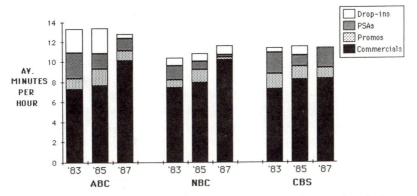

FIG. 7.19.   Minutes of nonprogram messages on Saturday morning television for ABC, NBC, and CBS, by year. (Information from Condry, Bence, & Scheibe, 1988.)

and drop-ins until 1987, when such messages nearly disappeared. Although the number of commercial minutes increased on all three networks, ABC showed the greatest increase in minutes devoted to product commercials (from 7.28 minutes in 1983, to 7.64 minutes in 1985, to 10.11 minutes in 1987).

There was steady decline in the frequency and number of minutes of PSAs on both ABC and NBC, but not on CBS. Drop-ins, which had been most frequent on ABC, dropped to almost nothing on both ABC and CBS; NBC, however, which had a low number of minutes of drop-ins in 1983 and 1985, actually increased their minutes of drop-ins slightly in 1987.

Toy ads increased on all three networks, with ABC having the highest frequency and proportion in all 3 years. NBC had the highest number of cereal ads, and CBS had the least, in all years. The average number of product commercials per hour increased each year on ABC and NBC, but not on CBS. NBC had the highest number of product commercials per hour in each of the 3 years, with 21.8 commercials/hour in 1987 (compared to 20.1/hour for ABC and 16.3/hour for CBS).

The average number of minutes devoted to program and nonprogram content on children's television has remained remarkably steady, at least since the early 1970s when Barcus began his research (Barcus, 1972). About 80% of the average hour is devoted to program material, with the remaining 20%, or 12 minutes, devoted to nonprogram material (including commercials, promos, PSAs, and drop-ins). Most of this nonprogram time is taken up by product commercials, especially commercials for toys, cereals, and heavily sugared snacks. Over the 3 years studied, on the average, there were 16–17 product commercials during an hour of Saturday morning television, taking up a little over 8 minutes, along with 8 or 9 other messages for promos, PSAs, or drop-ins.

Although the number of minutes of nonprogram content has stayed fairly constant over the past 5 years, the number of messages shown during those minutes has increased steadily. This is due largely to the increase in presenting shorter 10-second and 15-second messages, especially for PSAs and drop-ins. Furthermore, the proportion of both frequency and minutes of nonprogram messages that are taken up by product commercials (especially toy commercials) has risen dramatically in the past several years, although the proportion of time devoted to educational and informational messages (such as PSAs and drop-ins) has generally declined.

Aside from the descriptive value of these findings, one of the most important lessons to be drawn from these analyses is the value of updating information about the nature of television for children. Several generalizations from the findings of 1983 were no longer true in 1985; some of what was true in 1985 had changed again in 1987. Over the years of this study the number of minutes devoted to nonprogram content has remained remarkably steady, whereas the frequency of messages—across all categories—has risen significantly, so that children are being exposed to more commercial messages than ever before.

This type of descriptive information about the television environment is crucial for the study of children's television, especially as federal agencies, Congressional committees, consumer action groups, and television researchers continue the process of determining the extent to which such persuasive messages influence the beliefs, values, and behaviors of the children who see them.

Is Advertising to Children Effective?

The term *effective* requires definition. There are several possible ways of looking at it. There is evidence (reviewed by Atkin, 1982) that children exposed to the type of toy and food advertisement just described *desire* the products, *ask* their parents to provide these same products, and then *consume* them. As we saw earlier, each of these measures could be taken as an example of the effectiveness of commercials.

Commercials designed for children are effective in getting children to *recognize* and *want* or *desire* the products advertised (Caron & Ward, 1975; Donohue, 1975; Ward, Wackman, & Wartella, 1977). Children and parents name television as the major source of their information about products (Barry & Sheikh, 1977; Howard, Hulbert, & Lehmann, 1973; Ward et al., 1977).

Products for Children. We saw that edibles of one sort or another is the largest single category of products advertised on television, so it should not come as a surprise that ads for food, beverages, and other edibles are common (greater than half of all ads), on programs for children (Adler et al., 1980; Condry, Bence, & Scheibe, 1988; FTC Staff Report, 1978). Studies done in the late 1970s showed about 75% of ads on children's programs were for edibles. In our 1983–1987 survey of ads, 50% were of this type.

Desiring Advertised Products. Focusing on the kinds of food advertised on children's programs, heavily sugared candy and cereals, researchers have found that these ads have both specific and general effects. That is, watching the ads apparently influences what children think and feel about certain specific products, and about food in general. In research on specific desires promoted by ads, Atkin (1979) found a strong positive relationship between viewing television commercials and liking the 12 most frequently advertised foods. The effect was stronger for heavy viewers than light viewers. In addition, Atkin and Gibson (1978) found that 90% of children exposed to a "Pebbles Cereal" commercial wanted to eat the cereal compared to 66% of the group not exposed to this commercial. Similar findings for the influence of commercials on desire for a product have been demonstrated by Gorn and Goldberg (1977), Goldberg and Gorn (1978), and Resnik and Stern (1977).

Asking for Advertised Products. Children ask their parents for products advertised on television (Atkin, 1975b, 1975c; Clancy-Hepburn, Hickey, & Neville, 1974; Galst & White, 1976), and these requests result in a certain amount of parent–child conflict, especially when the child is young (Condry, 1978, FTC testimony). Finally, children are quite aware that although they may *want* many of the products on television, they will ask their parents for relatively few. In one study, children completing a projective technique (a story completion task) about a child watching television, indicated that they were aware of the large difference between *wanting* something advertised on television and *asking* their parents to buy the product. The children said that 90% of the time the child depicted in the story would "want" the product shown on television, but the child (presumably a projection of themselves) would only be willing to *ask for it* 60% of the time (Sheikh & Moleski, 1977).

Consuming the Product. Finally, to return to the primary consideration of advertisers, there is evidence that children consume the products advertised on television (Atkin, 1979, 1982; Sharaga, 1974). There is also research showing that brand name identification *increases* with age such that older children rather than younger children will ask their parents for specific brands of cereal and candy advertised (Ward et al., 1977). These requests, in turn, are related to actual consumption (Atkin, 1979).

Overall there is substantial evidence that after being exposed to television ads children *desire* the products, *request* the productions from their parents, and when they are successful in getting it, *consume* the products. By all of these measures we would have to say that advertising to children *is* effective in terms of the effects desired by advertisers.

Unintended Effects

There are many ways to be influenced by the persuasive messages of television that are not intended by those who design and show the ads. The same was true of programs. It is reasonable to assume that no network official ever intended for television watching to interfere with reading, or to stimulate violence. Network programmers were just "doing their job" collecting audiences to sell to advertisers.

In this section we consider three kinds of unintended effects of commercials that have been discovered in research: (a) the rapid paced format so attractive to commercial makers because of its attention getting and holding capacities may also be responsible for a certain amount of aggressive behavior in children; (b) the capacity of commercials to stimulate parent–child conflict, already noted; and (c) the fact that commercials display information that may be misinterpreted by the immature mind.

Formal Features and Comprehension.   In his research on the techniques used by advertisers, Barcus (1980) noted that many ads use unusual sounds and sights to grasp and hold the attention of children, and we saw in the last chapter how current-day researchers call these devices "formal features" (lively music, sound effects, unusual voices) and, studying program content, have shown that these are to be associated with high levels of attention as we noted in chapter 6.

Greer et al. (1982), for example, have shown that the formal features of "action" and "pace" are as common in ads for children as they are in children's programs. The rapid pace and action have the effect of drawing the child's wandering attention back to the screen. But Greer and his colleagues also found that these "high salient" commercials were associated with *aggression* in preschoolers, possibly through the mechanism of "arousal" discussed in chapter 4 (Zillmann, 1982).

Formal Features and Attention. As we also saw in our discussion of comprehension and attention to programs in the last chapter, the formal features of a program may serve to "signal" the kind of information that is about to come. Children use these features to determine whether a program is designed for them or not (Wright & Huston, 1983). A more recent study by this same research group (at the University of Kansas) has shown that children are able to discriminate the formal features of an advertisement for male toys from female toys (Huston et al., 1984).

Nutritional Information. A second type of unintended effect ads have on children is to influence a child's notion of "good nutrition." As we have seen, about half of the ads on children's programs are for (heavily sugared) food. One question that has arisen concerns the effect of these ads on "nutrition awareness" of children who watch them. In children's ads, children are most often shown having fun, enjoying food; the nutritional values of food are seldom mentioned. Although ads on children's programs often mention the importance of eating a "balanced" breakfast, it is unclear whether children understand what is meant by this term.

Children who are heavy viewers of television seldom mention "nutrition" as a central aspect they use when evaluating food (Atkin, 1975b; Leaman, 1973; Ward et al., 1977). Atkin (1979) found viewing of TV to be *unrelated* to "salience of nutrition" to the child, although he did find viewing related to "fun of eating cereal and candy," "the premium contained in the cereal box," and "the chewiness and lastingness of candy" (Atkin, 1979, p. 197).

This last set of attitudes about the "chewiness" and "lastingness" of candy are exactly what the commercials stress (Atkin, 1982), of course, and it is a cause for concern. It is exactly these features of heavily sugared food that dentists believe to be bad for teeth. The longer sugar stays in the mouth, for example, the greater the risk of tooth decay (FTC Staff Report, 1978).

Unintended Interpretations of Visual Messages. Although the advertisers have one thing in mind when they show a commercial, the manner in which it influences children may be on quite another level. The many ads for soft drinks worry some nutritionists because if exposed to this idea enough, children may come to think only of soft drinks when they are thirsty, instead of the healthier glass of water (Gussow, 1972).

In other instances, the intended message will be missed and another substituted by children who understand more of what they see than what they hear (because for many children language is not yet well developed). In one ad, marketed briefly, a naturalist was shown walking through the woods eating nuts and berries from the bushes and trees.

Children exposed to this ad were more likely to rate similar appearing *toxic plants* as edible (Poulos, 1975). Clearly, this outcome was not intended by the advertiser, and the commercial contained a "disclaimer" stating that not everything in the woods was edible. But verbal warnings or disclaimers, unless they are designed to be understood by young children, are often ineffective.

One study showed children a typical toy ad from Saturday morning television containing the common disclaimer "assembly required." Children of different ages were asked what this phrase meant. Although most third graders understood the meaning, few second and first graders had any idea what it meant. Then, these same researchers showed the same commercial, containing the disclaimer "you have to put it together." Now most of the first graders and all of the second graders understood the message (Liebert, Sprafkin, Liebert, & Rubinstein, 1977).

Children's Understanding of the Nature of Commercials

A basic tenant of communication theory is that awareness of the persuasive intent of a communicator may act as a "defense" against the message (Hovland, Janis, & Kelley, 1953). Adults *are* often aware of the nature of such transactions, but to what extent are children? To what extent are children aware of the selling–buying relationship and all that it entails? To what extent are children aware of the "selling" or "persuasive" intent of the commercial? If they are not aware of it, does this lack of knowledge make them unfairly vulnerable? We consider this issue again in the next chapter when we discuss government policy toward television ads.

What do children need in order for them to defend themselves against the unwanted influences of television ads? Two well-known researchers, one a communications expert and the other a developmental psychologist, argue that in order for a child to discount an influence attempt of the sort most common on television ads, the viewer must:

1. recognize the persuasive intent of the message;
2. realize that such communications may involve "biased" information;
3. be motivated to "counterargue," and
4. have the knowledge or experience necessary to provide adequate counter-arguments (Roberts & Maccoby, 1973, cited in Goldberg & Gorn, 1978, p. 25).

How Does the Understanding of the Nature of Commercials Develop?

There are two questions hidden in this one. First, when can children *tell the difference* between a commercial and a program, that is, how early is this discrimination made? And second, when do children learn that commercials are persuasive messages? A third question, important from the standpoint of social policy, is: Does having knowledge of the "selling intent" of an ad give children who possess it a "defense" against commercials, and so be less "vulnerable" to them? (FTC Staff Report, 1978.)

Discriminating Ads from Programs.   Several researchers have interpreted *shifts in attention* with commercial onset as evidence that children discriminate between commercials and programs (Gaines & Esserman, 1981; Ward, Levinson, & Wackman, 1972; Ward & Wackman, 1973). These studies show that even very young children *notice* that commercials and programs are different types of television content. Research by Levin, Petros, and Petrella (1982), for example, has demonstrated that preschoolers (3–5 years of age) are able to tell the difference between commercials and programs. The ability to make this distinction increases with age (Zuckerman, Ziegler, & Stevenson, 1978) and may be related to other cognitive abilities.

Selling Intent.   Other researchers have asked children directly about what they understand of the selling intent of a commercial (Blatt, Spencer, & Ward, 1972; Rossiter & Robertson, 1974; Ward, 1972; Ward & Wackman, 1973; Ward et al., 1977). Robertson and Rossiter (1974), for example, studied children's attributions regarding persuasive versus assistive intent in commercials. That is, to what extent are children aware of the fact that commercials contain information that can be used to *assist* purchase needs (assistive intent), compared to their awareness of the fact that commercials also intend to *persuade* the viewer to want the product. In a study of nearly 300 youngsters (all boys) from first, third, and fifth grades, Robertson and Rossiter (1974) asked about the intent of commercials, and about the degree to which the child saw them as "trustworthy, good sources of information, or untrustworthy."

Children in all three grades thought commercials were good at "helping you" with information about the product, but the understanding of the "other" purpose of the commercial, the persuasive intent, increased dramatically from first through fifth grade. First graders seem to have little grasp of this relationship, so, to the extent that such knowledge provides a "defense" against commercials, first graders would lack this defense.

These findings are supported by other research (Blatt et al., 1972; Ward & Wackman, 1973; Ward et al., 1977). One of the consequences of this increasing awareness of the persuasiveness and manipulativeness of the commercial for children is an openly expressed decrease in trust and liking for them (Robertson & Rossiter, 1974; Ward et al., 1977).

Defending Against Ads.   The final question about the knowledge of the nature of commercials concerns whether children who are fully aware of "selling intent" are any better able to defend against them. Does the knowledge of persuasive intent make the child any less "vulnerable" to the messages? Are people with knowledge of selling intent less manipulated or persuaded by commercials?

Although as children get older they are more knowledgeable and more "cynical" about commercials, there is little evidence that these same children are *any less persuaded* by them:

> Children's ability to recognize persuasive intent in commercials should not be taken as implying immunity to all commercials; clearly individual commercials may be highly persuasive for a given child, just as for adults. Attribution of persuasive intent merely signifies that the child has acquired the general capability to recognize commercial persuasion. (Robertson & Rossiter, 1974, p. 19)

On the other hand, the question of "defense" is a complicated one, requiring a more exact hypothesis before it can be answered definitively. No research has yet shown that children with a knowledge of selling intent are better able to "defend" themselves, perhaps only because no one has been able to define the terms with sufficient precision to study them. We return to this issue when we discuss social policy and government regulation in the next chapter.

THE EFFECTS OF TV COMMERCIALS

How do commercials work? How do they accomplish what they are designed to accomplish? What sort of influences do they have on those who view them? Let us return to the distinction between the *effects* and the *effectiveness* of ads. Recall that *effectiveness* refers to the question of whether a person exposed to the ad eventually comes to *want* the product, *buy* the product, and *consume* the product.

As we have noted, there is research showing that commercials are "effective" in this sense, in the sense of being successful in bringing about specific attitude and behavior change (Atkin, 1982; Coe & MacLachlan, 1980; Krugman, 1965; Sawyer & Ward, 1977; Vaughn, 1980; Ward et al., 1977). Most of the research on the effectiveness of a given ad is in the hands of the companies that produce and market the ads, and who measure their own effectiveness. This evidence is not public property. There are, however, theories of advertising effectiveness that have been published. In the next section we look at some of these theories.

Commercials may influence us in ways other than those that are intended, and we call these unintended consequences the *effects* of television ads. We should notice, at the outset, that an ad may have an "effect" on a person even though, in the eyes of the advertiser, it was not "effective." We begin, however, with a theory of ad effectiveness.

McGuire's Theory of Ads: Stages in the Persuasive Process

Several psychological models have arisen to explain the effectiveness of advertising (see e.g., Atkin, 1982; Roberts, 1978; Roberts & Maccoby, 1973; Robertson, 1979). We look at one proposed by William J. McGuire (1969). McGuire was part of the communications research group at Yale University directed by Carl Hovland during the late 1940s and early 1950s. This group of social psychologists was responsible for many of the early research studies on the topic of persuasion and propaganda. McGuire's model, then, is typical of the classic social-psychological models of the persuasive process.

In McGuire's model, an ad is *effective* if it passes through several stages of a decision-making process and arrives at the end point of the person *buying the product*. Each stage in the process is a decision that must be made or an event that must take place in order for a commercial to be successful. There are things the advertiser can do at each stage to maximize the likelihood of a successful outcome, and we consider some of these as we look at McGuire's theory. The stages in the persuasive process are called: *exposure, attention, comprehension, yielding, retention,* and *decision to buy.* Each stage in the sequence must be passed in order to go on to the next. Failure (a "no" answer) at any stage takes a person "out" of the process. The ad is effective if the viewer gets to the end of the sequence and answers "yes" to the final decision (i.e., to buy the product). Various parts of the sequence can be measured and studied to determine the functioning of separate aspects of the process.

Exposure.   This theory says that the decision-making process can be described as a "decision tree" with each branch representing a yes–no outcome. The first stage is *exposure.* This theory begins with the obvious by saying that only those who are exposed to an ad are likely to be influenced by it. To maximize exposure, the advertiser places an ad so to achieve the widest possible audience. For example, the ad should appear on all of the programs during which a desirable segment of the audience is known to be watching. For this reason, when "zipping" around from channel to channel, we often see ads for the same product at the same time on different television networks.

Attention.   Of those who are exposed, only some will pay *attention* to the ad in question. Many people use commercial time as an opportunity to talk, go to the bathroom, and in other ways turn their attention away from the television set. Factors that govern attention to the ad involve the "salient perceptual features" such as we saw described in chapter 6. When the advertisers want to get the attention of an audience they ring bells, blow up cars and buildings, rip clothing, and use all manners of unusual sights and sounds, especially sounds, to grasp attention.

Comprehension.   After attention, the next stage in the process is *comprehending* the message in its own terms, understanding what the advertiser wants you to understand of the product. For example: Some years ago a maker of paper towels marketed a brand with a character named "Aunt Bluebell." One of the refrains in the ad was Aunt Bluebell's line: "weigh it for yourself, honey." The line referred to the idea that this brand of paper towel was thicker and heavier than the other brands on the market, and thus it actually weighed more. One "theory" among advertisers is that simple quantitative claims, even if meaningless, are more easily comprehended than qualitative claims. It is better to say that a brand has 2 ounces more, or is "1 millimeter longer." Comprehending the ad about paper towels, in light of McGuire's theory, would be understanding this particular point: understanding that the ad was saying that Aunt Bluebell's brand of paper towel was actually heavier.

The viewer need not believe this claim in order to comprehend the ad; the viewer must only understand that this is what the message is about. Focus groups, small groups of individuals who view the ad and then are questioned afterward about it, are used by the advertiser to see that the ad was comprehended in its own terms. Ads that are not understood, or that are responded to differently than intended, may be redone.

Yielding. Although comprehension means understanding the message intended by the advertiser, *yielding*, the next stage in the process, refers to agreement with the message, believing it. A viewer might understand what was being claimed in the ad for paper towels just described, yet still want to know if there were other reasons, rather than thickness of the towel, that made Aunt Bluebell's paper towels heavier. Might the cardboard centerpiece of the roll be heavier, for example, making the entire roll heavier (without the papers being any thicker than others)? Those people who *yield* to the message are those who believe the claim made by the advertiser.

Retention and the Decision to Buy. The final two stages of the process described by McGuire take place some time after exposure, once the viewer is in the store ready to make a purchase. At this point, factors other than those in the ad may govern the response to the final two stages — factors such as package design and position in the store. Once in the store, the viewer must now *recall* the product at the proper time (here packaging plays a central role, especially for children). For children, characters associated with the product in the ad, e.g. the Toucan used to advertise "Fruit Loops," are put on the box to aid a recall. A child who does not read may still recognize "Fruit Loops" because of this cartoon character on the box.

Once the individual has recalled the product at the proper moment, when faced with the package array in the store, then the final part of the process, the *decision to buy* is at hand. The decision to buy may also be influenced by factors other than those in the ad, such as comparative price.

Other Advertising Theories:
Psychographics and VALS

McGuire's theory represents a classical approach, derived from historical social psychological research on attitudes and values. More recent approaches to explaining the effectiveness of ads stress "psychographics" where a file of the potential customer's "uses and gratifications" regarding the product is used to target the specific message of the ad to psychological characteristics of the audience.

For example, suppose an advertiser learned through questionnaire studies and focus groups that the customer for the product, in this case a brand of expensive dog food, buys the product for his or her pet as a treat about once a month. A "psychological" profile of the buyer could be provided, usually no more than a thumbnail sketch, but this could then used to design an ad to appeal to what is known about this group.

Assembling a set of psychological traits said to represent a group of consumers then, may be called a *psychographic* approach.

Typical of this approach is the set of psychological profiles called "values and lifestyles" or VALS. Consumers are described first as falling into one of two large groups (inner vs. outer directed) and then further subdivided into various categories (such as, for the outer directed, "achiever," "emulator," and "belonger," and for the inner directed, "societally conscious," "experiential," and "I-am-me.") Each of these *personality types* has a description. An "emulator" is described in the following way: "Chuck spends a lot of time polishing his new convertible. Seems he is always in debt buying things for the good life. He is determined to make it. Chuck wants to show how successful he is so he buys items displaying this desired status." An "achiever," also outer directed, is described as: "After getting his MBA, Lawrence landed a Fortune 500 corporation job and is aiming to be CEO. Lawrence, Kathy, and their family lead a happy, successful life. Financially well off, active, they want the best and newest innovations."

Advertisements are keyed to the description of the values and lifestyles of the potential customer, and would be different for an emulator versus an achiever. This approach uses psychological descriptions of the life situations of various customers to design exact appeals in the commercials.

Each of these theories seem to account for different aspects of advertising, yet something seems missing in them. For one thing, these approaches, especially McGuire's, are particularly cognitive and rational. The viewer not only pays attention, but thinks about the information provided—comprehends it, yields to it (or not), and so on. There is little room for emotions or feelings. Yet as we watch commercials on television, thousands of them, we have the sense that what is being manipulated here is not the cognitive, rational part of the mind but rather the emotional, feeling part. The VALS approach comes closer to this, to representing feelings and emotions, but it is not systematic or embedded in a broader theory of communications.

Persuasive Mechanisms: Memory

Over and above the rational decision-making processes described by McGuire, and the more affective needs and gratifications approach described by VALS, what can we discern about persuasive mechanisms involved in advertising from the material presented in this chapter? Let's begin by noting that persuasion in advertising is of a very narrow sort. Unlike the more complicated persuasive processes involved in changing political and social attitudes, advertisers simply want to manipulate *memory* of and *desire* for a product. This involves two different sets of mechanisms that are occasionally intertwined. Let's begin with memory.

Repeated exposure to a select audience is clearly one of the more important techniques used by advertisers to aid memory. Ads designed for particular audiences (i.e., toys for children, a variety of home products for women, beer and insurance for men) are targeted through specific programming to the intended audience and then shown over and over again. Repetition is a powerful mechanism when the object is simply to have the recipient remember the name of a product, and for this reason it is one of the most central of the persuasive mechanisms used in advertising.

Familiar music is another aid to memory that is part of both having the viewer remember the product by providing a catchy jingle that "sticks in the mind," and making the viewer want the product by associating the product with a well known and liked tune. We return to association when we discuss techniques that manipulate desire.

Finally, there are *visual memory aids.* The use of visual aids can be seen most clearly with children's ads, but the same techniques are used for adult products as well. A cartoon figure is often associated with a particular product, such as the Leprechaun that is used to advertise a brand of Keebler's cookies. This character is seen in the advertisement and is also prominently displayed on the box. Mothers of 2 year-olds who do not yet read are often surprised to have the child point to a particular food in the store. The child is reminded of the cookie by the character on the box, not the words. Distinctive labels and brand names serve the same mechanism for adults.

Persuasive Mechanisms: Desire

The techniques utilized by advertisers to create *desire* for a product are many and varied, and like exposure and repetition they are aimed at a specific target audience. What is persuasive for an adult may not have any influence on a child, what persuades men may not interest women or vice versa.

Positive association, a form of classical conditioning, is one of the most common techniques used across a variety of different types of ads to manipulate desire. The ad creates, with story or images, a positive feeling in the viewer and the advertiser hopes that some of this affection will be associated with the product by repeatedly presenting the two stimuli together. The use of familiar well-liked music is part of this process as well. Well-liked tunes are especially important to a generation raised on the ready availability of portable radios, and advertisers hope that some of these warm associations with the music will rub off on the product. In psychological terms, the warm feeling created by the music or the images is the "unconditioned stimulus" and the product is the "conditioned" stimulus. Like Pavlov's dog who heard a bell every time he was given food, eventually the bell alone brings about the same response (salivation) as the food. So it is with warm feelings and products. It is the advertisers' hope that eventually, through repeated association, the product alone will bring out a warm feeling and desire.

Identification is another powerful persuasive mechanism used in advertisements to create desire. A model person (a celebrity for example) is shown using the product. The advertiser hopes that because we identify with the person (or sometimes the type of person) depicted in the ad that we will desire the product in order to be like the model. Identification is the psychological process whereby we imitate the actions and characteristics of people we admire. The process begins in childhood with our parents and continues through life with different models all of whom are, for one reason or another, attractive to us. With age and experience these models change so that what is attractive to a child will not necessarily attract a teenager and so on. Advertisers use techniques such as VALS to determine the characteristics of models that their potential customers will find attractive.

Credibility is the final persuasive technique used to manipulate desire. Like identification credibility is a "source effect," that is, it is a characteristic of the source of the communication. But unlike identification that is based on attractiveness, credibility is based on the expertise of the model. A race car driver selling spark-plugs is more credible than a baseball player. Note that these two characteristics can vary independently of one another. A person can have prestige, that is the person could be an attractive model, a celebrity, or a person could be an expert without being especially attractive, without much prestige. More common, perhaps, is for a source to be both. A famous race car driver selling tires has both prestige and credibility.

These few persuasive mechanisms do not exhaust the list by any means, but they do seem to be some of the more important. Like the psychological mechanisms described earlier, each of these persuasive mechanisms has a research literature behind it. The parameters of the mechanisms, at least some of them, are understood. On the other hand there are reputed mechanisms that have little support in the research literature, even though they are widely believed to exist. In the next section we turn to the most famous of these false mechanisms, subliminal techniques.

Subliminal Techniques

Subliminal techniques in advertising refer to the idea that there is a way to present a "message" below (or outside of) conscious awareness that is, nevertheless, effective in making the viewer desire the product. The idea is that the conscious mind is prevented from "defending" against such techniques, because it does not *perceive* the message. Somehow the message goes right to the subconscious. Let's look at this myth, at how it came about in the first place and what is true and not true about it.

Legend has it that many years ago a theater owner in Fort Lee, New Jersey tried putting messages on film every 5 seconds at a level of one three-thousandths of a second, saying: "Drink Coca-Cola" and "Hungry? Eat popcorn." The story is that there was a huge increase in sales, and a new technique of advertising manipulation was born. Since that time, people claim to use subliminal messages to stop shoplifting in stores, and to help individuals lose weight, stop smoking, improve memory, lower blood pressure, increase sexual performance, and so forth. These techniques are called "subliminal" because the stimuli are reportedly presented so fast (for vision) or low (for hearing) that they cannot be perceived consciously, but they can, it is said, be "detected unconsciously" and thus have an effect. If this were true it would be an advertiser's dream and a consumer's nightmare. If it were true there would not be any way to defend oneself against such a technique, or to know that it was being used. Only it isn't true.

Research (see, for example, Dixon, 1981) shows that there are preconscious or unconscious processes. It is certainly *possible* to perceive and respond to stimuli that are presented "outside of conscious awareness." But this research *does not* support the notion that these "techniques" may be used for persuasive purposes. Someone may develop such a technique given time, but right now no such thing exists. Let's look at the truth.

The story about the movie theater in Fort Lee, New Jersey was reported in *Life Magazine,* in 1958 (Block & Vanden Bergh, 1985). There is reason to believe that something like this "experiment" did take place, although there is no credible evidence about the "findings." As we have seen, scientific research requires careful administration and design in order to be confident that the results are not in error. So, although the theater may have shown a movie with messages embedded in it so fast that the message could not be "recognized" by a viewer, there is no evidence that the claimed increase in Coca-Cola sales by 57.7%, or popcorn sales by 18.1% actually happened.

There is no evidence, that is, other than the word of a "marketing specialist" said to be responsible for designing and conducting the experiment. We do not know even if there was an actual increase in sales. According to the original magazine article on the topic, no "control" group was used (individuals who see the same movie without the "subliminal messages") for purposes of comparison. No actual "findings" were ever reported in any respectable scientific journal — about this so-called experiment. Over the years since this first report there have been many claims made about subliminal techniques, some of the most outrageous come from Wilson Bryan Key (1973, 1976, 1980). Rather than try to disentangle the assorted claims, let us instead begin with a definition and outline what is known about subliminal techniques.

Where does the word *subliminal* come from? What does it mean? Technically, *subliminal* means "below the limen." A limen is the limit of some dimension of a physical or perceptual ability. For every human ability there is a limit, usually an upper and a lower one, and for many years psychophysical research was devoted to establishing what these are (see Gleitman, 1986). In the auditory dimension, for example, there is a limen for volume — both at the quiet and loud ends. That is, there are sounds so quiet that they cannot be detected, and there are sounds so loud that they become painful — literally deafening. Detection of sound is determined, in part, by background noise. Some of the "subliminal" message techniques currently popular use background music or other sounds to "mask" the "subliminal" message, which would be detectable without the background. So any claim about a subliminal technique refers to using a stimulus that is below some limen of perception.

There are three basic questions to answer about subliminal techniques:

1. Is it possible to do such a thing at the visual and sound level?
2. Do advertisers use such techniques?
3. Do they work?

Is it Possible? Yes. There are several ways to present material on television, both visually and with sound, that might be said to contain "subliminal messages." With motion picture film, for example, it is possible to present written and visual material so quickly that the eye has difficulty detecting what was shown (although some people may notice that something happened). There are 24 frames to the second in a motion picture film so each frame is shown for 1/24th of a second. Either a picture or a word, flashed at that speed, would be difficult for most people to detect. The speed of detection depends on many things, of course, such as individual differences between subjects, the familiarity of the picture or word to be detected, the brightness and contrast of the stimulus, etc. But it is not unreasonable to say that there is a speed, for each person, at which a word, presented on television, is no longer detectable. As we have just seen, this point is the limit of perception, the "limen."

So, it is certainly possible to do what was claimed in 1958, it is *possible* to present a word or a combination of words, like "Drink Coke", on a screen so fast as to not be detectable by a sizable proportion of the audience exposed to it. It is also possible to present sounds either so low (in volume or pitch) that they could not be detected by the average person. So the answer to the first question is yes, it can be done, in both the visual and auditory dimensions.

Is it Done?   Probably. At least some have tried. In addition to the experiment just described (about which the theater subsequently refused to release any of the details), the House of Representatives Committee on Science and Technology had subcommittee hearings in 1984 on the topic of subliminal techniques. The FCC representative at the House hearings, Dr. John Kamp, reported several "experiments" to test whether such messages could be effective. A television station (WTWO in Bangor, Maine) tested the technique by monitoring reaction of viewers to flashes that stated "IF YOU SEE THIS MESSAGE, WRITE WTWO." After running this message, WTWO reported "no increase in incoming mail" (House Hearings of Subcommittee on Transportation, Aviation and Materials of the Committee on Science and Technology, U.S. House of Representatives, Aug. 6, 1984, p. 4).

Another television station, WTTV, broadcast a message "Watch Frank Edwards" and they later reported that the message had no statistically significant effect on the audience for the Frank Edwards program (De Fleur & Petranoff, 1959).

In 1957, in spite of not having any evidence that the technique worked, the FCC published a public notice expressing concern about the use of such techniques, and asserting jurisdiction. The 1957 FCC notice "clearly stated that the FCC considered the use of subliminal messages to be inappropriate by broadcasters" (House Hearings, 1984, p. 4).

The FCC's position was that the use of such techniques involves intentional deception and, thus, "is inconsistent with a licensee's obligation to broadcast in the public interest." In addition to this expression of disapproval by the FCC, the National Association of Broadcasters, in 1958, amended its "Television Code" to bar the use of subliminal messages.

In 1973 the issue came up again in a complaint to the FCC regarding an ad shown on television with the subliminal message "Get it" embedded in the ad. The advertising agency responsible admitted that such a message did exist, and sent a telegram authorizing stations to delete the message. The FCC used this occasion to clarify its position in a public notice stating: "We believe that use of subliminal perception is inconsistent with the obligations of a licensee. . .Broadcasts employing such techniques are contrary to the public interest. Whether effective or not, such broadcasts are intended to be deceptive" (Broadcast of Information by Means of "Subliminal Perception" Techniques at 44 F.C.C. 2d 1016, 1974).

So it is possible to present material on television so fast or quietly that it is not detected by the human eye or ear. There is even some evidence that people have tried doing this occasionally, with or without FCC approval, over the years.

Does it Work?   No. There is no credible evidence that such techniques work in the sense of "stimulating desire" for some product, or making a movie more arousing. As we noted earlier, there is substantial evidence for such a thing as subliminal perception, but there is no publicly available evidence that such techniques may be used to persuade. This does not stop the claims for the existence of such techniques on the part of the unscrupulous, nor does it prevent the guileless from exploiting the gullible.

In the Hearings of the House committee, several businessmen came foreward to describe how they use "subliminal techniques" to prevent shoplifting and to aid individuals in losing weight and attaining happiness. One witness claimed that "we have been able to demonstrate . . . a reduction of 60% in the annual turnover of employees in a chain of over a hundred supermarkets in which we had nine stores equipped with our experimental equipment" (House Hearings, Testimony of Dr. Hal Becker, p. 25).

So the long and the short of it is that although there may be such a thing as subliminal perception, in the sense that there are preconscious or unconscious processes, there is no solid evidence to support the claims that such processes may be used to persuade.

The funniest thing about this whole controversy, over and above the fact that the FCC has a rule against a technique it cannot prove to be actually effective, is that most advertisements use techniques that would have to be regarded as superliminal. When advertisers want to get our attention, as mentioned earlier, they ring bells, sound horns and gongs, flash lights, and blow up cars and buildings. There is nothing subliminal about most of the techniques used on television by advertisers.

SUMMARY

The amount of advertising in terms of time relative to the program content has remained more or less steady over the years since about the early 1970s, but the number of ads crushed into this time has increased steadily over these same years. In our research on this topic, we found an average of 30 nonprogram messages per hour, and wide variation over the day and week. The ratio of nonprogram to program content is lowest during the evening "prime-time" hours and on Saturday morning during the "children's hours." The largest number and greatest amount of time devoted to commercials is during the weekday afternoon, from 10 a.m. to 4 p.m. when the programming is primarily directed to women (soap operas dominate this time period).

Advertisements may be studied using the same content analysis techniques as were used with programs, although aside from sex differences in character portrayals, very few such content analyses of commercials are available in the literature. Scheibe's fairly recent analysis of character portrayals suggests that the ratio of men to women is more similar to everyday life in the ads than the programs. Few differences between the power or concerns of men and women appeared except when they were seen in a family context; there women were shown to have expert power while men had power of approval.

Our analysis of children's ads show a great increase in ads for toys in recent years, and a decrease in ads for cereals and candy. Much of the data was similar to our findings with ads in general: There are more ads per unit time, and more product commercials and fewer PSAs and promos than in times past.

There is substantial evidence that commercials are "effective" in the sense of achieving the goals set by advertisers. What effects ads have, over and above the intentions of the advertiser, are yet to be known. To hypothesize about these effects we must know both what is advertised and something about the characteristics of the recipient, the person who is exposed.

The persuasive mechanisms used in advertising are many and used for two basic purposes: to improve memory of and desire for a product. Psychologists have theories, as do advertisers, about why their techniques work. But, for the most part these theories stress the rational over the irrational, the conscious over the unconscious, the cognitive over the emotional. In the long run, an adequate theory of advertising must stress the emotional and unconscious factors in advertising, and it must explain the effects as well as the effectiveness of ads. In this chapter we have looked at what kinds of products are advertised to children and at some of the persuasive mechanisms involved. We have not discussed the broader ethical question of whether advertising is harmful to children, and that is the question we turn to in the next chapter.

PART III

REGULATIONS AND SPECULATIONS

The final two chapters of the book contain material that is in some ways different from the material contained in the first seven chapters. Most of the material in earlier chapters was based on evidence gathered from research laboratories involving well-established research paradigms. By contrast, most of the material in the last two chapters is either descriptive (e.g., of the regulatory process) or speculative. In my opinion this does not make the material any less reliable or truthful, but it does mean that it has a different basis in fact. In the first two parts of the book I was speaking as a scientist reviewing the work of other scientists. In this last part I am attempting to describe and report on the work of people who have tried to regulate the television industry, or who have tried to mitigate the effects of television through private, educational efforts.

Chapter 8 describes a series of efforts made by two governmental regulatory agencies (the FCC and FTC) to set up rules and regulations about the television industry's responsibility in programming for children and in manipulating children through advertising. Such an analysis first requires a brief description of the regulatory process itself, especially as it relates to the needs and special vulnerabilities of children. While First Amendment restrictions prohibit government intervention with regard to most of the content of television, television designed for children has received attention from regulatory agencies because of the susceptibility of children to persuasion designed by adults. Does this vulnerability result in harmful effects of television programs and advertisements on children? If so, should the government propose rules and regulations to mitigate such harm?

After reviewing the relevant laws and regulations, we look at several efforts by federal agencies to hold hearings on a variety of issues concerning the effect of television on children, and to propose a set of guidelines for the networks to follow. It is difficult to describe the outcome of these various efforts because although few rules were ever promulgated there have been changes in the content of children's television directly as a result of these regulatory efforts. The changes were made voluntarily, by the networks, after attention was drawn to certain problems as a result of the regulatory hearings. For example, all networks now insert a divider between programs and ads saying "we'll be right back after these messages." This was done, in part, because of testimony that children had difficulty telling the difference between program and advertising content, and that the failure to know the difference could result in unfair persuasion. In addition, most networks require that toy advertisements for children contain a "5-second island." That is, the last 5 seconds of a toy ad must show a "still shot" of the toy without adornments, sometimes called a "limbo" or "tombstone" shot, and that any disclaimers, like "parts sold separately," or "assembly required" must be given during these 5 seconds. This rule is now being challenged by advertisers because, as we saw in chapter 7, there are an increasing number of 15-second ads and advertisers want to know if they must still use the last 5 seconds for a "tombstone shot," or because the ad is shorter, can they reduce the 5-second island to 3 seconds, the same proportion of time required earlier for the 30-second ad.

In addition, every cereal ad on children's programs must comply with the "legal breakfast rule." That is, the cereal must be shown with milk, orange juice, fruit, and toast, and must say "part of this complete breakfast" or "part of this nutritious breakfast." These rules, adopted by the networks, were done to counteract the suggestion that toy ads often distorted the actual size or nature of the toy, and that a child could believe that the advertised cereal alone was sufficient for a nutritious breakfast. Both of these contentions were made by scientists at regulatory hearings, and although the agencies did not themselves require the rules, the networks adopted them anyway. So, although one view is that these regulatory efforts have resulted in few actual rules and regulations, the other view is that they have performed an important function by drawing attention to certain problems that the networks, in response, corrected. Whether the networks would have done so without pressure from the regulatory agencies or from private consumer

organizations like Action for Children's Television, is a matter of speculation.

Chapter 8 ends with brief descriptions of private (nongovernmental) efforts to counteract the influence of television through education,
through programs to mitigate the effects of violence, and through private consultation with the networks by social scientists. Although these
efforts are necessarily smaller, they are often effective and provide an
alternative to having the government use the regulatory system to counteract the influence of television.

Chapter 9 contains a little bit of everything. It serves as a brief summary and conclusion, at the broadest level, of what was said in the earlier
chapters. It is an attempt to put what I have said into some broader
context. It also contains some thoughts about aspects of television—
such as international television and educational television—that were
not included in the other chapters. Finally, chapter 9 contains some
speculations about the future of television in terms of new technologies just being introduced and in terms of the future directions of
research.

It was difficult to write this last part without being too redundant
with earlier parts of the book. I expect that research on imitation, disinhibition (or the stimulation of associative networks, as it is now called),
and arousal/desensitization to continue. I expect much more research
on attention to television, because that is the central variable of interest
to the programmers of television, and more research on the comprehension of television because that is the primary interest of many psychologists who study television. The future will bring more research
on the perceived reality of television, because that is an important question that is still largely unanswered. Finally, I expect the concept of
"scripts" to become a larger and more important part of future research
on television, because it is easy to conceptualize much of television content into these scripts, and because people may organize their own behavior along similar lines. But because I covered all of these topics in
the earlier chapters, I have only mentioned them in passing in the last
chapter.

I have discussed in more detail some research paradigms that are
relatively new and untested, such as B. S. Greenberg's notion of "drip
versus drench," and the notion that the value content of television may
be more important than the manifest content of role portrayals. These
ideas are so new that they have not resulted in much research as of
yet, but they deserve a mention because they may be an important part
of the future of television research.

Social Policy and the Regulation of Television for Children

And shall we just carelessly allow children to hear any casual tales which may be devised by casual persons, and to receive in their minds ideas for the most part the very opposite of those which we should wish them to have when they are grown up?

—Plato, *The Republic.**

Exploitation of children should be avoided. Commercials directed to children should in no way mislead as to the product's performance and usefulness.

—NAB Code of Advertising. (Cited in Adler et al., 1980, p. 311)

The children of a nation are its most precious resource, they are society's future. But children are delicate when young in some respects; they are unusually trusting. Children trust what adults tell them, and this trust is an important part of the child's capacity to effectively interact with and learn about the world. But this capacity for trust also means that children are easily manipulated and deceived, especially by unscrupulous adults. For these reasons, practically every society has rules about what Plato called the "casual manipulation" of children. In fact, the manipulation of children through advertising was banned in one of the earliest known legal codes. The code of Hamarabi made it a crime to try to sell something to a child (Rothenberg, 1975).

---

*translated by Francis M. Cornford (New York: Oxford University press, 1958) Book II, p. 69.

SOCIAL POLICY ISSUES

In the United States, as we saw in chapter 1, there are two government agencies with the power and responsibility to regulate television, to see that it is trustworthy. The Federal Communications Commission (FCC) has the power to regulate all of broadcasting, and the Federal Trade Commission (FTC) has the power to regulate the advertising content of broadcasting (and other media as well). As we saw also in chapter 1, these agencies have exercised their power to regulate very little. The one exception to this rule has been with regard to children. When questions arise about the influence of television on children, they become issues of social policy because they involve government agencies making rules to govern a particular segment of society.

A definition of social policy with respect to advertising is offered by Rossiter (1980). Social policy issues arise "when a specific advertising practice or an entire category of advertising is perceived as utilizing *means* or resulting in *ends* which are contrary to the ethical values held by some politically significant party" (p. 252).

Thus, something becomes a social policy issue when some powerful party, a group of consumers for example, becomes upset by some action or practice of a regulated industry — such as television (Wartella, 1988). Since the introduction of television into the United States in the early 1950s, three basic social policy questions have emerged regarding children: (a) How much time should be devoted during the broadcast day (or week) to programming exclusively designed for children? (b) Should the program content of television directed to children be regulated because of potentially undesirable effects of violent portrayals? (c) Should the advertising content of television directed to children be regulated because of undesirable health effects? Although relatively little has been done with regard to the first two of these issues, the third (concerning advertising), has received a good deal of governmental attention. We consider each of these three issues in this chapter, spending most of our time with the third — the problem of advertising.

In each of these cases it is the child's unique informational, emotional and intellectual needs (and shortcomings) that makes the issue worth considering. None of these issues would qualify as a social policy question for adults, although the problem of violent programming comes close. As we noted in chapter 1, there are constitutional limitations prohibiting any governmental interference in the programming content of television (beyond the broad injunction that broadcasting must "serve the public interest"). The only way violence in programming could be reduced, then, would be if the FCC decided that it was not in the public interest to have this type of programming.

Advertisements, on the other hand, have not been considered to be "protected" speech (Small, 1978), so government agencies can and do make rules about them. Even this degree of regulation has become legally clouded in the last few years because some courts have held that certain aspects of advertising do fall under the protection of the First Amendment. These findings were narrow in focus, however, and do not seem to dispute the fact that regulation of advertising in broadcasting continues to be a proper activity of federal agencies (see, for example, Bates v. State Bar of Arizona, 45 U.S.L.W. 4895 [U.S. June 27, 1977]; Virginia State Board of Pharmacy v. Virginia Citizens Consumer Council, 425 U.S. 748 [1976]—cited in The Federal Register, 4/27/78).

Social Policy Actors

When a social policy issue comes to the fore, who are the players in the drama? In all of the issues we consider in this chapter, the children of the nation are the *objects* of policy, and the television industry in the form of the major networks and the companies that advertise on them are the *subjects* of regulation. The two aforementioned federal regulatory agencies, the FCC and the FTC, are the makers of rules and regulation for the broadcast industry. In addition to these Federal rules, the broadcasting industry has its own self-regulatory guidelines.

Two industry groups responsible for publishing codes for the regulation of broadcasting are the National Advertising Division of the Better Business Bureau (known as the NAD), and the National Association of Broadcasters (NAB). The two codes share important characteristics in that both identify and forbid specific advertising or program practices and both are written in very general terms. Industry compliance with both codes is voluntary.

The *National Advertising Division* of the Better Business Bureau (NAD) forbids:

". . . language or production techniques which may exaggerate or distort the characteristics or functions of the product. . ."

". . . irritating, abrasive, or strident audio techniques which could overglamorize or mislead. . ."

. . . attitudes and practices inconsistent with generally recognized social values and customs" (cited in Adler et al., 1980, p. 305).

In a similar fashion, the National Association of Broadcasters (NAB) code states:

> Exploitation of children should be avoided. Commercials directed to children should in no way mislead as to the product's performance and usefulness. . . . no children's program personality or cartoon character shall be utilized to deliver commercial messages within or adjacent to the programs in which such a personality or cartoon character regularly appears. (cited in Adler et al., 1980, p. 311)

A major party in the formulation of social policy with regard to children has been various consumer groups, who petition the federal agencies to make rules on behalf of children. Action for Children's Television (ACT), for example, a group based in Cambridge, MA, has been especially active in petitioning the FCC and the FTC with regard to a variety of issues related to the quality of children's television.

In the following sections we consider in more detail the three basic social policy issues mentioned earlier to have arisen with respect to children and television: the amount of time devoted to children's programming, the effect of violence in programs, and the effect of ads.

How Much Air Time Should Be Devoted to Programming Especially Designed for Children?

In 1970, Action for Children's Television (ACT) proposed to the FCC that it require each station to provide daily programming for children totalling no less than 14 hours per week. In addition, ACT requested that all advertising for children be removed on the grounds that young children's limited intellectual development places limits on their ability to "defend themselves" against the influence of advertising. As a result of this petition (known formally as Docket #19142), the FCC held hearings about the effect of television on children in 1972, and in 1974 issued a report (FCC, 1974). Although the FCC did not implement the suggestion made by ACT, it did go further than ever before in defining children as a special audience with special needs, and it established requirements for television broadcasting directed to children.

In their 1974 report, the FCC suggested that the amount of violence on children's television programs be reduced, although we have already noted the ineffectiveness of this suggestion. In this report, the FCC also recognized the unique vulnerability of children, especially when it comes to advertising: "young children lack the necessary sophistication to appreciate the nature and purpose of advertising. . . the commission recognizes that. . . many children do not have the sophistication or experience needed to understand that advertising is not just another form of informational programming" (p. 39401 of FCC, 1974).

The report ended by making two suggestions about ads directed toward children: (a) a reduction in the amount of advertising allowable during children's programs; and (b) a clear separation of commercials during children's programs from programs. These suggestions were not implemented in the form of compulsory rules that require compliance under the law, but rather as new policies that broadcasters were asked to comply with voluntarily. At the time, however, the FCC warned that Docket # 19142 would remain "open" and new rules would be considered if children's programming did not improve. That is, if the industry did not respond voluntarily the Commission could and would resort to regulations. In 1978, the FCC reactivated the case to determine if broadcasters had complied with the 1974 report. Several studies were commissioned by the FCC comparing broadcasters performance (in 1978) with what it was in 1974. The conclusions of these studies were unequivocal: No significant increase in educational or informational programming for children had occurred since the 1974 report, but commercials were more frequently separated from programs than before.

Before any action could be taken, however, the political climate in Washington changed. A new Republican administration, the Reagan Administration, was elected and a new head of the FCC (Mark Fowler) was appointed. Chairman Fowler favored a "deregulatory philosophy" of government, so no new rules were ever promulgated. In late 1983, FCC docket # 19142 was finally closed (Kunkel & Watkins, 1985).

The Issue of Violence on Programming for Children

In chapters 4 and 5 we considered the many issues concerning the potential impact of violent programming on children. We saw that using a standardized measure of violence, Gerbner and his colleagues have demonstrated that children's programs have the highest rate of violence of any type of programming on television. This fact has not escaped the notice of people concerned about this problem.

In 1969, for example, the National Commission on the Causes and Prevention of Violence (the Eisenhower Commission, named for its Chairman Milton Eisenhower, President Dwight D. Eisenhower's brother) released a report on violence in the United States. In that report, the problem of violent television programming directed toward children was addressed as follows: "children can and do learn aggressive behavior from what they see in a film or on a TV screen, and they learn it equally from real life and fantasy (cartoon) models..." (National Commission on the Causes and Prevention of Violence, 1969, p. 168). The report went on to say that "much remains to be learned about media violence and its effects, but enough is known to require that constructive action be taken at once to reduce the amount and alter the kind of violent programs which have pervaded television" (National Commission, 1969, p. 172).

In 1969, before the report of the National Commission was issued, Senator John Pastore of Rhode Island, Chairman of the Senate Subcommittee on Communications, requested the Secretary of Health, Education, and Welfare (then Robert Finch) to conduct a study to determine—once and for all—the relationship between televised violence and aggressive behavior in children. The responsibility for this study was delegated to the office of the Surgeon General, administered through the National Institute of Health.

To date, the Surgeon General has issued two reports, one in 1972 and another in 1982. In chapter 5, we discussed the finding of both reports, especially the most recent. Summarizing the findings of both reports in the most recent overview volume, the (Pearl et al., 1982) came to the following conclusions:

> the consensus among most of the research community is that violence on television does lead to aggressive behavior by children and teenagers who watch the programs. This conclusion is based on laboratory experiments and field studies. Not all children become aggressive, of course, but the correlations between violence and aggression are positive. In magnitude, television violence is as strongly correlated with aggressive behavior as any other behavioral variable that has been measured. The research question has moved from asking whether or not there is an effect to seeking explanations for the effect. (p. 6)

In fact, even in the face of this widespread scientific conviction, the networks have done little to curb the amount or kind of violence shown on programs for children, as Gerbner's research (described in chapter 3) demonstrates. This kind of programming seems to be especially attractive to children and the networks have been unwilling to reduce it.

Advertising to Children

The advertising content of television is regulated primarily by the Federal Trade Commission (FTC). By law, an advertisement must be thought to be either unfair or deceptive before it can be reviewed by the FTC. For example, Section 5 of the FTC act (15 U.S.C. 45) declares unlawful the "unfair or deceptive acts or practices in or affecting com-

TABLE 8.1
A Framework for Classifying Policy Issues in Children's Television
Advertising (from Rossiter, 1980)

Proposition involves:	Means	Ends	FTC concept
Facts	False ads	Misleading ads	Deception
Values	Unfair means	Unfair ends	Unfairness

merce." Section 12 of the same act makes unlawful "the dissemination of a false advertisement."

In order to understand what these terms mean in practice, we need to return to Rossiter's (1980) definition of *social policy issues* as involving either means or ends. An issue could involve the ad itself (the means), or the outcome of the ad, regardless of the intention of the advertiser (the ends). In addition, regulatory issues can be further divided into questions of fact and value. Table 8.1 places these two sets of questions: means versus ends and facts versus values in juxtaposition, indicating the four broad types of social policy questions regarding advertising.

False Advertising.   An advertisement may be false if it involves an issue of fact that is limited to the ad itself (the means), regardless of its effects (the ends). Ads for psychic or occult services, for example, are forbidden on television because such services are considered invalid. That is, there is no credible scientific evidence for the effectiveness of such services. It is also against regulatory law to claim a drug has curative power it has not been shown to have. All such claims, false on their face, would be considered matters of fact and would fall within the overall FTC prohibition against false advertising.

Advertisers are, however, allowed a certain latitude with the truth. Some visual "tricks" are permitted because of the nature of television. Ice cream commercials, for example, may show scoops of mashed potatoes instead of real ice cream because under the hot lights of television real ice cream would melt. This and other tricks with food are permitted (Rossiter called these "white lies") because of the untempting appearance of real food under the glare of television lights. On the other hand, not all such deceptions are allowed. One well-known case at the FTC involved a soup company that placed marbles in the bottom of a soup bowl in order to make the soup appear "chunkier," more full of vegetables, than it actually was (the vegetables rested on top of the marbles, just visible under the surface of the soup). This practice was deemed "false advertising" because it made the soup appear quite different than it would when placed in an ordinary bowl. The company was ordered to stop the practice. The important point about false advertising, however, is that it concerns the claims (both voiced and pictured) made in the ad itself, and not the effect of the ad on the viewer.

Misleading Advertising. The second kind of deceptive advertising prohibited by the FTC involves the ends or effects of the ad. An ad that leads a viewer to a false belief, even though the ad is factually true, would fall under this category. The key issue is whether the average person viewing the ad is led to have a false or untrue belief. Moreover, a commercial may be deemed "misleading" if it is aimed at an easily misled minority such as children. "Children are the classic example of such an easily misled minority . . . (they) constitute an especially vulnerable and susceptible class requiring special protection from business practices that would not be unlawful if they only involved adults" (FTC Staff Report, 1978, p. 161).

One ad that was taken off the air because it was deemed to be "misleading" was an ad for "Wonder Bread." In this commercial, the theme "grow with Wonder Bread" was illustrated with special effects photography showing a child actually appearing to grow as he ate the advertised bread. The FTC held that this "visual representation" misled children to believe that "Wonder Bread" had the "extraordinary property to produce growth in children" (FTC Staff Report, 1978, p. 161).

Of course, an ad could be *both* false and misleading, but falling in either category alone would be enough to cause it to be prohibited. Note that both of these propositions involving deception are questions of fact that can be verified with research. It is possible to test the specific claims made in ads (about how high a plane can fly or how fast a car can move), and it is possible to determine the understanding of the viewer, even the child viewer, as well. Complaints involving issues of objectively determinable facts, such as false and misleading advertising, are easier to resolve than issues involving value judgments as in the case of the two categories of unfair advertising (Rossiter, 1980).

Unfair Means. Techniques used in ads may be forbidden because they are considered unfair—a question of values—and these issues can also be divided into means and ends. The current rules consider it unfair, for example, to use the host of a television program for children to sell a product to children, a technique known as *host selling.* Children are known to have especially strong attachments to television personalities (such as Captain Kangaroo, Mister Rogers, Big Bird, etc.), thus persuasion from characters such as these places the child at an unfair disadvantage because of the trust and affection children feel for them. For many children, a suggestion from a loved person is the same as a command. So host selling, although it was common in the early days of television, is forbidden today by both the FTC and the industry self-regulating codes, even though no claim of harm to the child viewer is made. The practice in and of itself is considered unfair, making it an issue of unfair means. (Samples of television for children from 1987, from the archive of television content described in chapter 7, contain several examples of host selling—e.g., characters from the "Flintstones" program selling "Pebbles" cereal during that program. So perhaps this rule, like many others, is no longer enforced by the FTC.)

Unfair Ends.   The final category of forbidden advertising is that involving the outcome or effects of an ad, even though the ad itself may be unobjectionable. Proprietary drug advertising (sometimes called "over-the-counter" or OTC drugs) falls into this category when it is directed toward children. The idea is that children exposed to OTC drug ads could end up with "excessive beliefs in the efficacy of these products" and they would be thus "predisposed toward requesting them or, when older, taking them when illness symptoms occurred" (Rossiter, 1980, p. 255). This is a value issue because the facts will not resolve it. It must remain a question of what one considers good and bad for children.

In general, FTC regulations and those of the industry tend to focus on means issues, on false and deceptive advertising, rather than on ends or effects of advertising issues (Rossiter, 1980). It is easier to forbid a specific practice such as outright deception than it is to forbid a certain outcome. On the other hand, "most cases heard by the children's advertising review unit of the NAD have involved advertisements that are alleged to result in beliefs about the product that are untrue. . .rarely have the advertisements themselves been false" (Rossiter, 1980, p. 257).

GOVERNMENT REGULATION OF CHILDREN'S ADVERTISING

In the decade of the 1970s both the FCC (as we have seen) and the FTC held hearings on the impact of television on children, and both agencies issued reports. In addition to these two regulatory agencies, the National Science Foundation (NSF) produced an excellent survey of the issues with regard to the effects of television advertisements on children.

We have already discussed the 1974 FCC report earlier in this chapter. Partly as a consequence of that report, and partly due to continued pressure from consumer groups, in 1976 the National Science Foundation undertook an updated review of the research literature (Sheikh, Prasad, & Rao had done one in 1974) on the effects of advertising directed to children. The results of this review were presented as an NSF report in 1977, and this report was later published as a book (Adler et al., 1980).

In doing this review, the NSF sought to encompass and summarize all of the important issues in the scientific and regulatory literature on the potential harmful effects of television advertising on children. In all, the NSF identified 10 issues it considered important. Each of these issues is considered below and categorized, as well, by Rossiter's fourfold categorization into false versus unfair, means versus ends.

Program–Commercial Separation

In the early days of television, actors and performers would simply pause in the middle of skits and say a "word" for those who sponsored the programs. Programs and ads were inseparable. Later, the ads became independent of the programs themselves, separately packaged and presented during "breaks" in the programming. During the FCC hearings in 1972, several social scientists raised the question of whether children understood the difference between commercials and programs, and if they did not, whether this constituted an unfair practice. Actually there are two questions hidden here: (a) Can children tell the difference between commercials and programs (and if not, what consequences follow for the child?). And (b) are children aware of the selling intent of ads in the sense of being aware that the purpose of the advertiser is to persuade?

The question of commercial/program separation is an issue of "unfair means." Lacking an understanding of the nature of the business transaction, and given their basically trusting nature, makes children easy targets for the huckster's charm. They may be led to want products they do not need, and according to many this represents an "unfair" contest. As one consumer advocate put it:

> Advertising to children much resembles a tug of war between 200 pound men and 60 pound youngsters. Whether called an unfair practice or thought subject to Fairness Doctrine interpretation, the fact remains that any communication that has a $1,000-per-commercial scriptwriter, actors, lighting technicians, sound effects specialists, electronic editors, psychological analysts, focus groups and motivations researchers, with a $50,000

budget on one end, and the 8 year old mind (curious, spongelike, eager, gullible) with 50 cents on the other, inherently represents an unfair contest. (Robert Choate, President of the Council on Children, Media, and Merchandising, 1976, cited in FTC Staff Report, 1978, p. 220)

Format and Audiovisual Techniques

A second issue outlined in the 1977 NSF report concerned the question of whether certain techniques commonly used on television have the potential to mislead children, "tricking" them into believing things that are factually untrue. An example would be the "Wonder Bread" commercial discussed earlier, where the visual trick of making the child in the commercial appear to grow could easily be misinterpreted by children who are unfamiliar with what can be done with special effects. As we noted earlier, this would be an issue of "unfair means." Ads for toys often fall into this category because they use special effects photography to make the toy appear larger or faster than it actually is.

Source Effects

A *source effect* refers to the influence of some trait of the person pictured in the ad, sometimes called the *source of the communication.* In general, the greater the prestige and credibility of the source, the more likely a listener is to believe the communication (Condry, 1962). Celebrity endorsements, historically used in advertising, would be one example of a source effect.

The question at issue with source effects is whether using celebrity endorsements represents an unfair practice, using unfair means, when it is done with children. Like many of these issues, the underlying question is whether children will be able to defend themselves in the face of such a technique, or whether their lack of experience makes them especially vulnerable. In addition, when the celebrities are fantasy characters, there is the fear that children will believe that in using the product they will be able to do as the character does. For example, children are more likely than adults to believe that if Superman advertises a certain tennis shoe, this means that if they wear that same shoe they will be able to fly.

Premium Offers

Long a mainstay of advertising, premium offers are especially effective with children who are not in a position to judge the facts about the product (Atkin, 1982). The social policy issue is whether premium offers wrongly focus the child's attention on wanting the prize, rather than on the qualities of the product. Because this is a value judgment and a question of the effects of the ad, premium offers would be classed as an issue of unfair ends.

Violent and Unsafe Acts

Few ads feature either violent or unsafe acts, and when they do it is often unintentionally. These displays are forbidden by both government regulatory policy and by the industry self-governing codes. It is interesting to note that no such restrictions apply to program material. Ads are forbidden to show violence and unsafe behavior presumably because of the possible harmful effects on viewers, even though programs may show these same acts without censorship. The same is true of drinking. Alcohol consumption (the act of drinking) is forbidden in advertising, although as we noted in chapter 3, alcohol is the most commonly used (and abused) drug on television programs.

Even though it does not often arise, the question of portraying violent and unsafe acts is an example of unfair ends, since the assumption is that the child will imitate what is seen and risk potential injury.

Proprietary Drug Advertising

Proprietary drugs are those bought over the counter, like aspirin or cough syrup, without requiring a prescription. As we noted earlier, at this time both the industry self-regulatory codes and the FTC regulations forbid proprietary drug advertising on television directed toward children. There are really two claims within this one proposition. The first is that children will be misled about the "commonality of use" and/or the "effectiveness" of such drugs, and this would be classified as a question of misleading advertising. The second claim is that children will be "pressured to make a decision they are not capable of making," and this claim falls under the category of unfair ends. Currently, the issue is moot because no such drugs are advertised on programs for children. OTC drugs advertised on other programs, even though they may be seen by children, are not considered unfair or misleading because they are not "directed" at the child audience.

Food Advertising

We saw in the last chapter that food advertising is the single most common type of advertisement on television, including children's programs. The issue about food advertising is focused as much on what kind of food is advertised as on what it will lead children to believe. Like proprietary drug ads, food ads are considered by some to be mislead-ing in that children who watch them are led to believe that the foods advertised on television constitute a good and healthy diet. Often they do not. The foods advertised on children's television are typically for heavily sugared cereals and candy, and the weight of medical and nutri-tional opinion is that these types of food are, eaten alone, nutritional-ly inadequate. Consuming them puts the person at risk for both tooth decay and obesity (for additional detail, see FTC Staff Report, 1978). Food advertising to children is thus alleged to be both misleading and unfair, although it is more an issue of value than of fact. That is, the argument is about what children ought to do, rather than whether the category is false or misleading.

Volume and Repetition

Both the overall number of ads and the number of times they are shown have drawn complaints from consumer groups, although the potential for harm is murky. As we noted earlier, children are exposed to some-where between 20,000 and 40,000 ads a year. Many of these ads urge the child to do things (such as eating candy) that may present a health risk. This issue of volume and repetition is not specific to any given ad, but rather refers to all of children's advertising in general. The claim here would be categorized as "unfair ends," exactly the kind of issue that is difficult if not impossible to resolve.

Consumer Socialization

A frequent complaint against TV advertising is that it "fosters undesir-able attitudes in children" by causing them to focus on crass commer-cialism (Rossiter, 1980, p. 261). This is an issue of "unfair ends." For some, it is unfair to advertise to children at all, making them want material things they do not need. Others have argued that advertising actually helps children by teaching them how to buy products, how to be good consumers (Ward et al., 1977). This is another value issue, and one that is focused on all of advertising, not any specific ad.

Parent-Child Conflict

The final issue identified by the 1977 NSF report was that advertising to children results in increased parent–child conflict. "There is a clear pattern of evidence showing that Saturday morning advertising has an important influence on children asking for cereal and toy products" (Atkin, 1975, cited in Adler et al., 1980, p. 206). Parents yield to some number of these requests and deny others (Caron & Ward, 1975; Robertson & Rossiter, 1974; Ward & Wackman, 1973). Apparently parents yield more to requests for food and cereal than for toys (Ward et al., 1977; Wells, 1965). Ward and Wackman (1973), for example, found that parents reported yielding 87% of the time for cereals, 63% of the time they were asked for snack foods, 42% for candy. Atkin (1975b) reported that a survey of 516 families revealed that parents yield to cereal requests 62% of the time. Wells and LoScuito (1966) reported parental acquiescence rates to be 69% for cereal and 57% for candy. Galst and White (1976), in a supermarket observation study, reported that parents yield 45% to their child's requests for products.

Children react with disappointment to denials of these requests (Atkin, 1975b, 1975c; Robertson & Rossiter, 1976) and the disappointment is strongest among the youngest children (Ward et al., 1977) and in those families with the closest bonds, or high levels of parent–child interaction (Robertson & Rossiter, 1976). Although this last result may seem paradoxical, it is not. One must first have an affectionate relationship before conflict of the sort described here can arise. Because parent–child conflict is a consequence or an effect of the ad, and is a question of values, this issue would be categorized as one of "unfair ends." Once again, as we noted with the last two issues, this problem involves all of advertising to children, not just a single category of ad.

Although the NSF regarded these 10 issues as potential issues of social policy, the NSF is not a policy-making or rule-making body. That is the task of the FCC and the FTC. In this case, after the publication of the NSF report the FTC decided to hold hearings on the matter.

FTC STAFF REPORT, 1978

In 1978, an advisory staff of the FTC, after reviewing the NSF report and other studies, and after reviewing the law in detail, proposed a set of regulations to govern advertising to children. Three particular rules were suggested:

1. Ban all televised advertising for any product that is directed to, or seen by, audiences composed of a significant proportion of children who are too young to understand the selling purpose of or otherwise comprehend or evaluate the advertising;

2. Ban televised advertising for sugared food products directed to, or seen by, audiences composed of a significant proportion of older children, the consumption of which products poses the most serious dental health risks;

3. Require televised advertising for sugared food products not included in (point number 2 above) which is directed to, or seen by, audiences composed of a significant proportion of older children, to be balanced by nutritional and/or health disclosures funded by advertisers (Federal Register, 4/27/78, p. 17969).

The Regulatory Process

Here it is worth digressing for a brief explanation of what happens when a regulatory body such as the FTC proposes such a set of rules. First, the proposed policy change must, by law, be given public notice. In this case, notice was published in the Federal Register of April 27, 1978. "Interested parties" are then given a chance to voice their opinions about the issues involved. This is also stated in the notice of rule making: "Any interested person may submit. . . data, views, or arguments on any issues of fact, law, or policy which may have some bearing on the proposed rule" (Federal Register, 4/27/78, p. 17969)

In addition to calling for public comment, a full range of issues that are under dispute is also published. In the case of children's ads, some of the related issues were as follows.

1. "Is there a specific age below which significant numbers of children are unable to understand the selling purpose of advertising? If so, what is the age?"
2. "Is televised advertising unfair (due to #1)?"
3. "How should the terms "directed to or seen by" be defined?"
4. "Will the proposed ban. . . adversely effect the quality or quantity of children's television programming?"
5. "Are there alternatives to the proposed regulation?" (All from Federal Register, 4/27/78, p. 17969.)

In many cases before the FTC, hearings are conducted before the entire commission, but in this case, perhaps because of the controversial nature of the regulations, an administrative law judge, Morton Needleman, presided over the hearings and questioned each of the people who testified.

The Hearing about Children's Ads

Hearings were held in both San Francisco, California and in Washington, DC for the Fall and Spring of 1978–1979. The hearings were held in widely separated locations, so that a wide range of opinion could be heard, and so the trip to testify would not depend entirely on those who could afford to come.

One researcher who testified, for example, was Dr. Charles Atkin of the University of Michigan. Dr. Atkin is recognized as one of the leading researchers in the field of the effects of advertising to children. After describing how his survey was done, Dr. Atkin discussed the relationship children feel with television characters:

> Children develop a close and personal relationship with characters heavily promoted in child-oriented commercials. There is considerable affection for these fantasy figures, and most children perceive this liking as returned by the characters. . . . More than half of the preschoolers think that commercial characters can see into their house from the TV set, and almost half think that they can talk back to these characters on TV. (Atkin, 1978b, p. 14)

Another of the studies done by Dr. Atkin involved asking children whether specific commercial characters were "real" people or "pretend" people. We saw in an earlier chapter how the question of perceived reality is an important one in research on television in general. The characters asked about in Atkin's survey were Burger King, Ronald McDonald, Captain Crunch, and Fred Flintstone:

> For Burger King, 45% thought he was real, along with 33% for Ronald McDonald, 21% for Captain Crunch, and 20% for Fred Flintstone . . . . substantial numbers of children perceived these characters as "real." (Atkin, 1978b, p. 16)

Does a child's belief that a character as "real" or "pretend" influence other things the child thinks about the message?

> There was a tendency for those children who perceived the characters as real to believe the characters were telling the truth (86% for the "real" vs. 76% for the "pretend" group), to believe the claims (67% vs. 54%), and to perceive the characters as knowing what's good for children (85% vs. 75%). (Atkin, 1978b, p. 16)

One interesting finding reported by Dr. Atkin in his testimony concerned the judgment of children about whether the character was "paid" for his endorsement:

Those children responding affirmatively that the characters were paid were compared to those responding in the negative with respect to their responses to other belief questions. Children who thought the characters were paid were more likely to believe the characters were telling the truth (81% vs. 68%), that hypothetical claims are to be believed (60% vs. 47%), and that fantasy figures know what is good for children to eat (81% vs. 61%). Thus contrary to adult behavior, children cognizant of the fact that actors are paid for their endorsements were actually more likely to accept commercial characters and their claims. (Atkin, 1978, p. 20)

Dr. Atkin's testimony is typical of many of the academic psychologists and researchers who testified, because they spent their time explaining what a child understands, and how that understanding changes over time. Many of the university based researchers supported contentions of the FTC Staff, because the research they had done was done on contract for the FTC, in order to supplement and amplify existing research.

The "Other" Side

Cereal manufacturers, advertisers, and network executives (through their representatives) also had a chance to voice their concerns at these hearings, and because they represent the "other" contending party, they were usually on the opposite side of the fence. One typical of the group was Fletcher C. Waller, at the time vice president and director of marketing services for General Mills, Inc.

About the allegations made as a basis for the proposed ban, Dr. Waller (1978) said:

These allegations are based on erroneous assumptions and inconclusive research.... We will demonstrate the care with which General Mills' advertising directed toward children is developed and show that our intent is to present the advertised products as clearly as possible and to do so within self-imposed guidelines. (p. 1)

Dr. Waller went even further. Not only was the FTC Staff wrong in asserting that advertising harms children, but, in fact, advertising is actually a *benefit* to both children and their parents. Advertising provides children with "information about the wide range of products available and provides them with a basis for making judgments or choices based on their preferences" (Waller, 1978, p. 14).

Moreover, Dr. Waller continued, advertising is actually an *advantage* to parents because, "Advertising to children results in lower prices for advertised products" (p. 16).

Judge Needleman often questioned those who testified in detail. One of the psychologists who testified, for example, was Dr. Herbert Ginsburg, a nationally known expert on the theory of Jean Piaget. Dr. Ginsburg had listed certain Piagetian concepts and discussed their implications regarding advertising. After presenting his testimony in written form, the following exchange took place:

Judge Needleman: "What is the relevance of the Piagetian concern with syncretism and television commercials?"

Dr. Ginsburg: The notion of syncretism asserts that the young child has a tendency to group together elements that don't necessarily belong together. In the case of television advertisements, they frequently associate. . . with the product, some product irrelevant emotional theme or other attributes so that with breakfast cereals, for example, the advertiser may attempt to associate things like. . . friendship among peers or. . . in one advertisement I saw, the relief of loneliness was associated with a breakfast cereal. Now for us, these associations are far-fetched. They don't go together very well. We know that one has little to do with the other. For the young child, because he has something of a tendency towards syncretism, those connections may be more easily accepted. (The child would have a greater tendency to believe that the association is a literal one. . . .)" (Testimony of Dr. Herbert Ginsburg, pp. 5782–5783)

Final Report

After the hearings were over, Judge Needleman issued a two-pronged report made up of the remaining *"disputed"* and *"non-disputed"* issues. That is, some of the issues were still "disputed" in the sense that the different parties in the case, the FTC Staff and their psychologists compared to the cereal companies, the television networks, and their psychologists, could not come to agreement about certain questions or problems, and the scientific evidence presented did not resolve the issue one way or the other. According to Judge Needleman, the three unresolved or *"disputed issues"* in the case were:

1. To what extent can children between the ages of 2 and 11 distinguish between children's commercials and children's programs, to the point that they comprehend the selling purpose of television advertising aimed at children?

2. To what extent can children between the ages of 2 and 11 defend against persuasive techniques used in these commercials, such as

fantasy or cartoon presenters, premiums, limited information, and various associative appeals?

3. What health effects, actual or potential, attach to any proven lack of understanding or inability to defend against persuasive techniques? (Federal Trade Commission, 1979, pp. 6–7, cited in Rossiter, 1980, p. 263)

These disputed issues are intertwined with one another, in the sense that they define a hierarchy (Rossiter, 1980). If children do not understand "selling intent," then advertising may be "unfair." But even if they do understand it, it may not mean that children can "defend" themselves against such ads. If not, then ads could have an unfair "effect," and this would be enough to ban them. But even if it could be shown that children understand selling intent, and if it could be shown that they are able to defend themselves against commercials, it still may be the case that exposure to ads has unwanted health consequences.

Judge Needleman called the first two "cognitive" issues because an affirmative finding on each would be reason enough for a regulation even if they were shown to have no behavioral consequences. The first two issues fall under the category of "unfair means." The final issue, on the other hand, is an "ends" issue, in the sense that it concerns itself with the question of the *end result* of television advertising on the health of those who are exposed to it.

If the hearings had gone on, these disputed issues would have been discussed and argued, more evidence would have been gathered and presented, and a final determination would have been made. But there were also questions that arose in the staff report and testimony which the Judge decided were not issues. These issues were either not in dispute, or, in the Judge's opinion and in light of the law, not worthy of debate. Five of these nondisputed issues are outlined here, from Rossiter (1980, p. 265):

1. TV advertising *not specifically designed* for children is not at issue. An example would be proprietary (OTC) drugs, which are forbidden on children's programs, but which children see when they watch prime time, or afternoon television. In this case, the Judge argued that the issues should be confined to those types of ads specifically designed for children.

2. The fact that "advertising does what it is intended to do" is not an issue. The fact that one of the aims of advertising is to present certain goods and services to children and that as a consequence children *want* the goods and services advertised, that children *request* them and *consume* them is not, in itself, an issue (Rossiter, 1980, p. 18).

3. Parent–child conflict is not an issue, although there was evidence that it does occur and is associated with advertising, the Judge felt it is "not especially severe nor long-lasting" (Rossiter, 1980, p. 19). The Judge's position was that some amount of parent–child conflict is to be expected in families and that the amount generated by television was not sufficient to cause alarm. The Judge is admitting that this happens, but denying that it is an important problem. This is, of course, a value judgment about how much harm must come about before an issue becomes a policy issue.

4. That eating too much sugar contributes to some health problems, was considered an issue (see the third item under disputed issues) but the evidence for some kinds of harm was better than for others. For example, the Judge suggested that the case for dental health (effects on the teeth) and obesity were well established, but not the case for coronary heart disease, diabetes, cancer, or hypertension.

5. Finally, the Judge threw out the issue of "psychological harm" by saying that it was not established that children's advertising led to psychological harm, unrealistic materialistic notions, or overstimulation of desires" (Rossiter, 1980, p. 20). This is similar to the "consumer socialization issue" of the NSF report, and to the second "nondisputed" issue previously cited. The Judge was willing to accept television as a part of the society and to argue that its aims were acceptable, broadly, to those who owned sets and had them in their houses. He would not allow the very existence of television, or its few *intended* effects, to be part of the case against children's ads.

So if the case had been continued, if the FTC would have gone on with the proposed rule making on children's ads, then the issues would have revolved around the two "cognitive" issues and the one "effects" issue adjudged to be worthy of continued debate. The FTC did not continue with the case, however, because the Congress removed the funding from the FTC specifically for the continued study of the proposal to regulate children's ads. That is where the process stopped.

SOCIAL POLICY IN THE FUTURE

The regulatory history of television, even that which is directed to children, is spotty at best. It consists of fits and starts—hearings and reports that begin with a bang and end with a wimper. Why is this the case? Two broad reasons suggest themselves. First, issues involving children keep coming back because of the importance of childhood itself, and because the values of regulators change with changes in federal administrations. Even if there is a chance that a powerful aspect of society such as television may be doing harm, that chance must be given serious consideration. This is why the issue of the potential effects of television on children cannot be ignored. It is not settled because there are many research questions still unanswered.

If the topic is so important that it won't go away, then why does it seem to keep going away? The broadcasting and advertising industries are very large and very powerful. They have a tendency to perceive any federal regulatory action as a threat and to respond accordingly. In each of the hearings and reports discussed in this chapter the television industry was well represented. They always spoke against regulation, claiming that there is no evidence that television is harmful, and generally opposed any future inquiry into the problem. When any particular set of hearings seems to be going poorly for the industry, as they apparently did with respect to the FTC hearings about children's advertising of 1979, then the industry is capable of exerting pressure on congress to bring an end to the process. So the reason these issues keep "going away" is that talking about them is opposed by a financially and politically powerful party—the broadcasters. At the moment industry forces have the upper hand because the Reagan administration is favorable to them and hostile to the consumer movement. This may change with a new administration, and under new leadership we may expect additional hearings, reports, and possibly rules. The problems will not go away. In the next sections of this chapter, we consider some of the potential issues of social policy that could occur in the near future.

The Relationship Between Programs and Ads

Both the industry self-regulating codes and government regulations specify the amount of advertising directed to children, in terms of the acceptable number of minutes per hour that are allowed (see chapter 7). But in recent years, as we saw in the last chapter, the distinction between what is an ad and what is a program has gotten murkier. Many ads are now for toys and games that have central characters who are also characters in television shows. In a sense, this makes the whole show an ad for the product, even if the product is not advertised on the show itself. This issue in turn is related to the question of the commercialization of children's television. No harm is alleged, rather the issue is one of "unfairness." Holding the attention of children with powerful but essentially meaningless devices, such as are used in television programs directed to children, for the sole purpose of marketing certain products, may be considered by some an undesirable practice (Tavris, 1988). This is an issue of values. It is not an issue that concerns the current political administration in Washington, but it may be of concern to future administrations.

Food Advertising

The effects of food advertising directed toward children are still not clear, in part because most research on the topic was ended when congress withdrew funds from the FTC. But like program–commercial relationships, the question of the influence of food advertising will not go away. Food is the largest single category of advertising on television, and food habits established in children often last for a lifetime. In particular, the negative health effects of food advertising to children must be explored in greater detail. How nutritionally undesirable are the foods children are encouraged, via television advertising, to eat? How likely are children who eat such foods to have specific health problems like cavities and obesity? As we have noted, this is one of the "still-disputed" issues left unresolved by the FTC hearings of 1978.

The answer to this kind of a question will not be simple. As we saw with the problem of violence, some children exposed to television are more likely to be "at risk" than others. What children are likely to suffer what harm from food advertising? In the FTC hearings of 1979, witnesses testified to the fact that health problems created by television often fall on those who have the lowest incomes thus who are unable to purchase additional foods to supplement the heavily sugared cereals advertised (Condry, 1978). Even if this were the only health effect of television advertising it cannot and should not be ignored. How great is the problem television creates in this regard, and what other actions could be taken to alleviate the problem? How many poor children are put at risk because of foods advertised on television, and what are the long term consequences to society of this number of people at risk? These questions and many others still need to be answered regarding the influence of food advertisements on television.

Violence on Children's Programs

Finally, the issue of violence on children's television will not go away. Violence is a problem in our society, not just on television. But it becomes an issue for television because it is so attractive, such a perfect attention grabber. Even for very young children, violence draws and holds attention. Because of this, in the face of many years of protest, networks have refused to abandon the violent program. To what degree this early introduction to power, physical power, influences the minds of children we may never know. But it does have an influence, as we saw in chapters 4 and 5. Because of this the issue of violence will be with us for quite a long time. But violence, unlike the other problems covered in this chapter, is an issue of free speech. The program content of television is not covered in any mandate of the regulatory agencies. So in the long run, we will have to deal with the issue of violence in other ways.

NONGOVERNMENTAL INTERVENTIONS

To this point, all of this chapter has been devoted to a review of government interventions with the networks and programmers to limit the potential effects of television on children. As we have seen, these various attempts have met with little success. In part this is due to the fact that the networks have never conceded that there is a relation between violence on television and the aggressive behavior of viewers, and they have been unwilling to reduce the amount of violence and mayhem in their shows (Eron, 1986). So it may be up to parents, teachers, and other authorities who deal with children to find ways of intervening between the child and the television set. Several teams of researchers, working from different perspectives, have tried such intervention programs, and their findings have been instructive. In the following sections we look at three kinds of efforts, first to mitigate the effects of violent television, second to teach "critical viewing skills" to children, and third to work directly with the programmers of television to improve the quality.

Interventions to Mitigate the Effects of Violence

A good deal of research has been directed to the family context of viewing, and on the uses and functions of television with the family (see McLeod, Fitzpatrick, Glynn, & Fallis, 1982, for a review). Some parents have rules about how much television can be watched, or what kinds of programs can be viewed. In a field experiment on children's creativity, however, Singer and Singer (1981) found that parents were better able to lure their children away from the television screen by changing their styles of interaction than by making rules to limit the viewing of their children (see also Desmond, J. Singer, D. Singer, Calam, & Colimore, 1985). Other families watch with their children and comment on the action on the screen. As we saw in chapter 6, coviewers' acts of mediation can make a considerable difference in what a child takes away from a television program (Collins, Sobol, & Westby, 1981; see also Salomon, 1977; Singer & Singer, 1976, 1983).

A broader approach to family mediation is taken by Bryce and Leichter (1983) and Leichter et al. (1985). They point out that television is on most of the time in so many families that it may be "embedded in the activities of their daily lives, unintentional, and unremarkable" (p. 315). Even if parents never explicitly discuss television itself, the child's learning from television may still be influenced by the family's style of interaction (Messaris, 1986).

Rothschild and Morgan (1987) report a study of parental mediation of television with adolescents. They studied family "cohesion" (e.g., maternal affection, shared activities, and satisfaction with time spent together) and "control" (e.g., parental rules, firmness, and disciplinary style) as they related to television viewing. Family cohesion functioned to intensify television's contribution, whereas control was related to television's impact in a negative way. Thus "adolescents who co-view with their parents who discuss television with them, and whose parents do not set rules about viewing seem most vulnerable to television" (p. 299).

Singer and Singer (1981) carried out a program of family intervention with a group of parents of preschoolers. Parents attended three 2-hour sessions a week apart, and then an additional session several months later. The parents were shown research findings on the role of television in promoting aggression, and then divided into three groups. One group was given suggestions on how to control their children's viewing habits, a second group was told how to stimulate creativity and imagination in their children, and a third group was taught how to help their children improve cognitive skills such as language acquisition. A control group was formed for purposes of comparison. The television regulation group was the least effective, they did not change their television habits and their children were no less aggressive after the intervention than before. The other two groups did a little better with some improvements in language skills and television habits, but with no decrease in aggression. The Singers concluded that training parents to control the television watching of their children may be less effective than offering them "games and exercises to encourage imagination and the use of language" (Eron, 1986, p. 157).

More recent attempts to study family mediation are described in J. Singer and D. Singer (1986, 1988). In addition to studying aggression, in their most recent studies the Singers have focused on a variety of cognitive variables such as the child's general information level, ability to separate reality from fantasy, specific knowledge of television techniques (such as "zoom" and "slow motion"), the ability to discriminate commercials from programs, and the ability to recall crucial details from a just witnessed program (Desmond, J. Singer, D. Singer, Calam, & Colimore, 1985; J. Singer, D. Singer, Desmond, Calam, & Colimore, 1984). Families who establish television rules, "who engage in active discussion with children, mediate their television use, view less television, and use less power assertion were correlated with the child's acquisition of greater general information and less aggression or motor restlessness" (J. Singer & D. Singer, 1986, p. 121).

A different type of intervention was attempted by Huesmann, Eron, Klein, Brice, and Fischer (1983). Working with first- and third-grade children over a 2-year period, these researchers selected 170 children who scored in the top 25% of violence viewers out of 700 children being studied in a longitudinal research project. Half of this "high-violence" group was assigned to an experimental treatment, the other half to a control group. The experimental group was exposed to training procedures designed to change their attitudes about the acceptability of aggression and the realism of television depictions of aggression. During the second year of the program, the experimental children were exposed to procedures designed to produce enduring attitude changes, such as "crediting the children for possessing attitudes it is hoped they will adopt, encouraging perceptions of personal responsibility, inducing the belief that one is participating out of free choice, and promoting the perception that the consequences of one's behaviors are important" (Eron, 1986, p. 159).

When these experimental subjects were examined 4 months after the second intervention, they were found to be significantly less aggressive than the control group. This lowering of aggression was found despite the fact that these children continued to be heavy television viewers.

Why was the Huesmann et al. (1983) intervention more successful than the intervention attempted by the Singers? Eron (1986) speculates that it is because in the Huesmann et al. study the researchers worked directly with the children specifically focusing on the types of attitudes and behaviors they wanted to change, whereas the Singer group worked with the parents and only indirectly with the children. Many of the parents in the Singer study resisted attempts to change their television habits, they had little motivation to institute change. By contrast, the children in the Huesmann et al. study were motivated to change. They were asked to develop arguments about the negative aspects of television violence, and they helped make a film to show other children how not to be fooled by television.

A second reason is that the Huesmann et al. group worked directly on the behavior they wanted to change. They taught the children that aggression is an undesirable behavior and an unacceptable way to solve personal conflicts. Finally, the Huesmann et al. group took much longer to induce the changes in the children. The time between the pre- and postmeasures was 3 years, whereas the entire Singer study was done over the course of 1 year.

So using these two studies as a guide, intervention programs to reduce the effect of television violence should (a) treat the children directly, (b) work on the specific attitudes and behaviors that one wants to change, and (c) extend the period of the intervention as long as possible. Single-shot attempts at changing attitudes and behaviors are doomed to failure, in part because aggressive habits are learned over a long period of time and deeply embedded in the structure of a person's behavioral repertoire. Changing these behaviors is no simple matter, but it can be done (see also Goldstein, 1981; Patterson, Chamberlain, & Reid, 1982).

Critical Viewing Skills and Media Literacy

A conceptually similar approach to intervention involving teaching children "critical viewing skills" is included under the broad rubric of "media literacy" (Reiger, 1988). Although not focused on violence per se, efforts by educators to teach children (Abelman, 1984; Anderson, 1983; Gumpert & Cathcart, 1985) and adults (Brookfield, 1986; Handron, 1988) about television are becoming more common. Gumpert and Cathcart (1984) for example, define media literacy as the "ability to meaningfully process mediated data" (p. 23). They suggest that there are a set of medium specific codes that influence our values, social relationships, and world view, a position also taken by Salomon (1979). Teaching children these codes so they will be more literate viewers is the general goal of media literacy programs (Burmester, 1984; Craig, 1985; Luke, 1985).

Many of these programs, like the one described earlier by the Singers, are designed to make participants more aware of research findings regarding the media, whereas others are designed to focus on specific program techniques (Barker, 1985; Singer, Zuckerman, & Singer, 1980) and the "semiotics" of broadcasting (Fiske, 1985). Still others use a "hands on" approach designed to allow children to learn first hand the nature of television's form and techniques (Baron, 1985).

It is perhaps too early to assess the value of these programs, and many of them are too short to be of value. As a reviewer of media literacy programs for the Surgeon General's report on television noted:

> Critical viewing skills appear to be a combination of reasoning skills and television viewing habits. Therefore the acquisition and regular use of critical viewing skills can be expected to require several months, maybe

several years of "training." The most fruitful approach appears to be the involvement of parents and teachers. (Corder-Bolz, 1982, p. 98)

Most of these efforts are in their infancy and they are designed more to teach than to evaluate the products of their teaching. Any new intervention program should have time to settle what is to be taught and how before careful evaluation is done of it, and media literacy is no exception to this rule. But the idea behind media literacy programs is an important one, because it offers an alternative route to intervention that does not involve censorship of the programs but rather education of the viewer. First questions of how this may be done must be settled, and then the effects of such interventions may be evaluated. But for now studies of "critical viewing" or "media literacy" offer at least the hope of mitigating the unwanted effects of television viewing on the young.

Private Interventions with the Broadcasting Industry

Many social scientists have worked with television programmers, not as part of a government program, but as scientists advising television programmers about television content. Dorr (1988) described the complexities of such a relationship: "the social scientist who attempts to work cooperatively with (the broadcasting system) soon recognizes some essential differences in the operative goals, values, knowledge, and skills of most social scientists and most broadcasters" (p. 291). Dorr suggested taking the perspective of an anthropologist: "the anthropologist's simultaneous respect for other cultures and identification with his or her own culture should be brought into play ... the values, language, roles, organizations, and interactional patterns in broadcasting differ from those in social science. These differences must be respected and treated as legitimate" (p. 293). The needs of broadcasters are often specific and the prescriptions of social scientists often too general to be of use.

> Social science itself, then, is at times an insubstantial base from which to provide advice to broadcasting. As a field it tends toward the general, while broadcasting deals in specifics. Research evidence itself is fragmentary and sometimes conflicting, and it rarely addresses the particular combination of elements in any specific instance of programming or scheduling ... social science is a limited source of wisdom when it comes to broadcasting decisions. (p. 297)

None of this makes Dorr pessimistic, but it does give her a perspective on the difficulty of the task.

When social scientists do succeed in cooperating with broadcasting, they will not radically alter television content or its scheduling. But if they are good, they will make some positive contribution to television and its viewers. Together with broadcasters they will have helped to create and broadcast television content that does more good and avoids more harm than it otherwise would. And this is a goal on which many people can agree. (p. 302)

Dorr is not the only researcher and teacher to have worked with the television industry to improve broadcasting. In the same book (Oskamp, 1988) there are also chapters by Harding (1988), Katz (1988), and Abel (1988), each in his own way providing a perspective on the relationship between broadcasters and researchers.

In short, there are many routes to achieving a social policy outcome of better television for viewers. The route described in most of this chapter, of having the government take care of it, may be the least productive. Private citizens, both as teachers and as researchers, have much to offer. Some intervention programs designed specifically to mitigate the effects of violence have been successful, and others designed to teach critical viewing skills are beginning to have an impact. Finally, researchers may work directly with the programmers themselves in the hopes of improving the content of television, especially for children.

In the last analysis, perhaps, it is parents who must be the most vigilant and concerned for the welfare of their own children. In a recent issue of *Journal of Early Adolescence,* Dorothy and Jerome Singer, leaders in the field, offer 12 practical suggestions for parents to use as guidelines in helping their children get the most out of television. These suggestions run from the very general ("start early to develop your child's good viewing habits") to the very specific ("Help children develop a balanced viewing schedule of action, comedy, fine arts, fantasy, sports, etc.") (Singer & Singer, 1987, pp. 365–366). But the general thrust is that parents can make a difference by being active rather than passive. By being part of the world of their children, and by noting how television is also a part of that world, parents can make a difference in the impact of television on their children.

SUMMARY

Social policy, then, may be viewed from a variety of perspectives. The most common definition involves some form of government intervention to improve broadcasting, and most of this chapter has been devoted to a study of several such attempts by government agencies, principally the FCC and the FTC, to regulate the content of television for children. Although these various attempts have resulted in some changes in rules over the years, none of them has had any large impact on the nature of broadcast television. More successful, although much smaller in scope, have been various private attempts to mitigate the effect of viewing violent behavior or to teach critical viewing skills. Similarly, social scientists, working directly with programmers, have had some impact on the nature of programming without involving the government in any form of censorship.

What lessons are to be drawn from this? I believe that two stand out from all the rest. First, education is better than censorship. Programs designed to treat children directly, to educate them about the nature of television and its impact, are easier to design and more likely to be successful than trying to force the networks and programmers of television to change their ways. As we saw earlier, such intervention programs should treat children directly and involve parents and teachers. Such programs should be designed to take place over an extended period of time in the hopes of bringing about long-term changes in attitudes and values. A part of such efforts might include improvements in the nature of television for children, but again rather than complain about what is there we should put our efforts into developing better programs.

The second lesson is related to this last point, we should focus on doing good rather than what does harm. The hope of all social policy is to improve the quality of programs on television, especially those designed for children. We do this best by focusing on that issue, the quality of children's programs, not on the question of harm. As we saw in this chapter, the question of harm is a difficult one to resolve. In part this is because of value differences that cannot be settled by research. What if it is the case that some children who view television develop poor eating habits, let us assume that this is true. How many children must be harmed in this manner to encourage a rule that would ban all cereal ads on children's programs? It is difficult to establish the case in the first place, and even if established it does not lead in any obvious way to a new rule or regulation.

This is not to say that "harm" should not be studied, but rather that we will make more progress trying to promote quality than we will in trying to establish harm (see Feshbach, 1988). So long as the debate continues to be about harm the quality of children's television will not improve. Let us shift the terms of the argument from harm to quality. If the children of this society are going to spend so many hours of their lives in front of a television set, the least we could do for them is to provide them with programs that stretch and expand their minds. This would surely serve the "public interest," however it is defined. We could see to it that at least some of the time children spend in front of a television set is as profitable to them as it is to the industry. We do less than this now, and more's the pity. We should be ashamed of what television has to offer children. Changing this will be no small feat, but it can be done if we will focus our attention on the main issue, the quality of the programs. We know a great deal about the needs of children of every age. Let us use that knowledge to make television a meaningful environment for children. As Dorr (1988) pointed out, this will involve compromises and a good deal of soul searching, but in the end it is a goal on which everyone involved—programmers, the public, social scientists, consumer groups, and government regulators—can agree.

The Future of Television

In Zaire, each television day begins with President Mobutu descending from the clouds
—The *New York Times* (12/28/86)

Imagery is the common language of the global village
—*Unknown*

Television is a device used for the purpose of communication. But how is it used? In this book, we have studied the way television is used in the United States. Here, as we saw in the first chapter, television has been used primarily as a marketing device, as a means of gathering an audience for sale to an advertiser. This use, in turn, determines the content, both the programs designed to attract and hold large audiences, and the advertisements. The content has "direct effects" on those exposed to it. We have seen what some of these effects are, described in terms of the way they arouse psychological mechanisms. The application of these basic psychological mechanisms should be universal, even though the content of television is different throughout the world. The direct effects themselves will be different depending on the information, but the way these effects work will be much the same.

People all over the world will imitate and be disinhibited by what they see on television, they will be aroused and desensitized by it. They will be informed and entertained, in their own way, as television has done in every culture since its inception. Those who are heavy viewers will live in the "mainstream" of the television world, and in so doing confuse some of the facts of television with the facts of everyday life in the world in which they live.

Television programs hold the attention of the young using lively and colorful cartoons with unusual sound effects and attention-getting formal features. Advertisements the world over use these same techniques. The variables we described in chapter 6 that are important to attention and comprehension of television should prove true the world over, even though the content may be different from country to country.

Age differences in the understanding of television will also be true wherever television exists. Television does not mean the same thing and is not used in the same way by a preschool child as it is by a child between the ages of 6 and 12. Television has yet a different meaning to teenagers, where, as we have seen, its role is limited. Most adults watch television for entertainment and information — and as a means of "unwinding" from a long day of work. The effect television has on adults is different than the effect it has on children, however, not only because they watch different kinds of programs but also because they have a different understanding of the world. We know very little about the role of television in the lives of the elderly, other than the fact that they watch more than any other age group, but in the long run we will learn that it serves different purposes and has different effects on individuals at this stage of life as well.

An Ecological Approach

When I began this book I had the idea of describing the impact of television on the human being. I wanted to describe the psychology of television. Throughout the middle chapters of this book I tried to do just this. I reviewed hundreds of studies that revealed several important psychological mechanisms. But in reading the research literature on television it became clear to me that, in the long run, in order to understand the influence of television on the human being or on a collection of human beings called a society, it would be necessary to take what J. J. Gibson (1986) described as an "ecological approach." Gibson was describing visual perception, not television per se, but his analysis is applicable to research on television.

From James Gibson's point of view, there are two factors to consider when trying to understand how perception works: the *person* (including his or her perceptual systems) on the one hand, and the *environment* to which the person is exposed, on the other. It is necessary to start with a precise definition of each. The psychology of television will tell us something about the variety of ways individuals react to the kind of material that is on television. But as we have seen, it will not tell us how many people might be disinhibited or aroused. It will not tell us about how different types of program content have different effects on individuals exposed to them. The psychology of television will tell us what may or could happen, but not what does.

An ecological approach begins with a comprehensive description of the environment and the organism. In this case, the environment is the content of television, the programs and the ads, described in terms of the appeal of selective aspects of it to selective members of the population. Gibson argued for a description of the environment from the viewpoint of the organism under consideration. We must do the same. We must look at programs on television from the standpoint of the audience exposed. Programs for children must be viewed from the perspective of children who watch, the same for programs for adults or the elderly. Predictions about the influence of television, television's direct effects, come from a confluence of these two factors: The nature of the information displayed, and the nature of the organism exposed.

Lifespan Television

In chapter 2 we reviewed information from the A.C. Nielsen Co. about the amount of television watched by the average American. We noted that the average number of hours viewed a week was different for each age and sex category. Future research on television will all begin with this fact, with not only the amount of television watched by people of different ages, but also with the relative amount of time it takes from their everyday lives, and the type of program popular with each age group. One way to remind ourselves of the power of this device is to look at the proportion of time watching television takes from each person's life.

We know that each person, no matter how poor or wealthy, has 24 hours in each day, 365 days of each year, and, generously speaking, 80 years to a lifetime. We know that people sleep an average of 8 hours a day, and that children go to school 9 months out of the year for about 6 hours a day, 5 days a week. Adults who are employed full time work for an average of 8 hours a day, 5 days a week. Putting these facts together with the viewing data reported in chapter 2, we can construct a figure showing the amount of time given to various activities in an ordinary day for an ordinary person. In doing this, we have constructed Fig. 9.1, which shows the "stream of television" through everyday life.

Television takes a substantial hunk out of everyone's life from about

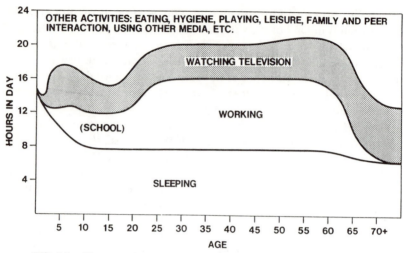

FIG. 9.1. Diagram of time spent watching television compared to other daily activities, across the lifespan. (Information from Robinson, 1972, 1981.)

2 years of age onward. As we have noted, children watch more television when they are very young (2–6 years) than they do during the middle years of childhood (6–12) years, and older people, 55 and over, watch the most television of any age group. It is interesting to note, however, that the largest *relative proportion* of the day used for television is for individuals who are in the young adult to middle-age group (18–55 years). For these adults who sleep 8 hours a day and work another 8 hours a day, there remains only 8 hours of conscious time left in the 24 hours allotted to us all. If the average American watches about 4 hours of television a day, this means that 50% of the conscious waking time of adults is taken up with televised material, more than any other demographic population.

The stream of time expended, however, is not enough for us to begin an ecological analysis because program preferences are different for people of different ages, and thus the information "available" to these different age groups is different. Table 9.1 was constructed from the data reported in chapter 2 on the types of programs watched by different groups in the population.

As we have previously noted, children prefer cartoons at the youngest age, and later situation comedies, drama, and movies. The drama children prefer is of the type "Walt Disney presents"—programs designed for children. Adults prefer adult drama, movies, entertainment, and informational programs. Men are less attracted to situation

TABLE 9.1
Top 15 Program Choices and Program Type by Age
and Program Type*

	Program Type					
Age	Information	Film	Drama	Sports	Sit-com	Cartoon
Children:						
2–11 yrs					67%	33%
12–17 yrs			7%		93%	
Adults:						
Women	7%	13%	27%		53%	
Men	7%	7%	13%	33%	40%	
All U.S.						
households	7%	7%	20%	7%	60%	

*derived from 1987 data presented in Table 2.6, chapter 2 (information from Nielsen, 1988).

comedies than women. Children do not watch or typically understand the news, in part due to their intellectual stage and motivational structure.

THE FUTURE OF TELEVISION RESEARCH

We have described the effects of television in terms of psychological mechanisms, causal routes, that associate some event on television with some structure in the human organism. The future will bring a more careful analysis of these mechanisms, more precise research that adds detail to our current understanding. I expect we will learn much about imitation, and especially the interesting question of the rate of imitation. That is, we will learn more of how many people, exposed to a particular dramatic event, are likely to imitate it. We will also learn more about the characteristics of these impactful events that makes them, and not others, candidates for imitation. The research on disinhibition will also continue, although as we noted in chapter 4, it is now called the "stimulation of associative networks." Much of this work will use the concept of "scripts" also introduced in chapter 4, and discussed again in chapter 5. These two notions are quite similar. The content of the "associative networks" that is stimulated by television may be in the form of scripts in which our behavior is coded. It is certainly true that much of television can be viewed in this manner, it is scripted. Moreover, it is true that many of these scripts are small, redundant stories that could easily become part of the cognitive repertoire of the viewer. Just how this happens, and what are the consequences will be two important questions for the future.

The study of arousal and desensitization will also continue in the future, because both questions are important to understanding the attention people pay to television, and attention is the primary concern of the programmers. The cognitive mechanisms of mainstreaming and resonance, will, I suspect, continue to be studied by Gerbner and his students, and these ideas may be merged with the notion of scripts and the notion of the stimulation of associative networks mentioned earlier.

I expect a great deal of advance in research on comprehension of television stories, and on the role of formal features of television in aiding comprehension. Research on the role of formal features of television programs in attention and comprehension will eventually tell us more about how and why people react to the structure of television, and in the long run, this research will be useful in designing programs that do a better job of informing as well as entertaining us. Programs designed for children already take advantage of this knowledge, and I expect that trend to continue. Finally, I expect a continued interest in the problem of the perceived reality of television. Things that we perceive as "real" or even "realistic" have a different influence on us than things that are perceived as unreal or fantastic, and yet the nature of that effect or the reasons for it are barely understood.

The future will bring a greater "fine tuning" of research linking the specific information contained in the television programs and ads that people watch to specific effects on their attitudes, values, and behaviors. The analysis of television's effects will become more age specific with different patterns of influence for children 2–6, children 6–12, adolescents, adults, and individuals over 55. Each of these age groups prefers different programs so each is exposed to different sorts of information, and each has specific needs and wants that are satisfied by television. Each of these groups has something different to learn from television.

In a recent article, Bradley S. Greenberg (1988) proposed a different approach to the study of television's content. He calls it the "drip versus drench" hypothesis, and future researchers may want to consider his proposal very seriously. Most content analyses look at the whole of television, at the number of shows featuring blacks, for example, as we did in chapter 3, and from this draw conclusions about the impact of television's portrayals of black people. But as Greenberg (1988) pointed out, one show like "The Cosby Show," a top-rated program currently on television, may overwhelm other portrayals of Blacks. Many more people watch "The Cosby Show" and many more may be influenced by it than by other, less popular, shows. Whereas the other shows represent a "drip, drip, drip" of influence, "The Cosby Show" "drenches" the audience. If so, it could have vastly more impact than the others. So Greenberg's proposal is that future researchers pay more attention to role portrayals that stand out, that are deviant and intense. They represent more important experiences. His argument is that the vast audience out there ignores most portrayals of most roles, and focus their energies and attention on just a few. Researchers would be wise to pay equivalent attention to these outstanding roles because they are the ones viewers are likely to imitate. According to Greenberg (1988):

> The drench hypothesis, in its current, primitive form, asserts that critical images may contribute more to impression-formulation and image-building than does the sheer frequency of television and behaviors that are viewed. The hypothesis provides an alternative to the no-effects hypothesis and to the view that the slow accretion of impressions cumulate across an indefinite time period. Finally, it also suggests that striking, new images can make a difference—that a single character or collection of characters may cause substantial changes in beliefs, perceptions, or expectations about a group or a role, particularly among young viewers. (pp. 100–101)

Finally, I suspect the future research on the effects of television will focus more on values than on attitudes or behaviors. Values are more difficult to analyze than attitudes or behaviors, but they may prove to have a deeper influence. There are two kinds of values on television, the explicit morals of stories and ads, and the implicit values of the images. The explicit values are codified in the network program practices divisions: Racism and sexism are not allowed, obscene language is not permitted, good must triumph over evil, crime doesn't pay (in the long run), and so forth. But it is the implicit values that are more important and these are barely understood.

Consider, for example, television's effects on values and beliefs about crime. Ask the ordinary man or woman in the street these simple questions: Is crime increasing nationally? Is crime increasing in your city? Is crime increasing in your neighborhood? The great likelihood is that most people will answer "yes" to the first two and "no" to the third. This was the finding of a survey done in Baltimore (reported by Glasser, 1988, p. 47), and it is worth taking a moment to think about these facts.

The truth is that crime statistics have been relatively flat since the mid-1970s (Curtis, 1985, p. 23; Walker, 1985, p. 3), and have even gone down in the last few years. People know about their own neighborhoods because they have direct experience with them, but about the broader society they have only indirect experience, and much of that from watching television. We noted this fact in chapter 6 when we were discussing the interesting difference between societal and personal attitudes. Television seems to have a stronger influence on more distant societal attitudes than on attitudes about our own personal lives where we have direct experience. This is not a trivial matter. If we are called upon to vote for more police or more education, which will we choose and why? We do not see hundreds of television shows about the need for better pay for teachers, but we do see hundreds, even thousands, of hours of violence and mayhem. We see dramatic presentations over and over again about the work of the police, because they are one of the most overrepresented occupations on television. But is the story told a true one? And if it is not true, does it influence our attitudes and beliefs anyway?

Most people believe that criminals get away with crimes because the courts let them loose, or because their prison sentences are too short. But as Glasser noted: "The facts are just the opposite. In most American cities only 15% to 18% of reported felonies ever result in arrests (Silberman, 1978, p. 76; Walker, 1985, p. 26, 102). Of that number, most people are convicted, and most go away for pretty long periods of time. There are three times as many people in prison today as there were 10 or 12 years ago, and we have the longest prison sentences of any industrialized nation in the Western world" (Glasser, 1988, p. 48). Why do we have these differences between what people believe is true and what is, in fact, true? Could television play a role in this?

It is certainly true that many television shows contain just these elements. Criminals are usually caught by the police (not true in reality, as we just noted) but on television they get away due to lenient and permissive judges. Cops never make mistakes on television, they know who's guilty before they catch them.

> Now of course the reality is exactly the opposite. That's why we have trials. If we knew who was guilty, we wouldn't need trials. That's why we require search warrants—because often the police don't know who the criminals are and would, if left to their own discretion, break down a lot of wrong doors. This is not fanciful. It happens. Search warrants impel the police to focus on people who are likely suspects by requiring some evidence prior to the search. And as most competent police officials know, search warrants do not hamper effective police work. But that's not the way it's shown on television. (Glasser, 1988, p. 49)

So this is not just a question of the way entertainment affects our attitudes and values, but rather a question of the role of this medium in a democracy. What is the responsibility of television in this regard? The television industry profits greatly from these biased messages about violence, does it bear any responsibility in correcting the false beliefs that it has encouraged? If not television, then who will correct these false impressions? Will the educational establishment do it? So far it has been reluctant to face television directly in the classroom. Should it be the responsibility of parents or other knowledgeable adults to monitor television and try to correct all of its little lies? The answer is that it is the responsibility of all of us, the programmers, the networks, the educational establishment, and parents alike, to see that television does not exert undue influence on our children or our social institutions.

It is not only the program content of television that we must consider either. Television advertisements tell us that when we want something to drink it should be a beer or soda, never water. If we want something to eat it must be processed food, never an apple. Television tells us that it is good to have "good breath" and bad otherwise, that if we are sleepy we should take a drug to wake up, and vice versa, that is, if we are too wide awake we should take a drug to go to sleep. In a recent study (Scheibe, Condry, & Christensen, 1988) we found that 85% of the messages on television about drugs were pro drug, what effect does this have on children who are told, also on television, "just say no to drugs?"

Television tells us that it is good to be thin and sleek, that fat people have to be ashamed of themselves. Television tells us that our hair should always be combed and we should always be on display. Television tells us all these things and many more by indirection, by the images it shows and the values it conveys.

Consider, for example, the problem of body image. In the past few years several researchers have reported that American's show a large discrepancy between their images of themselves and the actuality. Most people, especially young people, are unsatisfied with their bodies. They think they are too fat. This is particularly true of women.

Ideal body image is a social myth. It is not what we "naturally" prefer but what we learn is preferred by our society. But what if our preferences for a certain ideal profile are being manipulated by television? We have noted before that most of the people on television are thin and fit. On television thin is the ideal and someone overweight, even slightly overweight, is often ridiculed. Most of the people on television are in good shape because they are actors and actresses, it is part of their job to be in good shape. But what happens to people in ordinary shape who are constantly exposed to a sample of people who are thinner? Does it make them uncomfortable with their own bodies?

This is a nice example of the "value" aspect of television because it uses a value that is not a moral value, but simply a matter of taste. Furthermore, it is an example of the "latent" content of television as opposed to the "manifest" content. The manifest content is what is there, the actual story that is told. But the latent content is what is hidden beneath the surface, what is implied but not said outright. The value of being thin is not often stated explicitly, but it is implied in almost every scene. Thin people do well, they are happy, they look good in their clothes. It would be a surprise if this value did not influence the preferences and feelings of heavy viewers.

What other values does television portray? What other ways might people be influenced by the latent as opposed to the manifest content of television? How are our emotions and feelings influenced by the constant stream of images that is television? Most of the research to date has been on the manifest content, but I suspect the future will bring much more research on the latent content — on the message beneath the message. Most of the psychological research has been on rational cognitions, but I suspect the future will focus more on the irrational, the feeling part of the mind. Television's influence on this aspect of our lives is greatly understudied and may be the most powerful and lasting influence that television has.

International Television

The spread of television is world wide and has been continuous since television was first introduced. Across the world, the television industry takes many different forms, from completely private commercial enterprises, as in the United States, to wholly government owned and operated, as in the Soviet Union. Between these two extremes there are many different arrangements. Most countries have a mix of private and public television (Varis, 1984). In many countries the public television stations are not run by the government but rather supported by "user fees." These are taxes paid by television set owners each year that go to support the public broadcasting system. This is the case for the BBC in England, and NHK in Japan. These large corporations specialize in news and public affairs programming, much like PBS in the United States, although on a much larger scale.

Much of what is shown on private television networks across the world is imported from other countries, especially the United States and the Soviet Union. By contrast, the United States and Russia import very little television from other countries. The export or import of television around the world is a one-way street, at least for the moment.

For television to become more international, a single format for sending and receiving will have to be adopted. At this time there are several formats each of which is incompatible with the other. A program shown and taped in London, for example, must be "converted" to the American system before it can be shown on American TV. A single system could have been adopted when television was first developed, but it was not. With the arrival of new technologies, such as High Density Television (HDTV) once again there will come the opportunity to adopt a single format world wide. With a single format and the increased use of satellite transmitting, it will be possible to watch television from other countries "on line," that is, live. What effect would it have on American viewers if they could watch Soviet television? There are, of course, language barriers, but these can be solved, as it has been in the United Nations, with simultaneous translation.

When television was first invented, Marshal McLuhan predicted that it would turn the world into a global village. That has not happened yet, but the world is certainly moving in that direction. McLuhan's prediction was too broad. He should have noted that the first effect of television would be to turn the nations into villages, to make them more aware of themselves. When President John F. Kennedy was shot, an entire nation watched on television. As if we were in a single village where a leader had been murdered, we reacted to events as they happened. We saw them happen, we listened as our elders (Walter Cronkite, Chet Huntley, etc.) told the mournful story. We watched the funeral together, as if we were there. This had never before happened in the history of our nation. In the past, when leaders were murdered it took weeks for the news to travel, mourning was fragmented and discontinuous. This was immediate and visual, like in a village. We were there as spectators, participants, not just told of it after it was over.

This difference is an important one psychologically. It is the difference between perception and cognition. Perception is instant, generally accurate, and seldom "mediated" in the sense of interpreted. Perception is *direct*. Cognition is delayed and generally mediated. Cognition is indirect. One is not better than the other, they are just different processes. It is the difference between seeing something happen and reading about it in the newspaper. As television becomes more world wide our understanding of the world will become more perceptual, more direct and immediate than it is now.

Finally, television makes us more alike by what Gerbner called the "homogeneity" of attitudes and values produced by television. Our attitudes are shaped by the information we encounter in the world, and if that information contains systematic distortions, as it does with television, then some of those distortions will be reflected in the minds of people exposed. These may be most important for those things we understand least well, such as other cultures and environments much removed from those of our everyday lives. This homogeneity, however distorted, becomes part of our cultural life and those of us exposed to television share a commonality of outlooks more similar than would be expected from a large and diverse population. The global village works in both directions, by making the world we live in smaller and more immediate, and giving us, however inadvertently, a narrow and often inaccurate description of it.

New Technologies

Television itself is a new technology, as we saw in chapter 1. Forty years after its introduction it is still undergoing development and change. In the few decades since its invention television has gone from a grainy blurry picture in black and white to a brilliant sharp color picture. The broadcast of television has changed as well. At first television was broadcast like radio with the same limitations of being easily disrupted by electrical storms and having a limited range over which the signals could be received. Cable systems have brought television to widespread and remote locations, but even cable systems depend on a single receiver and a selection of program material to send over the cable.

Satellite transmission makes it possible for each homeowner to do his or her own programming by selecting the satellite to be watched. The Japanese have developed and refined a satellite broadcasting system that may put the current satellite receivers out of business because it functions like a broadcast transmitter and the receivers are much smaller and less of an eyesore. The system is much cheaper than the current satellite receivers, and it is capable of broadcasting in a high density format. Whether increased outlets will bring better and more diverse programming is a matter of debate. Some contend that it will (Blessington, 1988), and others argue that it has not done so until now and that it may not (Neuman, 1988). In the long run, however, an increase in available outlets, like radio, will lead to more selectivity on the audience and I believe it will result in greater diversity than we have now.

High Density Television (HDTV) is another advance just around the corner. The Japanese have a working system as do the Europeans (called MAC). Each of these systems broadcast television that has more than twice the number of "lines" as the current systems (around 1,100 lines, compared to the current 550 used in the American system, for example). This makes for a much sharper and clearer picture, close to the quality of 35 millimeter film shown in a movie theater. HDTV also allows a much larger screen without a loss of picture quality.

In addition to these advances in picture and reception quality, there have been and will continue to be advances in audience measurement, because this is the heart and soul of competitive commercial television. While this book was being written, the A.C. Nielsen Co. has introduced a new device for the measurement of the audience. This device, or ones like it, will eventually completely replace the old system of audience measurement. The new device, called a Peoplemeter, measures the actual number of people in the room watching television. Each person in the household has a unique number that must be punched into a hand-held device (and transmitted to a computer) as television is being watched. As we saw in chapter 2, the old system relied on a black box on the television set that recorded whether the set was on and what channel it was tuned into. The new system requires each person to press a button indicating that they are actually watching the program.

Since its introduction in late October 1987 the Peoplemeters have caused a certain amount of havoc in the television industry. The new system is recording a substantially smaller audience (on the order of 10% smaller) than the earlier system of measurement. Industry spokesmen have complained that the new system is difficult to use and may be underestimating the audience, but advertisers are happy to pay less (recall that advertisers pay "by the head").

In the long run, systems like the Peoplemeter offer advertisers a far more precise and exact way of knowing just who is watching their ads, and even whether those who watch actually buy the products. A new system being marketed by Arbitron not only measures the people in the audience, but it also has a "wand" that can be used to monitor the goods bought in the store. In this way advertisers will be able to tell the effectiveness of advertising in a far more precise manner than was heretofore possible.

Finally the continuing spread of VCRs will increase the selectiveness of viewing for households that have one, and as we noted earlier this includes more than 40% of the current households in the United States. The adoption rate of VCRs is paralleling that of television when it was first introduced, as we saw in chapter 1, and there is every reason to believe that this trend will continue. Having a VCR allows people to watch programs on their own time, when they want to rather than when they are shown, and it makes available the world of movies that can be rented and brought into the home. This should provide a strong boost to the movie industry that stands to make as much money on the sale and rental of videotapes as they do from ticket sales in the movie houses. One important consequence of many of these new technologies will be to increase the amount of choice open to viewers. This is especially important when considering the unwinding effects of television. As we noted in chapter 4 when we discussed arousal, the role of choice is especially important in providing televised material that is involving. If one of the main uses of television is to relax after a hard day, then the more choice available the better a person's ability to select material that will have this effect.

Critical Viewing: Television Literacy

One of the striking facts about television is how little the average public knows about the industry itself. It is true that television is a new industry, but it takes up a substantial proportion of our daily lives. We should be better informed about the nature of the industry and the nature of broadcasting itself. It may be particularly important for children to know how television is produced and how it should be interpreted. Yet although many high schools offer courses in literary criticism, and some even offer courses in computer literacy, few offer courses in television literacy. There are probably many reasons for this fact. The television industry is not especially informative about itself and teachers may harbor a dislike and a distrust of television. Students may be all too ready to bring television into the classroom to the distress of many teachers. But we would all be served by more information about the television industry, and children especially need to be informed about the nature of television broadcasting. Children need to develop critical viewing skills to help them interpret what is on, and these should be taught in primary and secondary schools. Children should have "hands-on" practice with using and making television, because such experience would be invaluable in helping them interpret what they see. In the early days of television this would have been an expensive endeavor but now with low cost cameras and VCRs it is possible for every school to offer children the experience of creating their own programs and ads. We need to stop avoiding a discussion of television in our schools and to address the problem head on. Let children discuss the programs they watch and help them understand the forces that produce them.

THE FUTURE OF PROGRAMMING

It is always a difficult business trying to predict the future, but some trends in programming seem likely to continue to develop into the foreseeable future. In the first place, the old "stand-bys" will be with us for quite some time (Comstock, 1988). Television will continue to offer drama, variety entertainment, situation comedies, news and sports. But there will be dramatic changes as well. For one thing, programs will become more selective, and they will be aimed at more precise segments of the audience. This is essentially what has happened to radio and it is reasonable to expect the same trend for television. Until recently, since television was restricted to the three major networks, the kinds of program were the same on all three because of a need to appeal to the largest possible segment of the audience. But with 10 or even 20 channels, broadcasting will diversify in an attempt to gather and hold a select part of the audience. Some of this is happening now. There are channels that appeal to religious people, news channels, channels for children, channels that show mostly sports, channels for adults only, and a channel (CSpan) that provides 24-hour coverage of Congress (when the House and Senate are not in session, CSpan covers committee hearings and interviews congressmen).

I expect this trend of increasingly select programming to continue, to the profit of an audience that will be offered more choice. (For an alternative view, see Neuman, 1988.) I expect programs for adults to become more "realistic" because of the power of the real (and the apparently real) to grasp and hold attention. I expect more news and special events to be produced, again because of the power of "real" television over drama. Finally, I expect better quality television for children.

Educational Television

Because the focus of this book has been largely on network television, I have not discussed the few excellent programs designed for children and available from the public broadcasting system (PBS). Two of the best of these "educational" television programs are "Sesame Street" and "Mister Rogers' Neighborhood." Although these two programs are very different in terms of style, format, and content, both are carefully designed for the needs and intellectual capacities of young children, and both are quite successful in reaching out to a child audience. Both programs are designed for and watched by preschoolers. "Sesame Street" uses a fast paced commercial-type format designed to get and hold the attention of the child viewer (Lesser, 1974). "Mister Rogers' Neighborhood," on the other hand, is much slower paced, but equally capable of holding a large child audience. Both programs, however, are designed to provide information important and useful to young children. "Sesame Street," for example, has a large research component, and the programmers go to great lengths to see that the lesson planned and shown is actually understood by children.

I expect the future to bring more programs of this type, perhaps designed for older children, but with a similar structure. That is, programs designed for a specific audience will be pretested to see that they are effective in both teaching the desired lesson, and in being able to compete with commercial programming. The coming of this type of program will be hastened if parents demand higher quality programs for children broadcast by their local stations. Station managers attend yearly conventions where they purchase programs to be shown during times when the networks have nothing to offer (e.g., 3–6 p.m. on weekday afternoons). If parents demanded that high quality children's programs be purchased for these time slots, at least some station managers would be responsive. As much as it may sound like a cliché, it is still true that the job of the station manager is to program in the public interest.

Finally, I expect the future to bring more programming designed specifically for the elderly. The elderly are a forgotten group on television in part because they are not as attractive as consumers. But children were once viewed in exactly this manner. As the population of the United States gets older, we should expect that programmers will rediscover this group and offer programs that are meaningful and attractive to them (e.g., "The Golden Girls") Because it will be able to offer a greater diversity of programming, and because we will be more and more able to program for ourselves, I expect that television will take more time from our lives in the future than it does now. But because greater diversity and control are helpful, I expect we will be more mindful (as opposed to mindless) viewers than in the past.

SUMMARY

From the perspective of the planet earth, we are just at the beginning of the age of television. We have just begun to scratch the surface of what television can do; we have just begun to study it, and to understand what it does to us. Television is, more than anything else, a series of images. But as human beings we thrive on images; we think in images, we are programmed through thousands of years of evolution to recognize and respond to images. "Imagery is the common language of the global village," as a correspondent on ABC's late night program "Nightline" once said.[1] And the imagery of television washes over us whether we are aware of it or not. It influences us whether we like it or not.

How do these images influence us? As we have seen throughout this

---

[1]I regret that I do not remember the correspondent's name, only his insightful phrase.

book, television has effects on our behaviors, our attitudes, and on our emotions; it effects how we act, think, and feel. Sometimes those effects are intended, as with the advertising, but often they are not. They are simply the consequence of the information available and the fact that we are creatures who utilize this kind of information readily. Maybe no one is to blame.

At its best, television is the most powerful medium of communication ever devised. It can help an entire nation mourn the loss of a president, as it did when John Kennedy was shot. It can inform us clearly about the workings of government, as it did during the McCarthy era, and later with the Watergate hearings and most recently with the Iran-Contra hearings. Television documentaries have the power to galvanize people into action as was the case with Edward R. Morrow's "Harvest of Shame" (about Migrant workers in the 1950s), and more recently Bill Moyer's "Crisis in Black America." Documentary is one of the most powerful things television does, and sadly it has done so with less and less frequency in recent years.

At its worst, television is as bad as its worst critics suggested it might be. In some countries television is used by petty dictators to make them appear godlike to an uneducated population; in others the information provided is what the party in power wants believed. Even in the most technologically advanced and well educated countries television is used to sell politicians like soap and deodorant.

In the words of Edwin Newman speaking on the PBS documentary on "Television": "television must have a brain as well as an eye." The eye can receive the message, but the brain must help us interpret it. The producers of television have a responsibility to provide this interpretation as clearly and forcefully as they know how. Without interpretation, pictures and images have the power to deceive, and with this power comes the temptation to manipulate.

The power of images to manipulate attitudes is most clearly shown in the use of television by political candidates. Almost as soon as television became a major force in the mass media, clever politicians started to use it to enhance their political careers. John F. Kennedy was the first "television president," in the sense of using the medium and the images it portrays to manipulate attitudes about him and against his opponent. The famous Nixon/Kennedy debates were rife with manipulation by Kennedy's staff who were well aware of the power of television images. President Jimmy Carter was also successful as a television image, although not as much as Kennedy. But his understanding of the importance of the medium was as great as Kennedy's, even if his accomplishments were less. Ronald Reagan is the most recent addition to the list of television presidents, and perhaps the most successful.

As I write this we have just ended one of the most negative political campaigns in memory. Political advertisements were effectively used to smear the other candidate rather than to put forward a given candidate's program, and it is a good bet that the future will hold more of the same. Although much of the public was revolted by the negative ads, they were nonetheless influenced by them. This is an old story in advertising. Surveys over the years have indicated that people do not like ads, they consider them intrusive and unpleasant, but they are still influenced by them. Once again, this is a question of the role of the medium in a democracy. Rational choice is the bedrock of a democracy, and if television may be used to undermine that choice, to appeal to emotion rather than reason, we may all be the loser.

Eventually, as a nation, we will have to overcome this childish attraction to form over substance. If we don't we may never elect another Lincoln—a shy and unattractive man who was uncomfortable whenever he was "on display." We must learn that substance is more important than form, and we must elect presidents on the basis of what they will do not how they look, or how well they manipulate the media.

In the long run, however, the direct manipulation of television by politicians and advertisers worries me less than the unintended effects of television. The images of television wash over all of us for many hours every day, some of them accurate and useful, whereas others are inaccurate and used nonetheless. I am reminded again and again of the beautiful, delicate, harmless tarantula. The fear it excites in us is not of its own doing. Nor was a false understanding of tarantulas particularly intended by those who designed the messages. But the information was there, and most of us exposed to it took it in and wove it into our understanding of the world.

It is not reasonable to ask television to be more realistic, to always tell the truth, whatever that is. But television could be more responsible in the way it portrays the "facts" of the world, it could balance some of its most common distortions by a dose, every now and then, of the truth. Television could offer us a wider and more representative sample of the world, and I think that eventually it will. But it is also possible for us to be better educated about the various ways the "truth" of television, however distorted and inaccurate, becomes the truth of our world. We need to experience the production end of television from as early in the schooling experience as is possible. Knowing how it is produced will make us more sensitive to the images and how much or little they tell us. We all need to be better informed about the effects of television, something I hope this book will remedy in its own small way. As television is better understood we will make better use of it, and it will control us less as we come to understand it better.

In a developmental sense television has grown from infancy to mid-dle childhood. It has yet to suffer the pangs of adolescence, it has certainly not yet "come of age." As we know it now, television is still a long way from maturity. But television is our child. We gave birth to it and we delighted in its early years; we embraced it with the great love of a parent for a brilliant if somewhat audacious child. Television, like our other children, will be around after we have gone. The best we can do is make intelligent use of it while we are here—to understand it and improve it, help it reach its full potential as we would with our children. In doing so, we will improve ourselves as well.

Television comes along at a particularly interesting time in human history. As a species we have just developed, through the use of our high intelligence, the means to destroy all life on earth. We have many thousands of these weapons and a great distrust of other people, the worst of all possible situations. But at this same time, also through the application of human intelligence, we have developed a means of communication that may help us understand each other, and ourselves, better than was ever before possible.

We live now at one of the great cusps of history, one of those points where our choices determine, moreso than usual, the quality of life the future has to offer. If we use this means of mass communication well, if we learn from it and use it to increase our understanding of the world and other human beings, we may avoid the disaster that has been pending since the middle of this century. For all the bad things one can say about it, the best thing you can say about television is that it may turn out to be the salvation of the human race. With its constant images it may help us gain a broader perspective on who we are and how, as a species, we share far greater commonality than difference. If the greatest evil is ignorance then the greatest good is communication. It won't make us love each other, but maybe it will help us understand that we are all in the same boat, we share the human condition. Television can combat ignorance or it can increase it. The choice is ours and how we use it will determine the future of the planet.

References

Abel, J. (1988). Making research useful to policymakers. In S. Oskamp (Ed.), *Television as a social issue* (pp. 315–323). Newbury Park, CA: Sage.

Abel, J., Fontes, B., Greenberg, B., & Atkin, C. (1980). *The impact of television on children's occupational role learning.* Unpublished report, Michigan State University, East Lansing, MI.

Abelman, R. (1984). Learning to learn TV cues and TVQs. *Television and Children, 7,* 13–17.

Abelson, R. P. (1976). Script processing in attitude formation and decision making. In J. S. Carroll & J. W. Payne (Eds.), *Cognition and social behavior* (pp. 33–45). Hillsdale, NJ: Lawrence Erlbaum Associates.

Adler, R. P., Lesser, G. S., Meringoff, L. K., Robertson, T. S., Rossiter, J. R., & Ward, S. (Eds). (1980). *The effects of television advertising on children: Review and recommendation.* Lexington, MA: Lexington Books.

Anderson, D. R., Alwitt, L. F., Lorch, E. P., & Levin, S. R. (1979). Watching children watch television. In G. Hale & M. Lewis (Eds.), *Attention and the development of cognitive skills* (pp. 331–361). New York: Plenum.

Anderson, D. R., & Collins, P. A. (1988, April) *The impact on children's education: Television's influence on cognitive development.* United States Department of Education, Office of Educational Research and improvement. Working paper #2.

Anderson, D. R., & Levin, S. R. (1976). Young children's attention to Sesame Street. *Child Development, 47,* 806–811.

Anderson, J. (1983). Television literacy and the critical viewer. In J. Bryant & D. Anderson (Eds.), *Children's understanding of television* (pp. 297–330). New York: Academic Press.

Andison, F. S. (1977). TV violence and viewer aggression: A cumulation of study results. *Public Opinion Quarterly, 41,* 14–31.

Arbitron Ratings, Inc. (1988). *An Arbitron diary of our television viewing.* New York: Author.

Arenstein, H. L. (1974). *The effect of television on children's stereotyping of occupational roles.* Unpublished master's thesis, Annenberg School of Communications, University of Pennsylvania, Philadelphia, PA.

Arlen, M. J. (1979). *Thirty seconds.* England: Penguin Books.

Aronoff, C. (1974). Old age in prime time. *Journal of Communication, 24*(1), 86–87.

Atkin, C. K. (1975a). Communication and political socialization. *Political Communication Review, 1,* 2–7.

Atkin, C. K. (1975b). *The effects of television advertising on children: Parent–child communication in supermarket breakfast cereal selection* (final report). Washington, DC: Office of Child Development, Department of Health, Education and Welfare. Resources in Education (ERIC Document Reproduction Service No. Ed 123 674).

Atkin, C. K. (1975c). *The effects of television advertising on children: Survey of children's and mothers' responses to television commercials* (final report). Washington, DC: Office of Child Development, Department of Health, Education and Welfare. Resources in Education (ERIC Document Reproduction Service No. Ed 123 675).

Atkin, C. K. (1978a). Broadcast news programming and the child audience. *Journal of Broadcasting, 22,* 47–61.

Atkin, C. K. (1978b). *Children's advertising rulemaking comment: A study of children and TV advertising.* Written testimony submitted to the Federal Trade Commission.

Atkin, C. K. (1978c). Effects of drug commercials on young viewers. *Journal of Communication, 28*(4), 71–79.

Atkin, C. K. (1979). Research evidence on mass mediated health communication campaigns. In D. Nimmo (Ed.), *Communication yearbook* (pp. 655–668). New Brunswick, NJ: International Communication Association.

Atkin, C. K. (1980). Effects of television advertising on children. In E. L. Palmer & A. Dorr (Eds.), *Children and the faces of television: Teaching, violence, selling* (pp. 287–303). New York: Academic Press.

Atkin, C. K. (1982). Television advertising and socialization to consumer roles. In D. Pearl, L. Bouthilet, & J. Lazar (Eds.), *Television and behavior: Ten years of scientific progress and implications for the eighties. Vol. 2, Technical reviews* (pp. 191–200). Rockville, MD: NIMH.

Atkin, C. (1983). Effects of realistic television violence vs. fictional violence on aggression. *Journalism Quarterly, 60,* 615–621.

Atkin, C. K., & Gibson, W. (1978). *Children's responses to cereal commercials.* Unpublished manuscript, Michigan State University, East Lansing, MI.

Atkin, C., & Miller, M. (1975, April). *The effects of television advertising on children: Experimental evidence.* Paper presented at the meeting of the International Communication Association, Chicago, IL.

Ball-Rokeach, S. J., Rokeach, M., & Grube, J. W. (1985). *Influencing behavior and belief through television.* New York: The Free Press.

Bandura, A. (1973). *Aggression: A social learning analysis.* New York: Holt, Rinehart & Winston.

Bandura, A. (1977). *Social learning theory.* Englewood Cliffs, NJ: Prentice-Hall.

Bandura, A., & Huston, A. C. (1961). Identification as a process of incidental learning. *Journal of Abnormal and Social Psychology, 63,* 311–318.

Bandura, A., Ross, D., & Ross, S. (1961). Transmission of aggression through imitation of aggressive models. *Journal of Abnormal and Social Psychology, 63,* 575–582.

Bandura, A., Ross, D., & Ross, S. (1963). Imitation of film-mediated aggressive models. *Journal of Abnormal and Social Psychology, 66,* 3–11.

Bandura, A., & Walters, R. H. (1963). Aggression. In H. Stevenson (Ed.), *Child psychology, 62nd yearbook of the National Society for the Study of Education, Part 1.* Chicago: University of Chicago Press.

Barcus, F. E. (1972). *Network programming and advertising in the Saturday children's hours: A June and November comparison.* Newtonville, MA: Action for Children's Television.

Barcus, F. E. (1977). *Children's television: An analysis of programming and advertising.* New York: Praeger.

Barcus, F. E. (1980). The nature of television advertising to children. In E. Palmer & A. Dorr (Eds.), *Children and the faces of television: Teaching, violence, selling* (pp. 273–286). New York: Academic Press.

Barcus, F. E. (1983). *Images of life on children's television.* New York: Praeger Publishers.

Barker, D. (1985). Television production techniques as communication. *Critical Studies in Mass Communication, 2,* 234–246.

Barnouw, E. (1966). *A tower of babel: A history of broadcasting in the United States to 1933.* New York: Oxford University Press.

Barnouw, E. (1968). *The golden web: A history of broadcasting in the United States 1933–1953.* New York: Oxford University Press.

Barnouw, E. (1970). *The image empire: A history of broadcasting in the United States from 1953.* New York: Oxford University Press.

Barnouw, E. (1982). *Tube of plenty: The evolution of American television* (rev. ed.). New York: Oxford University Press.

Baron, J. N., & Reiss, P. C. (1985). Same time, next year: Aggregate analyses of the mass media and violent behavior. *American Sociological Review, 50,* 347–363.

Baron, L. (1985). Television literacy curriculum in Action: A long-term study. *Journal of Educational Television, 11,* 49–55.

Barry, T. E., & Sheikh, A. A. (1977). Race as a dimension in children's TV advertising: The need for more research. *Journal of Advertising, 6*(3), 5–10.

Beck, K. (1978). Television and the older woman. *Television Quarterly, 15*(2), 47–49.

Becker, G. (1972). Causal analysis in R-R studies: Television violence and aggression. *American Psychologist, 27,* 967–968.

Belson, W. A. (1960). The effects of television upon family life. *Discovery, 21*(10), 1–5.

Belson, W. (1978). *Television violence and the adolescent boy.* Westmead, England: Saxon House, Teakfield LTD.

Bence, P. (1987). *From "Howdy Doody" to "Hulk Hogan's Rock 'n Wrestling": A 36 year history of children's network television.* Unpublished manuscript, Cornell University, Ithaca, NY.

Berkowitz, L. (1962). *Aggression: A social psychological analysis.* New York: McGraw-Hill.

Berkowitz, L. (1965). Some aspects of observed aggression. *Journal of Personality and Social Psychology, 2,* 359–369.

Berkowitz, L. (1969). The frustration-aggression hypothesis revisited. In L. Berkowitz (Ed.), *Roots of aggression: A reexamination of the frustration-aggression hypothesis* (pp. 1–28). New York: Atherton.

Berkowitz, L. (1971). Sex and violence: We can't have it both ways. (Some observations on the reports of the Violence and Pornography Commissions.) *Psychology Today, 5*(7), pp. 18–23.

Berkowitz, L. (1973). The control of aggression. In B. Caldwell & H. Ricciuti (Eds.), *Review of child development research* (Vol. 3, pp. 95–140). Chicago: University of Chicago Press.

Berkowitz, L. (1974). Some determinants of impulsive aggression: The role of mediated associations with reinforcements for aggression. *Psychological Review, 81,* 165–176.

Berkowitz, L. (1984). Some effects of thoughts on anti- and prosocial influences of media events: A cognitive–neoassociationist analysis. *Psychological Bulletin, 95,* 410–427.

Berkowitz, L., & Alioto, J. T. (1973). The meaning of an observed event as a determinant of its aggressive consequences. *Journal of Personality and Social Psychology, 28,* 206–217.

Berkowitz, L., Corwin, R., & Heironimus, M. (1963). Film violence and subsequent aggressive tendencies. *Public Opinion Quarterly, 27,* 217–229.

Berkowitz, L., & Donnerstein, E. (1982). External validity is more than skin deep: Some answers to criticisms of laboratory experiments (with a special reference to research on aggression). *American Psychologist, 37,* 245–257.

Berkowitz, L., & Geen, R. G. (1966). Film violence and the cue properties of available targets. *Journal of Personality and Social Psychology, 3*(66), 525–530.

Berkowitz, L., & Macaulay, J. (1971). The contagion of criminal violence. *Sociometry, 34,* 238–260.

Berkowitz, L., & Rawlings, E. (1963). Effects of film violence on inhibitions against subsequent aggression. *Journal of Abnormal and Social Psychology, 66*(3), 405–412.

Berry, G. L. (1980). Children, television and social class roles: The medium as an unplanned curriculum. In E. L. Palmer & A. Dorr (Eds.), *Children and the faces of television* (pp. 71–81). New York: Academic Press.

Berry, G. L. (1982). Research perspectives on the portrayals of Afro-American families on television. In A. W. Jackson (Ed.), *Black families and the medium of television* (pp. 47–59). Ann Arbor: Bush Program in Child Development and Social Policy, University of Michigan.

Berry, G. L. (1988). Multicultural role portrayals on television as a social psychological issue. In S. Oskamp (Ed.), *Television as a social issue* (pp. 118–127). Newbury Park, CA: Sage.

Beuf, A. (1974). Doctor, lawyer, household drudge. *Journal of Communication, 24*(2), 142–145.

Bjorkqvst, K., & Didrikkson, B. (1985, August). *Desensitization to film violence in aggressive and nonaggressive boys.* Paper presented at the meetings of the International Society for Research on Aggression, Parma, Italy.

Blank, D. M. (1977a). The Gerbner violence profile. *Journal of Broadcasting, 21,* 273–279.

Blank, D. M. (1977b). Final comments on the violence profile. *Journal of Broadcasting, 21,* 287–296.

Blatt, J., Spencer, L., & Ward, S. (1972). A cognitive developmental study of children's reactions to television advertising. In E. A. Rubinstein, G. A. Comstock, & J. P. Murray (Eds.), *Television and social behavior: Vol. 4. Television in day-to-day life: Patterns of use* (pp. 452–467). Washington, DC: U.S. Government Printing Office.

Blessington, J. P. (1988). Future visions of television. In S. Oskamp (Ed.), *Television as a social issue* (pp. 350–357). Newbury Park, CA: Sage.

Block, M. P., & Vanden Bergh, B. G. (1985). Can you sell subliminal messages to consumers? *Journal of Advertising, 14*(3), 59–62.

Blumler, J., & Katz, E. (Eds.). (1975). *The uses of mass communications.* Newbury Park, CA: Sage.

Bogart, L. (1972). *The age of television.* New York: Ungar.

Bower, R. T. (1973). *Television and the public.* New York: Holt, Rinehart & Winston.

Bower, R. T. (1985). *The changing television audience in America.* New York: Columbia University Press.

Breed, W., & DeFoe, J. R. (1981). The portrayal of the drinking process on prime-time television. *Journal of Communication, 31*(1), 58–67.

Briere, J., Corne, S., Runtz, M., & Malamuth, N. M. (1984, August). *The rape arousal inventory: Predicting actual and potential sexual aggression in a university population.* Paper presented at the annual meetings of the American Psychological Association, Toronto, Canada.

Broadcast of information by means of "subliminal perception" techniques. (1974). F.C.C. 2d 1016.

Brookfield, S. (1986). Media power and the development of media literacy: An adult educational interpretation. *Harvard Educational Review, 56*(2), 151–170.

Brooks, T., & Marsh, E. (1981). *The complete directory to prime time network TV shows 1946–present.* New York: Ballantine Books.

Brown, J. R., Cramond, J. K., & Wilde, R. J. (1974). Displacement effects of television and the child's functional orientation to media. In J. G. Blumler & E. Katz (Eds.), *The uses of mass communication.* London: Sage.

Brown, M. H., Skeen, P., & Osborn, K. K. (1979). Young children's perception of the reality of television. *Contemporary Education, 50*(3), 129–133.

Bryant, J., & Anderson, D. R. (Eds.). (1983). *Children's understanding of television: Research on attention and comprehension.* New York: Academic Press.

Bryant, J., Carveth, R. A., & Brown, D. (1981). Television viewing and anxiety: An experimental examination. *Journal of Communication, 31,* 106–119.

Bryant, J., Hezel, R., & Zillmann, D. (1978). Humor in children's educational television. *Communication Education, 28,* 49–59.

Bryant, J., & Zillmann, D. (1977). The mediating effect of the intervention potential of communications on displaced aggressiveness and retaliatory behavior. In B. D. Ruben (Ed.), *Communication yearbook 1.* New Brunswick, NJ: ICA–Transaction Press.

Bryant, W. K., & Gerner, J. L. (1981). Television use by adults and children: a multivariate analysis. *Journal of Consumer Research, 8,* 154–160.

Bryce, J., & Leichter, H. J. (1983). The family and television: Forms of mediation. *Journal of Family Issues, 4,* 309–328.

Buck, R. (1976). *Human motivation and emotion.* New York: Wiley.

Buerkel-Rothfuss, N., Greenberg, B., & Neuendorf, K. (1978). *Two seasons of family role interactions on commercial television. Project CASTLE:* (Report No. 8). East Lansing, MI: Department of Communication, Michigan State University.

Burmester, D. (1984). The case for video study. *English Journal, 73,* 104–106.

Busby, L. J. (1974). Defining the sex-role standard in network children's programs. *Journalism Quarterly, 41*(4), 690–696.

Busby, L. J. (1975). Sex-role research on mass media. *Journal of Communication, 25*(4), 107–131.

Butler, M., & Paisley, W. (1980). *Women and the mass media.* New York: Human Sciences Press.

Calvert, S., Huston, A. C., Watkins, B. A., & Wright, J. C. (1981). *The effects of selective attention to television forms on children's comprehension of content.* Paper presented at the meeting of the Society for Research in Child Development, Boston, MA.

Calvert, S., Huston, A. C., Watkins, B. A., & Wright, J. C. (1982). The effects of selective attention to television forms on children's comprehension of content. *Child Development, 53,* 601–610.

Calvert, S., & Watkins, B. (1979, March). *Recall of television content as a function of content type and level of production features used.* Paper presented at the Biennial Meeting of the Society for Research in Child Development, San Francisco, CA.

Campbell, T. (1982). *Formal cues and content difficulty as determinants of children's cognitive processing of televised educational messages.* Unpublished doctoral dissertation, University of Kansas, Lawrence, KS.

Campbell, W. J., & Keogh, R. (1962). *Television and the Australian adolescent.* Sydney: Angus & Robertson.

Cantor, J. R. (1978). Research on television's effects on children. *Phaedrus, 5*(1), 9–13.

Cantor, J., & Wilson, B. J. (1984). Modifying fear responses to mass media in preschool and elementary school children. *Journal of Broadcasting, 28,* 431–443.

Cantor, J. R., Zillmann, D., & Einsiedel, E. F. (1978). Female responses to provocation after exposure to aggressive and erotic films. *Communication Research, 5,* 395–411.

Cantril, H., Gaudet, H., & Hertzog, H. (1940). *The invasion from Mars.* Princeton, NJ: Princeton University Press.

Caron, A. H., & Ward, S. (1975). Gift decisions by kids and parents. *Journal of Advertising Research, 15*(4), 15–20.

Carruthers, M., & Taggart, P. (1973). Vagotonicity of violence: Biochemical and cardiac responses to violent films and television programs. *British Medical Journal, 3,* 384–389.

Cassata, M. B., Skill, T. D., & Boadu, S. O. (1979). In sickness and in health. *Journal of Communication, 29*(4), 73–80.

Castleman, H., & Podrazik, W. (1984). *The schedule book: Four decades of network programming from sign-on to sign-off.* New York: McGraw-Hill.

Catton, W. R. (1969). Outline of research required on effects. In D. Lange, R. Baker, & S. Ball (Eds.), *Mass media and violence: A report to the National Commission on the Causes and Prevention of Violence* (pp. 415–422). Washington, DC: U.S. Government Printing Office.

CBS, Inc., Office of Social Research. (1977). *Network prime-time violence tabulations for the 1976–77 season and instructions to coders, 1976–77.*

Ceniti, J., & Malamuth, N. M. (1984). Effects of repeated exposure to sexually violent or sexually nonviolent stimuli on sexual arousal to rape and nonrape depictions. *Behavior Research and Therapy, 22,* 535–538.

Chaffee, S. H. (1972). Television and adolescent aggressiveness (overview). In G. A. Comstock & E. A. Rubinstein (Eds.), *Television and social behavior: Vol. 3. Television and adolescent aggressiveness* (pp. 1–34). Washington, DC: U.S. Government Printing Office.

Chaffee, S. H., & McLeod, J. M. (1972). Adolescent television use in the family context. In G. A. Comstock & E. A. Rubinstein (Eds.), *Television and social behavior: Vol. 3. Television and adolescent aggressiveness* (pp. 149–172). Washington, DC: U.S. Government Printing Office.

Clancy–Hepburn, K., Hickey, A., & Neville, G. (1974). Children's behavior responses to TV food advertisements. *Journal of Nutrition Education, 6,*(3) 93–96.

Clark, D. G., & Blankenburg, W. B. (1972). Trends in violent content in selected mass media. In G. A. Comstock & E. A. Rubinstein (Eds.), *Television and social behavior. Vol. 1, Media content and control* (pp. 188-243). Washington, DC: U.S. Government Printing Office.

Cline, V. B., Croft, R. G., & Courrier, S. (1973). Desensitization of children to television violence. *Journal of Personality and Social Psychology, 27,* 360-365.

Cocks, J. (1983, December 26). Sing a song of seeing. *Time,* p. 54.

Cocks, J. (1985, September 30). Rock is a four-letter word. *Time,* pp. 70-71.

Coe, B., & MacLachlan, J. (1980). How major TV advertisers evaluate commercials. *Journal of Advertising Research, 20,* 51-54.

Coffin, T. E. (1955). Television's impact on society. *American Psychologist, 10,* 630-641.

Coffin, T. E., & Tuchman, S. (1972-1973). Rating television programs for violence: A comparison of five surveys. *Journal of Broadcasting, 17*(1), 3-20.

Collins, W. A. (1973). The effect of temporal separation between motivation, aggression, and consequences: A developmental study. *Developmental Psychology, 8*(2), 215-221.

Collins, W. A. (1979). Children's comprehension of television content. In E. Wartella (Ed.), *Children communicating: Media and development of thought, speech, understanding* (pp. 21-52). Beverly Hills: Sage.

Collins, W. A. (1982). Cognitive processing in television viewing. In D. Pearl, L. Bouthilet, & J. Lazar (Eds.), *Television and behavior: Ten years of scientific progress and implications for the eighties. Vol. 2, Technical reviews* (pp. 32-48). Rockville, MD: NIMH.

Collins, W. A. (1983a). Interpretation and inference in children's television viewing. In J. Bryant & D. R. Anderson (Eds.), *Children's understanding of television: Research on attention and comprehension* (pp. 125-150). New York: Academic Press.

Collins, W. A. (1983b). Social antecedents, cognitive processing, and comprehension of social portrayals on television. In E. T. Higgins, D. N. Ruble, & W. W. Hartup (Eds.), *Social cognition and social development: A sociocultural perspective* (pp. 110-133). London: Cambridge University Press.

Collins, W. A., Sobol, B. L., & Westby, S. (1981). Effects of adult commentary on children's comprehension and inferences about a televised aggressive portrayal. *Child Development, 52,* 158-163.

Collins, W. A., Wellman, H., Keniston, A. H., & Westby, S. D. (1978). Age-related aspects of comprehension and inference from a televised dramatic narrative. *Child Development, 49,* 389-399.

Comstock, G. (1978). The impact of television on American institutions. *Journal of Communication, 28,* 12-28.

Comstock, G. (1980a). *Television in America.* Beverly Hills, CA: Sage.

Comstock, G. (1980b). What children watch does affect how they act. *NCCT Forum, 3*(1), 30-35.

Comstock, G. (1988). Today's audiences, tomorrow's media. In S. Oskamp (Ed.), *Television as a social issue* (pp. 325-345). Newbury Park, CA: Sage.

Comstock, G., Chaffee, S., Katzman, N., McCombs, M., & Roberts, D. (1978). *Television and human behavior.* New York: Columbia University Press.

Condry, J. C. (1962). *Prestige vs. credibility in attitude change.* Unpublished master's thesis, West Virginia University, Morgantown, WV.

Condry, J. C. (1971, August). Broadcasting and the needs of children. *Clinical Pediatrics,* 459-461.

Condry, J. C. (1977). Enemies of exploration: Self-initiated versus other-initiated learning. *Journal of Personality and Social Psychology, 35*(7), 459-477.

Condry, J. C. (1978, November). *The effects of advertising on children.* Written testimony submitted to the Federal Trade Commission (FTC).

Condry, J. C. (1984). Gender identity and social competence. *Sex Roles, 11*(5/6), 485-511.

Condry, J. C. (1987). Enhancing motivation. In D. Kleiber & M. Maehr (Eds.), *Advances in motivation and achievement: Enhancing motivation* (Vol. 5, pp. 23–49). Greenwich, CT: JAI Press.

Condry, J. C., Bence, P., & Scheibe, C. (1988). Non-program content of children's television. *Journal of Broadcasting and Electronic Media. 32*(3), 255–270.

Condry, J. C., & Keith, D. (1983). Educational and recreational uses of computer technology. *Youth and Society, 15*(1), 87–112.

Cook, T. D., Kendzierski, D. A., & Thomas, S. V. (1983). The implicit assumptions of television research. *Public Opinion Quarterly, 47,* 161–201.

Corder-Bolz, C. R. (1982). Television literacy and critical television viewing skills. In D. Pearl, L. Bouthilet, & J. Lazar (Eds.), *Television and human behavior: Ten years of scientific progress and implications for the eighties. Vol. 2, Technical reviews* (pp. 91–102). Rockville, MD: NIMH.

Corteen, R. S. (1977, June). Television and reading skills. In T. M. Williams (Chair). *The impact of television: A natural experiment involving three communities.* A symposium presented at the annual meeting of the Canadian Psychological Association, Vancouver.

Courtney, A. E., & Whipple, T. W. (1974). Women in TV commercials. *Journal of Communication, 24*(2), 110–118.

Courtney, A. E., & Whipple, T. W. (1981). *Sex stereotyping in advertising: An annotated bibliography.* Cambridge: Marketing Science Institute.

Craig, R. (1985). J-Educators must deal with "A Nation at Risk." *Journalism Educator, 40,* 42–44.

Culley, J. D., & Bennett, R. (1975). Selling women, selling blacks. *Journal of Communication, 26*(4), 160–174.

Curtis, L. A. (Ed.). (1985). *American violence and public policy: An update of the National Commission on the Causes and Prevention of Violence.* New Haven, CT: Yale University Press.

Davis, R. (1971). Television and the older adult. *Journal of Broadcasting, 15,* 153–159.

DeFleur, M. L. (1964). Occupational roles as portrayed on television. *Public Opinion Quarterly, 28,* 57–74.

DeFleur, M. L., & DeFleur, L. (1967). The relative contribution of television as a learning source for children's occupational knowledge. *American Sociological Review, 32,* 777–789.

DeFleur, M. L., & Petranoff, J. (1959). A televised test of subliminal persuasion. *Public Opinion Quarterly, 23,* 168–180.

Denisoff, S., & Levine, M. (1971). The popular protest song: The case of "Eve of Destruction." *Public Opinion Quarterly, 35,* 117–122.

Dervin, B., & Greenberg, B. S. (1972). The communication environment of the urban poor. In F. G. Kline & P. J. Tichenor (Eds.), *Current perspectives in mass communication research.* Beverly Hills, London: Sage.

Desmond, R. J. (1986). *Adolescents and music lyrics: Research and speculation.* Unpublished manuscript, Department of Communication, University of Hartford, Hartford, CT.

Desmond, R. J., Singer, J. L., Singer, D. G., Calam, R., & Colimore, K. (1985). Family mediation patterns and television viewing: Young children's use and grasp of the medium. *Human Communication Research, 11*(4), 461–480.

Dillon, J. (1975a, June 30). TV drinking: How networks pour liquor into your living room. *Christian Science Monitor,* p. 6.

Dillon, J. (1975b, July 1). TV drinking: Do networks follow own code? *Christian Science Monitor,* pp. 12–13.

Dillon, J. (1975c, July 11). TV drinking does not mirror U.S. *Christian Science Monitor,* p. 4.

Dixon, N. F. (1981). *Preconscious processing.* New York: Wiley.

Dohrmann, R. D. (1975). A gender profile of children's educational TV. *Journal of Communication, 35*(4), 56–65.

Dominick, J. R. (1973). Crime and law enforcement in prime-time television. *Public Opinion Quarterly, 37,* 243–250.

Dominick, J. R., & Greenberg, B. S. (1970). Mass media functions among low-income adolescents. In B. S. Greenberg & B. Dervin (Eds.), *Uses of the mass media by the urban poor* (pp. 31–48). New York: Praeger.

Dominick, J. R., & Greenberg, B. S. (1972). Attitudes toward violence: The interaction of television exposure, family attitudes, and social class. In G. A. Comstock & E. A. Rubinstein (Eds.), *Television and social behavior. Vol. 3, Television and adolescent aggressiveness* (pp. 314–335). Washington, DC: U.S. Government Printing Office.

Dominick, J., & Rauch, G. (1972). The image of women in network TV commercials. *Journal of Broadcasting, 16,* 259–265.

Donnager, P. C., Poulos, R. W., Liebert, R. M., & Davidson, E. S. (1976). Race, sex and social example: An analysis of character portrayals on interracial television entertainment. *Psychological Reports, 38,* 3–14.

Donnerstein, E., & Hallam, J. (1978). Facilitating effects of erotica on aggression against women. *Journal of Personality and Social Psychology, 36,* 1270–1277.

Donohue, T. R. (1975). Effect of commercials on black children. *Journal of Advertising Research, 15*(6), 41–47.

Donohue, W. A., & Donohue, T. R. (1977). Black, white, white gifted, and emotionally disturbed children's perceptions of the reality in television programming. *Human Relations, 30,* 7, 609–621.

Doob, A. N., & MacDonald, G. E. (1979). Television viewing and fear of victimization: Is the relationship causal? *Journal of Personality and Psychology, 37*, 170–179.

Dorr, A. (1983). No shortcuts to judging reality. In J. Bryant & D. R. Anderson (Eds.), *Children's understanding of television: Research on attention and comprehension* (pp. 199–220). New York: Academic Press.

Dorr, A. (1986). *Television and children: A special medium for a special audience.* Beverly Hills: Sage.

Dorr, A. (1988). When social scientists cooperate with broadcasting. In S. Oskamp (Ed.), *Television as a social issue* (pp. 285–303). Newbury Park, CA: Sage.

Dorr, A., Graves, S. B., & Phelps, E. (1980). Television literacy for young children. *Journal of Communication, 30*(3), 71–83.

Dorr, A., Kovaric, P., Doubleday, C., Sims, D., & Seidner, L. B. (1985, August). *Beliefs about the realism of television programs featuring families.* Paper presented at the annual meeting of the American Psychological Association, Los Angeles, CA.

Dougherty, S. (1985, September) Parents vs rock, *People,* 46–53.

Drabman, R. S., & Thomas, M. H. (1974). Does media violence increase children's toleration of real-life aggression? *Developmental Psychology, 10*(3), 418–421.

Drew, D., & Reeves, B. (1980). Learning from a television news story. *Communication Research, 7,* 121–135.

Dubanoski, R. A., & Parton, D. A. (1971). Imitative aggression in children as a function of observing a human model. *Developmental Psychology, 4,* 489.

Edwards, E., & Singletary, M. (1984). Mass media images in popular music. *Popular Music and Society, 9,* 17–26.

Eisenberg, G. J. (1980). Children and aggression after observed film aggression with sanctioning adults. *Annals of the New York Academy of Science, 347,* 304–318.

Ekman, P., Liebert, R. M., Friesen, W. V., Harrison, R., Zlatchin, C., Malmstrom, E. J., & Baron, R. A. (1972). Facial expressions of emotion while watching televised violence as predictors of subsequent aggression. In G. A. Comstock, E. A. Rubinstein, & J. P. Murray (Eds.), *Television and social behavior. Vol. 5, Television's effects: Further explorations* (pp. 22–58). Washington, DC: U.S. Government Printing Office.

Ellis, G. T., & Sekura, F. III (1972). The effect of aggressive cartoons on the behavior of first grade children. *Journal of Psychology, 81,* 7–43.

Emery, W. B. (1971). *Broadcasting and government: Responsibilities and regulations.* East Lansing: Michigan State University Press.

Eron, L. (1963). Relationship with TV viewing habits and aggressive behavior in children. *Journal of Abnormal and Social Psychology, 67,* 193–196.

Eron, L. D. (1986). Interventions to mitigate the psychological effects of media violence on aggressive behavior. *Journal of Social Issues, 42*(3), 155–169.

Eron, L. D., & Huesmann, L. R. (1980a). Adolescent aggression and television. *Annals of the New York Academy of Sciences, 347,* 319–331.

Eron, L. D., & Huesmann, L. R. (1980b, August). *Integrating field and laboratory investigations of televised violence and aggression.* Paper presented at the meeting of the American Psychological Association, Montreal.

Eron, L. D., Huesmann, L. R., Lefkowitz, M. M., & Walder, L. O. (1972). Does television violence cause aggression? *American Psychologist, 27,* 253–263.

Federal Communications Commission (1974). *Children's television programs: Report and policy statement,* 39 Fed. Reg. 39396, 39401; 50 F.C.C. 2nd 1, 11.

Federal Trade Commission. (1978). *FTC staff report on television advertising to children.* Washington, DC: U.S. Government Printing Office.

Fernie, D. E. (1981, April). *Ordinary and extraordinary people: Children's understanding of television and real-life models.* Paper presented at the Society for Research in Child Development Biennial Meeting, Boston, MA.

Feshbach, S. (1972). Reality and fantasy in filmed violence. In J. P. Murray, E. A. Rubinstein, & G. A. Comstock (Eds.), *Television and social learning* (pp. 318–345). Washington, DC: U.S. Government Printing Office.

Feshbach, S. (1976). The role of fantasy in the response to television. *Journal of Social Issues, 32*(4), 71–85.

Feshbach, S. (1988). Television research and social policy: Some perspectives. In S. Oskamp (Ed.), *Television as a social issue* (pp. 198–213). Newbury Park, CA: Sage.

Feshbach, S., & Singer, R. D. (1971). *Television and aggression: An experimental field study.* San Francisco: Jossey-Bass.

Fiske, J. (1985, June). The semiotics of television. *Critical studies in Mass Communication,* 176–183.

Flavell, J. H., Flavell, E. R., & Green, F. L. (1987, April). *Young children's knowledge about the apparent-real and pretend-real distinctions.* Paper presented at the biennial meeting of the Society for Research in Child Development, Baltimore, MD.

Franzblau, S., Sprafkin, J. N., & Rubinstein, E. (1977). Sex on TV: A content analysis. *Journal of Communication, 27,* 164–170.

Franzwa, H. (1978). The image of women in television: An annotated bibliography. In G. Tuchman, A. K. Daniels, & J. Benet (Eds.), *Hearth and home: Images of women in the mass media* (pp. 272–300). New York: Oxford University Press.

Freedman, J. L. (1984). Effect of television violence on aggressiveness. *Psychological Bulletin, 96,* 227–246.

Freedman, J. L. (1988). Television violence and aggression: What the evidence shows. In S. Oskamp (Ed.), *Television as a social issue* (pp. 144–162). Newbury Park, CA: Sage.

French, J. R. P., Jr., & Raven, B. (1960). The bases of social power. In D. Cartwright & A. Zander (Eds.), *Group dynamics: Research and theory* (pp. 607–623). New York: Harper & Row.

Freuh, T., & McGhee, P. (1975). Traditional sex-role development and amount of time spent watching television. *Child Development, 11,* 109.

Friedlander, B. Z., Wetstone, S., & Scott, L. (1974). Suburban preschool children's comprehension of an age-appropriate information television program. *Child Development, 45,* 561–565.

Friedrich, L. K., & Stein, A. H. (1973). Aggressive and prosocial television programs and the natural behavior of preschool children. *Monographs of the Society for Research in Child Development, 38*(4), Serial No. 151.

Friedrich, L. K., & Stein, A. H. (1975). Prosocial television and young children: The effects of verbal labeling and role playing on learning and behavior. *Child Development, 46*, 27–38.

Friedrich-Cofer, L., & Huston, A. C. (1986). Television violence and aggression: The debate continues. *Psychological Bulletin. 100*, 364–371.

Furstenberg, F. F., Jr. (1971). Public reaction to crime in the streets. *American Scholar, 40*, 601–610.

Furu, T. (1962). *Television and children's life: A before-after study.* Tokyo: Japan Broadcasting Corporation.

Furu, T. (1971). *The function of television for children and adolescents.* Tokyo: Sophia University Press.

Futch, E., Geller, M. J., & Lisman, S. A. (1980). Analysis of alcohol use on prime time television. Unpublished paper, State University of New York at Binghamton, NY.

Gade, E. (1971, March). Representation of the world of work in daytime television serials. *Journal of Employment Counseling, 37–42.*

Gaines, L., & Esserman, J. (1981). A quantitative study of young children's comprehension of television programs and commercials. In J. F. Esserman (Ed.), *Television advertising and children issues, research and fundings* (pp. 96–105). New York: Child Research Service.

Galloway, J. J., & Meek, F. L. (1981). Audience uses and gratifications: An expectancy model. *Communications Research, 8*, 435–449.

Galst, J. P., & White, M. A. (1976). The unhealthy persuader: The reinforcing value of television and children's purchase-influencing attempts at the supermarket. *Child Development, 47*, 1089–1096.

Gantz, W. (1977). Gratifications and expectations associated with popular music among adolescents. *Popular Music and Society, 4*, 14–22.

Geen, R. G. (1975). The meaning of observed violence: Real vs. fictional violence and consequent effects on aggression and emotional arousal. *Journal of Research in Personality, 9*, 270–281.

Geen, R. G. (1976). Observing violence in the mass media: Implications of basic research. In R. G. Geen & E. D. O'Neal (Eds.), *Perspectives on aggression* (pp. 193–234). New York: Academic Press.

Geen, R. G., & Berkowitz, L. (1967). Some conditions facilitating the occurrence of aggression after the observation of violence. *Journal of Personality, 35*, 666–676.

Geen, R. G., & Rakosky, J. (1973). Interpretations of observed violence and their effect on GSR. *Journal of Experimental Research in Personality, 6*, 289–292.

Geen, R. G., & Stonner, D. (1974). The meaning of observed violence: Effects on arousal and aggressive behavior. *Journal of Research in Personality, 8*, 55–63.

Geen, R. G., & Thomas, S. L. (1986). The immediate effects of media violence on behavior. *Journal of Social Issues, 42*(3), 7–27.

General Mills, Inc. (1979). *The General Mills American Family Report 1978-79: Family health in an era of stress.* Minneapolis: Author.

Gerbner, G. (1961a). Psychology, psychiatry and mental illness in the mass media: A study of trends, 1900–1959. *Mental Hygiene, 45*, 89–93.

Gerbner, G. (1961b). Regulation of mental illness content in motion pictures and television. *Gazette, 6*, 365–385.

Gerbner, G. (1966). An institutional approach to mass communications research. In L. Thayer (Ed.), *Communications: Theory and research.* Springfield, IL: Charles C. Thomas.

Gerbner, G. (1969). The television world of violence. In D. Lange, R. Baker, & S. Ball (Eds.) *Mass media and violence: A report to the National Commission on the Causes and Prevention of Violence* (pp. 311–340). Washington, DC: U.S. Government Printing Office.

Gerbner, G. (1972a, September). Communication and social environment. *Scientific American*, pp. 152–160.

Gerbner, G. (1972b). Violence and television drama: Trends and symbolic functions. In G. A. Comstock & E. A. Rubinstein (Eds.), *Television and social behavior: Vol. 1. Content and control* (pp. 28–187). Washington, DC: U.S. Government Printing Office.

Gerbner, G. (1976). *A preliminary summary of the special analysis of television content.* Unpublished paper written for the Project on Human Sexual Development, Annenberg School of Communications, University of Pennsylvania, Philadelphia.

Gerbner, G. (1980a). Children and power on television: The other side of the picture. In G. Gerbner, C. J. Ross, & E. Ziegler (Eds.) *Child abuse: An analysis and agenda for action.* New York: Oxford University Press.

Gerbner, G. (1980b, January). Death in prime-time: Notes on the symbolic functions of dying in the mass media. *Annals of the American Academy of Political and Social Science, 447,* 64–70.

Gerbner, G. & Gross, L. (1976) Living with television: The violence profile. *Journal of Communication, 26*(2), 171–180.

Gerbner, G., & Gross, L. (1980). The violent face of television and its lessons. In E. Palmer & A. Dorr (Eds.), *Children and the faces of television: Teaching, violence, selling* (pp. 149–162). New York: Academic Press.

Gerbner, G., Gross, L., Eleey, M., Jackson–Beeck, M., Jeffries-Fox, S., & Signorielli, N. (1977a). The Gerbner violence profile: An analysis of the CBS Report. *Journal of Broadcasting, 21,* 280–286.

Gerbner, G., Gross, L., Eleey, M. F., Jackson–Beeck, M., Jeffries-Fox, S., & Signorielli, N. (1977b). TV violence profile no. 8: The highlights. *Journal of Communication, 27,*(2), 171–180.

Gerbner, G., Gross, L., Jackson-Beeck, M., Jeffries-Fox, S., & Signorielli, N. (1978). Cultural indicators: Violence profile no. 9. *Journal of Communication, 28,* 176–207.

Gerbner, G., Gross, L., Morgan, M., & Signorielli, N. (1980). The "mainstreaming" of America: Violence profile no. 11. *Journal of Communication, 30,* 10–29.

Gerbner, G., Gross, L., Morgan, M., & Signorielli, N. (1986). Living with television: The dynamics of the cultivation process. In J. Bryant & D. Zillmann (Eds.), *Perspectives in media effects* (pp. 17–40). Hillsdale, NJ: Lawrence Erlbaum Associates.

Gerbner, G., Gross, L., Signorielli, N., Morgan, M., & Jackson-Beeck, M. (1979). The demonstration of power: Violence profile no. 10. *Journal of Communication, 29*(3), 177–196.

Gerbner, G., Morgan, M., & Signorielli, N. (1982). Programming health portrayals: What viewers see, say and do. In D. Pearl, L. Bouthilet, & J. Lazar (Eds.), *Television and behavior: Ten years of scientific progress and implications for the eighties. Vol. 2, Technical reviews* (pp. 291–307). Rockville, MD: NIMH.

Gerbner, G., & Signorielli, N. (1979). *Women and minorities in television drama, 1969–1978.* Unpublished manuscript, The University of Pennsylvania, Philadelphia, PA.

Gerbner, G., & Tannenbaum, P. H. (1962). Mass media censorship and the portrayal of mental illness: Some effects of industry-wide controls in motion pictures and television. In W. Schramm (Ed.), *Studies of innovation and of communication to the public.* Stanford: Stanford University Press.

Gibson, J. J. (1986). *The ecological approach to visual perception.* Hillsdale, NJ: Lawrence Erlbaum Associates.

Ginsburg, H. (1978). *Children's advertising rulemaking comment.* Written testimony submitted to the Federal Trade Commission (FTC).

Glasser, I. (1988). Television and the construction of reality. In S. Oskamp (Ed.), *Television as a social issue* (pp. 44–51). Newbury Park, CA: Sage.

Gleitman, H. (1986). *Basic psychology* (2nd ed.). New York: W. W. Norton.

Goldberg, M. E., & Gorn, G. J. (1978). Some unintended consequences of TV advertising to children. *Journal of Consumer Research, 5*(1), 22–29.

Goldberg, M. E., Gorn, G., & Gibson, W. (1978). TV messages for snack and breakfast foods: Do they influence children's preferences? *Journal of Consumer Research, 5,* 73–81.

Goldsen, R. K. (1975). *The show & tell machine.* New York: The Dial Press.

Goldstein, A. P. (1981). *Psychological skill training.* New York: Pergamon Press.

Golinkoff, R., & Kerr, J. (1975). *Infants' perception of semantically defined action role changes in filmed events.* Unpublished manuscript, University of Delaware, Wilmington, DE.

Gore, T. (1987). *Raising PG kids in an X-rated society.* Nashville, TN: Abingdon Press.

Gorn, G. J., & Goldberg, M. E. (1977). The impact of television advertising on children of low income families. *Journal of Consumer Research, 4*(2), 86–88.

Granzberg, G., & Steinbring, J. (1980). *Television and the Canadian Indian.* Technical Report, Department of Anthropology, University of Winnipeg.

Graves, S. B. (1980). Psychological effects of black portrayals on television. In S. Withey & R. Abeles (Eds.), *Television and social behavior: Beyond violence and children* (pp. 259–289). Hillsdale, NJ: Lawrence Erlbaum Associates.

Greenberg, B. S. (1972). Children's reactions to TV blacks. *Journalism Quarterly, 49*(1), 5–14.

Greenberg, B. S. (1974). Gratifications of television viewing and their correlates for British children. In J. G. Blumler & E. Katz (Eds.), *The uses of mass communications: Current perspectives on gratifications research* (pp. 71–92). Beverly Hills: Sage.

Greenberg, B. S. (1975). British children and television violence. *Public Opinion Quarterly, 39,* 521–547.

Greenberg, B. S. (1980). *Life on television: Content analyses of U.S. TV drama.* Norwood, NJ: Ablex.

Greenberg, B. S. (1982). Television and role socialization. In D. Pearl, L. Bouthilet, & J. Lazar (Eds.), *Television and behavior: Ten years of scientific progress and implications for the eighties. Vol. 2, Technical reviews* (pp. 179–190). Rockville, MD: NIMH.

Greenberg, B. S. (1988). Some uncommon television images and the drench hypothesis. In S. Oskamp (Ed.), *Television as a social issue* (pp. 88–102). Newbury Park, CA: Sage.

Greenberg, B. S., & Atkin, C. K. (1977, May). *Current trends in research on children and television: Social behavior content portrayals and effects in the family context.* Paper presented at the Annual Meeting of the International Communication Association, Berlin.

Greenberg, B., & Burek-Neuendorf, K. (1980). Black family interactions on television. In B. S. Greenberg (Ed.), *Life on television.* Norwood, NJ: Ablex.

Greenberg, B. S., & Dervin, B. (1970). *Uses of the mass media by the urban poor.* New York: Praeger.

Greenberg, B. S., & Dominick, J. R. (1969). Racial and social class differences in teenagers' use of television. *Journal of Broadcasting, 13,* 331–344.

Greenberg, B. S., Fernandez–Collado, C., Graef, D., Korzenny, F., & Atkin, C. K. (1980). Trends in the use of alcohol and other substances on television. In B. S. Greenberg (Ed.), *Life on television.* Norwood, NJ: Ablex.

Greenberg, B. S., & Reeves, B. (1976). Children and the perceived reality of television. *Journal of Sociological Issues, 32,* 86–97.

Greenberg, B., Simmons, K., Hogan, L., & Atkin, C. (1978). *A three-season analysis of the demographic characteristics of fictional television characters. Project CASTLE* (Report No. 9). East Lansing, MI: Department of Communication, Michigan State University.

Greenfield, P., Bruzzone, L., Koyamatsu, K., Satuloff, W., Nixon, K., Brodie, M., & Kingsdale, D. (1987). What is rock music doing to the minds of our youth? A first experimental look at the effects of rock music lyrics and music videos. *Journal of Early Adolescence, 7*(3), 315–329.

Greenfield, P., Farrar, D., & Beagles-Roos, J. (1986). Is the medium the message? An experimental comparison of the effects of radio and television on imagination. *Journal of Applied Developmental Psychology, 7,* 201–218.

Greer, D., Potts, R., Wright, J. C., & Huston, A. C. (1982). The effects of television commercial form and commercial placement on children's social behavior and attention. *Child Development, 53,* 611–619.

Greer, L. D. (1980). *Children's comprehension of formal features with masculine and feminine connotations.* Unpublished master's thesis, Department of Human Development, University of Kansas, Lawrence.

Gross, L., & Jeffries–Fox, S. (1978). What do you want to be when you grow up, little girl? In G. Tuchman, A. K. Daniels, & J. Benet (Eds.), *Hearth and home: Images of women in the mass media.* New York: Oxford University Press.

Gumpert, G., & Cathcart, R. (1985). Media grammars, generations, and media gaps. *Critical studies in Mass Communication, 2,* 23–35.

Gussow, J. (1972). Counternutritional messages of TV ads aimed at children. *Journal of Nutrition Education, 4*(2), 48–52.

Halloran, J. D. (1969). (Ed.) *Findings and cognition on the television perception of children based on the prize-winning programs of Prix Jeunesse 1966.* Munich: Putrik and Clown Ferdl.

Halloran, J. D., Brown, R., & Chaney, D. C. (1970). *Television and delinquency.* Leicester: Leicester University Press.

Handron, D. (1988, October) *Promoting media literacy: methods and techniques.* Paper presented at the New York State Speech Communication Association, Ellenville, NY.

Hapkiewicz, W. G. (1979, Spring). Children's reactions to cartoon violence. *Journal of Clinical Child Psychology,* 30–34.

Hapkiewicz, W. G., & Roden, A. H. (1971). The effect of aggressive cartoons on children's interpersonal play. *Child Development, 42,* 1583–1585.

Harding, P. A. (1988). Social science research and media policy issues: A question of fit. In S. Oskamp (Ed.), *Television as a social issue,* (pp. 305–310). Newbury Park, CA: Sage.

Harris, L., & Associates, Inc. (1975). *The myth and reality of aging in America.* Washington, DC: National Council on Aging.

Hartman, D. P. (1969). Influence of symbolically modeled instrumental aggression and pain cues on aggressive behavior. *Journal of Personality and Social Psychology. 11*(3), 280–288.

Hartnagel, T. F., Teevan, J. J., Jr., & McIntyre, J. J. (1975). Television violence and violent behavior. *Social Forces, 54*(2), 341–351.

Harvey, S. E., Sprafkin, J. N., & Rubinstein, E. (1979). Prime time television: A profile of aggressive and prosocial behaviors. *Journal of Broadcasting, 23*(2), 179–189.

Hawkins, R. P. (1977). The dimensional structure of children's perceptions of television reality. *Communication Research, 4,* 299–320.

Hawkins, R., & Pingree, S. (1981). Uniform content and habitual viewing: Unnecessary assumptions in social reality effects. *Human Communication Research, 7,* 219–301.

Hawkins, R. P., & Pingree, S. H. (1982). Television's influence on constructions of social reality. In D. Pearl, L. Bouthilet, & J. Lazar (Eds.), *Television and behavior: Ten years of scientific progress and implications for the eighties. Vol. 2, Technical reviews* (pp. 224–247). Rockville, MD: NIMH.

Hawkins, R. P., Pingree, S. H., & Roberts, D. F. (1975). Watergate and political socialization: The inescapable event. *American Politics Quarterly, 3,* 406–422.

Head, S. (1954). Content analysis of television drama programs. *Quarterly of Film, Radio, and TV, 9,* 175–194.

Hearold, S. L. (1979). *Meta-analysis of the effects of television on social behavior.* Unpublished doctoral dissertation, University of Colorado, Boulder, CO.

Hennessee, J. A., & Nicholson, J. (1972, May 28). N.O.W. Says: TV commercials insult women. *New York Times,* pp. 12– 13+.

Hennigan, K., Del Resano, M., Heath, L., Cook, T., Wharton, J. D., & Calder, B. (1982). Impact of the introduction of television on crime in the United States: Empirical findings and theoretical implications. *Journal of Personality and Social Psychology, 3,* 461–478.

Herzog, H. (1944). What do we really know about daytime serial listeners? In P. F. Lazarsfeld & F. N. Stanton (Eds.), *Radio research 1942–1943* (pp. 3–33). New York: Duell, Sloan & Pearce.

Himmelweit, H. T., Oppenheim, A. N. & Vince, P. (1958). *Television and the child: An empirical study of the effects of television on the young.* London: Oxford University Press.

Himmelweit, H., & Swift, B. (1976). Continuities and discontinuities in media usage and taste: A longitudinal study. *Journal of Social Issues, 32*(4), 133–156.

Hines, M., Greenberg, B., & Buerkel, N. (1977) *An analysis of family role structures and interactions in commercial television.* Project CASTLE: (Report No. 6), Department of Communication, Michigan State University, East Lansing, MI.

Hirsch, P. (1980). The "scary world" of the nonviewer and other anomalies: A reanalysis of Gerbner et al.'s findings on cultivation analysis, Part 1. *Communication Research, 7,* 403–456.

Hirsch, P. (1981). On not learning from one's own mistakes: A reanalysis of Gerbner et al.'s findings on cultivation analysis, and a critique of mainstreaming, Part 2. *Communication Research, 8,* 3–37.

Hodge, B., & Tripp, D. (1986). *Children and television: A semiotic approach.* Stanford, CA: Stanford University Press.

Hoffner, C., & Cantor, J. (1985). Developmental differences in responses to a television character's appearance and behavior. *Developmental Psychology, 21,* 1065–1074.

Hollenbeck, A. R., & Slaby, R. G. (1979). Infant visual and vocal responses to television. *Child Development, 50,* 41–45.

Holsti, O. R. (1969). *Content analysis for the social sciences and humanities.* Reading, MA: Addison-Wesley.

House Hearing before the Subcommittee on Transportation, Aviation and Materials of the Committee on Science and Technology, U.S. House of Representatives, 1984, August 6. *Subliminal communication technology* (No. 105). Washington, DC: U.S. Government Printing Office.

Hovland, C. I., Janis, I. L., & Kelley, H. H. (1953). *Communication and persuasion.* New Haven: Yale University Press.

Howard, J. A., Hulbert, J. M., & Lehmann, D. R. (1973). An exploratory analysis of the effect of television advertising on children. *Proceedings of the American Marketing Association.* Washington, DC: American Marketing Association.

Howard, J. L., Reifler, C. B., & Liptzin, M. B. (1971). Effects of exposure to pornography. In *Technical report of the Commission on Obscenity and Pornography* (Vol. 8). Washington, DC: U.S. Government Printing Office.

Huesmann, L. R. (1982). Television violence and aggressive behavior. In D. Pearl, L. Bouthilet, & J. Lazar (Eds.), *Television and behavior: Ten years of scientific progress and implications for the eighties. Vol. 2, Technical reviews* (pp. 126–137). Rockville, MD: NIMH.

Huesmann, L. R. (1986). Psychological processes promoting the relation between exposure to media violence and aggressive behavior in the viewer. *Journal of Social Issues, 42*(3), 125–139.

Huesmann, L. R., & Eron, L. D. (1986). *Television and the aggressive child: A cross-national comparison.* Hillsdale, NJ: Lawrence Erlbaum Associates.

Huesmann, L. R., Eron, L. D., Klein, R., Bryce, P., & Fischer, P. (1981). *Mitigating the imitation of aggressive behaviors.* Technical Report, Department of Psychology, University of Illinois at Chicago Circle, IL.

Huesmann, L. R., Eron, L. D., Klein, R., Brice, P., & Fischer, P. (1983). Mitigating the imitation of aggressive behaviors by changing children's attitudes about media violence. *Journal of Personality and Social Psychology, 44,* 899–910.

Huesmann, L. R., Eron, L. D., Lefkowitz, M. M., & Walder, L. O. (1973). Television violence and aggression: The causal effect remains. *American Psychologist, 28,* 617–620.

Huesmann, L. R., Eron, L. D., Lefkowitz, M. M., & Walder, L. O. (1984). The stability of aggression over time and generations. *Developmental Psychology, 20,* 1120–1134.

Huesmann, L. R., Lagerspetz, K., & Eron, L. D. (1984). Intervening variables in the TV violence-aggression relation: Evidence from two countries. *Developmental Psychology, 20,* 746–775.

Huesmann, L. R., & Malamuth, N. M. (1986). Media violence and antisocial behavior: An overview. *Journal of Social Issues, 42,*(3), 1–6.

Hughes, M. (1980). The fruits of cultivation analysis: A re-examination of the effects of television watching on fear of victimization, alienation, and the approval of violence. *Public Opinion Quarterly, 44,* 287–302.

Huston, A. C., Greer, D., Wright, J. C., Welch, R., & Ross, R. (1984). Children's comprehension of televised formal features with masculine and feminine connotations. *Developmental Psychology, 20,*(4) 707–716.

Huston, A. C., & Wright, J. C. (1983). Children's processing of television: The informative functions of formal features. In J. Bryant & D. R. Anderson (Eds.), *Children's understanding of television: Research on attention and comprehension* (pp. 35–68). New York: Academic Press.

Huston, A. C., Wright, J. C., Wartella, E., Rice, M. L., Watkins, B. A., Campbell, T., & Potts, R. (1981). Communication more than content: Formal features of children's television programs. *Journal of Communication, 31,*(3), 32–48.

Jackson-Beeck, M. (1977). The non-viewers: Who are they. *Journal of Communication, 27,* 65–72.

Jaglom, L. M., & Gardner, H. (1981). The preschool television viewer as anthropologist. In H. Kelly & H. Gardner (Eds.), *Viewing children through television.* San Francisco: Jossey-Bass.

Janis, I. (1980). The influence of television on personal decision making. In S. B. Withey & R. P. Aubles (Eds.), *Television and social behavior: Beyond violence and children* (pp. 161–190). Hillsdale, NJ: Lawrence Erlbaum Associates.

Jeffries-Fox, S., & Gerbner, G. (1977). Television and the family. *Fernsehen and Bildung, 11*(3).

Jeffries-Fox, S., & Signorielli, N. (1978). *Television and children's conceptions about occupations.* Paper presented to the Airlie House Telecommunications Conference, Warrenton, VA.

Jeffries-Fox, S., & Signorielli, N. (1979). Television and children's conceptions about occupations. In H. S. Dordick (Ed.), *Proceedings of the Sixth Annual Telecommunications Policy Research Conference.* Lexington, MA: Lexington Books.

Johnson, W. O. (1981, August 11). You ain't seen nothin' yet. *Sports Illustrated,* pp. 50–64.

Johnston, J., & Ettema, J. S. (1982). *Positive images: Breaking stereotypes with children's television.* Beverly Hills, CA: Sage.

Joy, L. A., Kimball, M. M., & Zabrack, M. L. (1986). Television and children's aggressive behavior. In T. M. Williams (Ed.), *The impact of television: A natural experiment in three communities* (pp. 303–360). Orlando, FL: Academic Press.

Kanin, E. J. (1985). Date rapists: Differential sexual socialization and relative deprivation. *Archives of Sexual Behavior, 14,* 219–231.

Kaplan, R. M. (1972). On television as a cause of aggression. *American Psychologist, 27,* 968–969.

Kaplan, R. M., & Singer, R. D. (1976). Television violence and viewer aggression: A re-examination of the evidence. *Journal of Social Issues, 32,* 35–70.

Katz, E. (1988). The relationship between broadcasters and researchers. In S. Oskamp (Ed.), *Television as a social issue* (pp. 311–314). Newbury Park, CA: Sage.

Katz, E., Blumler, J. G., & Gurevitch, M. (1974). Utilization of mass communication by the individual. In J. G. Blumler & E. Katz (Eds.), *The uses of mass communications: Current perspectives on gratifications research* (pp. 19–32). Beverly Hills: Sage.

Katz, E., & Foulkes, D. (1962). On the use of the mass media as "escape": Clarification of a concept. *Public Opinion Quarterly, 26,* 377–388.

Katz, E., Gurevitch, M., & Haas, H. (1973). On the use of mass media for important things. *American Sociological Review, 38,* 164–181.

Katzman, N. (1972). Television soap operas: What's been going on anyway? *Public Opinion Quarterly, 36,* 200–212.

Kay, H. (1972). Weakness in the television-causes-aggression analysis by Eron et al. *American Psychologist, 27,* 970–973.

Kelly, H. (1981). Reasoning about realities: Children's evaluations of television and books. In H. Kelly & H. Gardner (Eds.), *Viewing children through television* (pp. 59–72). San Francisco: Jossey–Bass.

Kessler, R. C., & Stipp, H. (1984). The impact of fictional television suicide stories on U.S. fatalities: A replication. *American Journal of Sociology, 90,* 151–167.

Key, W. B. (1973). *Subliminal seduction.* Englewood Cliffs, NJ: Prentice–Hall.

Key, W. B. (1976). *Media sexploitation.* Englewood Cliffs, NJ: Prentice–Hall.

Key, W. B. (1980). *The clam-plate orgy and other subliminal techniques for manipulating your behavior.* Englewood Cliffs, NJ: Prentice–Hall.

Kippax, S., & Murray, J. P. (1977). Using television: Program content and need gratification. *Politics, 12,* 56–69.

Kippax, S., & Murray, J. P. (1980). Using the mass media: Need gratification and perceived utility. *Communication Research, 7*(3) 335–360.

Klapper, H. L. (1981). Children's perceptions of the realism of televised fiction: New wine in old bottles. In J. F. Esserman (Ed.), *Television advertising and children: Issues, research, and findings* (pp. 55–82). New York: Child Research Service.

Komisar, L. (1971). The image of women in advertising. In V. Gornick & B. Moran (Eds.), *Woman in sexist society* (pp. 207–217). New York: Basic Books.

Korzenny, F., & Neuendorf, K. (1980). Television viewing and self-concept of the elderly. *Journal of Communication, 30,*(1), 71–80.

Koss, M. P., Leonard, K. E., Beezley, D. A., & Oros, C. J. (1985). Nonstranger sexual aggression: A discriminant analysis of psychological characteristics of nondetected offenders. *Sex Roles, 12,* 981–992.

Krugman, H. (1965). The impact of television advertising: Learning without involvement. *Public Opinion Quarterly, 29,* 349–356.

Krull, R., & Husson, W. G. (1978). Children's attention: The case of TV viewing. In E. Wartella (Ed.), *Children communicating: Media and development of thought, speech, understanding.* Beverly Hills: Sage.

Krull, R., Watt, J., & Lichty, L. (1977). Entropy and structure: Two measures of complexity in television programs. *Communication Research, 4,* 61–85.

Kunkel, D. L., & Watkins, B. A. (1985). Children and television. *Washington Report, Society for Research in Child Development,* Whole Vol. 1, 4.

Landry, M., Kelly, H., & Gardner, H. (1982). Reality-fantasy discriminations in literature: A developmental study. *Research in the Teaching of English, 16,* 1, 39–52.

Langer, E. (1983). *The psychology of control.* Newbury Park, CA: Sage.

Langer, E., & Avorn, J. (1981). The psychosocial environment of the elderly: Some behavioral and health implications. In J. Seagle & R. Chellis (Eds.), *Congregate housing for older people.* Lexington, MA: Lexington.

Langer, E., Bashner, R., & Chanowitz, B. (1985). Decreasing prejudice by increasing discrimination. *Journal of Personality and Social Psychology, 49,* 113–120.

Langer, E., & Imber, L. (1979). When practice makes imperfect: The debilitating effects of overlearning. *Journal of Personality and Social Psychology, 37,* 2014–2025.

Langer, E., & Newman, H. (1979). The role of mindlessness in the typical social psychological experiment. *Personality and Social Psychology Bulletin, 37,* 2003-2013.

Langer, E., & Piper, A. (1988). Television from a mindful/mindless perspective. In S. Oskamp (Ed.), *Television as a social issue* (pp. 247-260). Newbury Park, CA: Sage.

Langer, E., & Rodin, J. (1976). The effects of enhanced personal responsibility for the aged: A field experiment in an institutional setting. *Journal of Personality and Social Psychology, 34,* 191-198.

Langer, E., & Weinman, C. (1981). When thinking disrupts intellectual performance: Mindlessness on an overlearned task. *Personality and Social Psychology Bulletin, 7,* 240-243.

Leaman, F. A. (1973). *Television's "fruitless" image: A cultivation analysis of children's nutritional knowledge and behavior.* Unpublished master's thesis, Annenberg School of Communications, University of Pennsylvania, PA.

Leary, A., Wright, J. C., & Huston, A. C. (1985, April). *Young children's judgments of the fictional/nonfictional status of television programming.* Presented at the Biennial Meeting of the Society for Research in Child Development, Toronto, Canada.

Lefkowitz, M. M., Eron, L. D., Walder, L. O., & Huesmann, L. R. (1972). Television violence and child aggression: A followup study. In G. A. Comstock & E. A. Rubinstein (Eds.), *Television and social behavior. Vol. 3, Television and adolescent aggressiveness* (pp. 35-135). Washington, DC: U.S. Government Printing Office.

Lefkowitz, M. M., Eron, L. D., Walder, L. O., & Huesmann, L. R. (1977). *Growing up to be violent: A longitudinal study of the development of aggression.* New York: Pergamon Press.

Lefkowitz, M. M., & Huesmann, L. R. (1980). Concomitants of television violence viewing in children. In E. L. Palmer & A. Dorr (Eds.) *Children and the faces of television: Teaching, violence, selling* (pp. 163-181). New York: Academic Press.

Leichter, H. J., Ahmed, D., Barrios, L., Bryce, J., Larsen, E., & Moe, L. (1985). Family context of television. *Educational Communication and Technology, 33,* 26-40.

Leifer, A. D., Gordon, N. J., & Graves, S. B. (1974). Children's television: More than mere entertainment. *Harvard Educational Review, 44,* 213-245.

Leifer, A. D., & Roberts, D. F. (1972). Children's response to television violence. In J. P. Murray, E. A. Rubinstein, & G. A. Comstock (Eds.), *Television and social behavior. Vol. 2: Television and social learning* (pp. 43-180). Washington, DC: U.S. Government Printing Office.

Lemon, J. (1977). Women and blacks on prime-time television. *Journal of Communication, 27*(4), 70-79.

Lepper, M. R. (1982, April). *Micro computers in education: Motivational and social issues.* Invited address to the annual meeting of the American Psychological Association, Washington, DC.

Lesser, G. S. (1974). *Children and television: Lessons from "Sesame Street."* New York: Random House.

Levi, L. (1965). The urinary output of adrenalin and noradrenalin during pleasant and unpleasant emotional states: A preliminary report. *Psychosomatic Medicine, 27,* 80-85.

Levi, L. (1969). Sympatho-adrenomedullary activity, diuresis, and emotional reactions during visual sexual stimulation in human females and males. *Psychosomatic Medicine, 31,* 251-268.

Levin, S. R., & Anderson, D. R. (1976). The development of attention. *Journal of Communication, 26*(2) 126-135.

Levin, S. R., Petros, T. V., & Petrella, F. W. (1982). Preschoolers' awareness of television advertising. *Child Development, 53,* 933-937.

Levinson, R. M. (1973). From Olive Oyl to Sweet Polly Purebread: Sex role stereotypes and televised cartoons. *Journal of Popular Culture, 9,* 561-572.

Leyens, J. P., Herman, G., & Dunand, M. (1982). The influence of an audience upon the reactions to filmed violence. *European Journal of Social Psychology, 12,* 131-142.

Leyens, J. P., Parke, R. D., Camino, L., & Berkowitz, L. (1975). Effects of movie violence on aggression in a field setting as a function of group dominance and cohesion. *Journal of Personality and Social Psychology, 32,* 346–360.

Liebert, D. E., Sprafkin, J. N., Liebert, R. M., & Rubinstein, E. A. (1977). Effects of television disclaimers on the product expectations of children. *Journal of Communication,* 27(1), 118–124.

Liebert, R. M., & Baron, R. A. (1972). Short-term effects of televised aggression on children's aggressive behavior. In J. P. Murray, E. A. Rubinstein, & G. A. Comstock (Eds.), *Television and social behavior. Vol. 2: Television and social learning* (pp. 181–201). Washington, DC: U.S. Government Printing Office.

Liebert, R. M., & Sprafkin, J. (1988). *The early window* (3rd ed.). Elmsford, NY: Pergamon Press.

Liebert, R. M., Sprafkin, J., & Davidson, E. S. (1982). *The early window* (2nd ed.). Elmsford, NY: Pergamon Press.

Linne, O. (1971). *Reactions of children to violence on TV.* Stockholm: Swedish Broadcasting Corporation (SR).

Linz, D. (1985). *Sexual violence in the media: Effects on male viewers and implications for society.* Unpublished doctoral dissertation, University of Wisconsin, Madison.

Linz, D., Donnerstein, E., & Penrod, S. (1984). The effects of multiple exposures to filmed violence against women. *Journal of Communication, 34,* 130–147.

Linz, D., Penrod, S., & Donnerstein, E. (1986). Issues bearing on the legal regulation of violent and sexually violent media. *Journal of Social Issues, 42*(3), 171–193.

Long, M. L., & Simon, R. J. (1974). Roles and statuses of women on children and family TV programs. *Journalism Quarterly, 51,* 107–110.

Lorch, E. P., Anderson, D. R., & Levin, S. R. (1979). The relationship of visual attention to children's comprehension of television. *Child Development, 50,* 722–727.

Lovaas, O. I. (1961). Effect of exposure to symbolic aggression on aggressive behavior. *Child Development, 32,* 37–44.

Loye, D., Gorney, R., & Steele, G. (1977). Effects of television: An experimental field study. *Journal of Communication, 27*(3), 206–216.

Luke, C. (1985). Television discourse processing: A schema theoretic approach. *Communication Education, 34,* 91–105.

Lyle, J., & Hoffman, H. R. (1972). Children's use of television and other media. In E. A. Rubinstein, G. A. Comstock, & J. P. Murray (Eds.), *Television and social behavior: Vol. 4. Television in day-to-day life: Patterns of use* (pp. 129–256). Washington, DC: U.S. Government Printing Office.

Maccoby, E. E. (1964). Effects of the mass media. In M. Hoffman & L. W. Hoffman (Eds.), *Review of child development research* (Vol. 1, pp. 323–348). New York: Russell Sage Foundation.

MacDonald, J. F. (1983). *Blacks on white TV: Afro-Americans in television since 1948.* Chicago: Nelson-Hall.

MacIntyre, J. J., & Teevan, J. J., Jr. (1972). Television violence and deviant behavior. In G. A. Comstock & E. A. Rubinstein (Eds.), *Television and social behavior: Vol. 3. Television and adolescent aggressiveness* (pp. 383–435). Washington, DC: Government Printing Office.

Malamuth, N. M. (1986). Predictors of naturalistic sexual aggression. *Journal of Personality and Social Psychology, 50,* 953–962.

Malamuth, N. M., & Briere, J. (1986). Sexual violence in the media: Indirect effects on aggression against women. *Journal of Social Issues, 42*(3), 75–92.

Malamuth, N. M., & Check, J. V. P. (1980). Penile tumescence and perceptual responses to rape as a function of victim's perceived reactions. *Journal of Applied Social Psychology, 10*(6), 528–547.

Malamuth, N. M., & Check, J. V. P. (1981). The effects of mass media exposure on acceptance of violence against women. A field experiment. *Journal of Research in Personality, 15,* 436–446.

Malamuth, N. M., & Check, J. V. P. (1985). The effects of aggressive pornography on beliefs in rape myths: Individual differences. *Journal of Research in Personality, 19,* 299–320.

Malamuth, N. M., Haber, S., & Feshbach, S. (1980). Testing hypotheses regarding rape: Exposure to sexual violence, sex differences, and the "normality" of rapists. *Journal of Research in Personality, 14,* 121–137.

Malamuth, N. M., & Spinner, B. (1980). A longitudinal content analysis of sexual violence in the best-selling erotic magazines. *The Journal of Sex Research, 16*(3), 226–237.

Mandler, J., & Johnson, N. (1977). Remembrance of things passed: Story structure and recall. *Cognitive Psychology, 9,* 111–151.

McArthur, L. Z., & Eisen, S. V. (1976). Achievements of male and female storybook characters as determinants of achievement behavior by boys and girls. *Journal of Personality and Social Psychology, 33,* 467–473.

McCabe, A. E., & Moriarity, R. J. (1977, March). *A laboratory/field study of television violence and aggression in children's sport.* Paper presented at the biennial meeting of the Society for Research in Child Development, New Orleans.

McCarthy, E. D., Langner, T. S., Gersten, J. C., Eisenberg, J. G., & Orzeck, L. (1975). Violence and behavior disorders. *Journal of Communication, 25*(4), 71–85.

McGuire, W. J. (1969). Theory-oriented research in natural settings: The best of both worlds for social psychology. In M. Sherif & C. W. Sherif (Eds.), *Interdisciplinary relationships in the social sciences.* Chicago: Aldine.

McLaughlin, J. (1975). The doctor shows. *Journal of Communication, 25*(3), 182–184.

McLeod, J. M., Atkin, C. K., & Chaffee, S. H. (1972a). Adolescents, parents, and television use: Adolescent self-report measures from Maryland and Wisconsin samples. In G. A. Comstock & E. A. Rubinstein (Eds.), *Television and social behavior: Vol. 3. Television and adolescent aggressiveness* (pp. 173–238). Washington, DC: U.S. Government Printing Office.

McLeod, J. M., Atkin, C. K., & Chaffee, S. H. (1972b). Adolescents, parents and television use: Self-report and other-report measures from the Wisconsin sample. In G. A. Comstock & E. A. Rubinstein (Eds.), *Television and social behavior: Vol. 3. Television and adolescent aggressiveness* (pp. 239–313). Washington, DC: U.S. Government Printing Office.

McLeod, J. M., Fitzpatrick, M. A., Glynn, C. J., & Fallis, S. F. (1982). Television and social relations: Family influences and consequences for interpersonal behavior. In D. Pearl, L. Bouthilet, & J. Lazar (Eds.), *Television and behavior: Ten years of scientific progress and implications for the eighties. Vol. 2, Technical reviews* (pp. 272–286). Rockville, MD: NIMH.

McLuhan, M. (1964). *Understanding media: The extensions of man.* New York: McGraw-Hill.

McNeil, J. C. (1975). Feminism, femininity, and television series: A content analysis. *Journal of Broadcasting, 19*(3), 259–271.

McQuail, D. (Ed.). (1972). *Sociology of mass communications.* Harmondsworth: Penguin.

Meehan, D. (1983). *Ladies of the evening: Women characters of prime time television.* Metuchen, NJ: Scarecrow.

Meehan, D. (1988). The strong-soft woman: Manifestations of the androgyne in popular media. In S. Oskamp (Ed.), *Television as a social issue* (pp. 103–112). Newbury Park, CA: Sage.

Melody, W. H. (1973). *Children's television: The economics of exploitation.* New Haven, CT: Yale University Press.

Meltzoff, A. N. (1988). Imitation of televised models by infants. *Child Development, 59,* 1221–1229.

Messaris, P. (1986). Parents, children, and television. In G. Gumpert & R. Cathcart (Eds.), *Intermedia: Interpersonal communication in a media world* (3rd. ed., pp. 519–536). New York: Oxford University Press.

Milavsky, J. R. (1988). Television and aggression once again. In S. Oskamp (Ed.), *Television as a social issue* (pp. 163–170). Newbury Park, CA: Sage.

Milavsky, J. R., Stipp, H. H., Kessler, R. C., & Rubins, W. S. (1982). *Television and aggression: A panel study.* New York: Academic Press.

Milgram, S., & Shotland, R. L. (1973). *Television and antisocial behavior: Field experiments.* New York: Academic Press.

Miller, M. M., & Reeves, B. B. (1976). Children's occupational sex-role stereotypes: The linkage between television content and perception. *Journal of Broadcasting, 20,* 35–50.

Morgan, M. (1980). Television and reading: Does more equal better? *Journal of Communication, 30*(1), 159–165.

Morgan, M. (1982). Television and adolescents' sex-role stereotypes: A longitudinal study. *Journal of Personality and Social Psychology, 43,* 947–955.

Morgan, M. (1987). Television, sex-role attitudes, and sex-role behavior. *Journal of Early Adolescence.* 7(3), 269–282.

Morgan, M., & Gross, L. (1979). Television, IQ, and school achievement. In S. Scheuyer (Ed.), *The TV annual 1978–1979.* New York: Macmillan.

Morgan, M., & Gross, L. (1982). Television and educational achievement and aspiration. In D. Pearl, L. Bouthilet, & J. Lazar (Eds.), *Television and behavior: Ten years of scientific progress and implications for the eighties. Vol. 2, Technical reviews* (pp. 78–90). Rockville, MD: NIMH.

Morgan, M., & Rothschild, N. (1983). Impact of the new television technology: Cable TV, peers, and sex-role cultivation in the electronic environment. *Youth and Society, 15,* 33–50.

Morison, P., & Gardner, H. (1978). Dragons and dinosaurs: The child's capacity to differentiate fantasy from reality. *Child Development, 49,* 3, 642–648.

Morison, P., Kelly, H., & Gardner, H. (1981). Reasoning about the realities on television: A developmental study. *Journal of Broadcasting, 23,* 229–241.

Morison, P., McCarthy, M., & Gardner, H. (1979). Exploring the realities of television with children. *Journal of Broadcasting, 23,* 453–463.

Mosher, D. L., & Anderson, R. D. (1986). Macho personality, sexual aggression, and reactions to guided imagery of realistic rape. *Journal of Research in Personality, 20,* 77–94.

Murray, J. P. (1980). *Television and youth: 25 years of research and controversy.* Boys Town, NE: Boys Town Center for the Study of Youth Development.

Murray, J. P., Hayes, A. J., & Smith, J. E. (1978). Sequential analysis: Another approach to describing the stream of behaviour in children's interactions. *Australian Journal of Psychology, 30*(3), 207–215.

Murray, J. P., & Kippax, S. (1978). Children's social behavior in three towns with differing television experience. *Journal of Communications, 28*(1), 19–29.

Mussen, P., & Rutherford, E. (1961). Effects of aggressive cartoons on children's aggressive play. *Journal of Abnormal and Social Psychology, 62,* 461–464.

National Commission on the Causes and Prevention of Violence (1969). *To establish justice, to insure domestic tranquility.* Washington, DC: U.S. Government Printing Office.

National Organization for Women, National Capital Area. (1972). *Women in the Wasteland Fight Back: A Report on the Image of Women Portrayed in Television Programming.* Washington, DC: National Organization for Women.

Neuman, W. R. (1982). Television and American culture: The mass medium and the pluralist audience. *Public Opinion Quarterly, 46,* 471–487.

Neuman, W. R. (1988). Programming diversity and the future of television: An empty cornucopia? In S. Oskamp (Ed.), *Television as a social issue* (pp. 346–349). Newbury Park, CA: Sage.

Newcomb, A. F., & Collins, W. A. (1979). Children's comprehension of family role portrayals in televised dramas: Effects of socioeconomic status, ethnicity, and age. *Developmental Psychology, 15,* 417–423.

Nielsen Report on Television. (1956). Northbrook, IL: A.C. Nielsen Co.

Nielsen Report on Television. (1960). Northbrook, IL: A.C. Nielsen Co.

Nielsen Report on Television. (1982). Northbrook, IL: A.C. Nielsen Co.

Nielsen Report on Television. (1984). Northbrook, IL: A.C. Nielsen Co.

Nielsen Report on Television. (1986). Northbrook, IL: A.C. Nielsen Co.

Nielsen Report on Television. (1988). Northbrook, IL: A.C. Nielsen Co.

Noble, G. (1975). *Children in front of the small screen*. London: Constable.

O'Bryant, S. L., & Corder-Bolz, C. R., (1978). The effects of television on children's stereotyping of women's work roles. *Journal of Vocational Behavior, 12*, 233–244.

O'Carroll, M., O'Neal, E. C., & Macdonald, P. J. (1977). Influence upon imitative aggression of an imitating peer. *Journal of Social Psychology, 101*, 313–314.

O'Donnell, W. J., & O'Donnell, K. J. (1978, Winter). Update: Sex role messages in TV commercials. *Journal of Communication*, 156–158.

Olivia, N. V. National Broadcasting Co., Inc. (1978). *California Reporter, 141*, 511–515.

O'Neal, E. C., Macdonald, P. J., Cloninger, C., & Levine, D. (1979). Coactor's behavior and imitative aggression. *Motivation and Emotion, 3*, 373–379.

Osborn, D. K., & Endsley, R. C. (1971). Emotional reactions of young children to TV violence. *Child Development, 42*, 321–331.

Oskamp, S. (Ed.). (1988). *Television as a social issue*. Newbury Park, CA: Sage.

Palmer, E. L., & Dorr, A. (Eds.). (1980). *Children and the faces of television: Teaching, violence, selling*. New York: Academic Press.

Palmer, E. L., & McDowell, C. N. (1979). Program/commercial separators in children's television programming. *Journal of Communication, 29*(3), 197–201.

Palys, T. S. (1986). Testing the common wisdom: The social content of video pornography. *Canadian Psychology, 27*, 22–35.

Parke, R. D., Berkowitz, L., Leyens, J. P., West, S., & Sebastian, R. J. (1977). Some effects of violent and nonviolent movies on the behavior of juvenile delinquents. *Advanced Experimental Social Psychology, 10*, 135–172.

Parton, D. A., & Geshuri, Y. (1971). Learning of aggression as a function of presence of a human model, response intensity, and target of the response. *Journal of Experimental Child Psychology, 20*, 304–318.

Patterson, G. R., Chamberlain, P., & Reid, J. B. (1982). A comparative evaluation of parent training procedures. *Behavior Therapy, 13*, 638–650.

Pearl, D., Bouthilet, L., & Lazar, J. (Eds.). (1982). *Television and behavior: Ten years of scientific progress and implications for the eighties. Vol. 2, Technical reviews*. Rockville, MD: NIMH.

Perloff, R. M. (1977). Some antecedents of children's sex-role stereotypes. *Psychological Reports, 40*, 463–466.

Peterson, M. (1973). The visibility and image of old people on television. *Journalism Quarterly, 50*, 569–573.

Phelps, E. (1976). *Comparisons of the personality traits of television characters who are portrayed in amicable and violent relationships*. Unpublished paper based on analysis of Cultural Indicators Project, Annenberg School of Communications, University of Pennsylvania, Philadelphia, PA.

Phillips, D. P. (1974). The influence of suggestion on suicide: Substantive and theoretical implications of the Werther effect. *American Sociological Review, 39*, 340–354.

Phillips, D. (1979). Suicide, motor vehicle fatalities, and the mass media: Evidence toward a theory of suggestion. *American Journal of Sociology, 84*, 1150–1174.

Phillips, D. (1980). Airplane accidents, murder, and the mass media: Towards a theory of imitation and suggestion. *Social Forces, 58*, 1001–1024.

Phillips, D. (1982). The impact of fictional television stories on U.S. adult fatalities: New evidence on the effect of mass media on violence. *American Journal of Sociology, 87*, 1340–1359.

Phillips, D. P. (1983) The impact of mass media violence on U.S. homicides. *American Sociological Review, 48*, 560–568.

Phillips, D. P., & Bollen, K. (1985). Same time, last year: Selective data dredging for negative findings. *American Sociological Review, 50*, 364–371.

Phillips, D. P., & Hensley, J. E. (1984). When violence is rewarded or punished: The impact of mass media stories on homicide. *Journal of Communication, 34,* 101–116.

Pingree, S. (1978). The effects of nonsexist commercials and perceptions of reality on children's attitudes about women. *Psychology of Women Quarterly, 2,* 262–277.

Pingree, S., & Hawkins, R. (1981). U.S. programs on Australian television: The cultivation effect. *Journal of Communication, 31*(1), 97–105.

Piper, A., & Langer, E. (1986). *Mindful televiewing.* Unpublished manuscript, Harvard University.

Potter, W. J. (1982). *An examination of selected dimensions of perceived reality of mass communicated messages.* Paper presented at the annual meeting of the International Communication Association, Boston, MA.

Poulos, R. W. (1975). *Unintentional negative effects of food commercials on children: A case study.* Media Action Research Center.

Poulsen, D., Kintsch, E., Kintsch, W., & Premack, D. (1979). Children's comprehension and memory for stories. *Journal of Experimental Child Psychology, 28,* 379–403.

Price, J. (1978). *The best thing on TV: Commercials.* New York: Penguin Books.

Prinsky, L. E., & Rosenbaum, J. L. (1987). Leer-ics or lyrics? *Youth and society, 18,* 384–393.

Quarforth, J. M. (1979). Children's understanding of the nature of television characters. *Journal of Communication, 29*(3), 210–218.

Rapaport, K., & Burkhart, B. R. (1984). Personality and attitudinal characteristics of sexually coercive college males. *Journal of Abnormal Psychology, 93,* 216–221.

Reeves, B. (1978). Perceived TV reality as a predictor of children's social behavior. *Journalism Quarterly, 55,* 682–695.

Reeves, B. (1979). Children's understanding of television people. In E. Wartella (Ed.), *Children communicating: Media and development of thought, speech, understanding* (pp. 115–156). Beverly Hills: Sage.

Reeves, B., & Greenberg, B. S. (1977). Children's perceptions of television characters. *Human Communication, 3,* 113–127.

Reeves, B., & Lometti, G. E. (1979). The dimensional structure of children's perceptions of television characters: A replication. *Human Communication Research, 5,* 247–256.

Reeves, B., & Miller, M. M. (1978). A multidimensional measure of children's identification with television characters. *Journal of Broadcasting, 22,* 71–85.

Rehman, S., & Reilly, S. (1985). Music videos: A new dimension of televised violence. *Pennsylvania Speech Communication Annual, 41,* 61–64.

Reifler, C. B., Howard, J., Lipton, M. A., Liptzin, M. B., & Widmann, D. E. (1971). Pornography: An experimental study of effects. *American Journal of Psychiatry, 128,* 575–582.

Reiger, R. (1988, October). *Teaching about television: New arguments and research.* Paper presented at the New York State Speech Communication Association, Ellenville, NY.

Resnik, A. J., & Stern, B. L. (1977). Children's television advertising and brand choice: A laboratory experiment. *Journal of Advertising, 6*(3), 11–17.

Roberts, D. F. (1978). *Children's information processing: Perceptions of and cognitions about television commercials and supplemental consumer information.* Written testimony submitted to the Federal Trade Commission.

Roberts, D. F., & Maccoby, N. (1973). Information processing and persuasion: Counterarguing behavior. In P. Clark (Ed.), *New models for mass communication research* (Vol. 2). Sage Annual Reviews of Communication Research. Beverly Hills, CA: Sage.

Roberts, E. (1982). Television and sexual learning in childhood. In D. Pearl, L. Bouthilet, & J. Lazar (Eds.), *Television and behavior: Ten years of scientific progress and implications for the eighties. Vol. 2, Technical reviews* (pp. 209–223). Rockville, MD: NIMH.

Robertson, T. S. (1979). Parental mediation of television advertising effects. *Journal of Communication, 29*(1), 12–25.

Robertson, T. S., & Rossiter, J. R. (1974). Children and commercial persuasion: An attribution theory analysis. *Journal of Consumer Research, 1,* 13–20.

Robertson, T. S., & Rossiter, J. R. (1977). Children's responsiveness to commercials. *Journal of Communication, 27*(1), 101–105.

Robinson, J. P. (1972): Television's impact on everyday life: Some crossnational evidence. In E. A. Rubinstein, G. A. Comstock, & J. P. Murray (Eds.), *Television and social behavior: Vol. 4. Television in day-to-day life: Patterns of use* (pp. 410–431). Washington, DC: U.S. Government Printing Office.

Robinson, J. P. (1981). Television and leisure time: A new scenario. *Journal of Communication, 31*(1), 120–130.

Robinson, J. P., & Bachman, J. G. (1972). Television viewing habits and aggression. In G. A. Comstock & J. P. Murray (Eds.), *Television and social behavior. Vol. 3, Television and adolescent aggressiveness* (pp. 372–382). Washington, DC: U.S. Government Printing Office.

Robinson, J., & Hirsch, R. (1969). Teenage response to rock and roll protest songs. In S. Denisoff & R. Peterson (Eds.), *The sounds of social change: Studies in popular culture* (pp. 103–115). Chicago: Rand McNally.

Rokeach, M. (1979). *Understanding human values.* New York: The Free Press.

Rosenbaum, J., & Prinsky, L. (1987). Sex, violence, and rock and roll: Youths' perceptions of popular music. *Popular Music and Society, 11,* 79–90.

Rosengren, K. E., Wenner, L. A., & Palmgreen, P. (Eds.). (1985). *Media gratifications research: Current perspectives.* Newbury Park, CA: Sage.

Ross, D. F., & Condry, J.C. (1985) *The effect of perceived reality on adults' responses to filmed and televised events.* Paper presented at the Annual Meeting of the American Psychological Association, Los Angeles, CA.

Ross, L. B. (1972). *The effect of aggressive cartoons on the group play of children.* Unpublished doctoral dissertation, Miami University, Miami, FL.

Ross, R. P., Wartella, E., & Lovelace, V. O. (1982, April). *A conceptual framework for describing children's television viewing patterns.* Paper presented at the biennial meeting of the Southwestern Society for Research in Human Development, Galveston, TX.

Rossiter, J. R. (1980). Children and television advertising: Policy issues, perspectives and the status of research. In E. Palmer & A. Dorr (Eds.), *Children and the faces of television: Teaching, violence, selling* (pp. 251–272). New York: Academic Press.

Rossiter, J. R., & Robertson, T. S. (1974). Children's TV commercials: Testing the defenses. *Journal of Communication, 24*(4), 137–144.

Rothenberg, M. B. (1975). Effect of television violence on children and youth. *Journal of the American Medical Association, 234,* 1043–1046.

Rothschild, N. (1979). *Group as a mediating factor in the cultivation process among young children.* Unpublished master's thesis. Annenberg School of Communications, University of Pennsylvania, Philadelphia, PA.

Rothschild, N. (1984). Small group affiliation as a mediating factor in the cultivation process. In G. Melischeck, K. E. Rosengren, & J. Stappers (Eds.), *Cultural indicators: An international symposium* (pp. 377–387). Vienna: Osterreichischen Akademie der Wissenschaften.

Rothschild, N., & Morgan, M. (1987). Cohesion and control: Adolescents' relationships with parents as mediators of television. *Journal of Early Adolescence, 7*(3), 299–314.

Routtenberg, A. (1968). The two-arousal hypothesis: Reticular formation and limbic system. *Psychological Review, 75,* 51–80.

Routtenberg, A. (1971). Stimulus processing and response execution: A neurobehavioral theory. *Physiology and Behavior, 6,* 589–596.

Rule, B. G., & Ferguson, T. J. (1986). The effects of media violence on attitudes, emotions, and cognitions. *Journal of Social Issues, 42*(3), 29–50.

Salomon, G. (1977). Effects of encouraging Israeli mothers to co-observe "Sesame Street" with their five-year olds. *Child Development, 48,* 1146–1158.

Salomon, G. (1979). *Interaction of media, cognition and learning.* San Francisco: Jossey-Bass.

Salomon, G. (1981). Introducing AIME: The assessment of children's mental involvement with television. In H. Gardner & H. Kelly (Eds.), *Children and the worlds of television. A quarterly sourcebook in the series, New directions in child development.* San Francisco: Jossey–Bass.

Salomon, G. (1983). Television watching and mental effort: A social psychological view. In J. Bryant & D.R. Anderson (Eds.), *Children's understanding of television: Research on attention and comprehension* (pp. 181–198). New York: Academic Press.

Sawin, D. (1981). The fantasy-reality distinction in TV violence. *Journal of Research in Personality, 15,* 323–330.

Sawyer, A., & Ward, S. (1977). Carry-over effects in advertising communications: Evidence and hypotheses from behavioral science. In *Cumulative advertising effects: Source and implication.* Cambridge: Marketing Science Institute.

Schachter, S. (1964). The interaction of cognitive and physiological determinants of emotional state. In L. Berkowitz (Ed.), *Advances in experimental social psychology* (Vol. 1, pp. 49–81). New York: Academic Press.

Schachter, S., & Singer, J. (1962). Cognitive, social, and physiological determinants of emotional state. *Psychological Review, 69,* 379–399.

Schachter, S., & Wheeler, L. (1962). Epinephrine, chlorpromazine, and amusement. *Journal of Abnormal and Social Psychology, 65,* 121–128.

Scheibe, C. (1979). Sex roles in commercials. *Journal of Advertising Research, 19*(1), 23–28.

Scheibe, C. (1983). *Character portrayals and values in network TV commercials.* Unpublished master's thesis, Cornell University, Ithaca, NY.

Scheibe, C., & Condry, J.C. (1988). *The structure of the television environment.* Unpublished manuscript, Ithaca College, Ithaca, NY.

Scheibe, C., Condry, J.C., & Christensen, T. (1988). *Anti-drug and pro-drug messages on television.* Unpublished manuscript, Ithaca College, Ithaca, NY.

Schneider, K. C., & Schneider, S. B. (1979, Summer). Trends in sex roles in television commercials. *Journal of Marketing, 43,* 79–84.

Schramm, W., Lyle, V., & Parker, E. B. (1961). *Television in the lives of our children.* Stanford: Stanford University Press.

Schuetz, S., & Sprafkin, J. N. (1978). Spot messages appearing within Saturday morning television programs. In G. Tuchman, A. K. Daniels, & J. Benet (Eds.), *Hearth and home: Images of women in the mass media.* New York: Oxford University Press.

Schwartz, L. A., & Markham, W. T. (1985). Sex stereotyping in children's toy advertisements. *Sex Roles, 12,* 157–170.

Seggar, J. F., Hafen, J.K., & Hannonen-Gladden, H. (1981). Television's portrayal of minorities and women in drama and comedy drama, 1971–1980. *Journal of Broadcasting, 25*(3), 277–288.

Seggar, J. F., & Wheeler, P. (1973). World of work on TV: Ethnic and sex representation in TV drama. *Journal of Broadcasting, 17,* 201–214.

Sharaga, S. J. (1974). The effect of television advertising on children's nutrition attitude, nutrition knowledge, and eating habits. *Dissertation Abstracts International, 35*(7), 3417.

Sheikh, A. A., & Moleski, L. M. (1977). Conflict in the family over commercials. *Journal of Communication, 27*(1), 152–157.

Sheikh, A. A., Prasad, V. K., & Rao, T. R. (1974). Children's TV commercials: A review of research. *Journal of Communication, 24*(4), 126–136.

Siegel, A. E. (1969). The effects of media violence on social learning. In D. Lange, R. Baker, & S. Ball (Eds.). *Mass media and violence: A report to the National Commission on the Causes and Prevention of Violence.* (pp. 261–284). Washington, DC: U. S. Government Printing Office.

Signorielli, N. (1978, April). *Television's contribution to sex role socialization.* Paper presented at the Seventh Annual Telecommunications Policy Research Conference, Skytop, PA.

Signorielli, N. (1985). *Role portrayal and stereotyping on television: An annotated bibliography of studies relating to women, minorities, aging, sexual behavior, health, and handicaps.* Westport, CT: Greenwood Press.

Signorielli, N. (1987). Children and adolescents on television: A consistent pattern of devaluation. *Journal of Early Adolescence, 7*(3), 255–268.

Signorielli, N., & Gerbner, G. (1977). *The image of the elderly in prime-time network television drama* (Report No. 12). Philadelphia: Annenberg School of Communication, University of Pennsylvania.

Signorielli, N., Gross, L., & Morgan, M. (1982). Violence in television programs: Ten years later. In D. Pearl, L. Bouthilet, & J. Lazar (Eds.), *Television and behavior: Ten years of scientific progress and implications for the eighties. Vol. 2, Technical reviews* (pp. 158–173). Rockville, MD: NIMH.

Silberman, C. E. (1978). *Criminal violence, criminal justice.* New York: Random House.

Silverman, L. T., Sprafkin, J. N., & Rubinstein, E. A. (1979). Physical contact and sexual behavior on prime-time TV. *Journal of Communication, 29,* 33–43.

Singer, D. G., & Singer, J. L. (1976). Family television viewing habits and the spontaneous play of preschool children. *American Journal of Orthopsychiatry, 46,* 496–502.

Singer, D. G., & Singer, J. L. (1984). Parents as mediators of the child's television environment. *Educational Media International, 4,* 7–11.

Singer, D. G., Zuckerman, D. M., & Singer, J. L. (1980). Helping elementary school children learn about TV. *Journal of Communication, 30,* 84–93.

Singer, J. L., & Singer, D. G. (1980). Television viewing, family style, and aggressive behavior in preschool children. In M. R. Green (Ed.), *Violence in the family.* Washington, DC: AAAS Symposium Series.

Singer, J. L., & Singer, D. G. (1981). *Television, imagination, and aggression: A study of preschoolers.* Hillsdale, NJ: Lawrence Erlbaum Associates.

Singer, J. L., & Singer, D. G. (1983). Psychologists look at television: Cognitive, developmental, personality, and social policy implications. *American Psychologist, 38*(3), 826–834.

Singer, J. L., & Singer, D. G. (1986). Family experiences and television viewing as predictors of children's imagination, restlessness, and aggression. *Journal of Social Issues, 42*(3), 107–124.

Singer, J. L., & Singer, D. G. (1987). Practical suggestions for controlling television. *Journal of Early Adolescence, 7*(3), 365–369.

Singer, J. L., & Singer, D. G. (1988). Some hazards of growing up in a television environment: Children's aggression and restlessness. In S. Oskamp (Ed.), *Television as a social issue* (pp. 171–188). Newbury Park, CA: Sage.

Singer, J. L., Singer, D. G., Desmond, R., Calam, R., & Colimore, K. (1984). *Family communication patterns and television use as correlates of children's cognitions, motor behavior, and comprehension of television.* Progress report to the MacArthur Foundation.

Singer, J. L., Singer, D. G., & Rapaczynski, W. (1984). Children's imagination as predicted by family patterns and television viewing: A longitudinal study. *Genetic Psychology Monographs, 110,* 43–69.

Singer, D. G., Zuckerman, D. M., & Singer, J. L. (1980). Teaching elementary school children television viewing skills: An evaluation. *Journal of Communication, 30,* 84–93.

Skeen, P., Brown, M. H., & Osborn, D. K. (1982). Young children's perception of "real" and "pretend" on television. *Perceptual and Motor Skills, 54,* 883–887.

Skogan, W. G., & Maxfield, M. G. (1981). *Coping with crime.* Beverly Hills: Sage.

Slaby, R. G., Quarfoth, G. R., & McConnachie, G. A. (1976) Television violence and its sponsors. *Journal of Communication, 26*(1), 88–96.

Slade, J. W. (1984). Violence in the hard-core pornographic film: A historical survey. *Journal of Communication, 34,* 148–163.

Small, F. (1978). Fairness and unfairness in television product advertising. *Michigan Law Review, 76*(3), 498–550.

Smith, D. G. (1976a). *Sexual aggression in American pornography: The stereotype of rape.* Presented at the annual meetings of the American Sociological Association, New York.

Smith, D. G. (1976b). The social content of pornography. *Journal of Communication, 26,* 16–33.

Smith, S. B. (1985, Jan. 6). Who's watching TV? It's getting hard to tell. *The New York Times,* pp. 1, 23.

Smythe, D. W. (1954). Reality as presented on television. *Public Opinion Quarterly, 18,* 143–156.

Snow, R. P. (1974). How children interpret TV violence in play context. *Journalism Quarterly, 51*(1), 13–21.

Sparks, G. G., & Cantor, J. (1986). Developmental differences in fright responses to a television program depicting a character transformation. *Journal of Broadcasting and Electronic Media, 30,* 309–323.

Stein, A. H., & Friedrich, L. K. (1972). Television content and young children's behavior. In J. P. Murray, E. A. Rubinstein, & G. A. Comstock (Eds.), *Television and social behavior. Vol. 2, Television and social learning* (pp. 202–317). Washington, DC: U.S. Government Printing Office.

Stein, N., & Glenn, C. (1979). An analysis of story completion in elementary school children. In R. Freedle (Ed.), *Advances in discourse processes* (Vol. 2). Hillsdale, NJ: Lawrence Erlbaum Associates.

Steinem, G. (1988). Six great ideas that television is missing. In S. Oskamp (Ed.), *Television as a social issue* (pp. 18–29). Newbury Park, CA: Sage.

Steiner, G. A. (1963). *The people look at television.* New York: Knopf.

Stengel, R. (1983, November 21). Evangelist of the marketplace. *Time,* p. 58.

Sternbach, R. A. (1966). *Principles of psychophysiology: An introductory text and readings.* New York: Academic Press.

Sternglanz, S. H., & Serbin, L. A. (1974). Sex role stereotyping in children's television programs. *Developmental Psychology, 10*(5), 710–715.

Steuer, F. B., Applefield, J. M., & Smith, R. (1971). Televised aggression and the interpersonal aggression of preschool children. *Journal of Experimental Child Psychology, 11,* 442–447.

Stone, L. E. (1985). *Child pornography literature: A content analysis.* Unpublished doctoral dissertation. International College, San Diego, CA.

Streicher, L. H., & Bonney, N. L. (1974, Summer). Children talk about television. *Journal of Communication,* 54–61.

Stroman, C. (1984). The socialization influence of television and black children. *Journal of Black Studies, 15,* 79–100.

Surgeon General's Scientific Advisory Committee. (1972). *Television and growing up: The impact of televised violence.* Washington, DC: U.S. Government Printing Office.

Surlin, S. H., & Dominick, J. R. (1970). Television's function as a "third parent" for black and white teenagers. *Journal of Broadcasting, 15,* 55–64.

Tada, T. (1969). *Image cognition: A developmental approach.* Tokyo: Nippon Hoso Kyokai.

Tan, A. S. (1977). Why TV is missed: A functional analysis. *Journal of Broadcasting, 21,* 371–380.

Tannenbaum, P. H. (1971). Emotional arousal as a mediator of erotic communication effects. *Technical reports of the Commission on Obscenity and Pornography* (Vol. 8). Washington, DC: U.S. Government Printing Office.

Tannenbaum, P. H. (1972). Studies in film- and television-mediated arousal and aggression: A progress report. In G. A. Comstock, E. A. Rubinstein, & J. P. Murray (Eds.), *Television and social behavior: Vol. 5. Television's effects: Further explorations* (pp. 309–350). Washington, DC: U.S. Government Printing Office.

Tavris, C. (1988). Beyond cartoon killings: Comments on two overlooked effects of television. In S. Oskamp (Ed.), *Television as a social issue* (pp. 189–197). Newbury Park, CA: Sage.

Taylor, B. J., & Howell, R. J. (1973). The ability of three-, four-, and five-year-old children to distinguish fantasy from reality. The *Journal of Genetic Psychology, 122,* 315–318.

Tedesco, N. S. (1974). Patterns in prime time. *Journal of Communication, 24,* 118–124.

Television and cable factbook 1983. (1983). Washington, DC: Television Digest.

Television and cable factbook 1986. (1986). Washington, DC: Television Digest.

Thomas, M. H., & Drabman, R. S. (1975). Toleration of real life aggression as a function of exposure to televised violence and age of subject. *Merrill-Palmer Quarterly, 21,* 227–232.

Thomas, M. H., Horton, R. W., Lippincott, E. C., & Drabman, R. S. (1977). Desensitization to portrayals of real-life aggression as a function of exposure to television violence. *Journal of Personality and Social Psychology, 35,* 450–458.

Thomas, M., & Tell, P. (1974). Effects of viewing real versus fantasy violence upon interpersonal aggression. *Journal of Research in Personality, 8,* 153–160.

Tuchman, G. (1974). Introduction. In G. Tuchman (Ed.), *The TV establishment: Programming for power and profit* (pp. 1–39). Englewood Cliffs, NJ: Prentice–Hall.

Tuchman, G. (1978). The symbolic annihilation of women by the mass media. In G. Tuchman, A. K. Daniels, & J. Benet (Eds.) *Hearth and home: Images of women in the mass media* (pp. 3–38). New York: Oxford University Press.

Turner, C. W., Hesse, B. W., & Peterson-Lewis, S. (1986). Naturalistic studies of the long-term effects of television violence. *Journal of Social Issues, 42*(3), 51–73.

Tyler, T. R. (1980). The impact of directly and indirectly experienced events: The origin of crime-related judgments and behaviors. *Journal of Personality and Social Psychology, 39,* 13–28.

Tyler, T. R., & Cook, F. L. (1984). The mass media and judgments of risk: Distinguishing impact on personal and societal level judgments. *Journal of Personality and Social Psychology, 47*(4), 693–708.

United States Commission on Civil Rights. (1977, August). *Window dressing on the set: women and minorities in television.* Washington, DC: U.S. Government Printing Office.

Varis, T. (1984). The international flow of television programs. *Journal of Communication, 34,* 143–152.

Vaughn, R. (1980). How advertising works: A planning model. *Journal of Advertising Research, 20,* 27–33.

Volgy, T., & Schwartz, J. (1980). Television entertainment programming and sociopolitical attitudes. *Journalism Quarterly, 57,* 150–155.

Wackman, D. B., Wartella, E., & Ward, S. (1977). Learning to be consumers: The role of the family. *Journal of Communication, 27,* 38–51.

Wadeson, R. W., Mason, J. W., Hamburg, D. A., & Handlon, J. H. (1963). Plasma and urinary 17-OHCS responses to motion pictures. *Archives of General Psychiatry, 9,* 146–156.

Walker, S. (1985). *Sense and nonsense about crime: A policy guide.* Monterey, CA: Brooks/Cole.

Waller, F. C. (1978). (Statement of Fletcher C. Waller, Vice President and Director of Marketing Services, General Mills, Inc. on advertising). Written testimony submitted to the Federal Trade Commission.

Walters, J. K., & Stone, V. A. (1971). Television and family communication. *Journal of Communication, 15,* 409–414.

Walters, R. H., & Thomas, E. L. (1963). Enhancement of punitiveness by visual and audiovisual displays. *Canadian Journal of Psychology, 17,* 244–255.

Ward, S. (1972). Effects of television advertising on children and adolescents. In E. A. Rubinstein, G. A. Comstock, & J. P. Murray (Eds.), *Television and social behavior: Vol. 4. Television in day-to-day life: Patterns of use* (pp. 432–451). Washington, DC: U.S. Government Printing Office.

Ward, S., Levinson, D., & Wackman, D. B. (1972). Children's attention to television advertising. In E. A. Rubinstein, G. A. Comstock, & J. P. Murray (Eds.), *Television and social behavior: Vol. 4. Television in day-to-day life: Patterns of use* (pp. 491–515). Washington, DC: U.S. Government Printing Office.

Ward, S., & Wackman, D. B. (1973). Children's information processing of television advertising. In P. Clarke (Ed.), *New models for communication research* (pp. 119–146). Beverly Hills: Sage.

Ward, S., Wackman, D. B., & Wartella, E. (1977). *How children learn to buy: The development of consumer information-processing skills.* Beverly Hills: Sage.

Warner, C. I. (1979). *The world of prime-time television doctors.* Unpublished master's thesis, University of Pennsylvania, Philadelphia, PA.

Wartella, E. (1988). The public context of debates about television and children. In S. Oskamp (Ed.), *Television as a social issue* (pp. 59–68). Newbury Park, CA: Sage.

Wartella, E., & Ettema, J. S. (1974). A cognitive developmental study of children's attention to television commercials. *Communication Research, 1,* 69–88.

Waters, H. F. (1982, December 6). Life according to TV. *Newsweek,* pp. 136–140.

Watkins, B. A., Calvert, S. L., Huston-Stein, A., & Wright, J. C. (1980). Children's recall of television material: Effects of presentation mode and adult labeling. *Development Psychology, 16,* 672–674.

Watkins, B., Huston-Stein, A., & Wright, J. (1980). Effects of planned television and programming. In E. Palmer & A. Dorr (Eds.), *Children and the faces of television: Teaching, violence, and selling* (pp. 49–66). New York: Academic Press.

Watt, J. H., & Krull, R. (1974). An information theory measure for television programming. *Communication Research, 1,* 44–68.

Weigel, R. H., & Howes, P. (1982). Race relations on children's television. *Journal of Psychology, 3*(1), 109–112.

Weigel, R. H., Loomis, J. W., & Soja, M. J. (1980). Race relations on prime-time television. *Journal of Personality and Social Psychology, 39*(5), 884–893.

Wellman, H. M., & Estes, D. (1986). Early understanding of mental entities: A reexamination of childhood realism. *Child Development, 57,* 4, 910–923.

Wells, W. D. (1965, June). Communicating with children. *Journal of Advertising Research, 5,* 2–14.

Wells, W. D., & LoScuito, L. A. (1966, August). Direct observation of purchasing behavior. *Journal of Marketing Research, 3,* 227–233.

Werner, A. (1971). Children and television in Norway. *Gazette, 16*(3), 133–151.

Wilder, J. (1957). The law of initial values in neurology and psychiatry: Facts and problems. *Journal of Nervous and Mental Disease, 125,* 73–86.

Williams, M., & Condry, J. C. (1988). *Living color: Minority portrayals and cross-racial interactions on television.* Unpublished manuscript, Cornell University, Ithaca, NY.

Williams, T. H. (1978). *Differential impact of TV on children: A natural experiment in communities with and without TV.* Paper presented at the meeting of the International Society for Research on Aggression, Washington, DC.

Williams, T. H. (1986). *The impact of television: A natural experiment in three communities.* Orlando, FL: Academic Press.

Williams, F., LaRose, R., & Frost, F. (1981). *Children, television, and sex-role stereotyping.* New York: Praeger.

Wilson, B. J., Hoffner, C., & Cantor, J. (1987). Children's perceptions of the effectiveness of techniques to reduce fear from mass media. *Journal of Applied Developmental Psychology, 8,* 39–52.

Wilson, C. C., & Gutierrez, F. (1985). *Minorities and media.* Newbury Park, CA: Sage.

Winick, C. (1985a). A content analysis of sexually explicit magazines sold in adult bookstores. *The Journal of Sex Research, 21,* 206–210.

Winick, C. (1985b). *Living with television, living without television.* New York: Television Information Office.

Winick, C. (1988). The functions of television: Life without the big box. In S. Oskamp (Ed.), *Television as a social issue* (pp. 217–237). Newbury Park, CA: Sage.

Winn, M. (1978). *The plug-in drug.* New York: Bantam.

Wober, J. M. (1978). Televised violence and paranoid perception: The view from Great Britain. *Public Opinion Quarterly, 42,* 315–321.

Wright, J. C., & Huston, A. C. (1983). A matter of form: Potentials of television for young viewers. *American Psychologist, 38*(7), 835–843.

Wright, J. C., Huston, A. C., Ross, R. P., Calvert, S. L., Rolandelli, D., Weeks, L. A., Raeissi, P., & Potts, R. (1984). Pace and continuity of television programs: Effects on children's attention and comprehension. *Developmental Psychology, 20,* 653–666.

Wright, J. C., Kunkel, D., Pinon, M., & Huston, A. C. (1987, April). *Children's affective and cognitive reactions to televised coverage of the space shuttle disaster.* Paper presented to the biennial meeting of the Society for Research in Child Development, Baltimore, MD.

Wright, J. C., & Vlietstra, A. G. (1975). The development of selective attention: From perceptual exploration to logical search. In H. W. Reese (Ed.), *Advances in child development and behavior* (Vol. 10). New York: Academic Press.

Wroblewski, R., & Huston, A. C. (1987). Televised occupational stereotypes and their effects on early adolescents: Are they changing? *Journal of Early Adolescence, 7*(3), 283–297.

Zajonc, R. B. (1986). The decline and rise of scholastic aptitude scores: A prediction derived from the confluence model. *American Psychologist, 41,* 862–867.

Zillmann, D. (1971). Excitation transfer in communication-mediated aggressive behavior. *Journal of Experimental Social Psychology, 7,* 419–434.

Zillmann, D. (1979). *Hostility and aggression.* Hillsdale, NJ: Lawrence Erlbaum Associates.

Zillmann, D. (1980). Anatomy of suspense. In P. H. Tannenbaum (Ed.) *The entertainment functions of television* (pp. 133–163). Hillsdale, NJ: Lawrence Erlbaum Associates.

Zillmann, D. (1982). Television viewing and arousal. In D. Pearl, L. Bouthilet, & J. Lazar (Eds.), *Television and behavior: Ten years of scientific progress and implications for the eighties. Vol. 2, Technical reviews* (pp. 53–67). Rockville, MD: NIMH.

Zillmann, D., & Bryant, J. (1974). Effect of residual excitation on the emotional response to provocation and delayed aggressive behavior. *Journal of Personality and Social Psychology, 30,* 782–791.

Zillmann, D., & Bryant, J. (1980). *Uses and effects of humor in educational television.* Paper presented at the Third International Conference on Experimental Research in TV Instruction, St. John's, Newfoundland, Canada.

Zillmann, D., & Wakshlag, J. (1985). Fear of victimization and the appeal of crime drama. In D. Zillmann & J. Bryant (Eds.), *Selective exposure to communication* (pp. 141–156). Hillsdale, NJ: Lawrence Erlbaum Associates.

Zorn, E. (1984, February 13). Memories aren't made of this. *Newsweek,* p. 16.

Zucchino, D. (1985, November 7). Big brother meets Twisted Sister, *Rolling Stone,* p. 22.

Zuckerman, P., Ziegler, M., & Stevenson, H. W. (1978). Children's viewing of television and recognition memory of commercials. *Child Development, 48,* 96–104.

Author Index

Subject Index